WINGS AND WARRIORS

Smithsonian History of Aviation Series
Von Hardesty, Series Editor

On December 17, 1903, human flight became a reality when Orville Wright piloted the *Wright Flyer* across a 120-foot course above the sands at Kitty Hawk, North Carolina. That awe-inspiring twelve seconds of powered flight inaugurated a new technology and a new era. The airplane quickly evolved as a means of transportation and a weapon of war. Flying faster, farther, and higher, airplanes soon encircled the globe, dramatically altering human perceptions of time and space. The dream of flight appeared to be without bounds. Having conquered the skies, the heirs to the Wrights eventually orbited the Earth and landed on the Moon.

Aerospace history is punctuated with many triumphs, acts of heroism, and technological achievements. But that same history also showcases technological failures and the devastating impact of aviation technology in modern warfare. As adapted to modern life, the airplane—as with many other important technological breakthroughs—mirrors the darker impulses as well as the genius of its creators. For millions, however, commercial aviation provides safe, reliable, and inexpensive travel for business and leisure.

This book series chronicles the development of aerospace technology in all its manifestations and subtlety. International in scope, this scholarly series includes original monographs, biographies, reprints of out-of-print classics, translations, and reference materials. Both civil and military themes are included, along with systematic studies of the cultural impact of the airplane. Together, these diverse titles contribute to our overall understanding of aeronautical technology and its evolution.

WINGS AND WARRIORS
MY LIFE AS A NAVAL AVIATOR

Donald D. Engen

SMITHSONIAN INSTITUTION PRESS

Washington and London

Copy editor: Ruth G. Thomson
Production editor: Jack Kirshbaum
Designer: Kathleen Sims

Library of Congress Cataloging-in-Publication Data
Engen, Donald Davenport, 1924–99
  Wings and warriors : my life as a naval aviator / Donald D. Engen.
     p.   cm.
  Includes index.
  ISBN 1-56098-795-2 (alk. paper)
   1. Engen, Donald Davenport, 1924– 99 2. United States. Navy—Biography.   3. United
States. Navy—Aviation—Biography.   4. Admirals—United States—Biography.   I. Title.
V63.E54A3   1997
359'.0092—dc21
[B]   97-17445

British Library Cataloguing-in-Publication Data is available

Manufactured in the United States of America
04 03 02 01 00 99 98 97 5 4 3 2 1

*To Mary, who shared this odyssey and made it possible,
and to Travis, Candace, Christopher, and Charles,
who brought laughter and fun to our lives*

CONTENTS

ACKNOWLEDGMENTS

In the course of writing this book I have benefited from the practical advice and words of encouragement of colleagues and friends, for which I am deeply grateful. I would particularly like to express my gratitude to Dr. Von Hardesty and Dr. Paul Stillwell for their encouragement and help in writing for publication. I thank Mark Hirsch and Jack Kirshbaum for believing there was a story to be told. Captain E. T. Wooldridge provided wise counsel and showed me how. I am grateful to the Admiral Dewitt Ramsey Trust for affording me the time to complete my work, and my sincere appreciation goes to Ms. Ruth G. Thomson for steadfastly enforcing the editorial rules of the road. Mary Baker Engen has admonished me to say that I wrote this book in spite of her, but that would be pure fiction. I am responsible for all dates, times, and descriptions, which have been drawn from my personal papers and letters, reports, log books, and official orders. Lastly, I wish to acknowledge those gallant officers and crewmen and now also crew women, alive and dead, who have served on aircraft carrier flight decks. It is they who make carrier aviation possible.

PROLOGUE

The full-throated roar of great reciprocating engines turning propellers on flight decks of aircraft carriers has given way to the body-penetrating continuous blast of sound, heat, and exhaust from jet engines. The hazards remain the same. This book chronicles the fast-moving twenty-five years of technological and flying development in the U.S. Navy from the 1940s into the 1960s while the jet revolution coursed through naval aviation and we forged our way with jet airplanes.

In the 1930s Royal Air Force engineer Flight Lieutenant Frank Whittle and German engineer Hans von O'Hain concurrently, but in isolation from each other, developed the jet engine. As the 1940s began, the military intelligence world spoke surreptitiously of new kinds of airplanes. Far-sighted people such as General H. H. Arnold found willing people like Lawrence Bell, along with his Bell Laboratories and the engineers of the General Electric Company, to lead the way to build the first jet airplane in the United States. U.S. Army and then Navy pilots flew the Bell YP-59 and a handful of captured German airplanes. From those efforts came a new breed of airplanes and pilots.

Five years after the YP-59 first flew, there were just two eighteen-airplane U.S. Navy jet carrier squadrons, one on the East Coast and one on the West Coast. The hybrid propjet, the Ryan FR-1, had led the way and did not prevail. At first, tactical concepts resided solely in the minds of adventuresome pilots, and the art of discovery was as important as knowledge. Progress was limited by lack of technology and by the quality of training. Navy leaders lacked the knowledge to use the new tools of jet aviation effectively. But carrier aviation was changing, slowly at first until 1949, and then, aided by the Korean War, much more quickly.

The 1950s were the golden age of jet airplane development with many new design concepts, and those airplanes had short useful design lives of a year or two. The Navy and the new Air Force improved on each other's airplane designs. North American Aviation swept the wings of its Navy FJ-1 in the late 1940s to give the Air Force the transonic F-86, and the Navy in turn adopted the F-86 design for its FJ-2 and -3 in the early 1950s. In the 1960s the Air Force extensively flew the Navy's F-4 and later the A-7.

Great change was required in the ships that launched and recovered World War II fighters and dive and torpedo bombers. The *Essex* class aircraft carrier of World War II evolved into the *Midway* class in the late 1940s, then into the *Forrestal* class in the late 1950s, the *Kitty Hawk* class in 1961, and the *Nimitz* class in 1978, which then led to the *Stennis* class of the 1990s. Along the way new catapults and arresting gear needed to be designed, and new means of communications and data transmission were needed. Carrier procedures changed, and jet blast deflectors, angled decks, steam catapults, and a mirror visual landing system were adopted. Most importantly, senior officers' knowledge on how jet airplanes could be used needed to be increased to make way for new warfare tactics and operating procedures.

New flying standards were set, and new air, ground, and flight deck procedures were devised to use these jet airplanes. Occasionally, it was one step forward and two steps back, while the Navy continued to hone and to improve jet flying procedures through the Korean War and the Cold War, with its numerous international conflicts small and large, and into the Vietnam War and beyond.

Individual naval aviators, flight and hangar deck officers, and crew developed new concepts. Truly, many contributed to jet aviation progress. Some were more fortunate than others and were in the right place at the right time. Some were less fortunate and happened to be in the wrong place at exactly the wrong time. All were driven by the desire to do better, to reach out for something new, and to excel.

I count myself fortunate to have been part of our jet transformation and to have been able to do the things I did and to observe others. I certainly did not see or do everything. I hope the reader will enjoy this one naval aviator's journey as I explain how the rough edges of a wartime naval aviator were rounded off and a dive bomber pilot became a fighter pilot, a jet fighter pilot, a test pilot, a squadron commander, an air group commander, and then an aircraft carrier commanding officer, all the while trying to contribute his best to carrier aviation. This is the story of the introduction of the jet airplane into the U.S. Navy as seen through my cockpit windscreen.

First, there was a great war. . . .

PART ONE
CHALLENGE AND CHANGE

1. CHALLENGE

The early morning sky was a brilliant blue as we flew across the Philippine Islands and over a few bright white cumulus clouds forming over the islands of Leyte, Cebu, Negros, and Panay. It was August 21, 1944. Ten Japanese freighters, our intended targets, were anchored in the blue waters of Iloilo harbor just ahead of us, their crews oblivious to what was about to happen. So far, this attack was to be a surprise.

Our twelve SB2C-3 Helldiver dive bombers from USS *Lexington* and VB-19 were picking up speed, tail high and nose down, as we descended through 12,500 feet for a high-speed entry into our dives and the first U.S. attack in the central Philippines. The coordinated attack was planned to be completed in three to five minutes, and very soon the idyllic harbor scene below would be shattered. With no air opposition yet, our SB2C-3s had just left the protective weaving cover of the accompanying VF-19 F6F Hellcat fighters, now diving to strafe the antiaircraft (AA) guns on the ships. Six TBF torpedo planes from VT-19 had already dropped lower to begin their own glide bombing attack. Our SB2C-3s, led by our executive officer, Lieutenant Don Banker, were in two divisions of six airplanes with Lieutenant Bill McBride leading the second division. In McBride's division, Lieutenant Emil Stella USNR, second section leader, gave me a right echelon signal. I slid my Helldiver down and behind Stella's tail, crossing under Ensign Al Emig's airplane to take my new position on Emig's right wing. My propeller moved inches below his underfuselage as I purposefully flew close. We both did this for fun. I knew my maneuver would raise his airplane a little for him to feel my closeness and smiled to myself. The signal from Stella told us both that we would be entering our dives to the left. There was no radio talk. I could see a small rivulet of red hydraulic fluid

5

seeping from the hinge line of Emig's right bomb-bay door, and I made a mental note to tell him when we returned to the ship. Helldivers leaked hydraulic fluid like sieves.

Each of us was now busy with our predive rituals as we flew in close formation. On the intercom, I reminded my gunner, Aviation Radioman Second Class Ted Stevenson, to clean up before our dive, but it was not necessary. He had rotated his seat 180 degrees to the rear and locked it in place to man his twin .50-caliber machine guns. I heard him cook off a couple of rounds as I opened the bomb-bay doors, set the selector switches, and armed the 1,000-pound semi-armor-piercing bomb. I recharged my two forward-firing 20mm cannon one more time just to be sure they would work.

McBride flew to bring our target ship into sight along his left side in the notch where the wing met the fuselage. When the target got there, he peeled off, rolling up and to the left and then down to drop away from us. His two wingmen followed smoothly. Immediately Stella turned, patted his head, pointed to Emig, and kissed off, pulling up and slowly rolling left until he disappeared. Three or four dirty, black puffs of five-inch AA blossomed off to the left of Emig and me. Seconds after Stella had kissed off, Emig looked at me and gave me the standard hand pat on the head and pointed forefinger, then hand to the lips to blow a kiss. He rolled left and quickly dropped below me as I watched his dive brakes open, noting the telltale red paint inside. In almost the same motion, I followed—the last one down. As I rolled inverted, I hung in my seat belt and watched with pride as all twelve of us plummeted simultaneously in our vertical dives in the classic helix formation that we had trained so hard to achieve.

McBride adjusted his dive slightly to pick our target, and we six drifted slowly away from the others, still flying vertically in close formation. I could see the fighters completing strafing runs and passing over and around some of the ships below, and now 40mm tracers were beginning to float up at us in their classic, detached sort of way. This was no longer a surprise party. I saw one or two torpedo planes low on the water, and then Banker began his pullout followed by the rest of his division.

Having no time to look at what they were doing, I placed my reflective gun sight pipper on the stack of the 15,000-ton freighter that McBride had picked and began tracking carefully. No wind. This attack was a piece of cake. McBride started his pullout, with streamers coming off each wing tip as his bomb went off amidships. The first bombs looked like hit, hit, close miss, as I released my bomb at 1,600 feet and pulled smoothly but hard into 5 g's. My vision grayed out slightly, and as soon as I saw I had it made, I released back pressure on the stick to come out of the dive right on the water. We headed northwest out of the harbor. Stevenson called that our bomb had hit amidships.

I took a quick look over my left shoulder and saw the large freighter engulfed in dirty gray and black smoke and the boiling water of exploding bombs. The ship would sink.

I turned my attention to getting out of the harbor, but everyone was pulling away from me. I could not figure out why. AA projectiles were flying through the air like golf balls, seeming to pass over and under my wings as their incendiaries burned out ahead. It was also unduly quiet! I checked the manifold pressure and rpm gauges to see with great consternation that I had 54 inches of manifold pressure and only 1,200 rpm. I should have had 2,400 rpm, and I was overtorquing the engine badly. If I did not do something quickly, I would blow a cylinder. I pulled the throttle back to 20 inches of manifold pressure to assess what was going on and reasoned that the Curtiss electric propeller must have oversped, hit the high stop, and bounced back to 1,200 rpm. Trying to increase rpm manually brought no response—the prop lever did not seem to be attached to anything. I tried the electric control toggle switch. No increase, but it would decrease—and did—another 100 rpm to 1,100! I was now stabilized at a maximum airspeed of 90 to 95 knots and in deep trouble. The Philippine Islands and 200 miles of Pacific Ocean were between me and *Lexington*.

I radioed Lieutenant Banker to tell him of my situation. He sent Ensign Bill Good back to escort me, while the group of F6Fs, SB2C-3s, and TBFs formed up to return to *Lexington* to meet the landing time and to be ready for the next strike. Bill began to weave above me so that he would not fall out of the sky, and I began to navigate through the Philippine Islands like Magellan did more than 400 years before, because I did not have the power to climb above 500 feet or fly over any island. We flew north around Cebu and then south into the Camotes Sea, passed south of Leyte, and flew out through the Surigao Strait trying to be unobtrusive. Fortunately, we saw no Japanese airplanes nor did they see us, and we departed the Philippines for *Lexington* and Task Group (TG) 38.3. With great fascination, I could almost count the propeller blades as they turned at 1,100 rpm.

Reaching the ship, I had another problem. My airplane would not stay in the air with both the wheels and the flaps down. The ship took Bill Good on board and asked me if I wanted to land in the water. That did not sound like a good idea to me, so I proposed an alternative. I would fly a loose pattern with my gear down to the cut and then throw my flaps down to make the landing. If I could not make the deck, I would make a water landing off the port side. The landing signal officer (LSO) and I had a little conversation about that, but he bought it, and I did just that. As I flew up the carrier's wake to the cut position with the landing gear down, the LSO threw a quick cut at me; I banged the flap lever down and pulled my throttle off. The flaps were still coming down as I caught the number 5 wire, and Stevenson made some comment such as "this was much nicer than landing in the water." In fact, we saved an airplane for another day and another strike. At the far end of the pipeline that can be important. As we were towed to the forward elevator to be sent to the hangar deck, I relaxed and thought of lots of things; one was how lucky I was to be in VB-19 and in *Lexington*. My mind drifted back. . . .

In the fourth grade I announced to my parents that I wanted to be a naval officer and go to sea. That became my goal in school. I had no great desire to be involved in aviation, but like every boy I was fascinated with it. My paternal grandparents lived in San Fernando Valley near the Burbank airport, where I frequently went to see Roscoe Turner with his lion Gilmore and other notable aviators. One night I even sneaked out of the house to watch Jimmy Doolittle take off in his GeeBee during one of the Bendix Air Races. In 1933 my father took me to Mines Field in Los Angeles for the National Air Races. There on the grass field in front of the Spanish-style control tower, Ernst Udet picked up a handkerchief with the wing tip of his biplane while flying inverted. That was thrilling. But I still had not put flying together with being the naval officer that I sought to be.

In May 1941 I graduated from high school in Pasadena, California, at the age of sixteen and set about obtaining an appointment to the Naval Academy from Carl Hinshaw, our Republican congressman. My father allowed me to attend a summer cram course at Mead Preparatory School in San Marino to prepare for the academic merit examinations for appointment to the service academies, after which I took the September competitive exams that were administered at the Federal Building in Los Angeles.

While waiting for those results, I enrolled for the freshman year of college at Pasadena Junior College, where I met Mary Baker and fell in love. She was sixteen and I was seventeen. When the Japanese attacked Pearl Harbor on Sunday, December 7, 1941, my parents, my brother, and I were preparing for church as we heard radio station KNX dramatically describe the attack that galvanized the United States.

Just five days after December 7, Representative Hinshaw sent a letter saying that he had awarded me a third alternate appointment to the Naval Academy. I also learned that, because of the war, I would probably gain entrance, provided I passed the entrance examinations. I was elated and continued to study for the examinations, which I took in late February at the Naval Reserve Armory in Los Angeles.

In early 1942 Southern California was in turmoil and near hysteria. One or two submarine-launched Japanese airplanes had attacked a coastal refinery. The entire West Coast of the United States was blacked out at night, and automobiles were not driven after dark or, if they were, only with parking lights or taped headlights. There were no street lights or illuminated advertising signs, and all store and house windows were carefully covered. The Army had deployed a few AA guns and large megaphone ears designed to detect aircraft engine noise, so that the searchlights, which were placed in strategic vacant lots and near large plants such as Firestone and Douglas Aircraft, could find the airplanes. The Army troops living in tents near their AA guns were stark testimony that we were at war. Rumors abounded, and the principal fear was that the Japanese would attack at any time. Men of all ages lined up to volunteer and fight.

The Japanese Americans on the West Coast were relocated, a euphemistic word for sent, to camps in the high desert. It is difficult today to understand the paranoia that was felt about the Japanese Americans. As a person who had grown up, been friends, and gone to school with many young Japanese Americans, I identified with them and could not believe that they or their parents were really threats or should be treated in this way.

In early April 1942 my world collapsed. I had failed the chemistry test on the entrance examinations and as a result could not enter the Naval Academy. I was determined to try again. However, in late April the Navy Department lowered the age to sign up for naval aviation from twenty-one to eighteen and also reduced the academic requirements from two years of college to a high school diploma. My immediate goal before my eighteenth birthday became to gain my parents' permission to join the Navy and to be at that recruiting office ready to sign up on that day. I talked incessantly of my goal with Mary Baker and with her father as well. He had been in the Great War of 1914–18 and was a strong but passive ally as I tried to gain my parents' permission to enlist in the naval aviation program.

Finally, my campaign proved successful. On my eighteenth birthday, May 28, 1942, with a handwritten note of permission from my parents to enlist as a seaman second class in the V5 Naval Aviation Cadet Program, I went to the recruiting office in the Los Angeles Federal Building on South Spring Street.

At the Navy recruiting office, after I took a series of written tests to determine aptitude, the recruiter said that the Navy was interested in me but that I must now have a comprehensive series of physical and psychological tests. If I passed those, I should bring to that office letters of recommendation, along with my letter of permission from my parents, and then I could enlist. Over the next week I dutifully went through the tests. Weight was my biggest challenge—I was skinny. But with the assistance of a propitious toe on the scale by an obliging corpsman, I made the minimum weight, after which I gathered letters of recommendation and appeared before a three-officer screening board of review. I met the board's criteria and enlisted as a seaman second class in the

Navy's V5 program on June 9, 1942, and went home to bask in the glory of acceptance. I was to be told later where and when I would be sent.

The Civilian Pilot Training (CPT) program had been organized under the newly formed Civil Aeronautics Board (CAB) in 1939. CPT, as it was called, was the brainchild of Robert H. Hinkley, the first chairman of the CAB. Seeing that there were just 21,000 civilian pilots in the United States, Hinkley persuaded President Roosevelt to develop a much larger pool of pilots to enhance air commerce. After 13 colleges demonstrated the success of such a program, a total of 400 universities and colleges eventually developed programs under the CPT umbrella. By mid-1942, CPT, which was part of the initial training process for Army and Navy aviation, enabled the services to cull the lowest 10 percent of the pilot candidates, thus enhancing the success rate of the more rigorous military flight training that followed.

In Southern California CPT was conducted at Santa Ana, Chaffey, Long Beach, and Pasadena Junior Colleges and provided seventy-two hours of ground instruction along with thirty-five to fifty hours of flight instruction, which led to a private pilot's license. In early spring 1942 Nick Lentine Flying Service contracted to supply Pasadena Junior College with CPT and moved its flying operations to Silver Lake, a dry lake near Baker, California, the southern entry point for Death Valley. Silver Lake was 100 feet below mean sea level, and the sun-baked surface was exceedingly hard and flat. There, it was not unusual to have clear weather with visibility of 70 miles.

I was told to report for ground school at Pasadena Junior College on Monday, July 6, 1942. Reporting in, I found I would be one of twenty-five primary CPT students. Earl Howard Floyd taught math and physics, Waldo Waterman taught civil air regulations, and Leland McAuley taught physical education and also tried to teach us to march in a semblance of order. Waldo Waterman had worked for Glenn Curtiss in San Diego in 1910 and had given my mother her first airplane ride 1921 in a J4 "Jenny" at the Long Beach airport. He was a colorful character, whom we worshipped!

We studied at Pasadena Junior College for two weeks; then, wearing civilian clothes, we boarded buses on Sunday, July 19, 1942, for Baker, California, and arrived at 4:45 P.M. to find the temperature to be 109°F. Each of us was assigned to one of three wooden-floored tents. I became fast friends with fellow primary CPT candidates George Kelly, Jack Barton, and Herb Biedebaugh. There was a secondary CPT, or advanced, class in Baker, as well. Among others in that class were Jack Scott and Ray Davis of Pasadena and Harry Evans of San Pedro. Baker had the distinction of being the only Greyhound Bus stop between Barstow and Las Vegas, and that was all it was—population 25, except for us.

Our routine was to rise at 0345, do calisthenics for ten minutes, wash up for another ten minutes, eat breakfast, and then ride a bus to the flight line on Silver Lake. There we flew between 0600 and 1030. That window of opportunity was small because the temperature rose to 125°F by 1030, and the 65-hp Continental engines on our J3 Piper Cubs would not allow both an instructor and student to become airborne in the same airplane at such temperatures. Ground school and athletics filled our afternoons, followed by dinner and bed. We flew seven days a week.

Harold R. Knorr, a young, quiet, and noncommittal man, was my instructor. We flew together for thirty minutes each day, and he had his hands full with me. He wrote these comments in my logbook rather consistently: "rough and abrupt" and "eager to learn." Those were occasionally punctuated by "uncertain," "banks too steeply," and "altitude variable." Nevertheless, I did solo on August 6, 1942, after seven hours and forty-five minutes of flight instruction.

Gradually, my flight grades improved, and Mr. Knorr began to think that I might become a pilot—someday. Ground school was a chore. Air conditioning was a thing of the future, and our classrooms in the back of Fehling's Soda Fountain were only partially cooled from the Death Valley heat by an evaporative cooler. Slowly we mastered the intricacies of meteorology, learned to recognize U.S. and enemy aircraft, memorized Morse code, and fathomed navigation.

As we flew more, we became bolder. I reported to my mother and father on August 24 that I had had my first dogfight with another student. He and I used the bent-wire gas sight gauges forward of our windscreens for sights and set about to see who was better. We did not prove anything, other than that an instructor is always watching when you least expect it. We were taken to task for unauthorized maneuvers, but the admonishment was light.

On Wednesday, September 2, 1942, I had my final check ride with Louis Regan, a Civil Aeronautics Authority (CAA) check pilot from Los Angeles. I was scared stiff but flew the one-hour flight as best I could. Mr. Regan passed me on that check ride, and at the end of thirty-six hours of flying I was qualified for a private pilot's license—which I neither applied for nor received. That would come thirty years later. Just as importantly, I learned that I had "made the academic and flying cut" and would be going to the naval preflight school at St. Mary's College in mid-September. With that good news and not a thought about the 50 percent staying behind, I paid my respects to my instructors, bid them good-bye, and returned to Pasadena in the same yellow school bus that had taken me to Baker.

The ensuing two weeks at home passed rapidly, and I was notified to join a draft of men forming up on September 16 in Los Angeles's Union Station to proceed by train to St. Mary's naval preflight school near Moraga, California.

On the appointed day we gathered in the cavernous Union Station lobby to bid our families good-bye. A Navy petty officer formed us into two rows and marched the loose semblance of an organization to the train, which then took some twenty-one hours to make the ten-hour trip to Oakland. Wartime train travel was a hazard when every other train seemed to have some mythical priority higher than that of the train in which you rode. Reaching Oakland at 1600 the next day, we rode silently in gray Navy buses to our new home.

St. Mary's College had been a De La Salle Christian Brothers school with the famous football coach Edward Patrick (Slip) Madigan. Three other Navy preflight schools had been established at the Universities of Iowa, North Carolina, and Georgia. Those four schools were modeled after MIT, which twenty-five years earlier, in World War I, had brought order out of academic chaos to Navy pilot training. The four colleges would turn out 5,000 naval aviation cadets every three months during the war. Eventually, a fifth preflight school was established in 1945 at the Del Monte Hotel in Monterey, California. The commanding officer at St. Mary's, whom, I might add, I never saw, was Captain G. W. Steele USN (ret), and his executive officer was Lieutenant Commander C. W. King USNR.

The athletic program, complementing the academic program, was the brainchild of Lieutenant Commander Tom Hamilton, who had arrived at St. Mary's in June 1942. He was a naval aviator and football coach at the Naval Academy and believed that body contact team sports such as football taught aggressive team spirit.

At St. Mary's a new cadet battalion of 200 men was formed every two weeks. On arrival in mid-September we were assigned to the 8th Battalion and quartered in Essex Hall, a new, three-story wooden barracks. Our first days at St. Mary's were a blur. Sore and light headed from medical shots and immunization, along with culture shock from strange surroundings and procedures, each cadet was an island unto himself, just trying to survive. One-half of us washed the windows on the previously unlived-in third deck, while the other half waxed and polished floors. We were taught to march in platoons, then companies, and then battalions.

The roster of cadets for each battalion was alphabetized with the As first and the Zs last. In this way I became fast friends with Gib Edwards, Harry Evans, Charles Epp, and others whose last names began with E. My former CPT compatriot, Irving Zelinka, from Los Angeles, was at the other end of the inoculation and pay lines and also at the far end of the barracks. He might as well have been in Russia.

After my swimming tests, I was placed on the St. Mary's preflight water polo team. Fellow cadet and former Olympic water polo player Deverre Christianson was to be the captain. It was not lost on me that only two teams would travel for games, the football team and the water polo team. I had already realized that we were to be in quarantine for four weeks and then have a six-hour liberty every other weekend. Clearly, we would not be going very far from St. Mary's unless there was some other way to do it. Water polo seemed to offer that opportunity.

The cadet routine was rigid: we rose at 0530 with fifteen minutes to shave and dress, marched to breakfast at the cafeteria-style mess hall, marched back to the barracks, dressed for gym, and performed fifteen minutes of calisthenics. Then one hour of organized team sports, such as football, soccer, combat track, or other body contact sports, was followed by one hour of individual sports, such as wrestling, boxing, obstacle course, or swimming. Then we showered and dressed and had an hour of military drill on the parade ground before marching to the mess hall for lunch. Following lunch, we marched to our classrooms for two hours of academic courses and then marched to the gym for two hours of our elected sports. We then showered and dressed to march to the mess hall for dinner. The food at every meal was high protein and plentiful. It dawned on us that we were not unlike cattle in fattening pens. We certainly put on weight and developed muscles. After dinner we marched to the barracks for two hours of individual study and finally thirty minutes of time to ourselves to write home. Lights went out at 2130, and I do not recall that any cadet had trouble sleeping. Our four-week quarantine period came and went.

A cadet's pay was $75 per month, and we were paid on the fifth and twentieth of every month. Being paid in the Navy was a time-honored ritual. The pay chit was a legal document, and woe be it to the cadet who did not meet the most exacting standards for filling out this 2½-by-6-inch white paper form. Pay chits came in pads. We would line up alphabetically, according to the pay list posted on a bulletin board, and someone in the As would pass back a pay chit pad. Each cadet would tear off a blank pay chit and pass the pad farther back and, using the back of the cadet in front of him as a writing surface, would fill out his pay chit only in black ink. As each cadet approached the pay table, where the disbursing clerk, disbursing officer, and pay master sat like three Supreme Court justices, he pressed his right thumb onto a large ink pad on the table and then placed it on the pay chit in the small box for that purpose. We cadets believed that someone actually compared those thumb prints to some master file. For the slightest digression from the norm on the pay chit, the cadet would be given a withering look by the supreme pay court and his pay chit would be ceremoniously torn in half with gusto, while he was sent in disgrace to the end of the line to try again. Each cadet was required to buy one $25 war bond each month and was given a $10,000 U.S. national life insurance policy, with his parents as beneficiaries. There were neither places nor time to spend our pay, and we always seemed to have money left over.

When several thousand young men participate actively in body contact sports that require great physical coordination, bones will be broken and ligaments torn. We had a goodly percentage of cadets limping or hobbling in casts or on crutches, wearing slings, or lying in bed, and the orthopedic doctors had a great learning opportunity. The walking wounded, as they were known, marched in their own formations to not slow the others, and those formations looked like a picture of dispirited retreat by the North or the South in the Civil War, which, incidentally, was still hotly debated each night after the lights went out.

The founding fathers of St. Mary's College had placed a large wooden water tank on the top of a commanding hill that overlooked the campus. That old water tank had stood for many years near a majestic grove of eucalyptus trees for all to see. By day no guard was required; no watch was set. From sunset until sunrise, though, was another matter, and pairs of cadets maintained a continuous watch over the tower at four-hour intervals, as if our very lives depended on our diligence. To fall asleep on watch was unthinkable and would have imperiled the nation and the entire Western world, along with earning a cadet eight demerits to match his heinous crime.

In October we learned that because of losses of pilots in the fleet our training would be accelerated and we would have our wings in six to nine months and be in the fleet soon after. On Friday, November 13, one-half of the 7th and the entire 8th Battalion were merged to become the 7th Battalion with a strength of 300 cadets and a graduation date of November 24. Several days before that date, I was told that I had been selected, along with Jack Scott, Jack Barton, Harry Evans, and fifty-six others to go to the Naval Reserve Aviation Base at Los Alamitos, California. We packed our bags and said good-bye to those who were going to the other elimination (E) bases (E bases were established under the Aviation Cadet Act of 1935 to weed out those who could not adapt to flying because of air sickness or lack of coordination). Jack Scott and I left St. Mary's by Navy bus for the Oakland airport at 0600 on November 25 to fly in a Western Airlines DC-3 to Burbank, California.

Eight days of leave in Pasadena with my family passed rapidly, while Mary Baker and I went on dates to Earl Carrol's Dinner Theater in Hollywood, to the Pasadena Civic Auditorium, where Tommy Dorsey's band played, and to Pasadena Junior College social functions. After the regimentation of St. Mary's, it was hard for me to adapt to the looser routine of life in Pasadena.

On December 3, 1942, my father drove me the 20 miles from Pasadena to the main gate of Los Alamitos, using one of his valuable gas-rationing B coupons. The route was the familiar one we had traveled to the beaches in previous years. Now, driving south on Bellflower Boulevard, we saw lines of

Navy SNV trainers on the airfield behind the Vultee plant. Occasionally, we would pass a group of U.S. Army trucks and an AA gun or searchlight in open fields, with tents nearby for the soldiers. The two-lane road to the main gate at Los Alamitos went through open farmland. My father said good-bye and left me at the gate because neither he nor I knew how to get a car pass. Carrying my bag, I walked down barren and treeless Lexington Drive the quarter of a mile to the administration building to report for duty.

The Naval Reserve Aviation Base had recently moved from the busy Long Beach airport to its new location at Los Alamitos. It was built on land appropriated from the Bixby Ranch and consisted of one large hangar with a control tower perched on the southeast corner, a just-completed administration building, a combination mess hall and enlisted barracks, a two-story aviation cadet barracks with four wings, a small bachelor officers quarters (BOQ) for the instructors, and a classroom building. A broad parade ground lay between Enterprise and Yorktown Roads, as well as a large supply warehouse, but not much else. Most importantly, thirty-five to forty bright yellow N2S and N3N biplanes were smartly lined up on the concrete ramp just to the south of the hangar.

We cadets from St. Mary's made up all of class 12A, the first flight class of December 1942. Half of us had been placed in the left wing—as class 12A L—and the other half in the right wing. On Sunday, December 6, we were given the option of going to Long Beach for church or remaining on the base without attending church services. Jack Scott, Mike Spooner, and I chose the better alternative, going to Long Beach in search of a church service—a form of freedom that we had not seen at St. Mary's.

The next day the liberal cadet policies changed. An obstacle course was being built, and we were to be bused to the ocean for one hour of swimming each day. However, after two weeks of swimming in the Pacific Ocean in December, that regimen was postponed until spring. Church in town for cadets was canceled, and we were told that we could receive visitors between 1330 and 1530 on Sundays only. The two wings of our class would alternate their flying every two weeks, and class 12A L would start flying in the mornings first. The high-quality food we had received at St. Mary's gave way to standard Navy chow: beans and minced meat on toast (affectionately called SOS, shit on a shingle, in Navy parlance) for breakfast, and lots of bread, meat, and gravy for lunch and dinner. Initially cadets and sailors intermingled in the chow lines, and by mid-December a cadet mess was established in a portion of the mess hall.

But we were happy because we were finally beginning our Navy flying careers. We marched to the supply department and were issued logbooks and flight gear consisting of a summer leather flying jacket, helmet, goggles, a sheepskin-lined winter flying jacket, boots, pants, summer and winter flying gloves, and a parachute bag in which to carry all of it. Each cadet had a tall, green metal flying locker in which he kept his gear. For ground school, we were given courses in Morse code, dead reckoning, and celestial navigation, and we studied the N2S-3 and N2S-4 Stearman biplanes that we were to fly. On December 11 one cadet hit the canvas-covered wind tee with his airplane, another landed on top of a second Stearman, and three cracked up while night flying. No one was hurt badly.

Ten days after reporting, I had my first flight in a Navy N2S-4 biplane with Lieutenant Bry. I did not ask questions, and he did not offer much conversation. He was a lieutenant, and I had never been close to one of those before. It had been two and a half months since my last flight in the J3 Cub, and my exhilaration was exceedingly high. The 240-hp engine and open cockpit of the Stearman made the flight awesome to me. Subsequently, Ensign Grow took over as my instructor.

When flying, cadets wore leather helmets and the gosport, a long flexible tube into which the instructor could speak, or shout, as the case may be. His voice traveled through a tube to a portion that bifurcated at the cadet's belly button and then went to each ear cup in the cadet's helmet. The gosport had been adopted from the British in late World War I and thereafter was used in all Navy training airplanes. It was an effective way for the instructor to communicate with his student. Luckily, the instructor could not hear comments that the cadet might mumble in return.

The Stearman and the N3N had inertial starters, as did the Waco and other airplanes of the 1930s. The plane captain would wind up the inertial starter's flywheel by means of a large crank that fit into the port side of the fuselage, just aft of the engine. That crank was hard to move, but gradually one could build up a head of steam and crank faster and faster. When the flywheel was up to speed, the plane captain would pull out the crank and hand it to the pilot, and the pilot would engage the starter. If the engine had been primed properly for the outside temperature and the temperature of the engine, it would catch and start handily. Occasionally, the pilot would use less or more than the best combination of gasoline priming, and an exasperated plane captain would have to climb back up to try again. We used the Navy standard rule of two: if you could not get the engine started in two tries, the pilot got out and cranked while the plane captain sat in the cockpit and started the airplane. That provided sport for the lineman and encouragement for the pilot to get it right the first time. It all seemed equitable, and it worked.

In mid-December I fell on the soccer field when I was tripped during a soccer game. Although I did not know it at the time, I had broken a small bone in my left wrist. The corpsman wrapped it in an elastic bandage, and I flew in great pain for several weeks because I was determined that I would not become a casualty to fall behind class 12A. To this day that wrist still bothers me.

On December 26, 1942, after exactly seven hours of dual instruction from Ensign Grow, I soloed. My check pilot, Ensign Schaffer, and I had flown to Mile Square Field near Santa Ana. He climbed out on the wing after I had made a landing and said, "OK, Cadet, get up in front and show me what you can do!" I took off with great elation and did stalls, spirals, and slips and made practice landings. I was really proud! As instructed, I then landed and picked up Ensign Schaffer, and I flew triumphantly back to Los Alamitos. By December 31 I had flown fifteen hours in the N2S.

Our cadet lives again gave way to routine. Rise at 0530, do calisthenics, eat, and alternately fly either morning or afternoon, with ground school during the other half of the day. We moved in our training through the instructional stages. Athletics remained very important, and we had good workouts every day. We had liberty every other Saturday afternoon, and if we were not scheduled to fly on Sunday, we were given liberty until 2300 every other Saturday night as well.

By mid-January we cadets of class 12A L could take up unwary sailors as passengers. Unknown to the sailors, each was the object of our game. The first cadet to return to the flight line with a legitimately sick passenger won. I am not sure that the sailors ever figured out that game.

With so much cadet flying, accidents did happen. On January 19 there were eight minor crashes on the field. Six were ground loops, and two airplanes nosed over. One of those involved a cadet who touched down near the end of the runway. His airplane then left the runway and tripped over the earthen dike for the base sewage treatment plant. The airplane pitched tail over nose slowly and fell inverted into one of the treatment ponds. The cadet was not injured, at least physically. In fact, he was just fine—until he undid his seat belt and fell head first into the pond.

The Navy had an inordinate interest in the Schneider test, a medical test taken periodically by airmen that entailed the measurement of the subject's blood pressure reclining and then again after brief exercise. Navy corpsmen administered those tests and, after consulting some mystical chart, would pronounce you fit or unfit to fly. Whenever the field was fogged in, which occurred frequently in January and February, we would be marched to sickbay for Schneider tests in lieu of flying. To this day, I still am not sure what that test demonstrated about healthy young males.

In January 1943 a cadet spun in over the field and was killed. His N2S crashed into the supply building roof, and the resulting fire destroyed all the seats for the still-to-be-built base movie theater. Shortly after that, another cadet spun in, missing the cadet barracks by 100 feet. He too was killed. Using those events as evidence that we were tired, we seized the opportunity to ask the commanding officer to abolish calisthenics at 0530 each morning. Two things happened. One, he relented on calisthenics—that was the good news; two, we were told that from then on no one was to fly over any building on the base while in the landing traffic pattern.

By the end of January we aviation cadets had mastered Morse code at the speed of eight words per minute and had mastered navigation as well. I had a total of forty-six Navy flying hours, having flown thirty-one hours in the N2S during January. Ensign Grow even began to compliment me occasionally on the odd maneuver. However, I did have one scare. I had been shooting landings at the Fullerton airfield, several miles north of Los Alamitos. In my concentration, I had cut an instructor out of the landing pattern without realizing it, and he had put me on report. I was sent before Lieutenant Blanchard, one of the most senior instructors at Los Alamitos. He listened to my side of the story and did nothing further, but that experience reinforced my feeling that you need to express yourself if you are correct. Going before Lieutenant Blanchard was my first and next-to-last brush with the aviation training discipline system.

Mary Baker and I continued to date on my occasional free Saturday. Her father had given her a 1941 yellow Chevrolet convertible the year before, and with her blonde hair she caught the attention of everyone when she picked me up at the gate! We would go into Long Beach. She was seventeen, and I was eighteen and deeply in love with her.

By February three or four of my classmates had washed out of the program to return to civilian life and to be drafted, and one or two of my friends had been killed in accidents. We began formation flying, and the precision required to fly a few feet from another airplane was stimulating. One unfortunate aviation cadet in class 11B was killed when he and another cadet locked wings while flying formation. One bailed out to live, but the other rode the two twisted, yellow-fabric-covered airplanes down.

Each aviation cadet was given one dual night flight and then three solo night flights. Those were exciting. We also learned about the physiology of the night world of rods and cones of the eyes and how to preserve night vision. Our flights at night in Southern California had to be coordinated with the U.S. Army. That coordination allowed the air defense troops to not go ballistic when they detected one of our airplanes and to not mistake it for a Japanese airplane. On February 15 I was flying at 3,000 feet on a dark night and was dutifully orbiting my assigned spot in the sky when all of a sudden fifteen multimegawatt searchlights turned on at once. I was the target. Those ears of the Army had been tracking my airplane, and through coordination, the searchlights hit me with enough light, I thought, to destroy my night vision for ten years. The piercing strobes of light played with me long enough to make me relax in the bright light, and then abruptly, in coordination, every searchlight went out at once! I was left in limbo over the blacked out city of Long Beach with my night vision totally destroyed and a scheduled landing time only ten minutes away. Suffice it to say, I recovered enough vision to land, but the experience made a lasting impression on me! That was my next-to-last flight at Los Alamitos. I had completed and passed the syllabus for primary training.

On Sunday, February 27, class 12A left Los Alamitos. Half a dozen of our classmates were left behind to join class 12B because they had not progressed with the norm of the class. Aviation training is very much like that. Most cadets met the stringent requirements of comprehension, hand-to-eye coordination, and other high motor skills in about the same time and sequence. But some never did and washed out. Learning to fly is an individual accomplishment. We were bused to the Santa Ana streetcar station in the midmorning of Sunday, February 21, to board two special redline electric street cars and to travel to Union Station in Los Angeles.

Mary and I had said our good-byes the night before, and she was to leave for Balboa Island and a school vacation on that Sunday. As our streetcar crossed Rosemead Boulevard en route to Los Angeles, I looked at the southbound cars lined up at the level crossing and saw Mary in her yellow convertible. I waved from behind my glass window, but she had no way of knowing that this particular streetcar held anyone she knew.

Union Station was still a busy place. Almost everyone was in uniform. Young men en route to their first military training marched through the gates, while scores of soldiers and sailors formed up after arrival. Our draft of cadets arrived in the early afternoon, and we were informed that our train would leave for Corpus Christi, Texas, at 2030. My parents and little brother had come to see me off for my first trip outside the state of California.

For this train trip, we were the troop train with top priority. Most cars were loaded with soldiers going to Texas. There were two cars for cadets from Los Alamitos, and we discovered that two additional cars behind us were filled with aviation cadets from Livermore, who were also bound for Corpus Christi. Jack Scott, Harry Evans, Gib Edwards, and I had a semiprivate compartment as did other cadets. Our Southern Pacific train took three days to get to Corpus Christi.

By 1943 the Navy had developed its training pipeline so that preflight schools first fed the E bases, and then the E bases fed the two centers for naval aviation training—Pensacola and Corpus Christi. Generally, the cadets from east of the Mississippi River went to Pensacola, and cadets from western states went to Corpus Christi. Cadets from the central states went to either Pensacola or Corpus Christi, depending on the needs of the pipeline. How fast you went through that pipeline depended on when you entered it and how good you were. While it only took me nine months from the start of preflight school to earn my wings, it took those who entered the pipeline four or five months later almost eighteen months. All of us were hostages to timing, and delays could be staggering, particularly when you wanted to fight the war.

2. TRAINING TO STAY ALIVE
MARCH 1943 TO JUNE 1944

In the Pacific the United States recaptured the Aleutian Islands, while Allied naval forces in the southwest Pacific moved forward to capture Rendova, Salamaua, and Lae. Rear Admirals Fredrick L. Sherman and Marc Mitscher were polishing multicarrier tactical skills and moved their task groups to place Marines ashore in the Marshall Islands. The first Japanese airplane was shot down using the Navy's new proximity-fused five-inch projectile, and the Vought F4U Corsair flew its first combat missions on Guadalcanal. In June 1944 Japanese and U.S. navies fought the decisive battle of the Philippine Sea.

In Africa General Eisenhower's forces captured Bizerte, and he later directed the invasions of Sicily and Italy. Round-the-clock bombing of German cities began, while there was relief in the air war over England.

In the United States the first U.S. Navy night-fighter squadron was commissioned, and helicopter flight was demonstrated for the military services. The first air-to-ground rockets were successfully fired. At the end of 1943 there were 21,621 naval aviators and 105,445 aviation ratings. There were twenty-nine aircraft carriers of all types, and the Navy was building light aircraft carriers on cruiser hulls. The first Navy-developed turbojet engine, the Westinghouse 19A, completed 100 hours of ground testing; McDonnell Aircraft Company was designing the FH1; and Ryan Aeronautical Company was completing design work on its dual reciprocating-and-jet-engined FR-1.

The naval aviation training system kept changing as it adapted to the needs of the fleet. Pensacola, the bastion of naval aviation, and Corpus Christi, the

newer training center, shared the advanced aviation training load in
Some 350 naval aviation cadets converged on Corpus Christi each month.
training complex of six naval air stations spread over two Texas counties. ↳
baniss Field was used for intermediate training; Rodd Field and Naval Air Station (NAS) Corpus Christi, or Main Side, gave P (patrol) boat and land-based
multiengine training. Main Side was also used for instrument training, which
later was moved to Beeville. Cudihy Field was used for torpedo training, while
Kingsville provided dive bomber and fighter training.

In the air, each cadet took intermediate training in the Vultee SNV, affectionately known as the Vibrator because of the penetrating noise of its fixed-
pitch propeller, and moved on to instrument training in the Link trainer and in
the backseat of the North American SNJ-4. Advanced training for fighters, dive
bombers, and torpedo bombers was given in the 480-hp North American
SNJ-3 or SNJ-4s. P boat training was given in Chance Vought OS2U float
planes, Consolidated PBY amphibians, and Beech JRBs and SNBs.

We cadets arrived in Corpus Christi at 1300 on Wednesday, February 24,
1943, and made the 15-mile bus trip south to NAS Corpus Christi. As a newly
liberated Californian, I found the oppressive humidity of the Gulf Coast, the
southern drawl of Texans, and the incessant cowboy music on the radio to be
strange. Texas was a foreign land to me. The now-standard new duty station
physical exam was administered, and those of us arriving at that time were
grouped into class 2D43C. The number 2 stood for the month of February, D
for the fourth class of the month, 43 for the year, and C for Corpus Christi. We
kept that class designator until we graduated three months later.

Orientation, organization, and leadership lectures were packed into three
days at Main Side, and Jack Scott and I learned from those ahead of us to order
our officer uniforms early from the tailor in Corpus Christi because it would take
eight weeks to get them. On our second day, we were given altitude chamber
indoctrination in which each cadet was told he would experience anoxia. When
he felt light headed, he was to put on his oxygen mask. Always in alphabetical
order, we were marched into the altitude chamber. With Harry Evans sitting on
my right and Gib Edwards sitting on my left, I and twelve others were taken to
18,000 feet. After a short period of time, Harry said something such as "I think
I am . . .," and he fell forward and passed out. We scrambled to put on our
masks, and then we helped Harry, who soon came around, totally oblivious to
the fact that he had passed out. The demonstration made its point.

Lieutenant Colonel R. C. Mangrum, the cadet brigade commander, had an
impressive presence because of his extensive combat experience. Lieutenant
Commander C. E. Dickinson, who had flown at the battles of Coral Sea and
Midway, lectured as well. We cadets frequently discussed the types of airplanes we wanted to fly and whether we wanted to be Marine or Navy officers
(the Marine Corps took 10 to 20 percent of the naval aviator graduating

classes). Jack Scott, Gib Edwards, Harry Evans, and I solidly opted for the Navy, with Jack and me asking for dive bombers, Gib fighters, and Harry P boats. We would learn of our fates in that respect later.

On Sunday, February 28, 1942, we moved to Cabaniss Field for four weeks of intermediate training emphasizing navigation in the classroom while flying the SNV. NAS Cabaniss was about the size of NAS Los Alamitos, and here we were first treated as potential officers. Initial ground school consisted of lectures on course rules for flying and ground indoctrination into the more complex SNV airplane, which was the first all-metal airplane we had flown. Later we were given five hours of ground school in dead reckoning navigation each day because we would be flying over water far more often than over land. Aircraft recognition by silhouette was continually stressed as were eye muscle and image retention training through the flashing of strings of up to twenty digits on a screen at .1 to .025 of a second. Later, I would wish fervently that more of our ships' gunners had spent time in similar recognition training.

Each cadet was given two or three dual flights in the SNV, with the same gosport communication as the N2S, and a check flight—mine was with Lieutenant Fliesbach. It was after three more hours of solo flight, though, that I received the only down check during my flight training. Early on the morning of March 13, I met my check pilot, Lieutenant Hines, at the flight assignment blackboard in the shade of the hangar. He had flaming red hair, which should have tipped me off as he briefed me while we walked down the flight line of SNVs to our assigned airplane. He spoke clearly of what he expected. I was to take off, fly to a nearby outlying field, shoot three landings, then climb to 3,000 feet, and demonstrate steep turns, chandelles, and level flight at different specified power settings and speeds. We then would return to Cabaniss Field.

I started the engine, taxied, and took off, listening by gosport to Lieutenant Hines's comments. When we were airborne, he told me to proceed to the outlying field and fly the prebriefed plan. On reflection, I think my first landing was passable but not my best. It was difficult to make the standard Navy three-point landing each time. The succeeding two landings were better. I continued to fly as I had been briefed. I thought it strange that Lieutenant Hines said nothing, no coaching, no remarks. I looked over the instrument glare shield in front of me and saw the back of his neck. It was very, very red! Obviously, he had reached some highly agitated state of which I had not been aware as I flew. He turned in his seat to look back directly into my eyes and motioned with his hands for me to return to Cabaniss and land. There was no doubt in my mind what he wanted. I landed and taxied to the flight line, whereupon Lieutenant Hines got out of the airplane, visibly exercised, and gave me a withering look and a thumbs down signal. He wordlessly stomped off toward the hangar with his seat parachute tucked into the small of his back.

I was shaken, and as I secured the airplane for the next cadet's flight, I saw that the gosport tube had come apart between the two of us. Lieutenant Hines had been speaking to me, but I had never heard a word. I was in deep trouble! I walked back to explain what I had found, but Lieutenant Hines was long gone. By my name he had left an unmistakably clear chalked arrow pointing down. I was shattered. I had watched my compatriots suffer through down checks followed by extra flying time and the required two additional up checks. That process seemed to take from several days to a week and led to worry, doubt, and unwanted attention. Some cadets worried themselves sick and withdrew from their friends, as if they were contagious. Those who recouped from their down check rejoined society later, but those who did not would leave the program and just disappear. Here I was in the same boat, and it had nothing to do with my flying ability.

I became mad because I knew how to fly. Perhaps I had a way to go, but the ignominy of the down and the way that it had been given without explanation caused me to muster all the spunk that an eighteen-year-old aviation cadet could and to march up on the never-before-trod-on sanctity of the hangar's second deck to see the chief flight instructor. I found Lieutenant Constantine in his office behind a mountain of scheduling papers and forms and respectfully unburdened myself by describing the flight, the separated gosport, and Lieutenant Hines's agitation. I then asked for two check rides that very day to resolve whether or not I could fly the SNV.

The chief flight instructor looked at me, mused for a moment, and asked me if I knew that I could be washed out if I was not ready for the two checks. I replied that, indeed, I did know that, and I wanted to continue my flying, but I was not going to sit around and worry about it, whereupon he agreed to my proposal. I flew the second check within the hour with Lieutenant Lou Chick, whom I would get to know years later. He gave me an up. On our return from that flight and before lunch, I was surprised to see my name on the blackboard scheduled with Chief Flight Instructor Constantine himself for my third check. I flew that check as well and will never know whether Lieutenant Constantine gave me an up for guts or for a flawless flight. But it was an up, and I continued my training. Wartime training was rushed and could be brutal. In one day my cadet career was threatened and satisfactorily resolved, at least up to that point.

We completed our intermediate flight training in three weeks instead of four. During that period I flew 26.3 hours. When added to my 74 hours at Los Alamitos, that gave me 100 hours of flying time, and I was beginning to feel very comfortable in the cockpit.

Class 2D43C left Cabaniss for instrument training at Main Side on Sunday, March 21. We still had no idea of what type of fleet flying we would be assigned or whether we would be Navy or Marine officers. However, at Main

Side, on Saturday, April 10, Jack Scott and I were notified that we would be graduated as naval officers. That was not an inconsequential event. First, we could see our goal, assuming we did not wash out. Second, we had to select our uniforms. That afternoon we went into town to the resident tailor to order our uniforms, which cost the then-princely sum of $191.25, for which the tailor accepted a $25 down payment, promising he would have the uniforms ready in six to eight weeks. We could pay the balance then, or he would loan us the money to be repaid in installments. We chose the installment plan.

With graduation now more a probability than a possibility, expectations were raised at home. Wartime travel was a major challenge. I did not know when I would graduate, so I discouraged Mary and my mother from coming to Corpus Christi.

Instrument training entailed intensive ground school instruction. We became acquainted with the Link trainer—a ground-based flight simulator that allowed students to practice instrument flight without the danger or expense of a real airplane—and learned to fly the Charlie pattern, a precisely defined and timed sequence of turns, climbs, and descents. Any pilot who learned and flew the Charlie pattern can still draw one and recite the requirements today. It was burned into our minds forever! We flew our instrument training from the back-seat of SNJ-3s and SNJ-4s while under white canvas hoods. The concentration and study required to master instrument flying were the most difficult that I had experienced to date. We would turn in at the end of a day totally exhausted, but we mastered flying the Adcock radio ranges and the red, blue, green, and amber airways that defined instrument navigation. We also mastered unusual attitudes and instrument landing approaches. When we finished the course on April 20, we were handed a small leather pocket folder that told all who should read it that we were qualified Navy instrument pilots. I now had a total of 119 Navy flying hours.

On Friday, April 23, our class learned in which specialties we would be trained, and Gib Edwards, Harry Evans, Jack Scott, and I were given our first choices. That night was our last as roommates as we packed our bags to go our separate ways in the Navy. I believe Gib Edwards was subsequently shot down and killed while in the fleet; Harry Evans died in 1951 as the result of an automobile accident near Moffett Field, California; and Jack Scott and I are still close friends.

The next day Jack Scott and I rode by Navy bus to the naval air station at Kingsville, Texas, and reported to Squadron 15 at the South Field. Kingsville was the advanced training base for fighters and dive bombers near Corpus Christi, where cadets received tactical indoctrination in those disciplines before being designated as naval aviators. Kingsville was much larger than Cabaniss but smaller than Main Side. Lieutenant Commander C. E. Dickinson was the squadron commanding officer, and Squadron 15 was composed of seven flights of twelve scout bomber trainees. On Monday we were given the ubiquitous change of station physical examination, and on Tuesday, April 27, twelve of us aviation cadets were formed into Scout Bombing Flight 48. Among those in my flight were Charles Fisher, George Peck, George Glumac, Bill Emerson, John Crocker, Robert E. Lee Duncan, and Jack Scott. Through quirks of timing we eight would later fly and fight in World War II in the same squadron.

I was made the flight leader, more because of luck than merit. By definition we were first class aviation cadets and were treated even more like officers. We flew all day with no ground school; our only other activity was one hour of athletics. On April 30 Lieutenant Ponton gave me a 1.3-hour checkout flight in the SNJ-4, and I soloed that afternoon to begin my advanced training.

During May I flew two to four flights each day under instruction in Flight 48 for a total of fifty-five flights and seventy-seven flight hours. It was hot, the sun shone, and we became intensely sunburned. Our noses peeled, our faces took on the texture of brown leather, and we tried Noxema and zinc oxide with little relief. We thoroughly enjoyed the flying and swam an hour each day both to exercise and to cool off. We were taught that the key to survival in combat was to fly tightly together to enable our gunners to defeat the attacking fighters. Our instructors drove that point home by playing the role of attacking fighters and trying to force us to break up our formations.

We flew gunnery flights over the Gulf of Mexico, shooting at towed 18-foot, silk, cylindrical sleeves with our single .30-caliber machine gun firing synchronously through the propeller. The projectiles of the belted ammunition were dipped in heavy, oil-based paint of a single bright color so that as the bullets passed through the sleeve, they left traces of color to register hits. The colors were red, blue, purple, plain (no color), green, and orange. We soon learned it was better to have plain belted ammunition because if doubt existed as to the color around a hole, the hit was marked as plain! Heated arguments were common.

We flew navigation flights over the Gulf of Mexico to learn how to return to our carrier. The importance of building team spirit and relying on fellow pilots was emphasized over and over again, and we were taught to entrust our lives to one another. Up before dawn, flying thirteen days with one day of rest, we moved rapidly through the syllabus. I turned nineteen on May 28, and on June 2 I flew my last training flight for a total of 204 Navy flying hours.

Jack and I left Kingsville on June 3 to return to Main Side for the administrative processing necessary for our June 9 graduation. Our uniforms were ready, but we still did not know where we would go after graduation. On June 8 we were told that we would be sent to Daytona Beach for operational dive bombing training, which set our spirits soaring.

One hundred thirty cadets waited at NAS Corpus Christi to receive commissions in the U.S. Navy and the U.S. Marine Corps. The pool of graduating cadets was unusually large because of delays in orders coming from the Bureau of Naval Personnel in Washington. Normally, we were told, both ensigns and second lieutenants were graduated together, but because of this large group, Navy officers would graduate on June 9 and Marine officers on June 13. We naval officers were separated into three groups, and at 0930, June 9, my group of twenty-seven new ensigns formed up in two rows under a clear blue sky, resplendent in our new summer dress whites. We stood before the large white naval air station administration building. Exactly one year to the day had passed since I had enlisted in the V5 program in Los Angeles and only twelve days since my nineteenth birthday.

Our graduation group was made up of officers from all training disciplines, a number of whom I had never met before. One of those was George Herbert Walker Bush, who had gone to E base at Minneapolis and had been in class 2C43C and at Cudihy Field for torpedo pilot training. Many years later, when he was vice president of the United States and I was administrator of the Federal Aviation Administration, we would reminisce about that graduation day when neither knew the other.

The ceremony was short, and Lieutenant Colonel Mangrum officiated as each of us was commissioned an ensign AV(N), U.S. Naval Reserve, and had our wings pinned on. After graduation we shook hands with each other and left in small groups for the BOQ. A few enterprising sailors arranged to be in the right place at the right time to be the first to salute the new officers and to earn the silver dollar we each had ready in our pockets for that event.

Jack Scott, Bill Emerson, and I headed for Corpus Christi to board a train for the all-night trip to New Orleans and then on to Daytona Beach. The horsehair coach seats were covered in well-worn, velvetlike material redolent of the heat of the June night and Texas. Even with the windows open and the acrid smell of burning coal from the engine up ahead wafting through the car, our spirits were not dampened. We moved toward Daytona Beach and operational training.

Arriving in Daytona Beach on Sunday, June 13, 1943, we stayed at the Williams Hotel, on the corner of Magnolia and Palmetto Avenues. The hotel's broad verandahs and nearness to the beach gave it a vacation atmosphere, which we enjoyed for two days before we had to report for duty at the naval air station Monday evening. The air station was several miles west of the city and just south of a large training center for the Women's Army Corps.

Operational training was the capstone to our formal flight training and provided an additional 100 hours of flying to forge us into deployable junior fleet pilots. Captain H. D. Felt, a scout bombing pilot with early war combat expe-

rience, was commanding officer of the air station and VSB-3, the scout bombing training squadron. Lieutenant Commander J. R. Penland, operations officer, was responsible for scheduling about eighty officer students in forty-five
SBD-1s, -2s, -3s, and -4s along with a dozen SNJs. VSB-3 in turn comprised
six minisquadrons. Each had eleven or twelve Navy and Marine trainee pilots,
an instructor pilot–commanding officer, and an assistant instructor to impart
the combat lessons learned at the battles of Midway and Coral Sea.

Jack, Bill, and I, along with two other Navy officers and five Marine officers,
were assigned to VSB-32. Lieutenant E. L. Anderson USN, a tall, impressive
veteran of Scouting Squadron 6 in USS *Enterprise* at the battle of Midway, was
our commanding officer. Lieutenant Junior Grade J. Hofmeister was our assistant instructor. All students were assigned ground duties to broaden our responsibilities as future squadron officers. Jack Scott was assigned as navigation
officer, and I was assigned as gunnery officer.

On June 16 we started flying first in SNJ-3s and -4s for carrier landing practice at the nearby Naval Auxiliary Air Station (NAAS) Banana River. The carrier pattern we were taught was a highly stylized box pattern to the left, flown
at precisely 175-feet altitude, and consisted of takeoff and an upwind leg, a
crosswind and then downwind leg, with a final turn to pick up the LSO and to
fly his signals to the cut point where the pilot then made his own landing.
Speed control was vital, and on the final turn we flew as close as possible to 7
knots (1 knot equals 1.15 statute miles per hour) above the stall speed of the
SNJs. Of the many signals two were mandatory: the cut and the wave off. You
obeyed those regardless or answered for your actions later. We always un-
buckled our parachutes and opened our canopies for easier egress in case we
had engine failure and made a water landing. We flew carrier landing practice
for nine days until the LSO was satisfied with our procedures and performance.

On June 24 we began to fly SBDs and then were assigned our rear seat men,
enlisted gunners also in training. The SBDs were scarred, weary survivors of
the Pacific battles, most with pre–World War II markings. The SBD-1s, -2s,
and -3s had telescopic gun sights and CO_2-actuated flotation balloons for aircraft recovery after water landings. Those balloons had a nasty habit of deploying during flight, so our gunners carried sharp knives to puncture them in
an emergency. The telescopic gun sight was a 16-inch-long, 2-inch-diameter
tube that protruded through the forward windscreen for the pilot to aim his
airplane for bombing or gunnery. Student officers were constantly reminded
of the hazard of target fixation while looking through the sight, but even so,
two or three pilots dived into the ground while we were at Daytona Beach.
Fleet pilots had complained about those telescopic sights for years, and finally
a new reflective glass sight was put into the SBD-4 to give the pilot greater pe-
ripheral awareness.

The SBDs had inertial starters like our earlier trainers, which our seventeen- and eighteen-year-old rear seat men wound with cranks. We used the same penalty system for those that could not start the engine, only now, because of the much heavier engines, pilots had to get it right on the first try. A usually successful first try brought a cloud of white smoke and a throaty roar and brief smile to the pilot for his accomplishment and to the rear seat man for his relief.

Dive bombing, developed by the U.S. Navy and Marine Corps in the late 1920s and early 1930s, was the most formidably accurate way of delivering a bomb. A dive had three parts: the entry, the dive itself, and the recovery. The length of time that you spent in the dive depended on the entry altitude and the ground or water below. In training we were required to pull out to be in level flight at 1,000 feet. As we became better, and particularly later in the fleet, we delayed our pullout until there was just enough altitude to be in level flight above the water. The late pullout improved chances for a hit and survival in combat, but being too late was disastrous.

Dive speed was stabilized at 250 knots by split upper and lower trailing- edge perforated flaps activated by the dive-flap lever on the left side of the cockpit. The landing flaps were simply the lower portion of the dive flaps. If the pilot inadvertently selected dive flaps in the landing pattern and did not close them immediately, he could fall out of the sky. Everyone seemed to do that once, but not twice.

First we dived individually on land targets. Then, as we improved our tech- nique, we dived in a column of three and then six airplanes. We entered a dive by flying to the target at 9,000 feet to bring it first along the left side of the en- gine cowl and then the fuselage until it was about to disappear from view in the notch of the wing and fuselage. Then the pilot rolled left until inverted and let the nose of the airplane fall to aim directly at the target. The dive was nothing more than flying vertically, just as you would do horizontally, except that you were hanging in your seat belt. As you passed 6,000 feet, you placed your pip- per in the exact position to account for any wind and movement of the target ship and held that until releasing your bomb at 2,500 feet by pulling a manual bomb release. The SBD had an external y-shaped yoke, hinged at its forward point of attachment to the fuselage, which held the single bomb and ensured that it would miss the propeller. In training we used a small, external bomb rack carried under the right wing. That rack held up to ten miniature practice bombs that showed telltale smoke on impact.

We pilots of VSB-32 spent hours and hours climbing to 9,000 feet and then flying down to 1,000 feet in vertical flight. Lieutenant Anderson would circle the target at 1,500 feet to observe and comment on our dives, calling out "three o'clock 50 feet" or, more frequently, "twelve o'clock 300 feet." Gradually, we improved until we were consistently inside 25 to 50 feet.

In 1943 Nazi U-boats were having a field day with Allied merchant shipping in the Florida Strait. On any given day or night in July, at least three abandoned merchant ships burned on the horizon off Daytona Beach. The crews were rescued and the ships left to burn and sink. It was not uncommon to walk along the beach at night and see the glow of a large number of burning ships on the horizon, but at night, from the air, the burning ships were like beacons on the dark sea. We carried 250-pound depth charges under each wing on navigation flights to attack any U-boats sighted, but to my knowledge none of us saw one.

As July progressed, most of us in VSB-32 became better pilots, but Ensign Coffin had particular problems. He failed to lock his tail wheel on landing and ground looped; he overused his wheel brakes taxiing and blew tires regularly, and one time he took off in his SBD without putting his propeller into low pitch for full power. We were on the flight line and heard the unmistakably different sound of less than full power. With eyes quickly riveted on his SBD, we watched in fascination as his airplane consumed the entire runway, skimmed over the airport barbed wire fence, and flew directly into a large wooden barn just off the airport property.

He hit the barn with a wallop, and dust and pieces of ancient wood flew everywhere, followed by a deafening silence. Crash trucks sped to the scene, and fortunately no fire ignited. Shoulder straps were new in aviation, and a few of our SBDs had them, but they were a real pain and prevented our reaching some levers and switches in the cockpit. Without saying much, we did not use them. Ensign Coffin was no exception, so when he hit the barn not wearing his shoulder straps, he was thrown forward to jackknife on the top of the stick. He received a black eye and a few bruises but nothing else. However, a large 4-by-4 timber came end first through the forward windscreen and smashed into the pilot's head rest, decimating it. Had he been wearing his shoulder straps, he would have been decapitated. His survival was proof positive to the rest of us that shoulder straps were not to be worn. That event also marked the end of Ensign Coffin's training as a dive bomber pilot, and he was shortly sent to an E base to be an instructor. Each pilot was a needed and useful commodity at that stage of the war and an asset the Navy could ill afford to lose.

We progressed to dive bombing a target boat that cruised Lake George, some 30 miles west of Daytona Beach. The 22-foot boat was manned by two sailors and had an armored upper deck and top. The boat generally held a straight course but on command would make turns to simulate a ship under attack. That target boat acquainted us with reading the wind signals on the water, target movement, and the hazard of lack of depth perception when diving over water. Occasionally, we would get a direct hit with our small practice bombs, and it must have been an earth-shattering experience for the boat crew because it was an unwritten law that any pilot getting a direct hit on the boat would deliver a case of cold beer to the crew. I think that beer helped keep the boat crew on that harrowing job.

In mid-July the U.S. Naval Academy class of 1944 came to Daytona Beach for aviation indoctrination, and in the process we lost two airplanes, two pilots, and two Naval Academy graduates when the SBDs they rode in dove into the water, just missing the target boat. An astute accident board investigation found that in both cases the new officers riding in the backseat had installed the removable control stick, most probably earlier in the flight when the pilots offered them an opportunity to fly the SBD in level flight. Later, when the pilots entered their vertical dives, the passengers rotated their seats 180 degrees to ride backwards for the thrill of the vertical dive and did not remove the aft stick. As the pilots tried to pull out of the dive, the passengers' control sticks hit the metal back of the aft seats, preventing the pilots from pulling out, and the airplanes dove straight into Lake George.

Another training squadron at Daytona Beach lost a pilot, Ensign Wilkins, while on a night glide-bombing flight when he and his rear seat man did not return. The next day we found where he had hit the trees near a land target without trying to pull out of his glide. Dive or glide bombing at night was an exercise in futility. We could see nothing at which to aim the airplane, and the only instrument to tell height above the ground was the barometric altimeter, which always lagged behind the actual altitude. Combat flying and combat training were daytime visual pursuits, and the war principally was fought that way. However, we heard stories that a Commander Gus Widhelm was experimenting with flying fighters at night farther up the East Coast.

On July 25 VSB-32 started its field carrier landing practice (FCLP) in the SBD at Banana River, and on July 27 ten of us naval officers from two training squadrons were told that we would be going to the Pacific Fleet for duty. That meant our departure from Daytona Beach was imminent, and we would soon be going to Glenview, Illinois, for carrier qualifications on either USS *Sable* or USS *Wolverine*—two coal-fired, paddle-wheel lake steamers converted to aircraft carriers. Our fellow Marine pilots also participated in FCLP, but they would go directly to their squadrons without carrier qualification. Our rear seat men had completed their training as well, but they were issued separate orders to different squadrons.

On Friday, August 6, 1943, we made our last dive bombing flight and prepared to leave Daytona Beach. We turned in our flight gear, said our good-byes to our instructors and those friends still training, and left by train on Sunday, August 8, for the two-day trip to Chicago. We were qualified dive bomber pilots and getting closer to the war that we sought. I felt that I could place a bomb accurately any place that I wanted to. In the forty-five days that I had been at Daytona Beach, I had flown 125 hours and had 329 hours of total Navy flight time.

Our train ride to Chicago was high class compared with our previous trips. John Crocker, Bill Emerson, Jack Scott, and I shared two adjoining compartments. We arrived on the morning of August 10 and rode the electric train 30 miles north to NAS Glenview. We checked in with the duty officer and were told to report for a flight physical and ground school the next morning at 0800. That evening we returned to Chicago to see the city lights, new naval aviators loose on the town. After Daytona Beach, Chicago was an entirely different place, and we found our way back to Glenview by 0400 the next morning.

The carrier qualifications training unit was under the command of Commander J. O. Vosseller, and the principal LSO at that time was Lieutenant Commander Charles Roemer, the former LSO in *Lexington*. The training at Glenview nominally entailed one day of ground school, a second day of FCLP, and a third day of carrier qualification. Jack Scott and I completed the training in forty-eight hours.

The two paddle-wheel aircraft carriers—USS *Wolverine*, formerly SS *Seeandbee*, and USS *Sable*, formerly SS *Greater Buffalo*—had been modified by removing their top decks to install 550-foot-long flight decks that were 26 feet above the waterline. The Navy could ill afford using its few real carriers in a training role, and Lake Michigan offered added wartime safety in which to conduct carrier qualifications. The two carriers coursed Lake Michigan by day and tied up nightly at the Navy Pier in Chicago.

On the morning of August 11, we were given the obligatory Schneider test and a brief ground school, after which I flew a one-hour flight in a tired, old SBD-2 to make field carrier landings, and the LSO considered me field qualified. The next morning Jack Scott and I became part of a flight of five student officers led by an instructor to fly to *Sable*. We flew without rear seat men because not many volunteered to fly with someone who was landing on a carrier for the first time. We flew first to Point Oboe, marked by a mausoleum near Wilmette on the western shore of Lake Michigan, and then 20 miles farther to *Sable*.

Identifying *Sable*, we passed up the starboard side and entered the landing pattern individually. Religiously completing my landing cockpit checklist while establishing a proper interval on the airplane ahead of me, I flew the pattern 150 feet above the water until I turned toward the ship abeam the LSO. When I saw the LSO's paddles, he picked me up, and we began our carrier landing mating dance—he gave signals and I followed. I flew up the wake until I passed over the fantail, and I wondered if he would ever give me a cut signal. He did! I instinctively chopped the throttle and looked ahead just in time to pull back on the stick and feel the hook catch a wire as my landing gear met the deck. My upper body was thrown forward because the airplane had no shoulder straps, but I easily rode out the arrested landing with elation. Completing all eight landings in the same manner, I returned to Glenview. It was just after 1000, the flight had taken two hours, and I was a carrier-qualified naval aviator!

Jack and I left Glenview early on August 13 for the train trip to Pasadena, California. There was no time for good-byes; we would see our Navy friends in San Diego. We were all headed in the same direction: to war in the Pacific. We felt like kings! We were ensigns, naval aviators, and fully qualified carrier pilots on our way to war. That was what we had wanted. You could not get much prouder or happier!

Much of my fifteen-day leave was spent trying to help my mother, who was working to support my younger brother and herself. My father had been called to active duty as a Navy chief petty officer and was on the East Coast. Between duties at home, I spent as much time with Mary as I could. After much planning on my part, I asked her to marry me—to which she said, "Yes." She was eighteen and I was nineteen. We did not discuss a date because she wanted to decide what to do about her schooling. She had been accepted by Stanford University where she wanted to study medicine. The remainder of my leave was spent in the glow of our engagement, after which Jack Scott and I rendezvoused at Union Station in Los Angeles and headed for San Diego on September 5, 1943. Arriving there, we walked to the waterfront, caught the Nickel Snatcher ferry near the naval district headquarters, and crossed the bay to NAS North Island.

NAS North Island was big. We marveled at the wartime hustle and bustle of cars with people, trucks with parts, and tractors towing airplanes in various stages of assembly down the streets. Everybody seemed busy. The aromas of paint and solvent so peculiar to airplanes filled the air as we walked down the street to report to Commander Fleet Air West Coast. We were told that a new air group was being formed and that all dive bomber pilots checking in at that time would go to NAS Los Alamitos to report to Scout Bombing Squadron 19 (VSB-19). Our orders were endorsed, and we retraced our steps to Los Angeles to report to VSB-19 the next day.

Los Alamitos, now an auxiliary air station, was still out in the sticks. Lexington Avenue, from the main gate to the administration building, was now tree lined. A gymnasium and swimming pool had been built, as well as a second hangar. The concrete aircraft parking ramp was no longer filled with yellow biplanes but instead with F6F-3 fighters, TBF-1 torpedo planes, and SBD-5 dive bombers. The former parade ground was now a parking lot. Los Alamitos had gone to war.

We reported to the squadron duty officer of VSB-19 in hangar 2 and met the squadron administrative officer, Lieutenant Ben Buttenweiser USNR. He was a diminutive man, a former stockbroker from Wall Street, and a bundle of energy. VSB-19, one of three squadrons in Air Group 19, was to have thirty-six SBD-5s. We made our perfunctory calls on the commanding officer, Lieutenant Commander Richard S. McGowan USN, and the executive officer, Lieutenant Billy Gates. Of the fifty-six officers and sixty-six enlisted men, fifty were pilots, six were ground support officers, fifty were radiomen gunners, and sixteen were maintenance and support petty officers. I was assigned as assistant navigation officer under Lieutenant Joe Williams, the navigation officer. Our entire world revolved around flying, working, and socializing in the squadron.

We learned that Lieutenant Commander Hugh Winters USN, commanding officer of Fighter Squadron 19, was also acting air group commander while waiting for Commander Carl Jung USN to assume the air group command. The Navy air group concept at the time was to streamline the squadrons to make them mobile and combat dedicated. Each squadron relied on a handful of highly qualified maintenance and ordnance senior petty officers, who worked with a carrier aircraft service unit (CASU) for the necessary maintenance support.

Scout Bombing Squadron 19 became Bombing Squadron 19 (VB-19) in September in a normal Navy-wide redesignation that seemed to change nothing else. The mix of experience in the squadron was a training challenge. Besides our skipper, who was the sole lieutenant commander, only three others in the squadron had combat experience. There were thirteen lieutenants, nine lieutenants junior grade, and twenty-eight ensigns. Our radiomen gunners came as recent graduates of the fleet gunnery school. Assignments of pilots and gunners were made in September, and the squadron tactical organization was created. I was assigned radioman gunner Ted Stevenson, with whom I was to fly for the next fifteen months. My tactical assignment was as the number 2, or right, wingman on Lieutenant Emil Stella, who in turn was the second section leader for Lieutenant Bill MacBride's six-plane division. In all, we were organized into eight divisions of six pilots, with two spare pilots, to fly our thirty-six SBDs.

My first familiarization flights began on September 8, and those were an open invitation to indulge in some time-honored but strictly forbidden flat hatting. One day I said hello to Mary at her large, Spanish-style, two-story house, which overlooked the Arroyo Seco Canyon and Rose Bowl in Pasadena, by flying down the Arroyo Seco along the treetops below the cliffs that defined the canyon, pulling up to clear the eastern cliff, and then flying low and fast over her house. She knew who it was, and so did her father.

That evening I drove to Pasadena to see Mary and knocked on the door to be greeted by her somber-faced father, who motioned me to come with him to the dining room. Once there, he pointed to a large crack in the wall and admonished me to never buzz the house again. I was suitably contrite and apologetic and allowed that I would not do that again. As Mary and I departed the house later, she started to laugh and told me that the crack had been there for ten years. Mr. Baker made his point, and I stopped flat hatting before I was caught.

Mary and I eloped to Yuma, Arizona, on September 23 because of my intense work schedule (Arizona did not require visits to city hall and blood tests before marriage). We were married in the county court house by a municipal judge. The witnesses were a charwoman, who temporarily put down her broom, and a handyman, who had been outside the judge's chambers. We then found a hard-to-come-by house on Balboa Island as our first home and set up housekeeping in that vacation atmosphere. An ensign's pay was not the greatest amount of money, but with base and flight pay plus subsistence and rental allowances, my total pay of $350 each month got us by—at least after I paid my loan to the Corpus Christi tailor.

The squadron moved directly into an accelerated training schedule of flying between thirty and fifty hours a month; each flight combined all training aspects—navigation, tactical division flying, defensive maneuvering, fixed and free gunnery, and bombing. We dived and dropped miniature bombs on towed sleds and oil slicks, and we bombed the Kearny Mesa Marine Corps Reservation targets. We almost lost two airplanes before we discovered that the expended brass cartridge cases from our two forward-firing .50-caliber cockpit machine guns could jam in the elevator controls under the floor boards.

Our dive bombing tactic was to approach the target at 13,000 feet in parade formation. Then each airplane would roll in sequentially until all airplanes were diving at once. We each would drop one practice bomb, then rendezvous, and go through the routine again, and again. One afternoon, while conducting dive bombing at Kearny Mesa, our flight leader, Lieutenant Gates, became furious with what he felt was our consistently slow rendezvous after each dive. On the 80-mile return flight to Los Alamitos, he placed us into an eighteen-plane right echelon parade formation and chewed on us using our brand new, four-channel, push-button VHF radios. The sun was setting, so our northbound direction of flight placed us all looking into the sun for the forty-five-minute flight to Los Alamitos. Lieutenant Gates was a hard, but deeply respected, taskmaster. Unfortunately, he was transferred to command another bombing squadron and was subsequently killed in combat.

On November 16, 1943, while bombing a slick off Huntington Beach, Ensign F. Leo Hart and his gunner, Theodore Scheck, were killed when Hart dove into the water after failing to pull out of the dive. Glassy water was a continuing hazard, and mistakes were fatal to dive bomber pilots. At a specific point in every dive you must have started your pullout—the trick was to know what that point was.

We lost another airplane in the water near Santa Catalina when the engine quit, but the crew were rescued. Several other SBDs were lost by other squadrons in the San Diego area at about the same time, and we did not know why. One day in December I was flying between San Clemente and Santa Catalina Islands when my engine abruptly quit. I cannot describe how loud that silence can be when you are over water, out of sight of land. I was determined to try everything before I hit the water; my third or fourth alternative was to use the electric fuel primer pump, which brought enough power from the engine to stay in the air. I held the primer on to keep the engine running at greatly reduced power while I limped back to Los Alamitos.

I was the first pilot to bring back an SBD-5 with that problem, so the next day Lieutenant Don Banker and I flew to the Douglas aircraft plant in El Segundo to talk with E. H. (Ed) Heinemann, a design engineer there. Ed was a tall, angular man; even without a college degree, he was a gifted natural aeronautical engineer, who had started with Jack Northrop and moved on to Douglas in the 1930s. Ed listened intently to my story and subsequently determined that during manufacturing a fuel line that passed through the firewall was being bent at more than the allowed maximum of 45 degrees. That bend caused a vapor lock, and the engine was starved for fuel. That manufacturing error was remedied, and we lost no more SBDs, at least for that reason.

Our training continued, and we became better and better. Each pilot could place his bomb on or near the bull's-eye of the target at will. Along the way some unlucky junior officers were caught flat hatting and paid the price by being placed in hack by the commanding officer. That meant being confined to a BOQ room for up to one week, depending on the severity of the offense. One pilot did a slow roll at 3,500 feet while over the water. There was nothing wrong with that, except this pilot failed to remind his gunner to lock his guns before the roll, and the gunner watched in amazement as his twin .30s cleanly departed the airplane and tumbled into the ocean. The pilot was court-martialed and fined some small amount of his pay as a penalty, and the event was over, but not forgotten.

In early January 1944 we flew our airplanes to NAS North Island and boarded USS *Altamaha*, a jeep escort aircraft carrier, for carrier qualifications. The night before we went to sea, four of us went into San Diego and walked into the first bar we saw. The others made it through the door past a very buxom blonde bouncer (there were no men around to be bouncers). As I approached, she leaned over, put her arm in the doorway, and said to me, "Not you, honey. You are under age!" My compatriots laughed and left me outside to nurse my wounded pride and to return to the ship thinking that life was not fair. I was nineteen and could fight for my country, but I could not enter a bar.

The next day we put to sea in USS *Altamaha* for three days while each of us made twelve carrier landings. The long ocean swells off the coast of California and the proclivity of the escort carrier (CVE) to roll made life difficult. Some sick pilots were glad to get into the air where the going was smoother.

Our training now was integrated, with the fighters, dive bombers, and torpedo bombers attacking sleds that were always towed behind the destroyers operating out of Long Beach. The ships received surprise AA tracking practice, and we gained a moving target. Lieutenant Don Banker, a Naval Academy graduate who had applied for and been accepted for flight training after serving his required two years at sea, now became executive officer. Banker graduated from flight training at Pensacola about the same time that many of the ensigns graduated. His lack of flight experience showed in the abruptness of his flying, and those who flew on his wing sometimes had a difficult time, but he was a fine officer and was well liked.

In early February 1944 we were alerted that we would deploy soon, and on February 16 we flew our airplanes to NAS Alameda, near Oakland, to be loaded in USS *Lexington*. *Lexington* had taken a Japanese aerial torpedo in the starboard quarter on December 5, 1943; now repaired, it was returning to Pearl Harbor to pick up Air Group 16 and proceed west again. After flying my airplane to Alameda, I returned to Los Alamitos to help with the squadron's move. Mary and I then drove our car north on Saturday and Sunday, February 19 and 20. We found a Quonset hut for transient officers at Alameda and spent two days touring San Francisco. On a dreary February 24 at 0900 we said our good-byes on the carrier pier at Alameda. Good-byes are hard. Wartime good-byes seem even harder, and Mary was pregnant with our first child. As luck would have it, our car was developing a flat tire, so Mary had to assault the Alameda ration board for a coupon to get a used tire, but she was successful. As the ship pulled out at 1330 under gray skies, I stood on the flight deck among closely packed airplanes and watched while we passed under the Bay Bridge, by Alcatraz, and through the Golden Gate. Mary drove back to Pasadena to live by herself in her father's house and to have our baby alone. Wars make strong people.

Lexington arrived in Pearl Harbor on February 28, 1944, where the carnage of December 7, 1941, remained evident. Three battleships, still capsized at their moorings with black oil oozing to the surface of the milky blue waters, were reminders of why we were fighting a war. As *Lexington* silently negotiated the channel to one of the H or hotel piers at Ford Island, the quartermaster of the watch on the bridge directed our attention to each sunken ship as we passed, saying "attention to starboard." Each time, the crew topside would stop all activity, face starboard at attention, and render silent tribute to those who had died in that particular ship. Once we had passed each ship, topside speakers would intone "carry on." Those acts of respect were great motivators.

After we moored, we immediately began to unload our air group equipment and airplanes by crane onto Ford Island. VB-16 took our SBDs because they were newer, and we were scheduled to receive the even newer SB2C-3s in several months. We would continue training in older SBDs at our new base at NAS Kahului, Maui. Air Force Pacific Fleet (AIRPAC) was headquartered on Ford Island. Our move to the Hawaiian Islands was part of the general plan to position trained air groups nearer the combat zone to defend Hawaii and to be poised for immediate deployment westward should combat losses require it. The normal combat tour for an air group was running about six months, while the carriers stayed on the line up to three years.

Radar was just coming into the fleet and was highly classified. We began radar training for our crewmen since our SB2Cs would have this new capability. A TBF was assigned to the squadron so that we could train several crewmen on one flight, and I, as well as several other pilots, flew that airplane. Our dive bombing training accelerated, and we again began coordinated squadron attacks, this time dropping live bombs on Molokini Rock between Maui and Kahoolawe. A well-coordinated attack of twenty-four fighters, twenty-four dive bombers, and eighteen torpedo bombers was as awesome to the friendly participants as it was to the enemy and could be accomplished in as little as four minutes. Some of our greatest thrills came from extricating ourselves from near simultaneous arrivals at the target.

One of the semiannual air defense exercises for Oahu was held at Pearl Harbor in March 1944 with the Navy attacking while the Army Air Forces defended. We enjoyed those exercises because they were tantamount to legalized flat hatting. Our particular target was Ford Island, which we aggressively attacked. While retiring with P-40s buzzing all about, I flew down Kapiolani Boulevard below the treetops. Fortunately, I saw the large pineapple-shaped water tower at the Dole plant just in time to miss it by inches, which made a lasting impression on me and allowed me to not make one on it.

In March two things happened: Lieutenant Commander McGowan was promoted to commander, and VB-19 began a slow transition to the SB2C. Before we received the newer SB2C-3s, we were given very old SB2C-1s to fly, which were plagued by maintenance problems. The SB2C-1 was deployed with VB-11 to the Pacific Fleet in February 1944. Because of the plane's large size and complexity, when compared with the older, more reliable SBD, it did not enjoy as good a reputation among ships' companies and staffs. Everyone referred to the SB2C as the beast. Its skin was aluminum except for fabric-covered ailerons, elevator, and rudder, and its sharp edges would bite pilots, aircrewmen, and maintenance men alike. The 3,000-psi hydraulic system was controlled by four garden-faucet-shaped valve handles positioned on the forward cockpit floor and was a nightmare after the simple on-demand hydraulic system of the SBD. The valves could isolate different parts of the hydraulic system, allowing the pilot to control combat damage. The bomb bay could hold a 1,000-pound bomb, and like the SBD it also had a yoke to move the bomb clear of the bay and propeller in the vertical dive.

Initially, we had six SB2Cs, four of which seemed to be unflyable at any given time, and so while slowly checking out in the SB2C-1, we continued our gunnery training in our SBDs. Ensigns towed target sleeves. Lieutenants and lieutenants junior grade did not. We ensigns towed and we towed. On April 12 I was to tow in an SBD and offered our first-class parachute rigger, Stopper Biesner, a ride. Parachute riggers were good people to know; they could do magic with their sewing machines. I briefed Stopper as we walked to the airplane and told him that I had determined that I could fly the SBD inverted without losing fuel pressure by using the primer. Also, I reasoned that a pilot could roll the SBD inverted without entangling the tail wheel in the towline and asked him if he was up for some inverted flying. He allowed that he was.

We took off with the tow and headed out to the gunnery firing area north of Maui while climbing to 8,000 feet. Lieutenant Bob Niemeyer flew by the tow to check it, and he and his division then climbed to begin making fixed gun firing passes. I was ready for them, and as Lieutenant Niemeyer rolled in for the first firing pass, I carefully rolled the airplane inverted and maintained level inverted flight. As the manifold pressure began to fall, I held the electric primer switch on to provide fuel to the engine and kept a watchful eye on the oil pressure. Niemeyer flew by my airplane, summarily announced that the gunnery flight was over, and told me to return to Kahului. I suspected that he was mad. Niemeyer told Commander McGowan, and Commander McGowan told me that I had earned three days in hack. Stopper Biesner went back to parachute packing after he and I convinced the commanding officer that he had no part in the event other than being an innocent rider. I read a lot, learned a lesson, and on the fourth day rejoined the squadron's social structure.

Our first new SB2C-3s arrived in mid-May, and by the end of May we had our full complement of thirty-six. The SB2C-3, a great improvement over the SB2C-1, had two Oldsmobile 20mm cannon mounted in the wing. In addition to the single bomb in the bomb bay, we could carry a 250-pound bomb under each wing, and our gunners had factory-installed radar. The R-2800 engine had a four-bladed propeller, which seemed to give the airplane greatly increased performance in cruise and climb. However, the airplane dived at 365 knots, much faster than the SBD. That speed meant that we would be less exposed to AA fire, but we would have to drop our bomb higher. On balance, the SB2C-3 was a delight to fly.

In mid-June we flew out to USS *Franklin*, then off Oahu, for carrier qualifications in our SB2C-3s. *Franklin* was deploying westward to the war, and the ship's air group was briefly off-loaded at Ford Island while each pilot in Air Group 19 made four landings. A big battle was taking place in the Philippine Sea, west of the Marianas, and the carriers had lost many airplanes and pilots. On June 20, 1944, we were alerted that we would be moving out immediately to go to the western Pacific as a thirty-airplane squadron instead of our current thirty-six. We would retain the same complement of pilots and aircrew. On the next day, June 21, we flew to Ford Island, shipped our gear by boat, and loaded on board USS *Intrepid* for transportation to the western Pacific. We were to be next up. At that time I had a total of eighteen flights and four carrier landings in the SB2C-3, but I had over 700 Navy flying hours and felt ready.

3. COMBAT
JUNE 1944 TO DECEMBER 1945

In the Pacific the Marianas were taken by U.S. forces as a prelude to the return to the Philippines, the epochal battle for Leyte Gulf, and the capture of Iwo Jima and Okinawa, but not before kamikaze pilots took a heavy toll on U.S. Navy ships. B-29s bombed Japan, and U.S., British, and Chinese forces defeated the Japanese in Burma. Toward the end of the war, the makeup of the Navy air group was altered to fifty-four fighters, twenty-four dive bombers, and eighteen torpedo bombers to meet the kamikaze threat in the planned invasion of Japan. Nuclear bombs were dropped first on Hiroshima and then on Nagasaki in August 1945, bringing Japanese capitulation as the Soviet Union declared war on Japan. The formal surrender ceremony in USS Missouri *was an event that brought rejoicing throughout the world.*

In Europe U.S. troops established the initial beachhead in Normandy in June 1944. The U.S. Navy captured the German U-505 submarine off Africa. The Allies occupied Athens, and Italy fell. German officers failed in an attempt to kill Hitler, while the Allied bombing campaign took a terrible toll on German cities. Allied ground forces from the west and the east overran Germany, which then capitulated in May 1945.

A merchant ammunition ship exploded with great force at Port Chicago, California, and 300 were killed. President Roosevelt was reelected to an unprecedented fourth term, only to die in June 1945. The chief of naval operations (CNO) drastically reduced pilot training in 1945, and at the end of that

*year there were 49,829 pilots, 241,364 aviation ratings, and 98 aircraft carri-
ers of all classes in the Navy.*

On June 24, 1944, a businesslike USS *Intrepid* sortied silently from Pearl Harbor, past the remaining sunken ships still oozing black oil and through the submarine nets to move west at 28 knots as a single ship. Speed and stealth were our defenses. We had no doubt where we were going. Certainly all the pilots and crewmen in Air Group 19 knew that their months of training were about to be tested as the days were filled with intelligence briefings and preparations for combat.

Later in July I learned that Mary had been admitted to the U.S. Army Hospital in Pasadena, California, on June 24 to have our baby. She had a most difficult delivery, which took three days, before our son, Travis, was born one month prematurely on June 27, 1944. The irony was that as *Intrepid* moved west, we crossed the international date line and moved our calendars from June 26 to June 28. Later, Mary did not think that was amusing.

On the morning of June 30, as we watched silently from the flight deck, *Intrepid* passed through the antisubmarine warfare (ASW) control point at Eniwetok some 900 miles east of Guam and entered the large lagoon to anchor. The coral reef and a few islands provided a compact administrative area, including a 4,000-foot crushed-coral landing strip. It was almost like an aircraft carrier. The ships of TG 58.2 were already anchored in the lagoon, and *Intrepid* entered to anchor alongside *Bunker Hill*. Other Task Force (TF) 58 task groups were still covering the invasion of Saipan or were en route from the recent battle of the Philippine Sea. The battle was a great success, but TF 58 lost 150 airplanes and a third as many pilots and was badly in need of reconstitution. Air Group 16 in *Lexington* had taken enough losses to be replaced, which was why we were there.

We began the logistics checkers game of moving people and airplanes, which lasted over the next nine days. On July 1 eighteen of our SB2C-3s were catapulted from *Intrepid* at anchor to fly to the Eniwetok coral strip and await further transfer to *Lexington*. For me the catapult shot itself was a highlight. The H-4 hydraulic catapult must have been near its and my airplane's limits to give the needed end speed to fly away. I remember the back-jarring jolt far more than I remember the short flight to the island.

Admiral Raymond Spruance was commander of the Fifth Fleet in USS *Indianapolis*, Vice Admiral Marc Mitscher was commander of Task Force (CTF) 58 in USS *Lexington*, and Rear Admiral Frederick Sherman was commander of Task Group (CTG) 58.3 in USS *Essex*. On July 5 TG 58.3 steamed into Eniwetok's lagoon fresh from supporting the Marines on Saipan and the battle of the Philippine Sea, and we had our first view of *Lexington* since the previous February as the ship anchored in the carrier row. Tokyo Rose had dubbed *Lexington* the Blue Ghost, a name that evoked great pride and satisfaction from the crew. The carrier was the only one of the *Essex* class in the task force that was painted with blue gray rather than zigzag camouflage paint. That color distinction also helped us pilots find the correct aircraft carrier.

On July 7 *Bunker Hill* sortied from Eniwetok with several destroyers to provide a deck for refresher landings for a few Air Group 19 pilots. Between Friday, July 7, and Sunday, July 9, Air Groups 16 and 19 moved between ships, and then *Lexington* got under way to recover our airplanes. The complex cannibals and missionaries game was completed, with the loss of one TBF on the catapult shot from *Intrepid*, and *Lexington* reentered the lagoon on July 9 to anchor and await departure with the others. The loss of the TBF was tragic because it carried the contraband whiskey for VF-19 and VT-19. There were no dry eyes in those squadrons after that airplane hit the water in the Eniwetok lagoon and the crew swam away.

About forty-five Air Group 19 ensigns lived in the junior officers bunk room on the 02 level in *Lexington*, which was forward, just under the flight deck, between the port and starboard catapults. It was true togetherness, and we affectionately called the bunk room boys' town. Each of us had a single 3-by-3-by-2-foot locker and one bunk in a triple tier. There were two small writing tables, which we moved to make room for the nightly crap game. Boys' town was for sleeping, not living, and we spent most of our time in our respective ready rooms, which were blessedly air conditioned. The rest of the ship relied on moving slightly cooler than ambient temperature air from one compartment to another to provide comfort. The officers' wardroom was amidships on the second deck, just below the armored hangar deck and abeam the island. Breakfast was served continuously for two hours after the ship's crew was secured from the daily sunrise general quarters, and there were two sittings each in the wardroom for lunch and dinner. During flight quarters the air group and air department officers could eat at any sitting. A long-sleeved wash khaki uniform was required at all times for officers, and that kept us prepared for the frequently unanticipated general quarters.

Much of the Fifth Fleet sortied from Eniwetok on the afternoon of July 14 and headed for combat. Arriving off Guam, *Lexington* and TG 58.3 supported the invasion of Guam from mid-to-late July. That was our warm-up to combat. The air group attacked targets around the Japanese airfield on Orote Peninsula and supported the Marines with on-call direct air support wherever they needed it.

On July 19 we lost two SB2C-3s. Ensign Paul Gevelinger and his crewman, Aviation Radioman Second Class Nichman, were killed when their SB2C-3 stalled after a deck-run takeoff and spun into the water forward of the ship.

That seemingly needless loss had a sobering effect on all pilots and aircrew-men because it reminded us that it was not just combat that had its hazards. In the afternoon Lieutenant Price Stradley's SB2C-3 was hit by small arms ground fire while providing close air support and was downed. He landed his airplane in the water two miles off Orote Peninsula. He and his rear seat man, Aviation Radioman Second Class Arno Droske, received minor injuries but re-turned to *Lexington* within two days to continue flying.

One task group remained to support the Marines while two others moved southwest to make the first strikes on Palau, and the fourth task group moved north to make the first attacks on Iwo Jima. Vice Admiral Mitscher employed this naval flexibility to great advantage to keep the Japanese off balance. En route to Palau, TG 58.3 refueled and rearmed at sea. Lieutenant Junior Grade George Lewis, our air intelligence officer, used that respite to brief all pilots for the coming attacks. He carefully gave us enough information to understand what we were going to see and to do; however, we were not told many intelli-gence matters because pilots and crewmen were the most liable to be captured.

On the afternoon of July 25, Lieutenant John Hutto, the only photo pilot of VF-19, brought back pictures of carefully camouflaged Japanese ships moored to the steep sides of small islands in the Palau group, and in the early dawn light of July 26, we launched to attack those and other targets. The fighters at-tacked the airfield, while the dive bombers and torpedo bombers attacked the ships. Many of the previously photographed ships were still there, and I at-tacked and sank my first ship, a small, 1,000-ton coastal freighter. The air group had a heyday in its first truly offensive combat flying. The opposition was principally AA from the many islands and ships. While launching to attack Palau, I first noticed Vice Admiral Mitscher sitting on the inboard side of his open flag bridge in a pedestal chair, alone, facing aft. He sat there for almost every launch and recovery, with his chin cupped in his right hand, his expres-sion and position never changing. He was—always—just there. We had heard of the respect that pilots held for Vice Admiral Mitscher, but because we were new, he was as much an unknown quantity to us as we were to him.

The process for striking new targets was simple in concept but complex in execution. The general objective was determined by the fleet commander's staff in coordination with Commander in Chief Pacific Fleet (CINCPAC). The when and how was determined by the task force commander's staff. The task group commanders' staffs coordinated within the assigned areas to be attacked, and the carriers were assigned specific targets. The size of a strike was con-trolled by the importance of the target, the aircraft available to fly, and the abil-ity of the carrier to launch them. That planning began days and weeks in ad-vance, but the details so critical to pilots became available several days before and particularly the evening before the first attack. The flight officer of each squadron would attend the evening air group planning session and complete his task of determining which pilots would fly and when. Our flying efforts were formulated when our flight officer, Lieutenant Bill Cravens, made up the next day's squadron schedule. He did a good job of keeping the number of strikes for each pilot equal regardless of rank. Key to good pilot morale was equity in scheduling, and an honest effort was made to keep all pilots equally exposed to combat with a fair mix of good and not-so-good targets and flights. Some of the more senior pilots occasionally would get the choicer opportunities, but generally the system worked.

Our lives centered on the ready room. There we received intelligence briefs, were briefed for our flights, and kept our flight gear on hooks along the bulkheads and our navigation plotting boards under our assigned seats. There we waited between flights, signed our airplane maintenance yellow sheets before manning our aircraft, debriefed when we returned, and filled out the yellow sheets after flights. Each pilot always did his own dead reckoning navigation because you never knew when you might have to come back alone or might be leading the flight home. In the ready room we received all preflight information from the air operations office (air ops) by teletype machine. The teletype machine, with its 3-by-3-foot, illuminated, yellow, translucent cloth screen, was our link to the world through air ops; it seemingly controlled our lives. The rotating squadron duty officer (SDO) was responsible for sitting at a desk at the head of the ready room, keeping the flight schedule up to date on the blackboard, talking to air ops as required to keep the information flowing, and ensuring that all pilots maintained decorum while in the ready room.

Before each flight the squadron maintenance officer would provide the side or identifying numbers of the ready-to-fly aircraft to flight deck control, which in turn spotted them for launch. The SDO would advise the pilots of the positions of the airplanes on the flight deck. Those details might seem irrelevant on a ship, but when it is pitch-black dark on a predawn launch or when a pilot must negotiate his way to his airplane around whirling propellers and treacherous slipstreams, the shortest way is the best way. The last thing we would do before running for our airplanes was to recheck the ship's current position and intended movement (PIM), and any further change would be flashed at us on a blackboard held by a flight deck crewman alongside the flight deck officer as he signaled us to launch. Navigation was a serious business, and the carrier pilot's plotting board was his life insurance policy. The entire fleet operated and flew in total radio silence. There were no radio navigational aids other than the mysteriously coded VHF homer wheel.

Airplanes were respotted on the flight deck for the next launch according to takeoff performance. That meant the fighters launched first, their deck runs starting from abeam the island, which gave them time to provide cover for the other airplanes as we rendezvoused. The TBFs were second in launch sequence because their large wing area and good aerodynamic lift required less deck run than the SB2Cs. The SB2Cs were parked farthest aft, which had its advantages and disadvantages for us dive bomber pilots. On the plus side, we had more time to preflight our airplanes or to switch to a spare airplane. On the minus side, the dive bomber pilot and his crewman always ate stack gas. That acrid, foul-smelling gas from the boiler fires far below the flight deck came out of the stack in the island and billowed across the after flight deck. The only person to eat more stack gas than a bomber pilot was the LSO. A good chief engineer never made visible, telltale smoke, particularly in wartime, but the clear stuff smelled just as bad. Finally, airplanes were always parked as far as possible from any five-inch gun mount because the concussion from the muzzle blast shredded our fabric-covered control surfaces.

On August 2 three task groups, each with two *Essex* class carriers and two CVLs (light carriers built on cruiser hulls), moved north to attack the Bonin Islands. Early on August 4 Air Group 19 launched to attack ships in the small Iwo Jima harbor. Lieutenant Don Banker led three divisions of six dive bombers each to the target area where Lieutenant Bill McBride's division went after a destroyer that was trying to sortie. We six dived in order; Stella, I, and Ensign Roy Majors were the last three down. We hit, stopped, and sank the destroyer, but I never saw Roy Majors again. He was right behind me in the dive but never joined up. The AA fire was intense, and Lieutenant Junior Grade Bill Emerson, flying wing on Don Banker, was hit in the engine during his dive, lost all power, and landed in the water. The wind and seas were high and obscured all detail on the surface of the sea, and in the melee none of us saw Bill's airplane hit the water. Two F6Fs from *Princeton* were the assigned rescue combat air patrol (RESCAP) and directed USS *Shark*, the rescue submarine, to Bill's area where he and his crewman, Aviation Radioman Second Class M. J. Harvey, were picked up. They spent the next twenty-five days on a submarine combat patrol in which *Shark* was depth charged many times by the Japanese. Bill felt that was double jeopardy, but he and Harvey were grateful for their rescue and eventually got back to Pearl Harbor where they were given a three-week vacation at the Royal Hawaiian Hotel. On October 23, during the submarine's next patrol, *Shark* was lost with all hands. We aviators had a great respect and empathy for submariners. Much later Bill Emerson and Harvey would relate how they climbed into their two-man raft after leaving the airplane and saw another SB2C dive vertically into the water. That was Roy Majors's airplane.

We returned from the strike believing Bill Emerson and Harvey were lost, and it was not until *Shark* surfaced to enter Pearl Harbor that we knew otherwise. Also, it was not until Bill filed his combat report in Pearl Harbor that we knew that he had seen Roy Majors go in. The air group was now regularly losing pilots, and we in boys' town developed a routine. When one of us was shot down, his personal effects were inventoried by the squadron, and the truly personal things were sent home. Each of us had little other than wash khaki shirts and trousers, socks, underwear, and toiletries, and those items would be handed out in the bunk room to those that were about the same size or could use the items. We did that in the case of Bill Emerson and Roy Majors. When Bill was reported to be alive later, we had to run around and collect all his things and put them back in his locker. He did not return to the ship until October 3, and I do not think we ever told him what we had done.

On August 4 I woke in boys' town to hear the hydraulic fluid humming as it coursed through the catapult tubes before a launch. The muted roar of the engines suddenly stopped before the launch, so I ducked out onto the port catwalk to see what was up. I heard a lone airplane engine droning somewhere off the port bow. It was so foggy that I could barely make out *Essex*, about 1,500 yards off our port beam. As I peered that way, I suddenly saw a Japanese Zero coming out of the mist at my eye level. Too late and too surprised to do anything, I watched with fascination as he flew at me and dropped his single 500-pound bomb, which then passed over me and across the flight deck to explode in the water on the starboard side. The Zero flew off, and no one fired a shot.

In the Pacific in 1944, the air war was generally fought in good weather in the daytime. On August 5 a fast-moving cold front compounded our problem in reaching the target at Chichi Jima, the island south of Iwo Jima, but many did get through to attack the airfield and ships there. Flying to the target was strictly a good weather proposition. We did not have the ability to cope with or to navigate through truly bad weather or fly great numbers of airplanes at night. The targets there were lucrative, but the AA fire was even more intense than it had been at Iwo Jima. Ensign John Cavanaugh's SB2C-3 was hit, and either he or Aviation Radioman First Class Michael Blazevich was seen to bail out. As the division completed its dives, a single chute was seen coming down inside Chichi Jima harbor. Every Japanese gun concentrated its fire on the chute and the person in it until the chute collapsed at about 400 feet and he fell to the water. Whoever it was, he was dead long before he hit the water. Two VF-19 pilots were shot down and lost as well.

Lieutenant Donald Helms's SB2C-3 also was shot down at Chichi Jima. He crashed into the heavy seas as he tried to land near another U.S. submarine that was patrolling to pick up pilots and crewmen. Don Helms was rescued and returned to *Lexington* a few weeks later in Eniwetok, but unfortunately Aviation Radioman Second Class Russell Snow was injured in the crash and died in the water before he could be rescued. That same afternoon Lieutenant Junior Grade Bob Smith's airplane was so damaged by AA fire that he was forced to make a water landing alongside a destroyer after returning as far as the task group. He and his rear seat man were returned to *Lexington* by high line and bosun's chair the next day.

The return of a squadron mate by high line was always an occasion. Pleased to see them, we gathered to cheer and to taunt them as they were swung across the 60 feet of water between *Lexington* and the destroyer. *Lexington* made fast the end of the high line, and fifteen or twenty men on the sending destroyer held the line taut between the ships. In that way the ships' rolls were accommodated without the person riding getting his feet or other parts wet. Everyone topside on both ships watched the sport and tried to coax the line-handling crew to give enough slack for a good dousing. In accordance with the then-accepted procedure, ten gallons of ice cream were sent back to the destroyer in exchange for each rescued aircrewman.

Flying from carriers was completely different from flying from an airfield. At an airfield pilots could launch on combat missions almost as they chose or were able to do so. Any pilot delayed in taxi or takeoff could take off later to join the flight. There was flexibility. On board ship flying involved much more process. The average combat flight lasted three to four hours. Three, at the most four, launches and recoveries were made each day. A task group had four carriers, and each carrier launched and recovered in coordination with the other three and complied with the tactical maneuvering of the task group. All turns into the wind for launch or recovery were made in unison with the carriers, battleships, and cruisers always within the screen of twelve to eighteen destroyers. There were just so many minutes for launches and recoveries. If airplanes were not ready or did not get airborne in time, then the flights proceeded without them. The process was not as haphazard as it may sound, but rather flexibly structured, and it worked well, but aircraft carriers did not provide squadron pilots the freedom to fly at will. On occasion, especially during an emergency, one carrier would take another's airplane on board to help. The task group would steam for days to get into position to launch aircraft and to attack a new target. Once there, we might stay for one, two, or three days and fly repetitive strikes, but the situation and the scenery were always changing for the carrier pilot. Also, we were always thrust into a hornet's nest of enemy activity. There were not many light flying days, but we would have layoffs of a week or so between major efforts.

By August the carrier task groups could use Ulithi for reprovisioning. On August 9 we anchored there, and along with thousands of others, we relaxed on the beach of the island of Mogmog, swimming and drinking beer. Two replacement pilots reported to VB-19 from a newly established replacement pool, and five replacement SB2C-3 airplanes were barged out to *Lexington* for us. The squadron was again back to thirty airplanes. VF-19 and VT-19 had also lost pilots and airplanes and were given replacements as well. We were combat experienced and were dedicated more than ever to finding and sinking Japanese ships.

We spent August 10–25, 1944, in Ulithi lagoon getting ready for the next big phase of the Pacific war, the attack to liberate the Philippines. Pilots and aircrew, those bearing the primary combat responsibility, were given time off to go ashore for athletics and a beer or two while staffs planned and ships re-provisioned. Frequently, after a few beers, things could get rough on the beach. One evening an LCM (landing craft medium), used to move the large liberty parties to and from *Lexington* and the other ships, was returning with a rowdy group. An ensign from USS *New Jersey* protested loudly when the aviators on board would not let the coxswain detour to drop him at the officer's ladder on his ship. As the LCM passed within 100 yards of *New Jersey*, the ensign was picked up bodily and thrown into the water to swim to the *New Jersey*.

At anchor we always played volleyball on the forward elevator, which was lowered to the hangar deck. That provided just enough space for a full court, where the net could be fastened at the proper height to the port and starboard tracks for the elevator cogs, and the three-sided elevator well kept the ball from being knocked over the side. The games were aggressive, and the rules were simple: no net burns above the elbow. Great volleyball rivalry existed between squadrons, the ship's crew, and Vice Admiral Mitscher's staff. Usually chief of staff Captain Arleigh Burke or staff air operations officer Commander Gus Widhelm played. During one such game with the staff, the ball bounced out onto the hangar deck and, before anyone could stop it, over the side. A volleyball was hard to come by and was not normally in the wartime supply system, so I ran quickly to the hangar deck edge and dived into the water to get it. I planned to swim to the Jacob's ladder at the after boat boom to avoid the officer of the deck at the quarterdeck because we were admonished to never swim around the ship because of pollution. I was swimming water polo style with the ball in front of me toward the Jacob's ladder when I saw a large, black, three-star admiral's barge bearing down on me. I thought that I was about to be apprehended by one very irate three-star admiral, so I swam all the harder to get to the Jacob's ladder. Unknown to me, Captain Burke had sent the barge around to pick me up. I misread his good intentions and hightailed it up the Jacob's ladder.

In-port periods were also the only time that movies were shown on the hangar deck for the crew. At sea no movies were shown, nor was volleyball played because every minute of every day was spent at the business of war, either attack or defend.

On August 26 Admiral Halsey assumed the fleet command from Admiral Spruance, and the Fifth Fleet became the Third Fleet. That meant Vice Admiral Mitscher became CTF 38, and Rear Admiral Frederick Sherman became

CTG 38.3. In our task group, the carriers continued to be *Lexington, Essex, Langley,* and *Princeton.* The entire task force was under way from Ulithi on August 31, 1944, with four complete task groups of four carriers each. It was an impressive sight to see sixteen carriers, eight battleships, ten cruisers, and some forty to fifty destroyers sortie from the lagoon to form up and proceed in different but coordinated directions. TG 38.4 was to go north to the Bonin Islands again, and the other three task groups moved west, first toward Peleliu and Palau and then to the Philippines. The flexibility of those task groups proved devastating to the Japanese.

We flew training flights and antisubmarine patrols to shake the sand and beer cobwebs out of our minds. There were no set numbers of flying hours for pilots to maintain proficiency; rather it was deemed more important that each pilot should get airborne once or twice to have a chance to bomb and strafe a sled towed behind his particular carrier and to make a landing or two.

Once that warm-up was accomplished, we moved into position to attack Peleliu and Palau. Shore installations, fuel and ammo depots, and airplanes on the airfields were left burning, but the Japanese seemed very much entrenched, and the AA fire was intense. Lieutenant Bill Cravens Jr. was shot down, and he and his crewman, Aviation Radioman Third Class Ira Gray, were rescued by the submarine USS *Grouper* off Peleliu and returned to us a month later. After three days in the area, we moved west toward our principal objectives in the southern Philippine Islands, while TG 38.4 returned from the Bonin Islands to support the invasion of Peleliu. We were ever mindful that this was the first time that we were attacking what had been a friendly country, and we strived to exercise caution to be sure that we hit only the Japanese and not the Filipinos.

On September 9 and 10 we struck targets on Mindanao. AA fire was light, few fighters were to be seen, and worthwhile targets were hard to find. The return to the Philippines was certainly anticlimactic when flying over the island of Mindanao. The lack of resistance that we found in the central and southern Philippines was the reason that the planned invasion of Palau was canceled, providing one more island that could be bypassed and many more Americans that would not be killed. All amphibious forces were to be focused instead on the next objective: the Philippines.

On September 12–14 we attacked the Visayan and central Philippine Islands. Japanese aircraft were abundant and aggressive, and we found many ships to sink. VF-19 shot down many Japanese airplanes and had a field day doing it. Lieutenant Robert B. Parker of VB-19, flying his SB2C-3, engaged a Zero, shot it down, and became our instant hero to flaunt before the fighters, and flaunt we did. Also, it was here over Iloilo that my propeller oversped, providing the previously told challenge of a return flight to *Lexington.* Our air group commander (CAG), Commander Carl Jung, was flying his F6F when his airplane was hit by ground fire, and he was forced to land in the water before he could return to *Lexington*. He failed to jettison his belly tank first, and in that landing, gasoline from that tank ignited. He seriously burned his hands as he swam out from under the ring of fire around the airplane. Commander Jung was transferred to a hospital ship, and Commander Hugh Winters became CAG. Lieutenant Commander Toby Cook became commanding officer of VF-19, only to be shot down and killed within days.

As September wore on, we moved up the Philippine Islands chain, attacking airfields and ships. The flying was constant and the fighting intense. The AA fire around Manila was considerable and accurate, but once you got through the heavy curtain of fire, the reward in large ships and other lucrative targets was great. Our losses were amazingly light, but other air groups did not fare as well. The Japanese took major losses in freighters, oilers, troop ships, and aircraft.

Fear can play a big part in combat. Almost everyone experienced fear from time to time and had to deal with it, and obviously some found it much harder than others. We junior pilots felt invincible even though our loss rate seemed to indicate otherwise. It was always the other guy who would get it—not me. One of our newer junior officers frequently jettisoned his bombs and returned to *Lexington* because of maintenance problems. He seemed to spend far more time flying in the assigned dud circle near the task group waiting recovery than he did in the company of his division. Finally, because of his unreliability, he was assigned and flew as a perennial spare pilot. When he flew in our division, out of meanness more than anything else, we junior officers would slide underneath his airplane when we checked our 20mm cannon. We always felt rewarded when we saw his airplane bobble up and down. That pilot finished the cruise but was sent off to be an instructor pilot at a primary training base on our return. I am sure that he regaled the people there with his combat exploits. He was our only true coward, but he could shoot craps like no one else and left the squadron relatively well off.

To ensure that the Japanese did not have ready access to reinforcements while the Philippines were being retaken, three task groups moved north under the cover of a typhoon to make the first attacks on Okinawa. The weather was lousy, and even though we had been at sea for many days and should have been used to deck motion, the storm-tossed seas made some pilots sick. We were used to the more placid South Pacific. On October 9 the seas abated, and on October 10 we found good flying weather for the first attacks on Okinawa. Each task group mounted some of the largest coordinated attacks up to that time, and we found good hunting in and around the waters of Okinawa. The fighters of the task groups shot down hundreds of airplanes, and the bombers and torpedo airplanes sank more than fifty ships. The preemptive strikes achieved their goal—we dealt the Japanese a surprise lesson in war and destroyed much of what could come south to interfere with the planned invasion of the Philippines.

When returning to the task group, a multiairplane formation could be easily identified by the aircraft lookouts in our ships. But woe be it to the single airplane returning! The rather doubtful recognition skills of the lookouts and the quick trigger fingers on the guns frequently provided the unwary returnee with an unwelcome Fourth of July greeting with him being the principal object of attention. On one such occasion, Ensign Wesley Koch and his gunner, Aviation Radioman Second Class Madrid, left their division formation and returned to the task group because of engine problems in their SB2C-3. As they approached the task group, first one and then many ships opened fire. Koch sought the safety of a large cloud nearby, and the firing stopped—until he popped out the other side of the cloud, when even more guns opened up on his airplane. Back into the cloud he went. That cat and mouse game went on for five to ten minutes while Koch tried to convince the force air defense officer that he was indeed one of ours and all he was trying to do was land on his carrier. He had a lose-lose situation. His choice seemed to be either to be shot down by his own force or to land in the water because his engine would fail. The situation was eventually sorted out, and Koch did land on *Lexington*, sadder but wiser.

Just as we arrived near Okinawa as a surprise, we left to move south and attack Formosa and Pescadores. We attacked targets there on October 12–14. Our charts and intelligence were poor, and flying over Formosa seemed confusing until we remembered that since leaving the States eight months before we had flown over water and around small islands. To see so much land seemed intimidating. We concentrated on attacking ships and found and sank many of them. The six of us in Lieutenant Bill McBride's division sank a large freighter and a troop transport in the Formosa Strait. We attacked airfields as well, but those were primarily the concern of the fighters, and we did not like to get in their way with all those .50-caliber bullets flying around.

One of the more spectacular attacks that we made was on the penstocks of a large hydroelectric plant on southern Formosa in an effort to deny the Japanese electrical power. Six of us dove and placed our bombs on the five 6-foot-diameter penstocks that fed water to the turbines 600 feet lower at the base of the mountain. We aimed to hit low on the penstocks, thinking the force of the water might yield even more damage. It did! The water display that resulted outdid any fountain I have ever seen.

On that flight Ensign Al Adlman dropped his bomb very high and pulled out to meet us at the rendezvous point. He was first there. He dropped so high that his bomb overtook Lieutenant Junior Grade Al Emig's airplane as he was dropping his bomb. Al caught sight of a 1,000-pound bomb passing over his right wing and, not wanting to be blown up, delayed his pullout until the bomb fell clear, but that move put him dangerously close to the ground. He returned to have a serious discussion with Adlman in the ready room.

Since early September the task groups of TF 38 had been under constant attack by Japanese land-based aircraft. Few task force ships had been hit, but we were at general quarters or our air defense stations more often than not. The pressure was telling, and it was almost a relief to get into the air to fly our offensive strikes. Finally, on the afternoon of October 14, the cruiser USS *Canberra* was hit by Japanese dive bombers. The cruiser went dead in the water and burned like a beacon throughout the night while the task group lay off to give support. Vice Admiral Mitscher's staff reasoned that the cruiser would be an attractive target for the Japanese the next day. He kept TG 38.3 just over the horizon while a cruiser attempted to take *Canberra* under tow. He was correct. Japanese aircraft came out to attack the next morning like flies coming to honey and were shot down. *Canberra* was towed slowly, first by another cruiser and then by a fleet tug, out of the combat area.

When you are fighting a war, you can lose sight of the fact that in each task group there are individual ships. In each ship are officers and men with families and loved ones thousands of miles away. Those men's lives are inextricably entwined and dedicated to form combat elements. Each man's life depends on his shipmate's dedication. Previous training and the threat that men faced together molded strong fighting units. From the admiral to the lowest seaman, some flew and faced that kind of direct combat daily, some saw the war as they were attacked and fought defensively, and some were so busy keeping the ship functioning that they did not become actively engaged in combat, but they risked their lives just as everyone else did. Each man had feelings, concerns, and fears to overcome. How they did that and how they worked together is what built esprit and combat effectiveness. As the individuals did for one ship, so the ships and units did for the mighty force. That force moved or stayed at will, with determination to fight the Japanese.

Underway replenishment was the secret of the staying power of the U.S. fleet, enabling one task group to rotate off the line to replenish while others continued their attacks; the constant pounding on the Japanese had the desired effect. On October 21 the air groups of the fast carrier force struck at Coron in the Philippines. Lieutenant Bill McBride's division attacked shipping in the harbor and tried skip bombing to place a bomb at the waterline of a large tanker, a new tactic to us. VT-19, with its torpedo delivery training, used that method with some success. We carried 1,000-pound semi-armor-piercing bombs with the fuses set at four to five seconds. As we fanned out in our six SB2Cs to bomb simultaneously from different angles, I came in low on the water just to the left of Emil Stella's airplane and released my bomb at 100 feet, well short of the tanker so that it would skip into the ship's side. Needless to say, my bomb hit short, and it skipped all right. It skipped over the ship and blew up harmlessly on the other side. So much for skip bombing, I thought. Some units achieved good results from skip bombing. I preferred dive bombing.

We had been at sea for almost two months, either attacking or being attacked. Vice Admiral Mitscher, whose presence in *Lexington* was revered by us pilots, had important intelligence he did not share. Admiral Halsey and he knew of the deploying ships of the Japanese navy from intelligence relayed by our submarines and from Japanese signals. The invasion of Leyte, to place General MacArthur's forces back on Philippine soil, was in the offing. The Japanese were responding, as expected, to our recent forays north and to the gathering U.S. amphibious forces.

On October 23 and 24 the fleet searched the waters of the Philippine Islands and to the north in the Philippine Sea for Japanese ships that might challenge the impending landing. So much happened on those two days and on October 25 that it is difficult to describe it all. Airplanes from the task groups found and attacked a Japanese surface force with the super battleship *Musashi* coming through the San Bernardino Strait on October 23 and 24. While leading our bombers on the first strike on that force, our commanding officer, Commander Dick McGowan, was forced to return to the force before reaching his target because of engine trouble. Others in the flight went on to attack while his wingman, Lieutenant Junior Grade Jack Scott, escorted him and Lieutenant Junior Grade Arni Jancar back to *Lexington* through heavy clouds and rain. Jancar made it on board, but McGowan's engine quit just short of the ship, and he landed in the water. He and his gunner, Aviation Radioman Second Class E. A. Brown, swam clear of the airplane, but McGowan, an accomplished Olympic swimmer, swam back to the airplane, as reported by Brown, to get something and went down with the airplane when it sank. We theorized that he was retrieving something from the cockpit and became snagged on the airplane, but that was never known. Brown was rescued by *Lexington*'s plane guard destroyer.

We dive bombers continued our searches for the Japanese carriers that were felt to be there. Lieutenant Stella's three-plane section of SB2C-3s was launched and flew adjacent 350-mile, single-plane searches to the north on October 23. Three hundred fifty miles over the water is a long way to go on a single-airplane mission, but we each did it. The R-2800 engine seemed to run rougher and rougher with each mile as Stevenson and I searched our sector, but we found nothing except empty sea for the 4½ hours that we flew that day before returning to *Lexington*.

On the morning of October 24, TG 38.3 was again sporadically repelling attacking Japanese airplanes when I came up on the flight deck for a breath of fresh air between attacks. The ready room could smell pretty ripe because of all our sweaty flight gear and cigarette smoke. As I looked out over the starboard side, I saw a lone Japanese Judy dive bomber coming out of the overcast skies over USS *Princeton*, 2,000 yards away on our starboard quarter. Not one gun in the task group fired. The Judy dropped a single bomb and flew over the horizon still without a shot being fired by our task group.

As I watched, the bomb exploded inside *Princeton*. Almost immediately a secondary explosion lifted up the entire aft elevator, and then it slowly rotated and fell back into the elevator well. *Princeton* slowly lost way as dark smoke billowed from the ship. An epic fight to save the carrier followed, and the cruisers USS *Santa Fe* and *Birmingham* took many casualties from exploding aircraft ammunition while alongside to fight the fires. Finally, with the press of the developing battle, *Princeton* became a tactical burden and was sunk on October 24, the first U.S. aircraft carrier to be lost since *Hornet* in 1943. *Lexington* took on board 152 mostly wounded *Princeton* survivors.

That afternoon Lieutenant Bud Thurmon's three-plane section split up and searched the same area that we had the day before. Thurmon found nothing, but he did sight VB-19's Lieutenant Junior Grade E. E. Newman and his gunner, Aviation Radioman Second Class R. S. Stanley, in the water. They had been shot down by a Zero as they returned from a strike on the Japanese force in the San Bernardino Strait. Thurmon alerted the destroyer USS *Dortch*, which rescued them. Lieutenant Junior Grade Hubert Walters found nothing on his search, and Lieutenant Junior Grade Stuart Crapser found the Japanese carrier fleet—in the sector that I had searched the day before. On October 24 Air Group 19 shot down sixty-one Japanese airplanes.

Crapser, who lived to retire as a school principal and naval reserve captain, was relatively taciturn about the events, but they were traumatic. To begin with, *Lexington* was under attack as Crapser took off, and his gunner, Aviation Radioman Second Class J. F. Burns, actually fired his guns at one attacking airplane while they were still on the flight deck. Burns described the subsequent flight in his own words in an informal squadron history.

> On the return leg, I picked up an indication on my radar screen and reported it to the pilot [Crapser]. We immediately changed course to investigate and through a hole in the clouds discovered a medium-size Jap carrier. A bit further on we found two more larger carriers and quite a few cruisers and destroyers— God, was I scared! My pilot gave me the location, and breaking radio silence I reported a "contact report" to our carrier base [using Morse code]. I didn't hear any receipt for our message, so I repeated it over and over. We climbed like bats out of hell to gain altitude, and Lieutenant Junior Grade Crapser said he saw some enemy fighters hiding in the clouds—I felt twice as scared. The whole task force opened up a full barrage of ack-ack, and it appeared to be a sky of solid flak—a ghastly sight. We got into position and nosed over. We were hit by some ack-ack, jarring the whole plane and putting us into an uncon-

trollable spin. I was hit by some of the stuff above my right eye. We were out of control, and I felt sure we were "going in." [Crapser then picked another ship as his target and dropped his bomb.] Lieutenant Junior Grade Crapser, by using all his strength, pulled the plane out in about a 12- or 13-g pullout, wrinkling the wings, and the tail and the ailerons were warped out of shape. The ack-ack was terrible, and it's a miracle that we came out of that alive. Six zekes jumped us when we cleared the formation and made individual runs on us. I called my pilot and yelled that there were fighters on our tail. As each plane came in, I opened fire. I set one of them afire but did not see him crash, but I officially got credit for a "plane." My pilot lost his helmet in that crazy dive, and he didn't hear me telling him about the fighters. He ducked for a cloud just in case, and we lost the fighters—Thank God. I can safely say that this was the most exciting experience I've ever had.

On Crapser's return to *Lexington*, he found that his bomb had not released and that his airplane was grossly overstressed from the high g pullout. The airplane was not repairable and was pushed over the side without fanfare. Called to the flag bridge to report to Vice Admiral Mitscher, he was severely reprimanded by the admiral for failing to receive an acknowledgment for his Morse code message before he hazarded himself in his attack. Mitscher reasoned that had Crapser's message not been received, as indeed it had, and if he had been shot down, the fleet would not have known of the presence of the Japanese carrier force until too late.

That sighting by Lieutenant Junior Grade Crapser and his gunner led to Admiral Halsey's choice to send his carriers north to pursue the attacking Japanese carrier force. Historians and strategists have criticized that decision, but at the time and in the heat of the battle, decisions are made and must be lived with.

The next morning, on my deck run for the launch to attack the Japanese carrier force, I looked up at Admiral Mitscher some 25 feet to my right as I was taking off and impulsively changed hands on the stick and gave him a smile and a quick right-handed salute. To my great surprise, he raised his head from the cupped hand that supported his chin, smiled back, and returned my unauthorized salute. That gesture meant a great deal to me. I have often wondered what he thought as he returned the salute on that fateful day.

We launched to attack before we knew the exact location of the Japanese carriers, and we rendezvoused and orbited 50 miles north of our task group while search planes located the Japanese carriers again. We did not have long to wait, and after about two orbits the assembled groups from *Essex*, *Lexington*, and *San Jacinto* flew to attack the Japanese fleet. Commanders Hugh Winters and David McCampbell, CAG 15 in *Essex*, sorted out the attacking order, and Winters retained the overall coordinating role. The melee began. The AA fire was stupendous, even to the 2,000-pound projectiles of the 16-inch rifles being fired straight up from the hybrid battleships *Ise* and *Hyuga*. You could see those projectiles before they burst, and after they burst, the sky was filled with large blue, green, purple, and red explosions. We in VB-19 were assigned the largest carrier, and I, along with eleven others, had the opportunity to make that long dive in the face of a great deal of AA coming up at us and to place our bombs on what we would learn later was the carrier *Zuikaku*. It was ironic that *Zuikaku*'s air group had attacked at Pearl Harbor and later disabled USS *Lexington* (CV-2), leading to that carrier's sinking in the battle of the Coral Sea. Now it was the new *Lexington*'s turn to return the favor! Our attacks, coupled with precise torpedo attacks by VT-19, culminated in the sinking of *Zuikaku* along with the carriers *Zuiho*, *Chitose*, and *Chiyoda*, as well as many escort ships.

The AA fire during those attacks was of an order of magnitude that far surpassed anything that we had seen before. It would be an understatement to say that it was impressive. On the pullout Stevenson called out a hit on the *Zuikaku* as I concentrated on getting as low as quickly as I could to avoid the deadly hail. I pulled out 25 feet above the water and headed for the bow of a battleship that I believed to be the *Hyuga*, which was 2,000 yards on the port beam of *Zuikaku* and steaming on the same course. I reasoned that if other ships were shooting at me, then they might as well hit the *Hyuga* as they tried to shoot me down. I flew under the raked bow of *Hyuga*, so close that I could see the rust on the anchor. As I passed, I looked up at the bridge to see Japanese officers in their dress white uniforms with swords. Just momentarily, as we flew by and Stevenson strafed them with his twin .30s, I thought about the officers back on the bridge of *Lexington* in long-sleeved wash khaki shirts, with battle helmets and kapok life jackets. We rendezvoused and returned immediately to *Lexington* to get ready to go again.

That afternoon I flew again, and that time we attacked the battleship *Hyuga*. By then, the Japanese carriers had gone down, and there was much less AA fire as we dive bombers placed our bombs on that lumbering behemoth. The battleship seemed to continue on unmindful of the attack. The ship took a terrific pounding but survived to escape under darkness and fight again, much later. On that strike Lieutenant R. D. Niemeyer's SB2C was hit by AA fire, and he and his gunner, Aviation Radioman Second Class A. D. Thorngren, were forced to land in the water near the remnants of the Japanese fleet. The situation near the Japanese fleet was so chaotic and confusing that they were hardly noticed, even though they were probably not far from many Japanese, also in the water. The destroyer USS *Bronson* came along that evening and rescued them to return them to *Lexington* later. It was a fact that neither the Navy nor the Japanese picked up enemy survivors in naval battles.

Forty-two years later I had cause to remember that day. President Ronald Reagan had appointed me administrator of the Federal Aviation Administration in

1984, and one day in 1986 the senior vice president for government relations for McDonnell Douglas called to ask if I would see a Mr. Kadota, the president for operations of a new Japanese airline that had just ordered a large number of DC-10 and MD-80 airplanes. I replied that I would, and later Mr. Kadota came to my office.

We were about the same age, and we chatted and had an interesting discussion about airplanes through his Japanese interpreter. As he left, he asked me to meet him at the Press Club that evening, in honor of the McDonnell Douglas order, and I accepted. That evening, as Mr. Kadota and I talked through his interpreter, the interpreter said, "Mr. Kadota was a kamikaze pilot, and he would like to know what you did in the war." I momentarily thought that Mr. Kadota had obviously not been a successful kamikaze pilot but replied that I had been in the U.S. Navy. Mr. Kadota asked again what I had done, to which I replied that I had been a naval aviator in the Pacific. Again, through the interpreter, he said, "No. No. What did you do?"

I looked him in the eye and said that among other things I and others had sunk a Japanese aircraft carrier. He asked immediately, "Which one?" I replied, "The *Zuikaku*." His eyes opened wide as he said, "That was my ship!" By then I was thinking of ways to move this conversation along to other topics because I did not want to embarrass him, but he expected a response. So I asked, "How long were you in the water?" He replied, "Five days." We both laughed. The intervening years had certainly altered our viewpoints, because I had tried to kill him, and certainly he would have gladly killed me if he could. Forty-two years later the experience seemed to create some bond between us. The bottom line was, I had helped save his life. He had never completed his World War II kamikaze mission.

On the evening of October 25 we knew that *Lexington* and TG 38.3 had played a major role in sinking four Japanese carriers. That important part of the battle for Leyte, fought in the Surigao and San Bernardino Straits, was of great interest, but it was someone else's concern, not ours. We knew the events made a good combat day for us. When you are getting shot at every day, each day can become a matter of survival, and a twenty-year-old lieutenant junior grade dive bomber pilot thinks tactically, not strategically. We knew there was much more to come.

In the aftermath of those wide-ranging major fleet actions during October 23–26, Air Group 19 and *Lexington* had expended so much ammunition that they had to withdraw to the west to rearm, refuel, and reprovision. Two of the task groups withdrew in the days immediately following the fleet battles, while the others continued to patrol in the event of additional attacks and to support the CVEs that had been so decimated by the Japanese naval surface force. In *Lexington* we had lost airplanes and pilots, and our bombs, ammo, and aviation gasoline were almost gone. Our food supplies had dwindled so that we were eating crackers with weevils, and we long ago had run out of milk and fresh vegetables. We ate thinly sliced roast beef and mashed potatoes with gravy for every meal. Fleet replenishment took the better part of a week to accomplish between continuing air attacks by the Japanese. VB-19 also received two new pilots and two SB2C-3s from a jeep carrier that embodied a new concept—a floating replacement pool.

On November 5, 1944, we were back on the line again and starting attacks on a few of the remnants of the Japanese fleets that had moved into Manila Bay. On the morning of November 5 we attacked Nielson Field at Manila to deny the Japanese air force the use of the field. On our approach to attack, and before we started our dive, I was flying close formation on Emil Stella in my number 2 spot, and in my line of vision was fellow wingman Lieutenant Junior Grade John Evatt. We were flying through heavy five-inch AA fire, and Evatt's airplane abruptly disappeared. John Evatt and his gunner, Aviation Radioman Third Class R. E. Hansen, were flying in their airplane one minute and gone the next. One of our fighters later said that he had seen an SB2C go in near Nielson Field. We made our dives on the hangars and strafed the few remaining Japanese airplanes on the field during our pullout, but we never saw Evatt and Hansen again.

One of the returning pilots reported a cruiser in Manila Bay, and that afternoon we launched again to attack that ship. On that launch I was the last to take off from *Lexington*. Shortly before I was to start my deck run, a Japanese Judy dive bomber flew overhead at high altitude, and all the ships, including *Lexington*, began firing their five-inch guns at it. As my time came to launch, I could see the visible agitation on the face and in the eyes of the flight deck officer as he looked at me after seeing the deck ahead strewn with empty five-inch brass shell casings from the rapidly firing guns. He gave me a quick turn up and launch signal and then ran down the deck ahead of me kicking brass out of the way. I let him head for the safety of the island before I began my takeoff roll, all the time wondering if the Judy was diving to plant a bomb on me and Stevenson. As I gained speed and came abreast of the number 2 twin five-inch turret forward of the island, both guns fired, and the concussion blew my airplane into the air some 200 feet short of the bow to fly down the deck for one of my shorter launch runs in combat.

Commander Winters led the coordinated strike groups into Manila Bay. Air groups from *Essex*, *Lexington*, *Ticonderoga*, and *San Jacinto* flew en masse. From 12,000 feet I could see the easily identifiable bifurcated after stack of the cruiser and knew it was the *Nachi*. Air Group 15 was told to attack first and placed two or three bombs on the cruiser, but it did not slow as it turned sharply to starboard. *San Jacinto*'s air group was directed to take a nearby destroyer,

Ticonderoga's to take ships inside the breakwater, and *Lexington*'s to attack *Nachi* again.

Lieutenant Commander Don Banker, now our commanding officer, led our twelve SB2C-3s into a dive while six TBFs fanned out to make torpedo attacks. All twelve SB2Cs were in the dive at one time. I was next to last; as bombs began hitting the cruiser, I could see several running torpedoes streaking toward the target. As I dove vertically, I saw Lieutenant Commander Banker's airplane start its pullout with white streamers coming from each wing tip, indicating a heavy pull, and then he suddenly began a series of snap rolls until his airplane hit the water inverted several hundred yards from the cruiser. It is tough to watch your commanding officer die, while you know that you still have to get your hit. The rest of us completed our dives, getting hits, as did the torpedo airplanes, and the cruiser abruptly broke into three pieces and sank in a matter of minutes. I pulled out over the spot where Lieutenant Commander Banker's airplane had hit and saw nothing but roiling water and some shark chaser dye, which was spreading slowly.

We rendezvoused and returned to *Lexington*, and I happened to be one of the first dive bombers to land on board. I was directed to report to the flag bridge to tell Vice Admiral Mitscher what had happened to Lieutenant Commander Banker. As I ducked into the island just aft of the medical station on the flight deck, I was struck by the sight of Stokes wire basket litters with bodies in them. They were stacked one on top of the other to about six feet high. Not knowing what had happened, I asked a sailor, and he replied that *Lexington* had been struck in the after island at the secondary conn station on the 05 level by a kamikaze airplane just an hour before. It was then 1530. I made my report to Vice Admiral Mitscher, who seemed to sink a little lower into the leather sofa on which he sat. He said, "Thanks." I realized that this had ended my report to him and left for our ready room where there was an awesome silence. VB-19 had taken heavy losses in the kamikaze attack.

Lieutenant Bob Parker, Lieutenant Junior Grade Bob Smith, Ensigns J. W. Gilchrist and R. W. Doyle, the latter two replacement pilots who had never had a chance to fly, and Ensign F. O. Jackson were all missing and presumed blown over the side. Lieutenant Junior Grade Chuck Fisher was badly burned and died that afternoon. Lieutenant Joe Williams, Lieutenants Junior Grade Ray Wicklander, Hubert Walters, and Bill Emerson, and Ensign Bob Griffin were burned on their hands and faces but survived. All had been standing on the catwalk aft and on the starboard side of secondary conn to observe the then-routine afternoon air attacks. On that one day VB-19 had lost two airplanes, eight officers and two enlisted men had been killed, and another five officers had been wounded. In total, *Lexington* had had 46 killed and 146 wounded by that kamikaze dive bomber.

Lieutenant Price Stradley became commanding officer of VB-19. Over the next two days, as the task group sailed for Ulithi, we held somber burial-at-sea services for the dead. Each body was sewn into a white canvas bag along with brass shell casings for added weight. The chaplains held services on the number 2 elevator for groups of six or eight. The Marine bugler played taps, and the Marine guard fired three volleys to mark each departure as the body was consigned to the deep. There is something very final about the swishing sound of a canvas-encased body sliding on pine board as the board is tilted to allow each body to slide out from under the flag. As at every Navy funeral, we sang the Navy hymn, which, by then, I had well memorized.

Lexington and the task group stayed on the line for a small amount of flying on November 6, after which we headed for the fleet anchorage at Ulithi. There the wounded were sent to a hospital ship, and we took stock. VB-19 was tactically decimated by its losses of the past five months. Someone decided that reconstituting with so many new pilots would be more difficult than bringing out a new air group from Honolulu and that this war tour would be over for us when the replacement group arrived.

There was one more change. Vice Admiral Mitscher relinquished command of TF 38 to Vice Admiral J. S. McCain and was to return to the United States. He had been deployed for a long time, and strain showed on his face and in his demeanor. Commander Winters learned that the admiral would leave the ship at 0345 on the morning of November 9 and passed the word to the ready rooms that, if we wished, we could muster on the hangar deck to see him off, but not to dress in uniform! Every single officer in the air group and the ship not on watch seemed to be there. Some were in pajamas, some in pants and no shirt, some in bathrobes—a motley but reverent group. There were so many of us that we formed two facing lines that snaked around and between airplanes from the flag entrance onto the hangar deck and ended at the port accommodation ladder, where the admiral would depart. Vice Admiral Mitscher came out on the hangar deck and seemed very surprised. Commander Winters said something to him, which I did not hear, and the admiral then walked the entire line in silence. It was eerie; no one said a thing—just respectful silence. The admiral was crying when he left us.

On November 13 the famed banjo player Eddie Peabody came on board *Lexington* with his band and put on a show that electrified the crew. He was the first and only USO personality that we saw. On November 20 a small Japanese submarine slipped inside Ulithi lagoon where TGs 38.1 and 38.3 were anchored, along with many support ships, and torpedoed USS *Mississinewa*, an oiler anchored 6,000 yards off *Lexington*'s starboard side. The submarine was sunk by destroyers, and *Mississinewa* was later repaired.

Air Group 19 was relieved in *Lexington* on November 23 by *Enterprise*'s Air Group 20, and *Enterprise*, in turn, transported Air Group 19 to Pearl Harbor, while we flew antisubmarine patrols. The ship would pick up a new air group there and return to western Pacific combat. We left our airplanes at Ford Island to be part of the airplane pool for other air groups in training and embarked in the CVE USS *Long Island* for transportation to San Diego. Upon arrival, just before Christmas, we all were given a thirty-day leave. A few of us were ordered to shore duty, but most of us were to return to combat in Air Group 19, and we were told to report to NAS Alameda after our leave.

There is no way to describe the joys of homecoming in enough detail to capture the emotions. My homecoming was absolutely great. Mary was living in a small house on Balboa Island, and I joined her there the day after I arrived in San Diego. It was the first Christmas for our five-month-old son, Travis, and he and I began to get acquainted.

My leave passed quickly, and Mary and I left the house on Balboa Island, piling all our possessions into her 1941 yellow Chevrolet convertible, and headed for Alameda. It is amazing how much you can get into a car if you have to. High chair, a fold-down baby buggy, silverware, pots, pans, sheets, blankets, clothes—it all fit with room enough for the baby. We looked like migrant workers as we drove from Pasadena to Alameda, where we found half a Quonset hut on the naval air station in which to live. Quonset huts were put together for temporary officer housing near the main gate.

We shared a Quonset hut with Lieutenant Junior Grade R. E. L. (Dunc) Duncan and his wife, Jane. The close friendships that had been fashioned during my previous training and then my combat cruise were the primary sources for our social life. Mary made immediate friends with Jane Duncan. Dunc was staying in VB-19, while I was one of ten VB-19 officers who were ordered to a new fourth squadron in Air Group 19, Bombing-Fighting 19 (VBF-19). The commissioning of that squadron was in keeping with the Navy emphasis on fighters preparing for the invasion of Japan. We needed the flexibility of high-performance airplanes that could drop bombs and then be fighters or just be fighters when needed.

Air Group 19 re-formed January 20, 1945, at NAS Alameda, and VBF-19 was commissioned on that day. Commander A. P. (Scoofer) Coffin USN, the first commanding officer of VT-19 in 1943, was our air group commander. VF-19, with Lieutenant Commander Joseph G. Smith USN as commanding officer, was to have the brand new F8F-1s when they became available in two or three months. VBF-19, with former VF-19 pilot Lieutenant E. L. (Lin) Lindsay USNR as commanding officer, would initially train in the F6F and then get the F4U. VB-19, with Lieutenant Robert D. Niemeyer USNR as commanding officer, was to get SB2C-4s. VT-19, with Lieutenant Commander Frank C. Perry USN as commanding officer, would get TBM-3s.

VBF-19 was planned to be a thirty-six-airplane squadron with sixty-four pilots during our 1945 training phase. Eleven pilots had come from VF-19, ten from VB-19, one from VB-1, three from VT-19, and thirty-nine from various shore stations, principally the training command. We had three ground support officers and seventeen key enlisted men. Maintenance of our airplanes would be provided by the ship or air station in which we were based. With the pilots' mix of experience, this squadron had a strong combat background. Second- and third-tour combat pilots provided the needed dos and don'ts, the street smarts, for a strong team. The marriage of VF and VB came with a few mixed emotions. Lin Lindsay tried not to have a bias toward fighters, while Don Helms, our executive officer, tried not to have a bias toward dive bombers. Initially, we were clubby and tended to stick with our old friends, but as we flew together, that changed. We were given a mix of thirty-one F6F-3s and -5s in which to start our training.

On February 6, 1945, the air group was directed by Commander Fleet Air Alameda to move to NAAS Santa Rosa, California, about 65 miles north of Alameda. We moved en masse over two or three days and settled into the area. NAAS Santa Rosa had been built six miles southwest of Santa Rosa in what had been open grazing land. It was a typical airfield for the time with two crossed 5,000-foot runways, a large parking apron, which accommodated all the air group's airplanes, two large open-air nose hangars, and an assortment of wood and tarpaper-sided buildings. It looked and was temporary. The populace of Santa Rosa had a strong bias toward the Army Air Forces because of an earlier training field there, and that did not go unnoticed as we looked for housing.

Housing in wartime was hard to find, particularly for migratory pilots. The naval air station's housing office kept lists of available apartments and houses. Mary and I, along with Dunc and Jane, found a resort cabin complex 15 miles east in the small community of Kenwood in the Valley of the Moon. Our cabin was situated partly over a stream and had one wood stove for heating and cooking. Mary really enjoyed that! Soon, we moved to the other side of Santa Rosa, to the Russian River area and the small resort community of Hacienda. That house was rustic, at best. We had to build a wood fire to heat any water, the ice melted quickly in the 25-pound ice box, and assorted snakes and varmints visited our house. The nearest telephone was 200 yards away, nailed to the trunk of a large, old redwood tree, and you could raise the operator by using the crank on the side of the phone. Myrt would answer—most of the time.

I first flew the Grumman F6F-3 Hellcat on February 8, 1945, at Santa Rosa, and I thought its improvement in performance over the more solidly flying SB2C-3 was spectacular. After the tenseness of the past six months, it was nice not being shot at, but still I found myself missing the thrill of combat. Also, I liked being alone in the airplane without the responsibility for a crewman. Dive bombing squadrons flew in two three-airplane sections to a division. VBF-19 now adopted the fighters' tactical division of two two-airplane elements. While we had thirty-six airplanes, our tactical organization blended bomber and fighter experience into thirteen divisions of four pilots. A few divisions even had a fifth, or spare, pilot. I became the second section leader in the seventh division led by Lieutenant W. S. (Bill) DeVaughn, a suave gentleman from Louisiana, who had come from the training command. Bill was as smooth on the ground as he was in the air and was much sought after by the ladies. In that arena he had an impressive record, too. His wingman was Ensign L. L. (Nick) Nichols USNR, and my wingman was Ensign Harry E. West USNR.

Lieutenant Lin Lindsay, an accomplished pilot, had shot down eight Japanese airplanes on our previous combat tour. He demanded that his pilots match his skills, which created safety problems because soon Lin's aggressive flying style led the squadron into accidents. It was not the more accomplished pilots but rather the younger pilots who got into trouble, and we lost four pilots and damaged a number of airplanes before four months of training passed.

The F6F-3 and -5 Hellcats were fine, combat-proven aircraft. We parked them on the ramp with the wings folded because space at NAAS Santa Rosa was at a premium. We used well-understood and time-tested flight deck signals and procedures to spread our wings when we departed the line and to fold them when we returned. Wing folding in an airplane can be serious business! Grumman designed the F6F wing fold to provide an aerodynamic load lock when spread. The wings would not fold in the air even if the mechanical lock slipped out of place. However, unlike the SB2C, each F6F wing had to be pushed by a ground crewman into the spread or folded position. The Pratt & Whitney twin-row R-2800-10 two-stage radial engine provided reliable performance all the way to 36,000 feet. Again, we were impressed.

In 1945 the Japanese were launching hydrogen balloons with incendiary and explosive loads to be carried by the prevailing strong winds across the Pacific to the United States, where they hoped the incendiaries would fall on cities and forests. Only occasionally were they successful, but the Japanese were far ahead of us in their meteorological knowledge of the upper winds. Still, several people were killed in Oregon and Northern California when they happened on those strange devices in the forests. As a result, VF-19 and VBF-19 stood continuous strip alert duty in our F6Fs to intercept and shoot down those balloons when coast watchers sighted them.

One spring afternoon I was standing the balloon strip alert when I was directed to launch for an intercept. I was given general directions on my six-channel VHF radio toward the coast and a spot over which the balloon had been sighted. There was no radar, and all sightings were visual. Passing 15,000 feet, I put on my oxygen mask and continued to climb until I spotted the balloon very high over the Russian River area. I continued to climb, trying to keep my eyes on the balloon, which was nothing more than a shiny speck. It was really high! When I got to 35,000 feet, I was carrying 2,350 rpm and 22 inches of manifold pressure in high blower, and that airplane was not going to go much higher. The balloon was still far above me when all of a sudden it struck me. I was chasing the planet Venus. I returned to Santa Rosà, I must admit, mumbling to myself and blaming myself and those who had directed the launch.

On April 1, 1945, we received a motley group of Corsairs—very old F3A-1s built by Brewster, FG-1s by Goodyear, and a couple of F4U-1Ds by Vought. But they were Corsairs, and we looked forward to flying them. By early June we had spent enough time in them to feel comfortable. We all had watched with envy as VF-19 was the first squadron to receive the new F8F-1 Bearcats. Its pilots were quick to demonstrate the phenomenal performance of the airplane and were, in fact, downright overbearing.

I do not recall who threw down the gauntlet for a commanding officer versus commanding officer dogfight-from-takeoff showdown, but the idea caught on like wildfire. Each agreed to the combat, and the rules were set so that Lin Lindsay in his F4U-1D and Joe Smith in his F8F-1 would line up on the runway at NAAS Santa Rosa and on a given signal release brakes; the first one on the other's tail would win. The VBF-19 crew waxed Lindsay's old F4U-1D until the chipped, worn blue paint and aluminum skin shined, and they prepped the engine for all the power it could give. Smith's crew were a little more confident with their brand new and powerful airplane.

On the appointed day all hands from both squadrons lined both sides of the runway as each commanding officer taxied his airplane to stop with wheels exactly on a broad white line painted across the runway for that purpose. Smith's Bearcat, with its R-2800-34W engine, was on the right. His engine purred and popped and sounded downright awesome. Lindsay's Corsair, with its much older and tired R-2800-10 engine, was on the left. His engine leaked a little oil as he sat on the starting line, but it ran smoothly, and the three-bladed prop just ticked over, waiting to respond. On signal, both pilots released their brakes and jammed on full power. The Bearcat slued to the right and seemed to bounce twice before leaping into the air sideways, as Smith retracted the landing gear to hold the airplane low on the runway and accelerated. Lindsay's Corsair was slower accelerating. He moved down the runway at almost the same speed but with his wheels on the ground. Initially, wing tip to wing tip, they slowly separated as they tore down the runway, until Lindsay sucked up his landing gear, dropped 10 degrees of landing flaps, turned 30 degrees to the left of the runway heading, then snapped the F4U around to the right with his right wing tip just inches from the ground, and fell victoriously on the tail of the Smith's F8F.

They disappeared over the horizon at less than 100 feet, and Lindsay won. VF-19 laid off us for a while after that.

In May we deployed to NAAS Arcata, California, to fire five-inch high-velocity aircraft rockets (HVARs) in our F6F-5s. Those new weapons had been developed by the Navy at the Naval Ordnance Test Station China Lake and were potent. They were designed to penetrate into the caves and bunkers of the Japanese and could easily open up a destroyer or a cruiser hull. These unguided rockets were relatively accurate. Initially, we were coaxed into the proper glide angle by ground range personnel, who sighted through a wire device that measured our dive angle. Before we left Arcata, we could hit with these powerful weapons, and we looked forward to using them.

On June 1, 1945, the air group conducted a coordinated attack on the battleship USS *Maryland* in the southern San Francisco Bay. I think Scoofer Coffin, who had many Hollywood ties, arranged for a Hollywood studio to film the air action for a movie. Cameras and crews were positioned in *Maryland*, as well as in a ferry that lay close by. Commander Coffin, a large, rotund naval officer, was gloved into his personal F8F-1 to circle above *Maryland* and provide tactical coordination. Each of the four squadrons flew as many F8Fs, F4Us, SB2Cs, and TBMs as they could get airborne and were led by our respective commanding officers. It was one of the most closely timed air group strikes that I had ever witnessed. In fact, it was so closely timed that most of us were scared pea green and wondered how no one was killed. With clockwork precision, dive bombers pulled out of vertical dives to pass between torpedo planes making or recovering from their simulated torpedo runs. The fighter-bombers and the fighters arrived at the target at the same time, making it difficult to tell who got there first. The attack was over in about sixty seconds. It was one of the best attacks that I have seen, and we heard later that the action was so fast that the film director asked for the proverbial "just one more," to which Commander Coffin replied, "Hell, no!"

Our social life centered mostly around small groups of officers, their wives, families, and girlfriends. We were fun seeking and lived a thrilling life at work, but our impending departure drove husbands and wives to seek each other's company. The officers club at the naval air station was rudimentary but functional, and we partied there on weekends. Also, on weekends Mary and I would visit squadron friends who lived nearby. We would picnic or swim in the Russian River. Mary was showing her pregnancy with our second child, and Jane Duncan looked the same with her first child. On occasion the two would drift down the Russian River, each in an inner tube, with much laughter.

We flew our FCLP at Cotati, a small airfield south of Santa Rosa. Our air group LSO would fly an airplane or drive a car there to spend the entire day waving airplanes. When concentrating on FCLP, flights of six of us would be scheduled from dawn to dusk to arrive at one-half-hour intervals and fly round and round the field at 200 feet. The LSOs evaluated each pass and kept cryptic comments in the LSO book for a debrief later that day. LSO language—special, descriptive, and pointed—has been derived over the years. Every LSO I knew seemed to come from the same mold—caustic and self-assured—and always had the last word. You never argued with the LSO. If you did, you lost because he could and would get you into trouble. Whenever there was a deck landing accident, the LSO's comment was always "well, he looked OK when he went by me."

There were many training accidents. No one wanted to be killed, but we flew with great abandon, egged on by Lindsay. We flew twenty-four airplane tail chases, and once Lindsay split us into two twelve-airplane columns, one doing loops through the other's horizontal circle. We chased each other under telephone wires and were encouraged to take on anything that moved in the sky. Seven pilots were killed before we left the States. At the end of June we made qualifying landings in our F4Us on USS *Takanis Bay* (CVE 89) off the coast of Northern California. Landing on a CVE was akin to using some but not all of an *Essex* class carrier deck. We had been spoiled by the roominess of *Lexington*, but all fifty-four pilots qualified in F4U-4s, and our deployment became more of a certainty.

We had finished over one-half of our training syllabus in a motley pack of F6Fs and F4Us. Now, we flew only our new F4U-4s in close air support training flights at the large Hunter Ligget target area south of Fort Ord, California. We were training to support the Marines and Army when they invaded Japan.

We had one more thing to do before we deployed west. In mid-July the squadron flew our F4U-4s south to NAS Twentynine Palms in the desert, over the mountains and north of Palm Springs. The Naval Ordnance Test Station China Lake had developed a large rocket dubbed the Tiny Tim, and we were to fire that weapon at Twentynine Palms. The Tiny Tim was to be the answer to hard Japanese targets, caves, and bunkers that we all knew would have to be attacked in an invasion of Japan, certainly if Saipan, Okinawa, and Iwo Jima were any criteria. Mary and I saw the deployment to Twentynine Palms as an opportunity for her to move south in preparation for our departure at the end of July, so we drove to Pasadena on July 10 and deposited Travis with my mother; then we both went to Twentynine Palms where I joined my squadron mates.

July on the desert was hot! The temperature frequently rose to 120 and 125°F. We flew from sunrise until midmorning and then quit for the day because our airplanes became so hot that our skin was seared if we touched the metal fuselage or wings. The base swimming pool became the center of our activities during the afternoons and the officers club during the evenings.

The Tiny Tim rocket was 11 feet long with an 11.75-inch diameter. It was all rocket motor except for the 500-pound armor-piercing bomb attached to the front end. Each airplane could carry one Tiny Tim, but it was a potent weapon!

It was dropped in a steep glide; to ensure the bomb cleared the propeller, the rocket motor was ignited after it dropped to the end of a six-foot lanyard fastened to the airplane. This large rocket fired with an impressive bang and a whoosh that could be heard over any engine noise and for miles around. If it did not hit, its noise certainly would scare the enemy to death. As the Tiny Tim dropped from the airplane, there was a large shift in the airplane's center of gravity so that the pilot had to push rapidly forward on the stick to prevent what felt like the start of an Immelmann. The whole squadron enjoyed our training. We should have fired Tiny Tims on the Fourth of July. Unfortunately, the Tiny Tim and other rockets were hazardous on decks and contributed to a great fire in USS *Franklin* in 1945.

Upon completion of my training at Twentynine Palms, Mary and I had a week to house hunt in Long Beach, where we had decided Mary should live to have our second child because of its proximity to the Long Beach Naval Hospital. With financial help from her father, we purchased our first house in Lakewood Village, not far from Los Alamitos. We paid the princely sum of $6,000 for the two-bedroom house and moved in before I returned to Santa Rosa for the squadron's move to Alameda preparatory to our departure.

On July 25, 1945, Air Group 19 loaded personnel and equipment, but no airplanes, in USS *Langley* at Alameda for transportation to our next training area, the Hawaiian Islands. VBF-19 left its airplanes for others to use and would pick up new F4U-4s when we arrived at our destination, NAS Kahului, Maui. We left August 3 and arrived in Pearl Harbor on August 8, 1945. Three years and nine months had passed since the Japanese had attacked Pearl Harbor, and most of the battleships had been righted or salvaged. USS *Arizona*, USS *Oklahoma*, and USS *Utah* still lay as mute testimony to that fateful day, and *Langley* rendered the time-honored recognition as the carrier silently moved by *Arizona* to take an assigned berth at Ford Island. We were flown to Kahului in a motley group of transport airplanes and upon arrival were given old F4Us to fly until the end of the month, when we would pick up brand new F4U-4s. Kahului was still a nice place to be.

In mid-August we heard that atomic bombs had been dropped at Hiroshima on August 6 and at Nagasaki on August 9. Then we quickly heard rumors of peace as we received our F4U-4s. All that news seemed so distant from what we were doing that we did not attach much significance to it. We were surprised and elated when, within a week after the second bomb had been dropped, Japan surrendered, and the peace that we all had fought for arrived.

The elation of victory soon disappeared, and rumor and uncertainty took over. Administrative rules for release from active duty were being promulgated, and in September our first group of pilots choosing to return to civilian life left the squadron. Their spots in the squadron were filled by newly trained replacement pilots, who did not have enough points for release from active duty. The squadron continued to train because we had nothing else to do, but our tactical abilities suffered as the combat experience drained away as more men opted to return to civilian life.

During August we went into extended preparation to take the air group on board ship, but which ship we did not know. We did day and night FCLP at NAS Kahului and Upolu Point. During one of those night FCLP sessions at Kahului, an unusual accident happened, which emphasized the strength and integrity of the F4U.

Ensign Nick Nichols was flying his F4U-4 in the low FCLP pattern over the cane fields. As he approached the flashlight-lit simulated carrier deck laid out on the runway, the LSO gave him a late wave off. He added full power for his wave off, but as he was flying near the stall speed of the airplane, the abrupt application of all that power caused him to do a one-half snap roll to the left into inverted flight. It was a classic torque roll at 50 feet. He knew he did not want to hit the ground that way and took off his power to roll the F4U upright. But he was headed 40 degrees left of the runway directly for the dark rows of airplanes parked on the ramp. The bright lights of the large nose hangars on the line loomed directly ahead. Nichols did not want to fly into those hangars and in one last desperate move added full power again. The F4U rolled inverted, and he hit a TBM parked in one row. The collision in turn threw him nose down and still inverted into succeeding rows of airplanes. He ploughed through line after line of TBMs, SB2Cs, and F4Us, spewing sparks and flames as he went, missed the F8Fs, and came to rest, still inverted. Fortunately, the flames were behind him in the carnage of airplanes.

People rushed to the scene to put out the fires and prevent further damage, believing that Nichols had surely been killed. Low and behold, as they worked their way to what was left of his F4U, Nichols undid his seat belt and, because he was inverted, fell out of what was left of his cockpit onto his head and knocked himself out. That was his only injury. He had totally destroyed six airplanes and damaged many others, but his F4U had held together and protected him. We were impressed, and Nichols was flying again the next night.

In August Air Group 19 conducted carrier qualifications on the CVE USS *Corrigidor* and in September on USS *Boxer*. Those were unsettling times for the squadrons. The massive loss of pilots as they opted to leave the Navy, our never-ending attempts to retrain new pilots, and fluid plans created great uncertainty. I began to catch the return-home fever as I watched Bill DeVaughn return to Louisiana and others leave. Although I had applied for a U.S. Navy commission and was told that I would receive favorable consideration, I began to doubt that I wanted to spend the next year at sea on a cruise around the world. Mary's time for the birth of our second child was drawing near. In October I applied for and received emergency leave to return to Long Beach for that event. I flew from NAS John Rogers as a passenger in one of the Mars flying boats for the fourteen-hour flight to Alameda and then caught a ride south to El Toro with a Marine pilot in a TBM-3.

My homecoming and our reunion were in time for the birth of our daughter, Candace, at the Long Beach Naval Hospital on October 12, 1945. We had time to get Mary home and somewhat settled before I left to rejoin the squadron and *Hornet* anchored in Monterey Bay, California, on October 28. In my absence Lieutenant Commander Lin Lindsay was relieved by Lieutenant Commander Robin Lindsey as commanding officer of VBF-19 on October 20, 1945. Lin Lindsay returned home to Montana. When I arrived in *Hornet*, I found even more officers had left the air group. The squadron was no longer the same, even though one or two of my closest friends, such as Jack Scott and Mel Chapman, remained.

On November 3, 1945, I and others in the air group launched in our airplanes from *Hornet* to our new home, NAS Barbers Point, Oahu. It was now planned that we would depart in USS *Valley Forge* for a victory world cruise in the tradition of President Theodore Roosevelt's great white fleet. In what seemed like desperation, I made the decision to return to Long Beach and civilian life. I succumbed to the emotions of post–World War II and lost sight of my long-term goal to be a naval officer. I declined the proffered regular commission for which I had applied and requested release from active duty.

My request was granted quickly because of my time in service and combat record, and I awaited detachment from VBF-19. I left the squadron after Thanksgiving, and Jack Scott came to the Pearl Harbor Navy Yard to say goodbye as I boarded USS *Nevada* for transportation to the States. It was a tough time. Jack and I said little and kept our thoughts to ourselves. We were from the same hometown, had joined the Navy together, trained together, fought the war together, and prepared to return to fight it again together. As *Nevada* began to leave the pier, both Jack and I watched the dark water grow between us. He waved and turned to go. Jack did make the around-the-world cruise in *Valley Forge*, not in VBF-19, but as aide to Rear Admiral Harold M. (Beauty) Martin. While on that voyage Jack contracted dysentery in Shanghai, and that illness led to other complications and a long hospitalization before he was medically retired as a lieutenant commander in 1948. Jack married and became a prosperous business man in Southern California, and we were good friends until he died in 1997.

I returned to civilian life like millions of others but started flying actively in the Naval Air Reserve at Los Alamitos.

4. CHANGE
DECEMBER 1945 TO MARCH 1949

The Allied military occupation of Japan began, and the United States granted independence to the Philippines while retaining bases there. The United States announced that it would maintain troops in South Korea until the Soviets removed their troops from North Korea, and President Truman stated the policy for Soviet containment in the world. The printed circuit was developed, and Richard Byrd led an expedition to the South Pole. The British mandate over Palestine ended, and the Jewish state of Israel was proclaimed. NATO was established to safeguard the West from Soviet aggression.

The Navy reduced aviation forces 80 percent to a total of 10,232 pilots, 56,767 aviation ratings, and 20 aircraft carriers of all classes by the end of 1949. The Coast Guard was transferred from the Navy Department to the Treasury Department. The squadron designations of VB and VT were abolished, and VA for attack was established. Lieutenant Colonel Marion Carl USMC made two shipboard catapult launches and four landings in the P-80A jet fighter, and later the FJ-1 and FH-1 airplanes, also jets, joined the fleet. The U.S. Air Force and the Joint Chiefs of Staff were established. In the Pacific VF-5A made the first jet carrier landings, and in the Atlantic VF-17A became the first jet squadron to be carrier qualified. Carrier air groups were designated to have three VF and two VA squadrons in austere times that saw the use, principally, of war surplus airplanes.

Mary, the children, and I lived in Lakewood Village as I prepared for civilian life. I applied to be a pilot for United Airlines and found a long line of former military pilots with experience in twin- and four-engine airplanes that I did not have. My background as a carrier pilot seemed extraneous, but United put me on its list, while I worked at the United Airlines reservation office in the Long Beach Hilton Hotel. Tiring of that, I took a job as a junior aeronautical engineer under Harold Cheney, chief engineer at the Consolidated Vultee plant in Bellflower, California, where I also had the promise to become a company test pilot when an opening developed.

I joined the Naval Air Reserve at Los Alamitos to fly F4U-4s on weekends with VBF-716, but this only heightened my desire to fly more, and I decided to return to active duty in the Navy. Mary knew how much I missed flying, and she, her father, and my father encouraged me to do what I had always planned. In retrospect, my search for a career was shared by hundreds of thousands of others returning after World War II. The focus of the war, now gone, left many in a void.

The process of regaining my commission seemed relatively complex, but with encouragement from those in the Navy with whom I talked, I applied and, in mid-April 1946, appeared before an evaluation board of five senior naval officers, who gave me a strong recommendation for augmentation into the U.S. Navy. While waiting for the Bureau of Naval Personnel in Washington, DC, to consider my request, I continued to work at Consolidated Vultee, where I was in the wings to be a backup test pilot on the XP-81. That airplane was an experimental fighter for the U.S. Army Air Forces that had a TG-180 gas turbine engine geared to a propeller in the nose and an I-40 pure jet gas turbine in the tail. Rube Snodgrass was the principal test pilot, and I followed him around like a puppy, but the opportunity to fly did not materialize.

In early August 1946 I was notified I had been accepted for a commission in the U.S. Navy and was recalled to active duty on August 30, 1946. I was a lieutenant junior grade, with a loss of several months lineal precedence to match my inactive service, but I certainly did not care. I was being given a second chance at a Navy career, and I could have walked on water. We spent September in Long Beach where I was temporarily assigned while awaiting orders. Those orders arrived by the end of September, and I reported to the Pilotless Aircraft Unit at NAS Mojave, California, where we lived in apartmentlike quarters on the naval air station. Living on the California high desert took a little getting used to, but once acclimated everyone became a high desert booster.

The Pilotless Aircraft Unit had been in existence in one form or another to develop experimental drone aircraft since the 1920s. The Naval Air Missile Unit in World War II developed large drones in attempts to blow up the seemingly impregnable Nazi submarine pens. Navy Lieutenant Joseph Kennedy was killed over the English Channel in 1944 while piloting a Navy PB4Y-1 drone loaded with tons of explosive. The Pilotless Aircraft Unit had been relocated from the Philadelphia area to Mojave, California, in 1945, and Captain

A. N. Perkins USN was commanding officer of both the unit and the naval air station. In addition, the Naval Air Facility Point Mugu, under officer in charge Lieutenant Commander L. G. Lehrer, reported to Captain Perkins.

On October 1 the Pilotless Aircraft Unit was deactivated to form the Naval Missile Test Center Point Mugu. We would move from Mojave to Point Mugu, California, north of Los Angeles, as facilities were built to support us. During the war the land had been appropriated from the Broome Ranch, and Point Mugu, relatively remote from Los Angeles, was the training ground for aircraft maintenance units being sent overseas. In 1946 Point Mugu was still primitive, and our offices were in Dallas tents on the flight line along with one large Nissen hut hangar. In the interim we continued to fly our project flights from Mojave.

At Mojave the officer roster was similar to that of a squadron. Lieutenant Commander J. T. Lake, operations officer, oversaw twenty project pilots. His officers flew the test flights for the projects of Commander Grayson Merrill, chief projects officer. The pilots were lieutenants or lieutenants junior grade, many former enlisted pilots, with a wide variety of flying experience in many different airplanes. Each pilot was assigned one or more projects and a project engineer. My project was the Gargoyle, a derivative of the winged bomb called the Bat. It was a remotely controlled glide bomb released at altitude from a carrier airplane and flown to a target by the pilot or a crewman. We had no telemetry then, and the instrumentation recording package was part of the payload, so we always had to find the missile after we dropped it to understand why it had not worked. The Gargoyle was hardly successful, and I spent far more time searching through the desert sagebrush for the few we dropped than I did flying them.

There were some twenty different kinds of airplanes at Mojave, and it was there that I first expanded my flying expertise to twin- and four-engine airplanes. I particularly liked the North American B-25 (Navy PBJ-1J). We flew six of them for our projects because they carried a good payload and were fast and reliable. We also had the four-engine PB4Y-1 (B-24) Liberator and the single-tail PB4Y-2 Privateer, as well as one P-80. There were F7Fs, SB2Cs, F8Fs, R4Ds (the venerable DC-3), twin-engine JRBs, and SNBs. There was even a captured German ME 163 rocket airplane sitting on the far end of the parking ramp. How it got there or where it went after we left it there in 1947 remains a mystery. The opportunity to polish our aviation skills and knowledge while flying a wide variety of airplanes made Mojave duty very attractive.

The P-80 was the first jet airplane that I had been near. It came to us mysteriously, without manuals or spare parts. Lieutenant Commander Wynn Junk was the project pilot and the only one to fly it, and I recall he was quite covetous of the few hours he could fly in an airplane that always seemed to need work. Wynn had gone through a transition school at Williams Air Force Base

(AFB) near Phoenix, and I set my sights on attending that school in the future. I would try to wait Wynn out.

For those people who have had the opportunity to live on the high desert, the dry air and clear skies are infectious. Mary, our two children, and I adapted to the characteristic winter high winds and bitter cold and liked it. Mary even devised her own way of ironing the children's clothes. She would carefully crease the trousers and smooth the dresses while they were still wet. She then would carry them outside in the bitter cold, and they would instantly freeze dry so that there was no need to iron them. When we left Mojave, we knew that we would miss that special place.

We junior pilots also flew a rotating pool of twenty TD2C target drone airplanes at Mojave to prepare them for fleet ship and aircraft target practice. They were small, fast, and highly maneuverable and were made with laminated wood for skin. Lieutenant Junior Grade Howard MacMillan and I flew many of those drones on their checkout flights to establish remote control continuity. The procedure was to fly the airplanes into view of a ground control officer, who would then take over control of the TD2C to do climbs, dives, and turns while advancing and retarding the throttle, all the while keeping the airplane within sight of the field. The pilot would sit in the cockpit, his right hand loosely around the stick and left hand near the throttle—just in case. The gut cruncher was the final remote-controlled dive from 2,500 feet toward the ground in a simulated attack followed by a pullout at 400 feet. None of us pilots liked that maneuver, but the ground controllers took delight in giving us a thrill. We did have the ultimate control in the cockpit; a mechanical disconnect lever located just above the throttle would give us total authority if our anxiety level went off the top of the scale.

We flew those TD2Cs from Mojave to Point Mugu where they were further deployed as AA gunnery targets. If they were not shot down, we would ferry them back to Mojave for another checkout and to be used again. Thus a steady stream of TD2Cs traveled between Mojave and Point Mugu. Occasionally, on the return flights, as a diversion, we would race each other as we ferried the airplanes.

During one of those races I learned two basic lessons that pilots who are lucky enough to survive unplanned maneuvers never forget. I was returning from Point Mugu, one clear winter's day, in my TD2C. The sky was blue, and visibility was 75 to 100 miles. It was the kind of day that makes you feel as if you are on top of the world. I was first back to Mojave and called the tower for permission for a low pass. The tower operator granted my request, and I descended to about 80 feet to fly by the tower parallel to the parking ramp. On the spur of the moment, I rolled the TD2C to fly by the tower upside down. I was fully inverted at 80 feet as I went by the tower when the engine quit! I had used up the fuel in the carburetor, and since it was not an upside down carburetor, the engine died. That was lesson number 1.

There I was, on my back at 80 feet with two hangars still to fly over. I could not roll the airplane upright because I would probably scoop out just enough to fly into the top of one of the hangars. My only option was to push forward on the stick, to fly inverted until I had crossed over those two hangars, and then to use whatever altitude that remained to roll upright. After that, I could sort out what to do with the engine. As I pushed forward on the stick to clear the first hangar, my airspeed began to bleed off. I held an altitude of about 100 feet until I cleared the second hangar roof. When I passed that, I rolled the little plywood-skinned airplane upright and stretched my glide, looking for a clear place to set it down with the landing gear up. Just as I was eye level with a barbed wire fence and about to discover how plywood reacts during prolonged contact with sand, the engine roared to life. I pulled up in a chandelle, turned downwind, and landed on the duty runway. Lesson number 2: I never made snap judgments like that again.

When I taxied into the line, not much was said. I guessed that not many had seen what I had done, and I walked back to the operations office, ashamed of the stupidity of my impulsive decision and action but glad to be alive. I glanced up at the pilot's roster board as I walked by it and saw a big underlined *lieutenant* by my name. I had been promoted to lieutenant, and that was my first notification.

On January 9, 1947, we closed NAS Mojave, and everybody moved to Point Mugu. A few sailors and I rounded up every stray dog that lived on the air station because they would either starve or become wild. Big and small, the dogs were coaxed into a Twin Beech, and I flew that last airplane from NAS Mojave with seven dogs of differing sizes and sexes as passengers. We let the dogs go at Point Mugu where they again found the sailors that had fed them previously and took up as before.

Housing was still not readily available in the area of Oxnard, California, and so Mary and I lived in one-half of a Quonset hut at Port Hueneme, some six miles west of Point Mugu. Our project flying was from the single Marsten Matting, or pierced steel planking, airstrip, and the conditions were quite rustic. The amount of flying that we did varied with the project requirements, but generally we were flying thirty to forty hours per month. The one project that seemed to garner the most attention was the Loon; at least it made the most distinctive noise. The Loon was a U.S.-manufactured version of the World War II German V-1 buzz bomb, which was being launched from the beach seaward as a cruise missile. Subsequently, Loons were launched many times from the submarine USS *Cusk*. We pilots flew chase in the F8F-1, with guns armed to shoot down the Loon should its guidance unit go astray. That never happened in my tenure, but I understand that later one project pilot had to tip an errant Loon into the ocean using his wing tip. Mostly, the Loon flights were very short and ended in self-destruction. Such was our missile expertise at that time.

As project pilots we built our skills and knowledge in aeronautical engineering and propulsion. Lieutenant Lloyd Garrison flew a project to further develop the pulse-jet engine, which was like the one used to power the Loon. This small podded engine developed great thrust through the opening and closing of inlet vanes in concert with pulses of burning fuel. The small pulse-jet engine was mounted centerline under a Douglas JD-1 airplane, and Lloyd would fly up and down the Pacific Coast Highway at low altitude with the pulse jet spitting fire and noise while he gathered data. Those flights were quite spectacular, and the motorists along the Pacific Coast Highway made random reports of seeing an airplane on fire. The residents of Malibu were less temperate in their comments.

An airfield was built on San Nicholas Island, one of the Santa Barbara Channel Islands, and a permanent Navy detachment was set up there to facilitate missile tracking. All personnel were moved by air. Later, facilities were developed to move heavy stores and equipment ashore by boat. Primarily, San Nicholas was used as an unofficial penal colony. Recalcitrant sailors, who were given courts-martial for civil or military infractions, were banished to San Nicholas to serve out their restriction. In today's environment that might not sit too well, but it worked then. I never heard anyone complain, because fishing and lobstering were favorite pastimes of those who spent time there.

Occasionally we made administrative flights to other airfields. On one such occasion I was to fly a Twin Beech to Alameda to pick up some aircraft parts. Our flight surgeon at Mojave and Point Mugu was Lieutenant Benjamin Franklin Edwards, a prince of a man. He heard that I was flying north and asked if I would give him a ride to Modesto, which was along the way. I agreed, and we set out on a bright sunny day with visibility in excess of 20 miles. It was so nice that we just enjoyed each other's company and chatted as we flew. Ben, like all flight surgeons, had taken some flight training and had a basic knowledge of flying, so he flew for part of the way. Finally, I saw the Modesto airport, and since it had no control tower, I cleared the pattern for other airplane traffic, and we landed. I taxied to the vacant parking ramp area, let Ben out of the airplane near some gas pumps, and then took off again to fly to Alameda. It took me longer to fly to Alameda than I thought it should have, but on arrival I picked up the parts and returned to Point Mugu. Several days later, when Ben returned from Modesto, he frostily informed me that I had let him out in Merced, not Modesto. He had to hitchhike 50 miles farther north to get to his destination. That did not spoil a good friendship, and we have had many laughs about the incident since then.

In May of 1947 I was ordered to the University of California at Los Angeles under the Navy's Holloway Five Term Program. Many young naval aviators of World War II vintage had entered the Navy with only a high school education. Vice Admiral Holloway, then chief of the Bureau of Naval Personnel, devised a program to give those naval aviators an opportunity to upgrade their college education and sent those who desired to go to colleges and universities for up to five semesters of study. The goal was to provide an educational upgrade within the officer corps, and many of us took advantage of the opportunity.

Returning to a campus was difficult for me until I was back in the swing of my studies. It was a nice interlude for Mary and me while I studied, and we enjoyed living in a house that we purchased in Westwood, a suburb of Los Angeles. In May 1948 Mary gave birth to our second son, Christopher, at the Long Beach Naval Hospital. I continued to fly the required monthly minimum of four hours in airplanes at Point Mugu where I felt that I could contribute more than just boring holes in the sky. In early September 1948 I completed my allotted three semesters of college and was told to report to Commander Fleet Air West Coast (COMFAIRWESTCOAST) at NAS North Island, where I would be further assigned to a fleet squadron. We sold our house and left Westwood to drive to San Diego with high hopes for our next duty station.

I reported to COMFAIRWESTCOAST in late September 1948. By now the air groups in the Pacific Fleet had been reduced to only a few. Gone were the many squadrons and air groups of World War II. The Ryan Fireball FR-1 airplane, the Navy's hybrid jet- and piston-powered airplane, had served its usefulness and was being phased out. VF-5A, then at North Island, had been flying the North American FJ-1 since the previous March. That squadron had a full complement of lucky pilots. In fact, it was exceedingly hard to gain an operational billet in any fleet squadron. I reported to the officer detailer and found that no fighter squadron billets were available. I would be lucky to find a billet in a torpedo squadron. Having flown many fighter airplanes, I was determined not to be sent to a torpedo squadron. I set about to persuade the officer detailer, Lieutenant Commander D. H. (Tex) Guinn, that he should send me to a fighter squadron. Through a lengthy process of negotiation, amounting almost to harassment on my part, over the course of four weeks of my schooling, I was able to wear him down. Finally, a lieutenant in VF-212 in Seattle contracted polio and died. I was assigned his spot as operations officer of that all-weather nightfighter squadron. Not wanting Tex Guinn to have a chance to change his mind, I grabbed the opportunity and then stayed as far away from him as I could.

I completed several more weeks of required antisubmarine warfare and radar training at the Fleet Airborne Electronics Unit Pacific at NAS Ream Field. Part of our ground training was learning procedures in the new Allied tactical publications. The United States had joined with our World War II allies and adopted mutual signals and terminology. The classic signal terms that we had learned and used for our alphabet during World War II, such as the phonetic Able, Baker, Cast, and Fox, were replaced with Alpha, Bravo, Charlie, and Foxtrot. Signal flags were no longer two blocked at the halyard; they were hauled close up. Our signalmen, officers of the deck, and pilots were having great difficulty mastering those changes, which we did not want anyway. Radio voice terminology changed dramatically as well. We pilots resisted but then reluctantly adopted the changes because we had no choice. Our airborne radars and shipboard equipment were much more capable than those of just two or three years before. Clearly, we were in a period of technological change, and we would soon be capitalizing on new forms of warfare.

Upon completion of my radar training course at Ream Field, Mary, our children, and I drove to Seattle and bought a house overlooking beautiful Lake Washington and NAS Sand Point. We paid the princely sum of $7,500 for three bedrooms, one bath, kitchen, living room and dining room, and a full basement, plus garage. I reported for duty to Fighter Squadron 212, part of Carrier Air Group 21, which was a three-squadron group: VF-211 flew F6F-5s, VF-212 flew F6F-5Ns, and VT-213 flew TBM-3s. Lieutenant Commander C. P. (Charlie) Muckenthaler was commanding officer, Lieutenant Commander J. J. Kinsella was executive officer, and I was the only lieutenant as operations officer. Lieutenant Junior Grade C. A. (Buck) Weaver, subsequently shot down and killed in the Korean War, was the flight officer. Charlie Muckenthaler had been a night-fighter pilot during the war and represented the squadron's total practical experience in night fighters. We had twenty other lieutenants junior grade, ensigns, and midshipmen pilots for this eighteen-airplane squadron.

Commander Harvey P. Lanham USN was the air group commander. He had been an air group commander at the end of the war and had served a tour in Washington before returning to the fleet for another tour as air group commander. In the late 1940s and early 1950s, many of the more senior naval aviators had two or more opportunities for aviation commands while all officers were virtually frozen in their current ranks until the personnel turmoil associated with the end of the war could be dealt with. In my case, I had been promoted to lieutenant at the age of twenty-one in 1946, and I remained a lieutenant until I was twenty-nine in 1954. The lieutenant commanders and commanders were more fortunate in their timing. However, I must admit that being a lieutenant was good because it ensured me flying billets in the fleet, which was what I wanted. Those below the rank of lieutenant had to claw their way to find a seat in a squadron and at times just to stay in the Navy.

In 1947 and 1948 new student aviators completed their training and received their naval aviator wings but continued active duty as flying midshipmen. They served in that position for two years before being promoted to ensign. Some midshipmen opted to be ensigns in the Naval Reserve, which meant they left active duty after serving an obligated two or three years. Many of those new pilots were my age, twenty-four. I did not recognize it then, but the guts-to-brains ratio was more heavily skewed to guts than to brains at that age. I had the advantage of being a seasoned lieutenant with five years of flying experience and 1,500 Navy flying hours. Timing and experience have everything to do with flying careers in the Navy, and age has less to do with them. Experience really counts.

Charlie Muckenthaler enrolled Lieutenant Junior Grade Buck Weaver and me in the Fleet All-Weather Training Unit at Barbers Point for night-fighter training. Consequently, I left for Pearl Harbor and Barbers Point almost before Mary and I were settled in our home. Fleet All-Weather Training Unit Pacific (FAWTUPAC) was the primary instrument training facility for all Pacific Fleet pilots. It was the only training facility that provided upgrading in instrument flying, and pilots came from all over the Pacific Fleet to learn that trade. There was a follow-on course to be a night-fighter pilot.

For the thirty-six years of naval aviation to date, instrument flying still had not been fully mastered by all to provide a true fleetwide operational capability. World War II was principally a daytime visual flight rules (VFR) war for carrier pilots, mostly because the Pacific Fleet had enjoyed good flying weather in the South Pacific. Instrument skills initially taught and learned in flight training became rusty in carrier aviation. In 1948 the fleet needed good instrument pilots, and a stronger Navy corporate philosophy embraced flying in weather as never before.

To go to FAWTUPAC was to sit at the knees of the great ones who had experience, wisdom, and thorough instrument flying knowledge and ability. One might question the efficacy of going to Hawaii for all-weather training, but it was ideally suited. Because of the good weather there were no training delays, and the black nights and broad, open-ocean environment provided areas for training not available elsewhere. Similar training was offered in Key West for the Atlantic Fleet.

Captain Paul Ramsey was commanding officer of FAWTUPAC, and his executive officer was Commander Bill Martin, one of our preeminent night-fighter pilots. In 1943–44 Lieutenants Martin and O'Hare were contemporaries in the Navy's development of the tactics of fighting at night. Pilots flew with pride in FAWTUPAC, and the eagerness and experience of the instructors made the entire experience a valuable one.

Training at FAWTUPAC was serious business, and there was heavy emphasis on the physiology of night vision. Basic instrument skills are axiomatic if one is to survive on black nights over the sea. Instrument training in the type of airplane to be flown was achieved by flying in pairs with one pilot chasing the other for one-half of the 1.5 hour flight and then switching roles. Basic air work was taught in the backseat of the SNJ, just as was done in the training command. Realism in instrument flying was the watchword. We covered the inside window screen of the Twin Beech airplanes we flew with green Plexiglas, and the trainee pilot wore red goggles. The result was total blackness outside; the trainee could see nothing. A safety pilot or instructor would sit in the copilot's seat without goggles and provide safe separation from others doing the same training. To save time, an additional student pilot would ride as a passenger, observing the other student pilot's performance until it was his turn to fly. The instructor pilot flew in the left seat.

We used the same green-red system in the F6F-5Ns. A safety pilot would fly wing on each pilot who was under the hood and warn him by radio if he was getting near another airplane or was in danger of hitting the water or ground. Normally, you let the pilot sort out his own problems as long as you could before you let him take off his goggles. Pilots learned to be more self-reliant in flying at night and on instruments.

Basic radar fighter direction was provided from a radar site at Barbers Point. An additional advantage to being in Hawaii was that ships undergoing training there could also provide fighter director control. Thus, not only pilots, but also fighter directors, were being trained. Sometimes the arrangement did not work all that well, and occasionally we felt as if we were the trainers rather than the trainees, but on balance the operational environment of working with the destroyers and cruisers was an advantage for the fleet.

The concept of using destroyers as picket ships for returning airplanes and/or air-sea rescue had been developed to an art form in World War II. With the advent of radar, those ships could be deployed toward the intended target and with fighters assigned from a nearby carrier could also provide more remote early warning and air defense. That concept of using picket ships led to the airborne pickets or early warning airplanes much later.

In 1948 we had a three-category instrument-rating system. A student graduating from flight training would be issued a red instrument card, which allowed him to fly on instruments in U.S. airspace and to make instrument approaches to airfields that had ceiling and visibility of 500 feet and 1 mile or greater. A white card was issued to pilots who had 1,000 hours of flight time and had demonstrated their abilities to fly approaches at a ceiling and visibility down to 200 feet and ½ mile. The ultimate card, the green instrument card, was usually only obtained through a formal course such as the one given at FAWTUPAC. The green card permitted the very experienced pilot, after he had demonstrated his skills, to fly in all weather. He was given the authority to clear himself to fly when filing a flight plan. At FAWTUPAC only the instructors had green instrument cards. When I left FAWTUPAC on January 23, 1949, with a white instrument card, I had the flying skills and knowledge that have stood me in good stead the rest of my life.

Just before I returned to Seattle, one of those policy decisions that seemed to crop up from time to time in the postwar era was rendered in Washington. The standard daytime fighter airplane for the Navy was the F8F Grumman Bearcat, still a magnificent performer below 15,000 feet. But it could still sometimes float up the deck after the LSO's cut, with the hook just missing the arresting gear wires, to hit and trip on the wire deck barriers rigged forward of the arresting gear. When the F8F did this, it could turn turtle to slam into the deck, forcing a tall pilot to become shorter. The F8F seat was only moderately adjustable and could be raised or lowered only by tilting the forward part of the seat up or down. The incidence of neck injuries in F8F barrier engagements was high enough for the flight surgeons and physiologists to become concerned.

In 1948 some wise aviation physiologist decreed that all Navy fighter pilots must be no taller than 5 feet 11 inches. Charlie Muckenthaler was 6 feet 3 inches, and I was 6 feet 2 inches. Others in VF-212 were over 6 feet tall. Since I was in Hawaii and the commanding officer had to report who and how many pilots in his command were over 5 feet 11 inches, Charlie called Mary at home. He explained carefully the reason for the call and what administrative actions might occur if a pilot were over 5 feet 11 inches. He told her how he himself had miraculously shrunk to the standard height of 5 feet 11 inches and asked Mary how tall I was. Mary is certainly no dummy, and she knew the lengths to which I had gone and how much I wanted to be a fighter pilot. So she promptly replied, "5 feet 11 inches, I think." It turned out that no one in VF-212 was taller than 5 feet 11 inches in the report that was sent to COMFAIRWEST-COAST. I believe that the Navy physiologists found the answers to the question were just as preposterous as we felt the question had been. Eventually, a rollover bar was put on the F8F, the doctors forgot their concern or they were transferred, and we fighter pilots grew back to our normal heights.

When I returned to Seattle, I found the squadron had made good progress in fulfilling the individual pilot training requirements. Flying at night in Seattle in late January and early February presented some weather challenges, but our skills matched those—except for ice. The F6F-5N, designed to be used in the South Pacific, had no ice protection, and so we assiduously avoided clouds with visible moisture in them. Other than that, the squadron flew the weather well.

At night we would sit in the ready room in the hangar wearing red goggles for thirty minutes before each flight. Once adapted to darkness, we would stumble toward the line shack wearing our red goggles. The line shack was, in reality, an office on the ground floor of the hangar with a door leading outside to our parked airplanes. Individual airplane line maintenance records were kept on clipboards in the line shack. There we accepted the assigned airplanes and then went outside to grope farther in the dark to find our airplanes. The red goggles could now come off; however, only our red flashlights were allowed on the flight line.

Once we strapped into the airplane and started, we taxied out to fly together in sections of two airplanes, carefully missing the small snow berms and the dim blue lights of the taxiway. After completing our checklists, we pulled up short of the runway for magneto checks. As each pilot checked his mags, we could tell what he was doing by the color of the engine exhaust flames streaming back on either side of the fuselage. Blue exhaust flames showed a high power setting. When a pilot had completed the magneto checks, a blossom of bright yellow exhaust flames signified that he had throttled back. In that way the flight leader knew exactly what was going on and did not have to wait for or use radio confirmation. The airplanes took off individually at thirty-second intervals to fly into the darkness and climb to 1,500 feet on the runway heading. The leader allowed one minute for each airplane in the flight after the pilot reached 1,500 feet and then made a standard rate turn, 90 degrees in sixty seconds, to the left to a prebriefed and usually reciprocal heading. Each succeeding pilot turned to join as the airplane in front of him was 45 degrees off his left nose. As each airplane joined the group, the last pilot to join would turn his exterior lights to dim.

Inside the airplane the cockpit was a glow of red light. Each instrument was lit individually, and red floodlights could be turned on to bathe the side panel switches, knobs, and circuit breakers in red light. A red filter was placed over the eight-inch radar screen to mute the normally green phosphorescent color of the main radar bang, which would move back and forth to leave range dots and images of targets on the vertical or distance scale. Those dots would gently fade away with time until illuminated on the next sweep of the radar. A pilot could choose the mapping mode and navigate his airplane in relation to the coastline below, if he chose. The leader normally did that, and each wingman flew a parade formation on the left or right side of the leader, not relying on radar until he left formation. Once the division of four was formed, the flight leader would break up the flight into twos, which then would proceed to assigned areas for intercept operations. The dark night gave smooth flying conditions, and cockpit heaters made the cockpits relatively comfortable. Each pilot sat, a separate entity, in his red enclosed cocoon monitoring his instruments and radar.

To practice night intercepts, two airplanes worked together. The target airplane held course, speed, and altitude. The attacking airplane would separate and drop down 500 feet for safety separation reasons to proceed outbound for five or ten minutes. The attacking airplane would then turn toward the target airplane, acquire the target on radar, and make the intercept to get behind and identify the target. The pilot would then simulate firing his six .50-caliber wing-mounted guns for the kill.

Night flying was very satisfying. It was intensely challenging and took a high level of skill to master. My love of flying still remained, but now I was more satisfied than exhilarated after completing a flight. Those of us who flew night fighters acquired a more businesslike disposition than we had had when flying day fighters. We each deeply enjoyed what we were doing, but gone were the carefree times of flying in and around the clouds, except on rare day-time test flights. Flying at night took total concentration if you were to stay alive for long.

One very black night, Charlie Muckenthaler showed me something that I had not seen before. We were flying individually and conducting separate radar mapping flights. I was a little bored with radar mapping, and when I picked up an airborne target on my radarscope about 15 miles away, I decided to make an identifying run on the target. As I closed to two or three miles, I picked out the wing and tail lights of the target and saw it was another F6F by the geometry of the lights. I commenced a simulated firing pass on my newly found and, I thought, unsuspecting target. It was Charlie Muckenthaler. Charlie watched me start to slide into a firing position, and when I was fully committed, he banked violently toward the direction of my attack and turned out his lights.

Where there had been red wing tip, white turtleback, and white tail lights, there was nothing! The radar target was fast disappearing on the left side of my radar screen. Now at a great disadvantage because he could see my lights but I could not see his, I turned my lights out, and we went at it. There were two F6Fs milling about in the black night sky somewhere over the Strait of Juan de Fuca, each trying to acquire the other on radar to get into firing position. One of us would acquire the other on radar momentarily and then lose him again. Charlie, the veteran night-fighter pilot and the professional, gave a fine performance. We milled about in the sky for fifteen minutes. After a couple of head-on passes, we scared ourselves; each lost the other, and we drifted off to continue our individual radar mapping exercises. I was to use that lights out tactic a number of times in later years to good advantage.

The secretary of defense in 1949 was Louis Johnson. The challenge handed him by President Truman was to downsize the military forces. His decisions must have been difficult, but the ruthlessness with which he made them had a traumatic impact on the personnel in the Navy. I am sure that those who made seemingly simple decisions in Washington did not recognize the chaos that could be created when the impact of those decisions rolled across the land to the Pacific Fleet. Our forces literally reeled from the rate of the change. We seemed to hurry up and wait like never before. Bases were closed and then re-opened. There was no new aircraft procurement, or if there was, it was to buy twelve or twenty-four airplanes. Some wise naval officers in the Bureau of Aeronautics in Washington, DC, did see the need for change. They fought the budget battles valiantly, trying to continue to provide new technology, but their efforts were thwarted by the secretary of defense. His plan was not fully understood at the fleet level, at least not at the lower echelon of the Pacific Fleet, and morale in aircraft squadrons plummeted.

As quickly as Air Group 21 had been established, it was disestablished. With no warning, at the end of February 1949, the secretary of defense decreed that more naval air stations were to be closed, and Sand Point was one of the first to go. In early March ferry pilots showed up and began to fly away our F6F-5Ns, and the squadron was disbanded. Good-byes at such times are usually minimal, and the squadron, which had been a closely integrated one, disbanded with little fanfare. We had an air group party at the NAS Sand Point officers club, and we all prepared to leave. Lieutenant Commander J. J. Kinsella, Lieutenants Junior Grade A. L. Degroff and W. O. Teague, and I from VF-212, Lieutenant H. H. Avants from Air Group 21 staff, and Lieutenants Junior Grade W. M. Gortney, C. H. Klindworth, and D. L. Christianson from VF-211 were ordered to COMFAIRWESTCOAST in San Diego for further assignment. We did not know it at the time, but there we would join VF-5A after completing jet transition training. The Navy was about to bring jet airplanes into the fleet in far greater numbers, and that transition would lead to some of our finest and most interesting flying.

Mary and I, with our three children, had four days to get to San Diego. Owning a house and leaving it in an economy of base closings can be financially catastrophic, and it was. We left our house and our furniture and drove nonstop for San Diego to comply with the orders. Our good friends Lieutenant Bob Hobsen and his wife, Ethel, were staying in Seattle because he was doing postgraduate work at the University of Washington. They agreed to oversee the company that would pack up and move all of our furniture and belongings to us in Coronado, California. They did, and we were eternally grateful for their above and beyond duty. Eventually, after eight or nine months, a real estate agent managed to sell our house at a financial loss. But at least it was sold, and we did not have to make payments on a house in which we did not live. At the time I could not believe that the secretary of defense had any idea of the havoc created by his decisions.

PART TWO

GOLDEN JET AGE

5. JETS
MARCH 1949 TO JUNE 1950

The NATO alliance grew in strength. The Greek civil war ended with the defeat of communist rebel forces. Soviet/U.S. relations were strained when a Navy PB4Y-2 Privateer was shot down by Soviet aircraft over the Baltic Sea with the loss of ten lives. The Chinese Communists drove the Chinese Nationalists from the mainland of China and proclaimed the Peoples Republic of China. The United States recognized the new state of Vietnam and sent military advisors in support, and North Korea continued to build a mighty army.

The program to build a large, new flush-deck carrier, USS United States, *was summarily canceled by Secretary of Defense Louis Johnson. An Air Force and Navy roles-and-missions struggle ensued and spilled over into a series of hearings before the House Armed Services Committee. Deemed the revolt of the admirals by the press, the end result for naval aviation was a more clearly defined role and more strength. The U.S. Air Force flew a P-80 across the country in three hours and forty-six minutes.*

In 1949 there were 12,131 pilots, 73,631 aviation ratings, and 18 aircraft carriers of all classes in the Navy. Lieutenant J. L. Fruin of VF-171 became the first U.S. pilot to use an ejection seat. A one-year officer-exchange program was initiated between Navy, Marine, and Air Force squadrons. There were four jet squadrons in the Navy, two in the Atlantic Fleet and two in the Pacific Fleet, but more were on the way as F9F and F2H jet airplanes began coming off the production lines.

Between 1943 and 1949 members of a small but growing group of naval avia-
tors were fortunate enough to be in the right place at the right time to fly jets.
At first, a few experimental test pilots like Najeeb Halaby, Jim Davidson, Bob
Elder, Fred Trapnell, Marion Carl, and Turner Caldwell occasionally flew the
U.S. Army's YP-59 and XP-80. Then several of those airplanes were trans-
ferred to the Navy for carrier suitability tests. In 1945 the Ryan FR-1, with its
Wright R-1820 reciprocating engine forward and an I-16 jet engine in the tail,
was introduced to VF-66 for fleet evaluation and then was phased out in 1947.

In 1948 VF-5A in the Pacific Fleet was assigned eighteen FJ-1s, and VF-17A
in the Atlantic Fleet was assigned a similar number of FH-1s. Those squadrons
began forging new tactics. Little, if any, information was exchanged between
the two fleets. Just getting airborne and staying up in a jet were challenges.
Commander E. P. Aurand and Lieutenant Commander R. M. Elder of VF-5A
made the first fleet carrier landings in USS *Boxer* in March 1948, and in May
VF-17A became the first fleet squadron to be fully carrier qualified. But flight
operations at sea were confined to four-to-six airplane detachments temporarily assigned to a carrier and were minimal. The jet airplane and carrier marriage was a slow and painful one. In 1948 VF-52 became a Pacific Fleet jet
training squadron flying twenty-four Air Force P-80s to increase the number of
pilots qualified in jet airplanes, and by early 1949 the squadron transitioned
some sixty-five pilots into jet airplanes. Most of those pilots, with their new jet
knowledge, returned to flying F4Us, F6Fs, and F8Fs because there were not yet
enough jet airplanes to form other squadrons. This was a time of slow learning.

In early 1949 there were three jet squadrons in the Navy and a total of seventy-five naval aviators actually flying jet airplanes in the two fleets. While
there was progress in assimilating knowledge, the small number of jet airplanes in the Navy kept the few jet pilots an elite group, and not much was
known about flying jets or was shared outside those three squadrons. In 1949
the Naval Air Force Pacific Fleet had shrunk to four active aircraft carriers and
four carrier air groups.

That was the Navy jet picture as we pilots from VF-212 arrived in San
Diego to be assigned to VF-52 as part of a nineteen-officer jet-transition training class that began March 9, 1949. Our subsequent duty would be determined
by how well we adapted and performed in our jet transition training. VF-52
had a number of seasoned pilots. Commander Edward J. Pawka was commanding officer, and Lieutenant Commander A. D. Pollock was his executive
officer. Lieutenant Commander Red O'Neil was operations and training officer,
and Lieutenant Commander James Davidson, the pilot who made the first jet
carrier landing in 1943, and a 1944 graduate of the Empire Test Pilots School
at Farnborough, England, assisted him. Other highly qualified and dedicated
lieutenants and lieutenants junior grade, such as Wayne Cheal, Don Lanning,

and Chuck Deasy, were also in the squadron. All told, VF-52, as the only jet training squadron, represented the resident knowledge on jet training in the Navy.

Our transition class seemed to be a motley crew insofar as we arrived from many different sources. One was a ferry pilot, several were from staffs, and the rest were from fleet squadrons. Lieutenant H. H. Avants and I were two of the lieutenants. Another was Lieutenant George Watkins from the COMFAIR-WESTCOAST staff. George and I both hailed from Pasadena, and Mary had gone to school with his younger brothers. Another lieutenant in the class was Leonard (Tiny) Granning from VF-191, a squadron scheduled to receive jet airplanes later in the year.

As we started our ground school, there was a change to standardized jet engine nomenclature throughout the Navy and the Air Force. The I series of engines became the J series, with the last numbers delineating the amount of thrust in the engine. Also, in the Navy the P-80 became the TO-1.

In the first week of our course, we spent forty-five hours learning the theory of the J-33 jet engine and listening to lectures on the handling characteristics of the jet airplane. During the second week I first flew the TO-1, and what an experience that was! The airplane was quiet and smooth and gave a feeling of great power once you became airborne. The excessively slow acceleration on takeoff and the small amount of fuel on board were another matter. Probably the single most impressive piece of equipment to me, other than the airplane itself, was the Air Force's automatic direction finding (ADF) radio. That was a major step forward for us Navy fighter pilots and did away with the need for an Adcock radio-range orientation to find an airfield when flying on instruments.

During the training I flew twenty flights for a total of twenty hours in the TO-1. Most of those flights were in company with my instructor, Lieutenant Junior Grade Don Lanning. Learning the art of cruise control, that is, managing the fuel carried and burned, was kept foremost in our minds. We were fascinated to see how fast the fuel disappeared as we watched the fuel counter gauges rapidly click over the gallons we were burning. The airplane was a dream in which to perform acrobatics. Although we had little unsupervised flight, on occasion I sneaked time to fly in the brilliant white cloud mountains and valleys that developed over the mountains to the east of San Diego. The increased thrust with speed in the TO-1 seemed staggering and provided power in a way that I never before thought possible. I felt free!

Formation flying was an absolute delight in the TO-1. A pilot could fly and maintain a precise formation position within inches of another airplane. If you placed your wing very close, you could literally cause the leader's wing to move because of the aerodynamic interaction between wings. We found the venturi effect, created between the two wings, actually prevented them from touching, unless a pilot purposely overpowered it. The beauty was that there was no propeller to chew up another airplane's wing or fuselage. Each flight was scheduled for one hour, and we had to be on the deck with 75 gallons or about 450 pounds of fuel remaining to account for any delay that might occur at the field.

Several transition pilots had problems. The TO-1 had a great tendency to porpoise when landing if a pilot's speed was the least bit fast and if he let the nose wheel touch the ground before the main landing gear. The resulting porpoise of nose wheel–main gear–nose wheel could be divergent (that is, self-perpetuating) if left uncorrected and almost always resulted in the nose landing gear collapsing and the airplane sliding ignominiously to a stop on its main landing gear and nose. That happened twice to pilots in our class.

We completed our transition training on March 29, and immediately Hal Avants, Bill Gortney, Carl Klindworth, Don Christianson, and I received orders to report to VF-51 in Air Group 5. All five squadrons of Air Group 5 and the air group staff were located in a 1930s-style hangar just across the road from Victor's Bar in the BOQ, which we frequented each afternoon after flying. Administrative offices were on the second deck, maintenance offices were on the first deck, and each squadron had a representative portion of the hangar floor to work on airplanes.

VF-51 was proud of being called the first jet squadron in the Navy. Those on the East Coast in VF-171 could argue that point, but at that time VF-51 was the jet squadron to be in, certainly on the West Coast. Commander E. P. Aurand was commanding officer, and Lieutenant Commander R. M. (Bob) Elder was the executive officer. The squadron had an amazing array of talent and names, who all made their mark on naval aviation. Among them were Lieutenant Commanders John Magda and Ed Holley, Lieutenants Vince Kelly, Ralph Hanks, Bud Sickle, and Don Davis, and Lieutenants Junior Grade Nello Pierozzi, Taylor Brown, Paul Davidson, Malcom Vail, and Bob Oechslin.

When I joined VF-51, Bob Elder had recently returned from a USS *Boxer* deployment to Alaska with four FJ-1s to develop cold weather tactics. The trip was successful, but the flying was sporadic—a disappointment to the pilots. Their complaint principally focused on the lack of knowledge that the carrier's officers had concerning jet operations. Shortly after we joined VF-51, the names and faces began to change—it was transition time. Bob Elder was acting commanding officer until his detachment, when Lieutenant Commander Dave Pollock of VF-52 took command. Six new lieutenant commanders joined the squadron. More lieutenants junior grade, ensigns, and midshipmen from Air Group 21 and elsewhere went through the transition course in VF-52 and joined the squadron. During that spring, VF-51 became a sixteen-airplane squadron with twenty-four pilots; the rank structure was unusual in that there were seven lieutenant commanders, one lieutenant (me), six lieutenants junior grade, and ten ensigns and midshipmen. Inequities in rank distribution still remained from the chaos after World War II.

Every pilot enjoyed flying the FJ-1. It sat high off the ground on tricycle landing gear. In the air it looked good and was a fine flying airplane. A gas guzzler, it carried only some 3,000 pounds of fuel internally. We pilots felt as if we had a fuel emergency as soon as we took off, so most of the time we flew within 200 to 300 miles of NAS North Island. The biggest challenge was that the FJ-1 did not have an ADF radio, as the P-80 did, and we had to use a four-course, Adcock low-frequency radio-range orientation for descent to the field if the visibility was bad. By early 1949 the airplanes were well used and tired, and it was difficult to get more than four or five in the air at any given time.

On May 23 I was flying an FJ-1 when I sensed rather than knew something was wrong. I looked out at the right aileron, and instead of seeing a well-defined trailing edge, I saw a complete blur. In fact, the trailing edge of the aileron seemed to have grown to be two inches thick. That was my first encounter with aileron buzz or flutter! There was no force feedback of aileron movement to my hand on the stick, and yet I was in imminent danger of losing the aileron. I immediately slowed, and the aileron buzz stopped, so I cautiously returned to the field at low speed and landed. On inspection back on the ground, I found I could move the aileron tab three-eighths of an inch because the hinge was so worn. The danger was that this flutter would continue until the aileron hinge failed, and then the aileron would leave the airplane, most probably followed immediately by the wing. The tab was repaired, and I reported the event to the squadron at an all-pilots meeting.

Two weeks later Lieutenant Hal Avants was flying alone near the Coronados Islands at what we estimated to be 450 knots at 10,000 feet in another FJ-1. His airplane abruptly disintegrated in the air, killing him instantly. We recovered nothing. In reconstructing the accident, we had only one short unintelligible radio transmission from Hal. We theorized that the tab was excited to a buzz, and then the aileron failed. Next the wing folded over Hal's head onto the fuselage, and the airplane exploded into small pieces and fell into the sea. I was certainly more fortunate than he.

It was and still is a matter of form that each Navy pilot keeps a confidential sheet on file in the administrative offices of his squadron. That sheet identifies whom the pilot wants to inventory his personal effects in the event of his death and other personal data such as next of kin, insurance policies, their location, etc. Hal Avants had named me to inventory his effects. Such an inventory becomes a solemn duty as you catalog personal effects of a friend and squadron mate who was flying with you in the morning but is gone in the afternoon. Loose change or car keys held in his hand not so long ago; the letter home, written but not yet mailed, and the letters received but not yet answered; the personal things, such as razor, toothbrush, and soap; and the uniforms and many small things that had been his. The commanding officer and I both wrote letters of condolence to Hal's family. The Navy sent his effects home in the standard wooden cruise box, and we continued our flying in earnest.

With the end of World War II, gone were the thousands of airplanes in the aircraft inventory, and the Navy reverted to procuring small numbers of airplanes for specific squadrons, as had been done in the 1930s. In 1949 fifty-two F9F-3s, powered by the Allison J-33 centrifugal-flow engine, were to be assigned only to VF-51 and VF-52. Those F9F-3s came off the production line before the F9F-2, with its axial-flow J-42 Nene engine. Upon receipt of those airplanes, VF-52 reverted to its fleet fighter role in Air Group 5 and sent the TO-1 airplanes along with a number of its officers and enlisted men to Whiting Field, Pensacola. That cadre of officers and men and those airplanes formed the nucleus of the jet training unit there, under the Naval Air Training Command, to begin more formal jet transition.

I flew my first flight in the F9F-3 in mid-June 1949, and two weeks later Lieutenants Junior Grade Leonard Plog, Paul Davidson, Malcomb Vail, and I were ordered to Bethpage, New York, to pick up four brand new F9F-3s. The airplanes we had flown to date did not have ejection seats, and as a result pilot casualty rates were climbing. So we first went to the Naval Aircraft Factory in Philadelphia to be fleet guinea pigs for the new and still untried (in the United States) British Martin Baker ejection seat, now being installed in the F9F. There we found a 96-foot training tower that stood like a giant guillotine outside several workshops.

The Martin Baker seat was essentially a seat sitting on a 40mm shell filled with slower burning propellant and fitted with tracks to guide the seat upward and clear of the airplane. The 40mm shell fired when the pilot pulled a face curtain to its full length down over his head and face to protect himself from severe wind blast injury at high speeds. Before the shell fired, the cockpit canopy jettisoned aft. Then the force of the powder charge propelled the pilot clear of the airplane. The pilot then undid his seat belt and shoulder straps to kick himself clear of the seat and manually pulled his parachute ripcord. The Martin Baker seat was an ingenious development and improved over time to ultimately save over 6,000 pilots' lives during some forty-two years. Our view in 1949 was that this seat was to be used in an emergency. Not one of us looked forward to the honor of firing the seat on the ground.

Being the senior officer, I approached the tower first. The grains of powder propellant were carefully measured out and weighed according to our body weight to give each of us one-half to three-quarters of a full shot. I sat in the seat while my compatriots and passersby gathered to watch the show. Some of them opened lunch sacks to sit in the shade and munch while watching. Having been briefed and fully strapped in, I positioned myself and on signal pulled the face curtain over my helmet in one full stroke. Nothing happened! I was sitting on a seat whose cartridge supposedly had been fired, and no one wanted to come near me. A loud voice said, "Do not move!" That was irrelevant—I was not about to move. I still firmly clasped the face curtain over my head and face to keep my arms from being broken should the seat accidentally fire. After some consultation, one person with a very long pole approached me cautiously. Using a metal hook on the end of the pole, he fished around behind the seat until he could mechanically insert the safety pin into the cartridge on the seat. Then everyone, especially me, relaxed enough to get me out of the hot seat.

Hours later the problem was determined to be a bad firing squib, and we set about to duplicate the morning exercise. This time I firmly grasped the face curtain and on signal pulled as hard as I could to make sure that the thing fired. It did, and in a fraction of a second the seat compressed my spine, now elongated from the pull, and propelled me up the tower to stop some 48 feet above with a great display of smoke and noise.

After being let down by some ratchet-and-pulley arrangement, I told my friends to not pull so hard, and they fared much better than I. Still later, I found that I had compressed a disk in my spine, but I never doubted that I would use the ejection seat. Weeks later squadron executive officer Lieutenant Commander Bill Sisley also injured himself on the same tower, and Lieutenant Commander Dave Pollock said that he would never use the seat but would choose to bail out. Dave was killed four years later when he did just that from an F9F-6 that he was flight testing at Patuxent River. He chose to not use the ejection seat and hit his head on the leading edge of the stabilator; he never opened his parachute.

Within a day we left Philadelphia by train for Bethpage to pick up our new F9F-3s. The checkouts went quickly and smoothly under the tutelage of Grumman test pilots Connie Converse and Corky Meyer. The four of us then left for Patuxent River, our first stop on the return flight.

At Patuxent River I found that I had a hydraulic leak in my left main landing gear retracting cylinder. It was not encouraging to have problems on the very first stop, but through the wizardry of Ralph Clark, the resident Grumman representative at the Naval Air Test Center, we took the cylinder apart in the evening, and he fixed it in time for me to leave with the others the next day. On the next stop at Dobbins AFB in Marietta, Georgia, I found on landing that my speed brakes would not retract. Those were located aft of the nose wheel and forward of the main landing gear on the fuselage centerline and were effective enough to prevent me from taking off. After consulting Grumman's erection and maintenance handbooks, which I carried in the ammo cans, but making no headway, I told my squadron compatriots to go on ahead to San Diego.

Over the next two days, an Air Force tech sergeant and I struggled to solve the vexing problem. Finally, he said, "If it does not bother you to not have speed brakes for the rest of the trip, I think I can fix it." I replied that "was OK with me," and he proceeded to attach the up hydraulic line to the down side and the down hydraulic line to the up side. I turned up the engine, and those speed brakes firmly slammed up. I then completed my flight across country to San Diego after additional stops at NAS Dallas, Texas, and Williams AFB, Arizona. Because good fuel planning information was not available at the time of my trip, I vowed to do something about that problem in the future.

It was deemed important to get the F9F-3 on board ship as soon as we could with one-half of the squadron pilots to qualify in September and the other half somewhat later. We flew FCLP at Ream and Brown Fields, two airfields near the Mexican border, for the remainder of July and through August, to fly on board USS *Boxer* on September 16. Commander E. S. Keats, our CAG, qualified, as well as Commander Harvey Lanham, who was soon to relieve him. Each pilot made four carrier landings, and those landings were the first for the F9F-3.

Much of the flight testing on the F9F-3 was done concurrently with the fleet introduction, and the pilots of VF-51 and VF-52 found themselves gathering valuable information expected to be available from Patuxent River. That was not much of a problem because at that time the squadron had more jet experience than the test center. However, Dave Pollock expressed his concern to Commander Naval Air Force Pacific Fleet about the volume of data constantly being requested by the test center from our squadron. He felt, correctly, that the burden of providing that information detracted from the training. The situation illustrated the need for earlier and more complete testing of new airplanes.

Because of my all-weather training, I developed and wrote a doctrine for instrument-flying procedures for jet airplanes over the summer of 1949. Very little was known and nothing had been written about flying jet airplanes in weather or on instruments. We discovered our attitude gyro instruments were inadequate at high altitude because the gyros precessed inordinately at high true airspeeds. No one had previously cataloged this as being a concern. As a result of my work, in September 1949, Lieutenant Commander Dave Pollock nominated me to take the first jet airplane to the CAA-sponsored and Navy-supported Landing Aids Experimental Station (LAES) at Arcata, California, for low-visibility landing operations and evaluation.

The development of airplane avionics and particularly ground-based support systems for air navigation had been virtually on hold during World War II. We had flown with what was available. The CAA had developed an instrument landing system (ILS) just before the war started, and that system had been used by large airplanes, particularly in the Army Air Forces. Concurrently, the Navy developed the radar concept of ground controlled approaches (GCA). The Navy and the Air Force used GCA extensively, particularly in single-engine airplanes.

A controversy over GCA versus ILS raged back and forth, and proponents for each spoke in acrimonious hearings in Congress. Finally, Congress decreed the airspace in the United States to be a civil, not a military, airspace and noted the need for better air navigation coordination between civil and military aviation. The CAA took the lead and in May 1948 established the civil Air Navigation Development Board, with military representation. That board decreed the use of ILS for civil aviation and GCA, or precision approach radar (PAR), for the military. Regardless of the system used, the pilot's ability to see the runway after completing the approach remained a challenge.

LAES Arcata was created under the auspices of the CAA to evaluate visual pilot aids. To facilitate testing there, the Navy GCA unit from Gander, Newfoundland, was mustered out of the Navy en masse and rehired as civilians at LAES Arcata. Pilots flying the development programs there relied on them for guidance to find the runway approach lighting under evaluation. That GCA team was indeed the finest GCA team in the United States.

Petty Officer First Class L. L. Kasper, one of VF-51's leading mechanics, was flown to Arcata in a Twin Beech along with some key tools and ground-handling equipment to support my F9F-3, and I flew the airplane north. We planned the flights to arrive September 18. Cross-country flying was not something that we jet pilots did frequently, so I enjoyed the sixty-five-minute flight from San Diego to Alameda and became the first to land at that naval air station in the F9F-3. The airplane elicited a great deal of interest, and after some delay, I flew to Arcata. On arrival I noticed a large number of onlookers lining the airfield boundary and suddenly realized that this was not only the first jet to be tested there but also the first jet the local citizens had seen.

Arcata, California, said to be the foggiest place in the Lower Forty-Eight, was selected as the ideal site to test airplanes in reduced visibility. A large number of different Navy and civil airplanes were undergoing test and evaluation there. I began flying on September 19 in good weather because the scientific and support staff of LAES felt a certain amount of apprehension about the handling of the jet airplane. The responsibility was mine to show that we could use a jet airplane like any other airplane. The differences were more mental than actual and were focused on the higher landing speeds and the shorter time of flight due to high fuel consumption. The runway was 5,000 feet long and ample, considering the prevailing wind from the west, and the landing aids all were gathered at the east end of the single east-west runway for the same reason. The one drawback was the west end of the runway. It stopped a few feet before a sheer cliff, which dropped 100 feet to the Pacific Ocean. One did not want to land long. Over the course of two days I made four flights and won over the LAES staff to accept the F9F-3 as a normal airplane. We then settled down to fly only when the weather produced less than 200-foot ceilings and ¼ mile or less of forward visibility.

It took the better part of a week's flying until on September 26 we achieved the first really low visibility passes for the F9F, flown to a measured ceiling of 40 feet and ¼ mile of forward visibility. The F9F performed flawlessly, and I made a number of approaches and landings to evaluate the Calvert, Air Line Pilots Association (ALPA), and slope line approach visual systems.

That night, after midnight, a heavy pea-soup fog settled over the field, and everyone was called back to the field to start flying again. A FAWTUPAC F7F-2N took off first, and I was to be second to fly. The visibility was really poor as I donned my flight gear and then literally began to feel my way to my airplane on the ramp. I heard the F7F-2N making an approach and could see nothing. Obviously the pilot of the F7F could see less. It was pitch black with dense fog. I heard the F7F touch down not too far away and realized, with great alarm, that the touchdown was hard and definitely not on the runway. It was considerably closer to me, probably on the taxiway to my right. I heard a muffled explosion and then the grinding and screeching sounds of metal sliding on concrete while bits and pieces of airplane broke off. The sound was coming my way, and I turned and ran as the F7F must have slid by me to hit airplanes on the ramp as it ploughed on. Each impact with another airplane made a distinctive sound, and after the third or fourth airplane was hit, I saw a faint orange glow as airplanes began to burn. It was so foggy that I never saw flames—only the glow.

The fire and crash crew could not find the F7F for five minutes even though it had blown up on the parking ramp within 100 feet of the control tower. Eventually, the fire was extinguished, and the FAWTUPAC pilot, a lieutenant junior grade, who survived, was found in a hangar where he had run in a state of shock. That ended flight operations for that night. FAWTUPAC convened an aircraft accident board and over the course of the next ten days determined that pilot judgment was a principal factor in the accident. The preponderance of evidence was that alcohol was a contributing factor. The pilot had been in town at a local watering hole when recalled to fly.

When the fog lifted the next day, Petty Officer Kasper and I found that the top of the right wing of the F7F had struck a glancing blow on the bottom of the left wing-tip tank of my airplane. There was no visible damage other than the imprint of a large nut on the upper skin of the landing gear well, but that clearly indicated that we should drop check the landing gear before the next flight. Necessity being the mother of invention, we persuaded a California highway crew that was working on a bridge north of Arcata to bring its crane to the airfield. There we put nylon straps under the wings of the F9F and gingerly lifted it clear of the ground. The sight of that huge highway crane lifting a jet fighter was incongruous, but it worked! I used a tall ladder to climb up into the cockpit and started the engine to get the hydraulic power we needed. I then found that the left main landing gear would not retract. Otherwise all else was fine.

The next day, September 28, I flew the airplane to San Diego with the left main landing gear down and the nose and right landing gear up. It looked funny, but again it worked, and I traded airplanes at the squadron and returned to Arcata that same day to continue our tests. Over the course of the next week, I flew many day and night flights, making landings down to measured ceilings of 0–25 feet and less than 1/16 of a mile of forward visibility. It was rewarding bad-weather flying, and we dramatically opened peoples' eyes to the capabilities of these heretofore fair-weather jet airplanes.

The citizens of Arcata treated Kasper and me like royalty during our stay. We could not buy a drink or a dinner in town. Wherever we went, those fine people made us put our money away, and we were treated to real Northern California hospitality. We returned to San Diego to find notoriety and acclaim, which I subsequently used up.

In October, within days of returning to NAS North Island, and while still bathing in the light of recognition for my work in Arcata, I made the classic aviator's mistake and landed with my wheels up. There were extenuating circumstances, but no pilot can blame others for his mistakes. I made the mistake, and I had to bear the shame, even though there was little damage to the airplane. Two things happened as a result of that wheels-up landing. First, Chet Huntley, then the Richfield radio news reporter in California (and later one-half of the duo on the Huntley-Brinkley Report), dutifully reported on the 10 o'clock evening news that the "fog pilot," on whom he had reported favorably just days before, landed in a "new kind of fog." Second, from then on, every time someone had a problem with landing gear, I was called to the tower as the expert. I enjoyed neither one of those distinctions.

There were no such things as instrument letdown procedures or letdown plates, as they were called for jet airplanes. I set about in earnest to derive procedures that would enable the squadron to make instrument approaches to NAS North Island and to an aircraft carrier when we were at sea. I envisioned a standard approach for every radio range, unlike the older system, in which the orientation of the preferred leg for Adcock ranges could vary significantly. Using the San Diego radio range near Lindbergh Field as a fix, I designed a letdown procedure that permitted the pilot to fly over the radio range at 20,000 feet and, in a new teardrop flight path, to descend to the lowest permitted altitude to fly directly to the airfield. We avoided that part of the radio range used by the airlines and other propeller airplanes so we could have near simultaneous use. Besides, there was virtually no civil air traffic above 10,000 feet. Additionally, there was no radar, and all flight separation was maintained solely by time and procedures. We could put two, four, six, or eight airplanes down below the weather and in position for a GCA pickup easily. The CAA showed absolutely no interest in those procedures as long as we stayed away from the standard instrument approach to Lindbergh Field.

Commander Harvey Lanham, now the CAG, persuaded USS *Boxer* and *Valley Forge* to install low-frequency homer beacons. That was a major departure because previously ships did not want to be identified, but by doing so, we could use our instrument procedures at sea. Using time to maintain our own separation, we could descend to 200 feet above the water to fly our carrier pattern. In very low visibility, we could identify the ship or ship's wake in time to see the LSO. It was as rudimentary then as it seems now, but it worked. We could fly on board the carrier in poor weather. Slowly we built our confidence and, just as importantly, the ship's confidence in us.

In the fall of 1949 we conducted gunnery training at 15,000 feet, firing on sleeves towed by JD-1 airplanes from VU-3. The F9F-3 was armed with four 20mm cannon mounted in the nose. Those cannon were the only armament; there were no bombs and no rockets. The expended brass cartridges and steel belting links were saved inside the nose cover, to be retrieved at the end of a flight. That helped maintain the center of gravity of the airplane within limits and prevented the expend d brass from entering the engine with catastrophic results.

When not conducting gunnery training, we flew intercept operations against other aircraft under control of Combat Operations Center Point Loma and USS *Valley Forge*. It was painfully slow training the combat information center (CIC) controllers on board the ship to understand the new capabilities, as well as the limitations, of jet airplanes. The principal difficulty lay in the controllers' lack of sensitivity to time and distance. The jet airplane used much more airspace and needed to be positioned more precisely to gain visual identification in time to complete a successful intercept.

After World War II the great Convair B-36 bomber was developed and, from that, the B-36B, RB-36B, and B-36D. The B-36D had six integral, wing-mounted, pusher reciprocating engines and also a twin J-47 engine jet pod mounted under each wing outboard of the number 1 and 6 engines. The B-36 was the original aluminum overcast to us fighter pilots. It was big, and the Air

Force was proud of it. The B-36 and aircraft carriers were key objects in the all-consuming roles-and-missions debate between the Air Force and the Navy when interservice debate rose in crescendo in 1949 and spilled out of the newly created Department of Defense. Virulent arguments were leaked to the press by both the Air Force and the Navy, and it became clearer that naval aviation was fighting for its life. Finally, when Secretary of Defense Louis Johnson summarily canceled the aircraft carrier *United States* five days after its keel laying, Secretary of the Navy John L. Sullivan resigned in protest, and the Navy's admirals rose up in arms in what history has termed the revolt of the admirals. The centerpiece of the Air Force's attack on the role of naval aviation was the B-36, an airplane described as flying above and beyond radar detection, higher than current fighters could fly. The B-36, said the Air Force, produced such great wing and engine wake vortices that, should an attacking airplane fly through them at high altitude and high speed, the attacking airplane would shed its wings. The Air Force maintained that the B-36 needed no fighter protection.

The leaks of information, charges, and countercharges caused Carl Vinson, chairman of the House Armed Services Committee, to announce in June 1949 that he would convene a full investigation. The Air Force flew the B-36 throughout the world, and the Navy flew its F2H and F9F . ;hters higher and higher, while the press played up and intensified the now-public debate. Pictures of the nation's capital were taken by an F2H from an altitude above 40,000 feet, and those pictures magically appeared on the wall of a restaurant in Washington, DC. Emotions ran high—especially in the Navy. Eventually, Chief of Naval Operations Louis Denfield was fired by Secretary of Defense Johnson, and Captain Arleigh Burke, along with his small staff in the Pentagon, was actually held incommunicado for hours under interrogation at the direction of the secretary of defense for aiding and abetting. Famed naval aviator Captain John Crommelin spoke out publicly, using a privileged letter between Secretary of the Navy Matthews and Vice Admiral Gerald F. Bogan, and was fired. Vice Admiral Bogan retired early. Congressional B-36 hearings began on August 9, 1949, and continued for months.

Vice Admiral Arthur Radford, first as deputy chief of naval operations (air), and then as CINCPAC, walked a fine line and was a key player in the acrimonious debate. In the late summer of 1949 Commander Pete Aurand, then of Naval Air Force Pacific Fleet staff, orally gave Commander Harvey Lanham the task of showing that the claims of the Air Force were not valid, and he in turn tasked VF-51 and VF-52. Pete Aurand knew the Air Force was flying B-36s on training flights over U.S. cities, among them San Diego, using them as mock targets. In September and October of 1949 we prepared for and flew a series of intercepts on those B-36 bombers as they approached San Diego.

We Navy pilots entered that contest with great enthusiasm and stood strip alert at NAS North Island. We launched when directed by the air defense controllers at Combat Operations Center Point Loma or in *Valley Forge*, and if they could not see the B-36s on radar, we could see the giant contrails marking their flight path. After takeoff, we would climb to intercept altitude and make our simulated firing pass. The purpose was to fly at the same altitude as the B-36 to show that we could fly there and in its wake to show that our wings would not come off as claimed. Key to that was our gun camera film. We were unarmed, of course, but carefully framed the B-36 in our sights and then picked one engine as an aiming point to show photographic proof of the simulated firing passes. The film showed the result.

The strip alerts and intercepts were great fun and good practice. We would intercept and fly close by the B-36 to let the Air Force pilots know that we were there. As soon as we returned, our gun camera film was developed and flown to Washington to be used by the admirals in testimony before Congress.

The revolt of the admirals subsequently was resolved in Washington. Senate hearings were adjourned October 21 after the Senate Armed Services Committee intervened, defining again the Department of Defense Act. There would be further Department of Defense personnel changes the next year, mostly because of Louis Johnson's high-handed approach to naval aviation, but at the end of 1949 Admiral Forrest P. Sherman, then CNO, set about to redefine naval aviation as an integral part of the Navy and Marine Corps. Meanwhile, we in the fleet squadrons continued about our business of flying airplanes.

The B-36 intercepts showed a shortcoming in the F9F-3—frequent loss of cabin pressurization. The canopy of the F9F was hydraulically actuated to slide aft and open when the pilot moved a lever on the left side of the canopy rail. As a matter of policy, we made all landings and takeoffs with our canopies open for water survival reasons. After taking off and closing the canopy, we found the rubber pneumatic seal around the canopy, designed to inflate and provide pressurization for cockpit climate and altitude control, would fail to keep the pressure above 35,000 feet. This required that pilots pressure breathe, a process designed to force oxygen into the lungs. Instead of taking a deep breath and relaxing to exhale, the pilot would relax so his mouth opened, and oxygen under great pressure was forced into his lungs until he closed his mouth. Then he would forcefully exhale to do it again and again with great effort.

Losing cabin pressure was not necessarily dangerous; it was annoying. Of more concern to me, I found that my left wrist, broken back in my aviation cadet days, would ache in the extreme as I developed the bends from loss of pressurization. My wrist would become immobile from the pain of the nitrogen bubbles in the joint, which made flights a lot less fun. We found a simple solution for the loss of cabin pressurization, and that solved my problem with the bends as well. We shut our cockpits before takeoff and took pliable adhesive cloth tape used by our aviation ordnance men for sealing gun ports and taped ourselves inside the cockpit. The tape provided the necessary seal, and we could complete our B-36 intercept flight in pressurized comfort. We removed the tape before opening the canopy for landing. Of course, we said nothing of our pressurization problems to the Air Force.

To plan for fuel to be used on a flight, we used unwieldly tables in the back of the aircraft's handbook. That was difficult, and the data were not accurate. In the fall of 1949 I set about to devise a better method. I reasoned that we could make a cruise-control planning device patterned after a language verb wheel used in schools. It could be small, fit in a flight suit pocket, and be easy to use. But first the fuel data in our handbook had to be improved. With help from Dave Pollock, Howie Boydstun, Jim Davidson, and others who had done airplane performance testing, I created cards for pilots of VF-51 and VF-52 to fill out on each flight. I asked my fellow pilots to record fuel-use figures at exact altitudes in 5,000 feet increments from sea level to 35,000 feet. Over several months I accumulated enough valid fuel data for an accurate picture and put this information in a printed format that would fit on a four-inch-diameter circular verb wheel. By dialing a desired altitude in one window, you then could easily read the fuel required, time to climb, and pounds of fuel burned each minute at any engine power setting.

We were fortunate to have an overhaul and repair facility at North Island, and its engineering section manufactured 100 of those fuel computers. The end product was quite novel and good, and each pilot flying the F9F-3 got one. By then the F9F-2, with its J-42 engine, was arriving in the fleet, and our sister air group, Air Group 11, was flying them. We needed more data, but help was on the way.

Unbeknownst to me, Theron (Tee) Davison of the Naval Air Test Center Patuxent River also was working on a cruise-control computer. When produced later, it had more and better logarithmic information on it and a navigation circular slide rule as well. Tee Davison and the Tactical Test Division subsequently produced many different cruise-control computers for other models of airplanes and did a great service for naval aviation. Eight years later when Tee and I worked together at Patuxent River, I found that he still kept one of my cruise-control computers. One of my computers is also on display at the National Naval Aviation Museum in Pensacola.

In 1949 the Air Force and Navy began an exchange program for a few pilots, which had a beneficial impact on the development of jet airplanes in both services and helped infuse in each organization the thinking of the other. Where flag and general officers previously had been pitted against one another, squadron level pilots now cooperated as never before. The first Navy pilots to go on such exchanges from the West Coast were Lieutenants Bud Sickle and

Don Davis. Captain E. H. (Ted) Connor USAF came as an exchange officer to VF-51.

Ted Connor was a great asset. A Military Academy graduate, he was a former P-80 pilot who understood Air Force fighter tactics. Ted came from the Air Force environment in which pilots only flew airplanes, and he was surprised to be made squadron ordnance officer. He joined right in, learned well, and became an important part of VF-51. His enthusiasm after his first carrier landing was something to behold! Later, he and I roomed together on deployment to the western Pacific and became close friends.

On January 5, 1950, we began flying squadron tactics and FCLP to refresh ourselves for a short trip at sea in USS *Valley Forge*. Those occasional and short carrier trips proved that one of the great challenges to operating jets on a ship was the ship itself. Little was known in *Valley Forge* of jet airplane capabilities and limitations. The CIC was the central part of the operations division of the ship. The thinking in CIC was strictly World War II—crewmen standing behind transparent plastic boards writing backwards to show aircraft position and tactical plot for intercept officers standing in front of them. Located nearby was a small air operations office where the daily air operations schedule was managed and relayed to ready rooms.

No pilot from the Navy's few jet squadrons had yet reported to the carriers for duty. CIC poorly understood speeds, turning radii, and altitude capabilities of jet airplanes. As a result, we provided hours of training intercept services to help build CIC's knowledge. There was no height-finding radar, and the altitude of a target airplane was estimated by using the radar transmission nulls and lobes. Some controllers were good, but most were poor. If a pilot valued his life, he maintained a healthy mistrust of the radar controller's ability to know where he was, how much fuel he had, and whether or not he could get back to the ship.

The radar controllers, in particular, did not understand how altitude affected range and endurance. We pilots measured fuel in pounds and minutes, and the controllers measured it in gallons and hours. We would climb to 35,000 feet, and they would vector us to intercept a bogey at sea level and then wonder why we never had enough fuel. If we had stopped to think about it, no airplanes other than ours were flying as high. Soon, it was recognized that all the bogeys were low, so we flew low. However, it was the pilot's responsibility to not run out of fuel, and frequently the intercept controllers seemed determined to trick us in that matter. The suspicions that grew in pilots' minds did little to enhance ship-squadron team spirit. It seemed to us that there never would be full understanding of jet operations in *Valley Forge*.

If *Valley Forge* CIC was difficult to train, destroyer CICs were nearly impossible, but there were funny moments too. One time, while providing speed calibration and radar services, I was at 10,000 feet maintaining a steady course and speed toward the ship. My blip was moving across the CIC radar screen in a straight line. Without saying a word, I pulled up into a loop, and the radar blip stopped moving and then started again. The controller, without benefit of altitude information, excitedly asked on the radio what I had done. I replied, "Nothing." Only later did he figure it out.

Not just *Valley Forge* CIC needed indoctrination. Air ops needed help in planning schedules and determining capabilities. The air department thought jets always needed something special. Jets were a pain. The supply department thought jets needed an inordinate number of spare parts. *Valley Forge* could support three or, at the most, four days of operations before needing to replenish its aviation gasoline stores. As jets entered service, the logisticians believed that a common aviation gasoline fuel would solve logistic problems. However, the jet engines consumed aviation gasoline far faster than the piston engines did, and soon we ran the other airplanes out of fuel as well. Captain H. B. Temple, commanding officer of *Valley Forge*, and his officers needed to understand the importance of increased wind across the deck for arrested landings and catapulting. That need for greater education and knowledge was constant. Fortunately, we did not kill any pilots during the ship's learning process, but we sure came close.

To be fair, the jet squadrons also had much to learn. For example, we needed to learn how to cope with the use of 115/145 aviation gasoline at sea instead of the JP-1 jet fuel we burned ashore. JP-1, a simple kerosene, had more British thermal units (Btu's) and hence more energy than aviation gasoline. It cost 11 cents a gallon instead of the 22 cents for aviation gasoline and weighed a tenth of a pound more per gallon. So at sea, burning gasoline, we had less thrust at higher price of operation. Also, aviation gasoline gave off a toxic lead byproduct when burned that covered turbine blades and tailpipes alike, creating health hazards for our maintenance crews. To combat toxicity and loss of performance, Allison engineers devised a method of throwing walnut shells into the intake as an engine was running on the deck. Those shells disintegrated on impact with the compressor-wheel blades and did not hurt them but subsequently scoured the turbine blades, removing the lead deposits. Thus burning aviation gasoline was a penalty that we did not relish accepting, but no alternative seemed to be available.

In February 1950 seven pilots led by Commander Harvey Lanham prepared to make the first night jet carrier landings. Up to that point, it had been thrilling enough to make carrier landings in the daytime, let alone on a black night. Commander Lanham chose from VF-51 Lieutenant Commanders Pollock, Sisley, and Thompson, and me as the only lieutenant, and from VF-52 Commander E. J. Pawka and Lieutenant Commanders Boydstun and Davidson. The air group's LSO was Lieutenant Leroy R. (Tom) Mix, and his assistant LSO was Lieutenant Junior Grade Emmett B. Boutwell. Both did a stellar job using fifteen or so flashlight-sized bulbs in each of two angular metal wands arranged in such a way that their glow reflected toward the pilots from the metal angle iron. The Navy had used ultraviolet light and reflective paddles and clothing before, but the flashlight bulbs gave better definition. Besides, the ultraviolet light was hard on the LSO's eyes. Tom Mix placed a 24-volt battery between his feet, hooked the wands to the battery, and then held one wand in each hand to give standard daytime signals.

We practiced night FCLP at Brown Field, south of San Diego, for four nights, while maintaining our day-landing currency, and made our night carrier landings on USS *Boxer* on February 28. At sea there was no horizon to visually orient yourself, and we did not have radar altimeters. After each catapult shot, the glow of the flame coming from our tailpipes would blossom on the water, and that glow and the reflection of our wing lights on the water were all that we could see other than the red glow inside our cockpits. That was true of the entire landing pattern until we sighted Tom Mix's wand signals and flew in response. We saw high, low, and fast signals, but I do not think we ever saw a slow signal! Especially designed dustpan lights were mounted on the landing deck edge to provide an artificial glow over the landing area, which still looked like nothing more than a black hole. There were no centerline or other deck edge lights to help, and beyond the last of the eight arresting wires on the straight flight deck were the three wire barricades waiting to end your flight ingloriously.

We each made our landings and achieved notoriety in *Time* and *Life* magazines, but other than a few dusk landings much later that year we did not fly at night again. However, the qualification was one more proof that the jet airplane could be used like any other airplane. Commander Lanham was doing his best to have us challenge other firsts to bring the jet airplane into tactical utility.

In February and March 1950 we moved on to air-to-air gunnery training at El Centro, California, and to cross-country flights for familiarization with the cruise-control computers. The cross-country flights went well for all except Lieutenant Commander Harley (Tommy) Thompson and his wingman, who landed by navigational mistake at Luke AFB, Arizona, shortly after it was deactivated and abandoned. Not one person was on the airfield. No one would have been the wiser had not Tommy blown a tire on landing. He survived the taunts later after his return to the squadron.

We stopped flying in mid-April 1950 to board *Valley Forge* and to prepare to be the first air group with jet airplanes to deploy to the western Pacific. Over a two-week period, all airplanes, parts, and special handling equipment needed to support the air group for six months were stuffed away in nooks and crannies in the ship. No one stopped to think about what the air group with jet airplanes was doing in the Atlantic Fleet. It was almost as if they were in a different navy. We departed San Diego on April 30, 1950, to relieve USS *Boxer* and Air Group 19 as the only U.S. aircraft carrier deployed to the western Pacific.

Deployment is hard for all, but it is particularly hard for wives. Children seem to accept that Dad is going away for six months or a year because they do not have much choice. Wives do not have much choice either, but most seem to understand. These are magnificent women who stay behind to handle difficult situations and to carry on the leadership of the family. Some do better than others. Mary always did a great job, but she had many trials and problems to solve. She persevered and became stronger. Without such wives, naval officers could not go to sea successfully.

Valley Forge operated offshore for two days before we left the safety of alternate fields in Southern California. The carrier was continuing to have problems with short-cycle flight operations. The fact that the jets had to land one hour after being launched was like a sword dangling over everyone's head. We experimented and finally settled on one hour and fifteen minutes as the cycle time for the F9F-3 and doubled that for the propeller-driven F4U and AD airplanes. *Valley Forge* had one other new aircraft. We had on board an HU-1 detachment of two HO3S-1 helicopters. That aircraft would eventually change flight operations as much as the jet airplane.

Rear Admiral John M. Hoskins, commander of Carrier Division 3, and his staff, were embarked. Rear Admiral Hoskins had been the prospective commanding officer in USS *Princeton* in 1944, on board while waiting to take command, when the carrier was hit and subsequently sunk in the battle for Leyte Gulf. At that time he lost one of his legs below the knee and fought the medics to continue on active duty as the only one-legged officer in the Navy. That certainly did not seem to slow him down. Because of Rear Admiral Hoskins's continuing concern for the lack of knowledge about jet operations in the ship, he was very cautious. He directed that either Harvey Lanham or Dave Pollock remain on deck during all air operations. Commander Lanham, in turn, designated Lieutenant Commander Howard (Howie) Boydstun from VF-52 and me to fill a new position whose title he chose: landing control officer. He directed that for the rest of the cruise either Howie or I would be in Primary Fly with the air officer whenever VF-51 or VF-52 airplanes were flying. Our presence supported the air officer, but it also gave Commander Lanham and Dave Pollock more flexibility. The landing control officer was a ready source of jet knowledge for the air officer, and depending on our knowledge of each individual pilot's skills, we could advise him on how real a fuel emergency might be.

Primary Fly is the place where the air officer controls all flight operations onto or off the ship. The air officer is also responsible for the movement of all aircraft on board the ship. He is crucial to good operations, and his officers and men enable the complex tasks such as maintenance turn ups, major aircraft checks, armament loading, fueling, and a myriad of other jobs that must be done before and after airplanes fly. On board a ship, each function requires a great deal more coordination than on land. The air officer also is responsible for the catapults, the arresting gear, and the elevators.

Primary Fly in *Valley Forge* was nothing more than a wide spot in the port fore-and-aft walkway around the island, two decks above the flight deck and one deck below the bridge. There was room for four people, just. Commander J. P. (Blackie) Wienel, the *Valley Forge* air officer, was an experienced carrier pilot with a wry wit. On reflection, those qualities are essential in any air officer. If it rained, he got wet. If it was hot, he sweated. If it was cold, he froze. It was windy when we were recovering aircraft, and not windy when we were not. Primary Fly was open to all the noise and elements, and you could reach out and almost touch the folded wings of airplanes as they taxied by. All radio communications between airplanes and the ship were through CIC, and any flight information, such as fuel remaining or a potential emergency, was first received there and then passed to Primary Fly by talkers—men with sound-powered phones.

If Howie and I were to do our jobs, we needed more accurate and timely information from the pilots. To gain that, we borrowed a brand new, twenty-channel, spare squadron aircraft radio and installed it in Primary Fly. That was a great innovation and almost caused the supply department to go berserk. Either Howie or I had to sign for custody of the radio in case it disappeared. That radio, alone, did more to enhance the flow of information to Primary Fly than anything since the dark ages. Howie and I would spend many long hours with Blackie Wienel during the cruise, and we learned a great deal from him. We all became good friends. It was about this time that Commander Lanham asked Dave Pollock to assign me to fly as his section leader for the remainder of the cruise.

Valley Forge and Air Group 5 made the obligatory arriving carrier attack on military facilities on Oahu on May 8, and our unit of aircraft carrier, light cruiser, and eight destroyers entered Pearl Harbor on May 9. Our stay in Honolulu was short, and after loading stores and ammunition from the Naval Ammunition Depot Pearl Harbor, we sortied for continued training in Hawaiian waters. Admiral Hoskins was not going to let us fly without having the option to use land-based airfields should an emergency so dictate.

Valley Forge and the escorting destroyers left Hawaii and made their way west while we flew only when within 200 miles of the island bases at Johnston and Kwajalein. Obviously, the air group was not going to be flying a great deal on this peacetime cruise. That fact became a great concern to the commanding officers of the squadrons and to CAG. Also, each jet squadron had an operating budget for fuel that would allow each pilot between four and ten hours of flight time per month, neither one of which was a satisfactory figure. When we did fly, though, the spectacular Pacific Ocean views from high altitudes were much more dramatic than I had remembered when flying at the much lower altitudes during the war. The deep blue of the Pacific gave way to lighter blue and then to green and to milky white as the water shoaled on each atoll. Clouds seemed more sharply defined and set off the blue water, the white sands, and the green coconut palms on the atolls. It seemed strange to be deployed and not to be at war, and I found vivid memories flashing through my mind. At times it was hard to believe that someone would not start shooting soon.

On May 21 I was not flying, and I did not have the landing control duty. I was in the starboard bow 40mm gun sponson just below the flight deck, which was a great place to observe the launch because each airplane would burst into view with much smoke and noise as it was catapulted. I felt the thump of the starboard catapult, and in two seconds an F9F-3 flashed over my head. Instead of flying away, the airplane dropped like a rock. I watched spellbound as the F9F hit the water just ahead of the ship with a mighty roar and splash, followed by sudden silence as the water enveloped it. With a speed of 25 knots for launching aircraft, *Valley Forge* bore down on the floating F9F. I saw the pilot, uninjured, stand up in the cockpit, and I recognized Lieutenant Wayne Cheal of VF-52. As he and his airplane passed directly below me, the cockpit was full of foaming white water, and Wayne stepped out of the cockpit as the ship's side hit the left wing to slew the airplane around. I was about to dive in to help him when I saw that he was clear of the airplane and swimming away from the fast-moving ship. He needed no help from me. Wayne was rescued, and we had one less F9F for the cruise. On the same day that Wayne went in the water, VF-53 put an F4U into the barricade on a recovery.

On May 25 USS *Valley Forge* and USS *Boxer* exchanged air strikes to give the task groups training in AA warfare tactics, and on the next day the ships entered Guam's Apra Harbor. A turnover between Navy task groups is always a chance to see friends, and the relieved ship passes on valuable information to the relieving ship. After the ships' boats were in the water, I went to *Boxer*, where I visited Lieutenant Buck Weaver, an old friend from VF-212; Commander Frank Perry, former commanding officer of VT-19 and now commanding officer of VF-192; and a number of other pilot friends. Much of the talk I heard in *Boxer* concerned the jets and our operations, since those pilots had never seen them in action before. This time the exchange of information could help both air groups.

Entering port brought mail as well, and it was a time for catching up with family and the rest of the world. I received twelve letters from Mary. Besides the family news, I learned that Lieutenant Junior Grade Don Lanning, my jet transition instructor in VF-52, had been killed in a TO-1 accident at Pensacola.

Time in port, particularly turnover times between two carriers, also can be raucous. The evening of May 26 found the off-duty officers of the two carriers and their air groups at the Orote Peninsula officers club. This was the same place on which I had dropped bombs in anger six years before. The Orote Peninsula officers club clearly reflected the unhurried island life of Guam, but that night it was filled to the brim with thirsty officers renewing friendships, and the place was booming! We had a good party and eventually made our ways back to our ships.

The next morning Rear Admiral Hoskins, as well as the carrier division (CARDIV) commander in *Boxer*, received semaphore messages from the Commander Naval Forces Marianas via the harbor master's signal tower on Orote Peninsula. Ours read:

From: COMNAVMARIANAS
To: COMCARDIV 3
The unseemly conduct by your officers at the officers club last night cannot be condoned. Take your ships and take your air group and leave my harbor.

We left.

While en route to Manila we flew when within range of airfields at Guam, Leyte, and then Nielson Field near Manila. *Valley Forge* entered Manila Bay and anchored near NAS Sangley Point at Cavite, and more old memories of the war flooded back. Manila harbor still was filled with Japanese ships. Their hulls rested permanently on the bottom with their hundreds of masts rising above the water like some great denuded forest. After liberty for all hands in Manila, the task group moved north to Subic Bay where there was no airfield. The amount of flying that we were doing at sea was just not enough to keep us pilots current. We were averaging about 5.5 hours of flying per month per pilot, and it did not seem likely that the hours would increase. So we launched some of our airplanes to go to Clark AFB about 80 miles east of Subic Bay.

We departed Subic Bay in mid-June, conducted two days of air operations en route, and entered Hong Kong harbor on June 20. Rear Admiral Hoskins was still leery of the ability of *Valley Forge* to provide a responsive flight deck for the jet aircraft, but his staff seemed to be more comfortable. Hong Kong, like Manila, had suffered the ravages of war, but unlike those in charge of Manila, the British had made great progress towards repairing that damage. American sailors and officers were warmly welcomed, and every merchant had his hand out to offer tailor-made suits, shoes, ladies' dresses, coats, lingerie, watches, and rings, all for cash.

On June 22, our last night in port at Hong Kong, I drew duty as the senior shore patrol officer in Kowloon, just across from Victoria. It was quiet until trouble erupted at the Red Lion Tavern, several blocks from the Star Ferry landing. My two assigned petty officers and I ran the distance and arrived to find a full-scale fight between Chinese, U.S. sailors, and British soldiers that started when a Chinese customer stuck his hand into the cash register behind the bar. We waded in and cleared the tavern of American sailors just as the Chinese police arrived en masse with Sten submachine guns at the ready. The fight then stopped even faster than it started!

Valley Forge and the accompanying destroyers left Hong Kong harbor on June 23 and conducted joint air operations with the carrier HMS *Triumph* on June 24 and 25. *Triumph* carried two types of aircraft: Fire Flys and Sea Furys. Two events occurred on June 25. Lieutenant Junior Grade Tiffany, of the air group staff, went into the water in an F9F-3 on a catapult shot and was rescued. Since there would be no replacement airplanes for the cruise, we were down two airplanes. More importantly, later that day we learned the North Koreans had invaded South Korea at 0400 that morning. While this event had not been totally unanticipated by the intelligence community, I had the feeling of "oh, oh, here we go again!" This peacetime cruise was about to become another war cruise. The next day our task group refueled and resupplied at sea to receive food and stores while en route to Subic Bay for a full load of ammunition. We would wait there while the United States determined what its role would be in a war in Korea.

It did not take long to find out. On June 27 we were under way and en route to Sasebo, Japan. Not wanting to unduly alarm the Soviets and Chinese, Vice Admiral Arthur D. Struble, then commander of the Seventh Fleet, directed hospital ship USNHS *Solace* to join the task group, and we all proceeded north with the lights of every ship blazing away. At night the hospital ship in its brilliant white paint with a giant red cross on each side of the hull looked like a festive cruise ship. The Seventh Fleet flagship joined our task group near Taiwan, and our destination was changed to Buckner Bay, Okinawa. Rumors abounded. We would fight only if attacked. We were being shadowed by submarines. The Air Force had shot down a North Korean airplane.

We flew over Taiwan on the way north to give visible notice that the Seventh Fleet was on its way to Korea. Two persistent submarine contacts were depth charged between Taiwan and Okinawa with no known results. We heard that the Royal Navy would be supporting a combined United Nations naval force to be formed in defense of South Korea. HMS *Belfast*, *Triumph*, and two destroyers were en route. We arrived at Buckner Bay on June 30 and the next day sortied for Korea, now as TG 77.4, part of TF 77.

The Air Force was already committed and was flying sorties in support of the South Koreans. All civil radio stations were transmitting music as if nothing was happening. Our families in the States were going about their normal business. Mary was driving to Montana and then on to Minnesota with the children for a summer visit with relatives and was probably now sitting in her aunt's living room, trying to find out exactly what I was doing. The events seemed unreal to us all.

6. WAR AGAIN
JUNE 1950 TO DECEMBER 1950

On June 25, 1950, North Korea invaded South Korea, setting off a chain of events that soon involved the United States and other nations in another war in the western Pacific. Following President Truman's authorization to use U.S. forces in support of South Korea, USS Valley Forge, *along with the British carrier HMS* Triumph, *moved north to engage the North Koreans. Later, USS* Boxer *transported Air Force P-51s and L-5s and Navy replacement aircraft to Japan, and USS* Philippine Sea *with Air Group 11 arrived in the Seventh Fleet. U.S. Air Force and Army units were transported in ships, and a massive airlift was begun from the United States. The 1st Marine Aircraft Wing was transported to Japan in USS* Badoeng Strait, *and other naval aviation commands in Japan were strengthened. Greece and Turkey also committed forces to help defend South Korea in what became the first United Nations war.*

Naval aviation force levels stood at 9,481 pilots, 63,505 aviation ratings, and 15 carriers of all types. The bikini bathing suit was out of fashion, and haircuts were short. Trade shipments to Communist China were barred; President Truman approved development of the hydrogen bomb and ordered the Army to seize the railroads in the United States to prevent a general strike. Across the Atlantic, General Eisenhower became supreme allied commander in Europe, and riots broke out in South Africa against the policy of apartheid.

In June 1950 our intelligence information on North Korea was strictly World War II vintage and woefully inadequate. Navy intelligence officers tried to obtain what they could from the Fifth Air Force in Japan, but that overburdened organization had little to offer. We knew what equipment the North Koreans were supposed to have, but we knew very little about ground or air military units or where they were deployed. We were given civil aviation sectional charts and civil world aeronautical charts with which to plan our attacks. The sectional chart of northeastern Korea had a white blank spot, about the size of a silver dollar, in the eastern mountains of Manchuria. That area was simply annotated on the chart as an area not yet charted and accentuated the strangeness of our situation.

The Air Force squadrons in Japan and Okinawa were fully committed to stop the North Korean army juggernaut that had rolled across the thirty-eighth parallel early on June 25. We heard that those squadrons were providing sorties in support of the troops in South Korea. No one was flying north of the thirty-eighth parallel yet, and TF 77 was ordered to prepare to make the first strike on the capital city of P'yŏngyang, the east coast port city of Chinampo, and Haeju, south of P'yŏngyang. Royal Navy airplanes from HMS *Triumph* were assigned Haeju as their target. *Valley Forge* would target P'yŏngyang and Chinampo. Those first strikes were to be as hard hitting as possible to carry the message that the U.S. and the U.K. forces, as designated United Nations forces, were aggressively entering the war started by the North Koreans.

USS *Valley Forge* and HMS *Triumph* rendezvoused and with escorts proceeded north into the Yellow Sea to a position slightly above the thirty-eighth parallel, where we would launch to make the first combat sorties into North Korea. *Triumph* and *Valley Forge* operated as separate task groups, and at 0300 on July 3, 1950, we Navy pilots arose, ate breakfast, and went to the ready rooms to brief for the start of our part of the Korean War. I was scheduled to fly as section leader for Commander Harvey Lanham, who would be the airborne coordinator of the initial strike. Commander Lanham planned to reassign targets of opportunity should the prebriefed airfields not appear sufficiently important. Lieutenant Commander Bill Lamb of VF-52 was in tactical command of the high cover, and a total of sixteen F9F-3s would be in the air. VF-53 and VF-54, each with eight F4U-4s, and VA-55, with twelve AD-1s, under the leadership of Lieutenant Commander Doug Hodson, would be the main attack group. That group was appreciably slower, so it took off first. The jets planned to overtake the main group and provide flak suppression as the main attack group began its initial runs.

The jets launched eastward into the half-lit, early dawn sky and rendezvoused en route to coast in across the western, low, flat islands and marshlands of North Korea. No one shot at us. I could see large ships anchored in Chinampo harbor, and many plumes of steam clearly marked busy locomotives in the early morning. Each engine pulled long strings of loaded railroad cars to destinations inland, and the country appeared to be oblivious to the attack that would start in minutes.

The F4Us and ADs began a long, fast, descending run-in to attack the main airfield at P'yŏngyang as our F9F-3s purposefully overtook them. Our F9Fs split into four divisions of four to comb the area for airplanes and to strafe any opposing gun emplacements on the airfield before the F4Us and ADs attacked. Lieutenant Junior Grade Leonard Plog and Ensign Eldon W. Brown of Lieutenant Commander Bill Sisley's division each reported making firing passes at airborne Yak fighters, and I could tell by their excited comments on the radio that each had made a kill. Everyone else was too busy with their responsibilities to say much. My job was to stay with CAG, regardless, and to provide extra eyes and support for him. I saw one Yak-9P that I was tempted to chase, but CAG pulled John Nyhuis and me back and kept me in position as his section leader. After CAG saw that the attack was going as planned, he let it continue without retargeting, and his section and mine dropped down from 20,000 feet to join the fray.

John Nyhuis and I made a strafing run from north to south on the airfield. Each of us could pick individual targets, and I used the large concrete parking ramp in front of the control tower as my general target and strafed and burned one Yak-9 fighter and a DC-3 look-alike on the first pass. John Nyhuis also strafed and left two airplanes burning. There was a lot of excited chatter on the radio about various targets, and there was very little AA that I could see, as we wheeled in the air over the airfield, craning our necks for more airborne airplanes. The aerial war in North Korea, at least the early phase, was over almost before it began. The North Korean air force never launched more than hecklers again.

The F4Us and ADs completed their attacks on the hangars, airfield facilities, and airplanes on the ground. Their 1,000-pound bombs were decimating those facilities, and although it was July 3, not July 4, I caught myself thinking that those were high-order fireworks and that we had front row seats for a most unusual show. For twenty minutes we wheeled in and out of the low hung clouds over P'yŏngyang in complete aerial domination, and when our ammunition had been fully expended, we rendezvoused and departed to arrive back at the ship in time for the scheduled recovery. We vaguely heard our British friends over Haeju on our common VHF frequencies, and they were much more reserved on the radio than our pilots seemed to be.

Our low flying caused us to use more fuel than planned, but each pilot had enough to make the recovery in *Valley Forge* as the jets overtook the returning force and landed first. The first Navy jet combat sorties were completed without incident and without damage to any U.S. aircraft. The ready rooms were full of excited pilot chatter as we were debriefed, and those who had not yet flown prepared for the next combat strike into North Korea.

I was fortunate that CAG flew on both the first morning flight and an afternoon flight, too, because that meant that I would fly twice. That afternoon we attacked P'yŏngyang airfield again, as well as a nearby major rail yard. John Nyhuis and I strafed another Yak fighter on the airfield and a locomotive that gave off a satisfyingly large cloud of steam as my 20mm cannon projectiles penetrated the outer skin and tubes of the boiler. On that flight I realized that this war was to be different from World War II. North Korea was too small a country to provide much in the way of large targets for long. That fact was further emphasized when John Nyhuis and I flew over a yellow 1941 Chevrolet convertible that was roaring down a dirt road, creating a high dust plume behind that could be seen for miles. The convertible's top was down, and a uniformed figure was hunched over the wheel, driving like Barney Oldfield. John and I wheeled up in the sky, reversed course, and rolled in on the Chevrolet from 5,000 feet. Yes, this was going to be a different kind of a war.

I stood the landing control duty in Primary Fly so that Howie Boydstun could fly on the second strike that first morning and again in the early morning of July 4. In addition to the fireworks over North Korea, we had our own fireworks back in *Valley Forge*. July 4 was one of those days that aircraft carriers do not like to have. During the first recovery that morning, an AD with minor AA damage came in high and fast and after the cut floated over the wires and barriers to pass by Commander Blackie Wienel and me in Primary Fly at eye level. Blackie hit the emergency alert switch to announce heads up on the flight deck for all to hear and to enable them to take cover wherever they could find it. The AD landed with a thunderous smash on top of the air group airplanes parked farther forward on the flight deck. Parts, propeller blades, and dust flew in all directions, and when everything came to rest, not one person had been hurt. The AD ended up askew on top of another AD, and both pilots eventually climbed out of their airplanes uninjured.

That "act" was followed by an F4U with moderate battle damage that could not lower one main wheel. The pilot made his approach for landing after all aircraft were on board. His hook caught a cross-deck pendant as his right wing slammed to the deck. No sooner had that occurred than the HO3S-1 helicopter manning the plane guard station aft of *Valley Forge* reported an engine failure and hit the water in a great splash. The helo pilot was rescued by the plane guard destroyer, while the mess on the flight deck was sorted out. Finally, another AD floated over the wires after the cut but remained low enough to hit all three barriers and then to end up in a mess of wire spaghetti on the flight deck just below Primary Fly. Again, no one was injured, but it was not a good day.

No one had been shot down in combat on July 4, but we managed to lose three aircraft and damage seven others in the second day of combat! For my way of thinking, that was not the way to start a war. It was immediately apparent that, among other things, a vital need existed for additional intelligence and better coordination. It was evident, too, that we would need to repair the airplanes that had been damaged because we had no replacements. The pilots of the air group also needed to do some deep thinking about carrier procedures. What was happening was a manifestation of our lack of flying earlier on the cruise. That lack continued to haunt us until August, when we had built up greater currency in the air. After our first days of combat, *Valley Forge*, in company with *Triumph*, returned to Buckner Bay, Okinawa, to prepare better for much more combat.

The F9F-3 was designed from World War II fighter experience, when the Navy was still trying to figure out what a jet fighter should be. Its four 20mm cannon were quite effective against many targets, but Rear Admiral John Hoskins must have pondered that he might have been better off with more F4Us and ADs. The jets provided an entirely new warfare capability and an effective deterrent to strikes against the force, but they used too much aviation gasoline, and we still had no jet fuel on board the ship. The tender loving care required by the jets was appreciably greater than that needed by airplanes deployed in World War II. But Rear Admiral Hoskins also knew that this was the first deployment of any Navy jet airplanes in the Pacific and that the war was providing valuable opportunities to test new procedures and the efficacy of those jet airplanes. He probably spent many sleepless nights, certainly in the early stage of the Korean War, weighing the pros and cons of the mix of aircraft with which he could fight this war. Soon, his answer to the need for jet airplanes would be a resounding "yes, we need them." Ultimately, the war forced a faster rate of introduction of jet airplanes and improved ordnance-carrying capability and taught us many lessons to hasten jet airplane acceptance.

By mid-July the war was going badly on the ground for South Korean and United Nation forces. The North Koreans marched south past Osan, and the Air Force had its hands full trying to interdict their supply lines from the north. Our TG 77.4 sortied from Buckner Bay on July 16 and moved north into the Sea of Japan to cover a diversionary landing of the 1st Cavalry Division at P'ohang on the east coast of South Korea. That flanking maneuver was designed to put more pressure on the North Koreans as they continued their determined drive south toward Pusan. HMS *Triumph* with the escorts moved into the Yellow Sea. North Korea was no more than 150 miles from east to west and some 240 miles from north to south. Its small size made us wonder all the more how a country could mount such a determined advance. We placed a carrier off each coast of North Korea so we could squeeze the North Koreans harder. The Air Force was fully engaged in supporting the South Koreans at the front, and naval aviation forces were to carry the war to North Korea.

With the landing of the 1st Cavalry Division on the east coast of South

Korea, we then moved up the east coast to target our efforts on port complexes of Wŏnsan and Hamhŭng, north of the thirty-eighth parallel, and those were virtually destroyed. Our intelligence was still poor, and returning pilots constantly brought in new information. We virtually did our own real-time intelligence gathering. A returning VF-51 pilot reported a large oil refinery in Wŏnsan. A subsequent strike by the F4Us and ADs destroyed that target, probably one of the largest we had seen to date.

For the remainder of July Air Group 5 attacked new and different target complexes along the east coast of North Korea. Also, we set about to deny the North Koreans use of their transportation system, so vital to the support of their war in the south. Our F9F-3s provided new combat tactics, and we honed our ability to conduct road and railroad recce flights by flying at treetop height to clear all transport from a specific stretch of road or railroad track and to deny the vehicles and trains early warning of impending attack. A typical two-airplane combat recce flight would yield three or four trucks, a bus, and perhaps a locomotive. There was no aerial opposition in August 1950. John Nyhuis and I adopted this technique: I flew very low at about 50 feet, and he would loiter behind me at 400 or 500 feet; the instant I saw something, I would call him, and he would be in position to attack before the truck or tank could get off the road and hide in nearby trees. That worked well, but I frequently returned to the *Valley Forge* with Korean mud from my 20mm projectiles splashed onto the underside of my fuselage.

As the war progressed, our flight deck procedures and flying became more polished. We overcame the tactical rustiness from our previous lack of flying. We fighters launched in tactical divisions of four and then split into two groups of two after we struck at our major target. Our greater speed allowed us to cover much more area in less time than the propeller-driven airplanes. Of course, we had less time in the air as well, and that drove the need for better coordination. It also created challenges back at the ship for jet launch and recovery in coordination with the much slower propeller-driven airplanes. New single- and double-launch-and-recovery cycles were devised as a means to dovetail the differing operating requirements.

By late July the North Koreans pushed the South Koreans and our U.S. ground forces back almost to Pusan, the southernmost port in South Korea. We shifted our road recce into South Korea to support the Air Force. Its pilots were having to fly their combat sorties from Japan because Korean airfields were no longer available. Anything moving on the roads 23 miles north of Pusan was North Korean. That was our rule of engagement.

John Nyhuis and I flew our road recce flights and marveled at the large number of bits and pieces of P-51s and P-80s strewn beside the roads of South Korea and across the nearby countryside. Shiny aluminum wings and fuselages of

Air Force airplanes stood out in marked contrast to the lush green countryside. Those airplanes were shot down or were brought down by the nearly invisible wires purposely stretched across valleys or roads by the North Koreans. We were alert for the wires, but we still flew low. On one road recce flight, using our technique of low-high, I was flying at 50 feet, following each turn in the road, and John was higher, a mile behind me. I came around a small mountain to be face to face with a North Korean truck coming down the road from the other direction. I saw the look of surprise on the truck driver's face, and I am not sure who was more surprised, he or I. The truck driver jammed on his brakes and skidded to a stop as I whizzed past, too quickly to shoot. A company of soldiers had camouflaged the truck with an improbable entire tree in the truck bed and was hiding under it. I quickly called John Nyhuis, and he dispatched the truck and the platoon.

As we flew more and more in the south, the F9Fs were coming back with the odd rifle bullet hole in the wing or fuselage. One pilot came back with a big chip out of the armored glass in front of his face from a single rifle bullet. The propeller-driven F4U-4 was a World War II design, which initially had had an engine-oil-cooler bypass installed to prevent ground fire from downing an otherwise good airplane. (That is, the World War II pilot had been able to bypass the oil cooler if that vulnerable part of the engine was hit by ground fire.) That feature was removed from the F4Us in the late 1940s because it was thought to add needless cost and complexity. That decision was coming home to haunt the Corsair pilots. Their airplanes would be hit by nothing more serious than a single rifle bullet, and then their engines would seize when all the engine oil leaked from the oil cooler. They then would be forced to land behind enemy lines minutes after being hit. The amazingly versatile helicopter performed many miraculous pilot saves, but at that juncture in the war helicopters could not be positioned close enough to the action to always be effective. We were losing many F4U pilots and hoped they were being captured, not killed out of hand.

We had a small Marine photo airplane detachment in Air Group 5. In late July one of those pilots, Captain Dave Booker, was shot down about 30 miles north of Seoul. Dave crash landed his F4U-5 photo airplane late one afternoon, setting off a monumental search and rescue effort, which failed because of impending darkness. The next day the first airplanes airborne could find no sign of Dave. Several weeks later we heard him speak on Radio P'yŏngyang during a propaganda program. We recognized immediately that he was just telling us that he was alive, and whatever inane statement the North Koreans attributed to him was meaningless. Dave was the first pilot from *Valley Forge* known to be captured.

As July ended, *Valley Forge* and *Triumph* went into Sasebo, Japan, for ammunition and resupply. On August 1 the first naval aviation support from the

States arrived. USS *Philippine Sea*, with Air Group 11 embarked, entered Sasebo harbor to coordinate combat information and operating procedures with *Valley Forge* and the task group commander's staff. They were a welcome addition to our meager naval aviation forces. We saw a number of old friends and acquaintances when Rear Admiral Hoskins sent us to *Philippine Sea* to provide our combat lessons learned to date. Commander Solly Vogle was commander of Air Group 11, Lieutenant Commander Tom Amen was commanding officer of VF-111, Lieutenant Commander John Butts—an old friend from VB-19 days—was commanding officer of VF-112, and Lieutenant Commander Jerry Lake—from my days at Mojave—was executive officer of VA-115. There were many other friends as well—Lieutenant Junior Grade William Barnes from VBF-19, now in a VC-3 detachment and flying F4Us, and Lieutenant C. A. (Buck) Weaver, friend from VF-212 days. Later, Buck would be shot down and killed.

Both *Valley Forge* and *Philippine Sea* were under way on August 3. We returned to the Yellow Sea for eleven days, and the *Philippine Sea* started combat operations in the Sea of Japan. During that time Commander Solly Vogel was shot down and killed. We also saw the senseless brutality of the Korean War. As we steamed at our launch position off the west coast of Korea, near the thirty-eighth parallel, we found the sea littered with hundreds of bodies of men. Each had been tied back-to-back with another man and shot in the head. Those bodies must have come from a river, or perhaps they were captives that had been taken to sea and executed. We could not tell if they were North or South Koreans. Regardless, that sight was a grim reminder that being captured was certainly not in one's best interest.

On August 12 Commander Harvey Lanham's division was launched in the late morning to coast in over the southwestern part of North Korea. We were on a road and railroad recce flight and split into two sections. CAG and Ensign Lou Simmons went north. John Nyhuis and I conducted our road and rail recce farther south near Kumch'on, where we found two heavily armored trains moving south through the delta toward Seoul. We immediately stopped them by strafing the locomotives. We were working over the remaining cars when John advised me that 40mm AA from the heavily defended trains was coming very close to me. I acknowledged his transmission, and we pulled up to put some distance between ourselves and those shooting on the ground before returning to our attack from a different direction. I never heard from John Nyhuis again. He simply disappeared after he made that radio call and never answered my subsequent attempts to raise him on the radio. I looked for an airplane on the ground or evidence where one might have crashed; there was none. John had simply disappeared. I called CAG, and he and Lou Simmons came down to look. We found nothing. Finally, reaching a low-fuel state, we departed for the ship. I hoped that John might have had radio failure and returned to the ship, but he had not. John Nyhuis had been shot down.

The next strike to be launched that day contained a search and rescue group of ADs and F4Us that returned to the area of Kumch'on, but no sign of John's airplane could be found. The next day I flew to the same area to look again but found nothing. To this day I do not know exactly what happened. He was simply missing. On the evening of August 13 *Valley Forge* headed toward Sasebo for brief resupply and needed repairs to the catapults and arresting gear. After a few days I wrote John's parents in Walla Walla, Washington, to tell them what I knew.

Returning to sea, Air Group 5 worked the east coast of Korea for the rest of the month, first to the south and then back up north again. While we hoped that the troops would hold and eventually break out of the Pusan perimeter, it was easy to see that North Korea was effective in sending so many troops and supplies to the south under the cover of darkness. Our four-plane night-fighter detachment from VC-3 under Lieutenant Commander Bill Henry proved invaluable at interdicting large truck convoys at night. Frequently, they would hit the lead few trucks and then the rear few trucks, to trap the remainder on the narrow road until daylight, when the first day strikes would finish off the convoy.

One day Lieutenant Commander Harley Thompson, operations officer in VF-51, attacked a train that happened to have explosives in it. His 20mm shells laced into one rail car, and as he flew over it, it disintegrated, blowing wood and rail-car parts everywhere. Harley's F9F-3 flew through the blast and out the other side, and when he had collected his senses and evaluated his situation, he found he was in deep trouble. He had one piece of 4-by-4 lumber stuck in the leading edge of his wing; there were holes in the fuselage and the wings; he was losing hydraulic fluid, as well as fuel, from some gaping holes that he could not see. He had almost blown himself out of the sky, but his engine was still running.

Harley, some said understandably, let the world know that he had a problem. On the VHF radio he broadcast, "I'm hit! I'm hit! I'm going in. I can't make it." All this was given in one continuous stream of chatter as he headed toward the Sea of Japan. No one could offer help because he would not stop talking on the radio. However, he did remain airborne, and when he finally paused long enough for someone else to have a chance to talk, I heard the cool crisp voice of one of our HMS *Triumph* Royal Navy friends, a Sea Fury pilot somewhere over the horizon, come on the radio. He said, "I say, old chap, why don't you shut up and die like a man." Harley made it back to the ship with some masterful flying, but it seemed that subsequently he talked less on the radio.

The North Koreans continued heavy use of their roads for resupply of their forces in the south during August 1950, and we stepped up our assault efforts on the roads. A typical combat recce flight would garner each section of two airplanes three or four trucks, a bus, and, if lucky, a locomotive. There was no aerial opposition. We had the skies to ourselves, and the Air Force stayed close to the battlefront. The automatic antiaircraft (AAA) fire was definitely becoming more accurate, and it seemed as though every person on the ground had a rifle. We could see individual soldiers shooting at our airplanes when we flew low.

There are always anomalies when a war first starts. Peacetime administrative requirements are still in effect, even though you are fighting a war! Reports, accident investigations, and all manner of administrative minutiae confound those in battle until some higher echelon provides relief. We had to conduct an aircraft accident investigation if a .50-caliber bullet hit an airplane; other peacetime reports seemed just as pointless, and there was the continuing need for written examinations for promotion and the completion of required correspondence courses. Dave Pollock completed his written examinations for promotion to commander in the wardroom of *Valley Forge* between combat flights and was promoted at the end of August. I was fulfilling my correspondence course requirements from the U.S. Naval War College for promotion to lieutenant commander, and the course on international law particularly troubled me. It just did not ring true with respect to what we were doing in Korea. I was about to quit the course in disgust when fortunately the Navy did away with such requirements for promotion.

August brought another challenge. USS *Valley Forge* was limited in its air operations by the capabilities of its H-4 catapults and its arresting gear. Our jet airplanes always taxed those capabilities to their limits, and as a pilot you could feel the punishment in your body on the catapult shot or arrested landing. The ship could make 30 knots, but we needed in excess of 35 knots of wind across the deck so that we would not exceed the airplane's or the ship's catapult and arresting gear capabilities. In August some days the F9Fs could not fly because there was not enough wind across the deck, so we would simply stand down. That happened infrequently, but we pilots in VF-51 and VF-52 took some heavy ribbing from our friends in the F4U and AD squadrons when it did.

Commander Harvey Lanham's division now consisted of himself; his wingman, Ensign Bob Zaijicheck of VF-52; me from VF-51; and my wingman, Ensign Lou Simmons from VF-52. We had so few pilots that the intermingling of VF-51 and -52 pilots in the division was a means of sharing the combat sortie load.

By the end of August more and more pilot rescues and recoveries were being made by helicopter pilots. One of those rescued was VA-115's Lieutenant Commander Jerry Lake. Jerry was shot down and crash landed on a sandbar in the middle of a river in North Korea. He held off a platoon of North Koreans with his .38-caliber pistol, even though wounded, while his compatriots overhead tried to keep the enemy out of the river by strafing them. An HO3S heli-

copter made it in and picked up Jerry in a hail of enemy fire to return him behind our front lines. Many heroic tales, such as that one, did much to sustain
the morale of the pilots. Helicopter pilots were special people, and tales of their
exploits cannot give them the praise they deserve.

General MacArthur planned the invasion of Inch'ŏn in a bold move to cut
off the North Korean army south of Seoul. We moved to the Yellow Sea to support that invasion, which was scheduled for September 15. While our operations in the Yellow Sea were not challenged by the Chinese or the Soviets,
everyone was edgy about operating in this landlocked area. Late on the afternoon of September 4 a radar target was detected moving south seemingly out
of Darien in Manchuria. CIC reported to Rear Admiral Hoskins that the bogey
was tracking south over the Yellow Sea, approaching the force on a direct
course. *Valley Forge* went to general quarters in preparation for an air attack,
and an airborne division of four F4U-4s led by Lieutenant Junior Grade
Richard Downs of VF-53 was directed to intercept the bogey.

Faced with this oncoming threat, Rear Admiral Hoskins gave the order to
the flight leader to make an identification pass and if fired on to return the fire.
The bogey was identified as a twin-engine Tupelov bomber, a Tu-2, with Soviet markings. Downs made the first pass, and as he flew by the Tu-2, its tail
gunner opened fire. Downs then instructed his following wingman, Ensign Edward Laney, to fire back. Laney's 20mm fire was very effective and took large
pieces out of the Tu-2. On fire, the bomber dove toward the water and then
crash landed not far from an American destroyer in our screen. The destroyer
pulled the only surviving crew member out of the water, but he promptly died.
The destroyer reported that from the papers in his flight suit and from his appearance he was a Soviet pilot. Air Group 5 had just shot down a Soviet bomber!

Messages then flew thick and fast to Pearl Harbor and on to Washington.
President Truman had been scheduled to make a speech before the United Nations denouncing the aggression in South Korea, and the State Department had
one glorious mess on its hands. The Seventh Fleet had shot down a Soviet airplane that we thought was attacking *Valley Forge* in the Yellow Sea. In fact, the
airplane might have been going to attack, but we would never know for sure.
The commander of the Seventh Fleet directed that the body of the Soviet pilot
be transferred to the fleet flag ship, where it was temporarily interred in the re-
frigerated meat locker.

Diplomats being diplomats, things were not resolved quickly. Washington
and Moscow exchanged views, and the president did speak at the United Nations. Notes were exchanged. The Soviet pilot's body was transferred to *Valley
Forge*'s meat locker. The Soviets would not admit that one of their airplanes
had been flying over the Yellow Sea with the intent of attack, let alone that it
had been near the U.S. task force. More diplomatic meetings were held, and

more notes were exchanged. After weeks of this, the supply officer in *Valley Forge* palmed off the Soviet pilot's body on an unsuspecting supply officer in Sasebo, where there was a much larger refrigeration facility. We never learned if that vexing diplomatic problem was ever resolved, and I would not be surprised if that Soviet pilot's body was still in limbo.

Not all of our losses were in the air. On September 12 one of our ordnance men, Petty Officer Third Class Dominguez, and an ordnance striker were loading 20mm cannon ammo into one of our F9Fs on the forward hangar deck when one of the high explosive incendiary rounds blew up and killed Dominguez. There was no further damage. His death was particularly sad because just six hours after the accident the squadron received a Red Cross message that his wife had just given birth to an eight-pound baby boy, their third child. Petty Officer Dominguez had only $1,000 of life insurance so all of us in VF-51 chipped in and raised another $2,000 for his family. Life on board an aircraft carrier is tremendously complex and is not just about flying airplanes. Those sailors who maintained the airplanes and the many officers and enlisted men who manned the absolutely vital nonflying positions in our aircraft carriers deserved special credit.

General MacArthur's invasion of Inch'ŏn went down in history as a classic operation on September 15. The U.S. and South Korean Marines stormed Wolmi-do Island off Inch'ŏn in the morning and took it in a matter of hours. In the afternoon the Marine Corps and the Army stormed ashore with strong close air support. The F4Us and ADs from the carriers *Valley Forge*, *Boxer*, and *Philippine Sea*, along with Marine F4Us from the CVEs *Badoeng Strait* and *Sicily*, provided the close air support. *Boxer*, with Air Group 2 embarked, had just arrived from the States the night before and had no jet airplanes. The F9F-3s of *Valley Forge* and F9F-2s of *Philippine Sea* flew interdictory reconnaissance north and south of the landing. Over 200 ships were brought together under the command of Vice Admiral A. D. Struble as commander of Joint Task Force 7. After the landing the ground troops moved across Korea, cutting the lines of supply for the North Korean army and enabling the U.S. and South Korean forces to break out of the Pusan perimeter and join them by September 27. More than one-half of the North Koreans were killed or captured.

On October 6, 1950, *Valley Forge* entered Sasebo harbor for our first port visit in a month. Everyone was grumpy from the daily flying routine, and the wardroom crackers had weevils. We would break the crackers in half to knock out the weevils before we ate them. After you have been at sea for a month, land can have a definite and different identifiable smell. Once ashore, trees and flowers have individual smells, and you detect the slightest whiff of perfume almost immediately. The Sasebo port visit was good but seemed too short as *Valley Forge* left on October 11 for our return to combat.

The rate at which we were flying was such that the ship had to refuel every third day to maintain the required supply of aviation gasoline. The jets still were using most of the aviation gasoline. We would rearm every other refueling day, now that there were sufficient ammunition ships deployed. Air Group 5 continued to pound the targets in North Korea, and Lou Simmons and I spent a lot of time on road reconnaissance. The weather turned much colder, and, in a way, that was a blessing at sea because we had more thrust in our engines and good wind for our jet launches and recoveries.

The days droned on. War fighting is not much fun. The thrill of coasting in over a hostile coastline and attacking a large target complex, or looking for an enemy fighter airplane with which to test your skills, can break the monotony, but the thrill soon disappears as the daily dirty drudgery of strafing trucks and looking for soldiers on the ground to kill, as they try to kill you, begins to dull your mind. One day melds into another, and administrative duties on board ship become chores to take your mind off tomorrow. At night you dream of improbable war fighting situations and wake to begin another day of the same slugging dirty war.

During September and October our losses in the air continued to mount. Air Group 5 now had some fourteen pilots, well over 10 percent of all our pilots, missing or presumed captured. We knew nothing of what had happened to that group, other than Marine Captain Dave Booker. We naval aviators were attacking targets in North Korea along the Manchurian and Soviet borders and were ranging the length and breadth of the Korean peninsula from the front lines near the thirty-eighth parallel to Sinanju and the Chosŏn Reservoir in the north. But our combat area was becoming smaller as the United Nations forces were moving north for the first time.

The ground forces rapidly fought their way north in October, and each day we would be provided new exclusion areas for our recce flights. The F4Us and ADs did a masterful job of keeping up with the land battle and providing close air support. P'yŏngyang fell on October 19, and the North Korean government moved to Sinŭiju, just across the Yalu River from Manchuria. Our assigned areas for road and rail recce grew smaller and smaller as the ground forces moved north. The targets also proved more elusive to hit as the assigned roads and rail lines were more and more in the rugged mountain terrain of the far north. By late October there were literally too many U.S. airplanes for too small an area. USS *Boxer* suffered a reduction gear casualty to one of the propeller shafts in September and was limping along on three screws. The ship left the line for much needed repair.

Howie Boydstun and I continued to alternate in Primary Fly for the landing control duty every other day. Either he or I still were with Commander Blackie Wienel during all air operations. Rumors concerning *Valley Forge*'s return to the United States began, and sailors and officers alike would pass on any word that had the slightest connotation of our returning to the States. But official word never came. Finally, on October 29, *Valley Forge* was ordered to retire to Sasebo, and we thought that we might be going home at last—but not yet.

We had heard nothing from the U.S. forces ashore in Korea as to our missing pilots. The lack of information was so troubling that CAG asked the CARDIV staff to send someone into Korea to make contact with the U.S. forces to find out about our fourteen missing pilots. On October 29, the day before we arrived in Sasebo, Lieutenant Junior Grade John Ford of VF-53 and I were selected to go to Korea to establish contact. Other carriers had had losses as well, and they needed the same information. The air war was slackening, and this was the time to see what we could do.

John Ford and I were given simple but flexible orders to proceed to Korea by whatever means we could find to visit and revisit any place that we chose in North or South Korea in search of information on our missing Navy pilots. We were directed to return to *Valley Forge* no later than November 4, 1950, just a short six days hence. Carrying one small bag each and with our .38-caliber pistols strapped to our chests under our flight jackets, we flew to the U.S. Air Force base at Itazuke, Japan, on the afternoon of October 30, 1950. On arrival we found a C-47 about to fly to Taegu, South Korea, and boarded it shortly after dark. Within five minutes after takeoff, there was a big thud. Almost immediately the cockpit cabin door burst open, and the copilot, with blood all over his face and upper body, staggered back into my arms. A duck (I did not know they flew at night!) had come through the right forward windscreen and hit him in the face, knocking glass into his eyes, but most of the blood belonged to the dead duck. I climbed into the copilot's seat to help with the radios, and the pilot returned to Itazuke. We spent the remainder of that night arranging another flight the next day.

On October 31 we caught another flight to Ashiya, Japan, where we left on a Marine Corps four-engine R5D (the military air-transport version of the civilian Douglas DC-4 airliner) with a load of C rations headed for Wŏnsan, North Korea.Wŏnsan had been captured in mid-October and was a Marine Corps airfield and staging base. While we were in the air, the airplane was diverted to Yonpo, an airfield north of Wŏnsan near Hamhŭng. Our R5D was one of the first U.S. airplanes to land at Yonpo, and as we taxied up to stop on the war-littered concrete apron before some heavily bombed hangars, we could see Marines running about on the edges of the airfield fighting with the North Korean defenders, who still held part of the field. John and I helped unload the C rations to an eagerly waiting Marine platoon leader and then explored one of the hangars. We had bombed and strafed them just weeks before. Inside were several damaged Soviet Yak-9 fighters and a Stormovik dive bomber, which we eagerly explored.

Hearing the start-up roar of the R-2800 engines on the R5D, we ran for the airplane before we were left behind. The airplane flew the short 40-mile flight to Wŏnsan, where it was to load up immediately with wounded to return to Japan. John and I were left to our own devices. We would have to find our way to Seoul the next day. The night was bitterly cold, and seeking shelter in Wŏnsan was all about survival. We found the "Wŏnsan Hotel," which had been some kind of North Korean military administration building. The building was now devoid of all glass in any window and was totally air conditioned in the frigid November air. "The management" advertised a "swimming pool" in the entrance courtyard, which was nothing more than a giant crater made by a 2,000-pound bomb, now filled with ice-covered water. A Marine sergeant took pity on us and rounded up two sleeping bags, and we bedded down on the floor of an empty room on the second story. We had no sooner settled down than we heard a loud explosion down the hall. Arising to see what was happening, we found that one Marine had shot another in the head with a .45-caliber pistol in a dispute over a late-night poker game. The Marine MPs took over, and we retired again.

On the morning of November 1, after a C ration breakfast, we left Wŏnsan for Seoul on a C-119, the Fairchild-built, twin-engine, twin-boom air transport. On arrival at Kimpo, the major airfield there, we went into Seoul in search of the Fifth Air Force escape and evasion team, which we had learned was headquartered there along with the Army graves registration team. John and I carried a great amount of data about each missing Navy pilot. We had service numbers, aircraft numbers, engine numbers, and machine gun and cannon identification serial numbers of the aircraft they were flying when shot down, along with exact geographic coordinates positioning their crashed airplanes. We met with some initial success, sad but at least productive, and were able to identify five of our Air Group 5 pilots as having been killed in action. Each had been buried as an unidentified Navy pilot near their airplane, and aircraft engine or cannon nomenclature plates were tacked onto the crosses marking their graves. The other nine Air Group 5 pilots still had to be listed as missing or captured. We made sure that the escape and evasion staff and the graves registration staff had those pilots' names, positions of the crash sites or location of the wreckage, if known, and all aircraft and component serial numbers.

I specifically looked for any information on John Nyhuis. Zeroing in on the area in which he was shot down, we combed the files for any possible geographic match. However, no pilot's body or wreckage had been reported in that particular part of North Korea. There still was no sign of John. I left the pertinent data with the graves registration troops in Seoul and asked that a search be conducted. They assured me that they would send a team to the area where he had disappeared.

A most important aspect of our visit was meeting a Captain Doyle, an Air Force officer, who was heavily involved in the secret business of escape and evasion. We established the start of a strong working relationship between the Navy and the Air Force for the future. We learned that pilots shot down and captured who were able to escape within hours stood a good chance of evading and returning through the front lines. A number of pilots had done so; unfortunately not one was from Air Group 5.

John Ford and I spent two of the coldest nights of our lives in an Army tent in Seoul. We never removed our clothes or our long underwear. On November 3, with our principal task completed, we caught a ride in a C-54 (the Air Force version of the Navy R5D) carrying a load of carbine ammunition destined for the front lines, then very fluid and far north in Korea. The C-54 landed at a makeshift dirt strip near the river at Sinanju, just behind the front lines. We very quickly determined that as pilots on the ground we had made a gross tactical blunder. Everyone seemed to be going the other way—south! Those who could walk were walking. Those who were wounded were waiting to be moved back, and they spoke of the Chinese forces having entered the war the night before. They talked with wide eyes of wild Chinese cavalry troops on shaggy ponies charging with the riders blowing their bugles. There seemed to be mass confusion as to what was going on, and even David Duncan, the *Life* magazine photographer, with his *Newsweek* reporter sidekick, was looking for a way south out of there.

Unarmed, except for our .38-caliber pistols that we still carried under our flight jackets, John and I reasoned that we Navy pilots wearing flight jackets were clearly marked people who were in the wrong place at the wrong time. After helping to load as many wounded as possible into the C-54 under the direction of a couple of hard-working Army nurses, we also climbed back on board our C-54 and flew as passengers back to Ashiya, Japan. From there to Sasebo we traveled on a Navy PBM flying boat that landed in Sasebo harbor, returning us to *Valley Forge* just in time to meet our Cinderella date of November 4.

John Ford and I reported our trip and our findings to Rear Admiral Hoskins and Commander Lanham, and I am pleased to say much good came from our efforts. Prisoner-of-war (POW) and missing-in-action information started flowing between the Navy carriers and the land forces in Korea. Captain Doyle later visited *Valley Forge* at the invitation of Rear Admiral Hoskins and provided first-hand knowledge that the carriers had never had before. John Ford's and my initial reward for the trip was to return in time to go to sea the next morning without so much as a beer, but our real reward was the knowledge that we helped break the logjam of information on our missing pilots.

The entry of the Chinese into the war was the reason for *Valley Forge*'s early sortie from Sasebo, and we returned to Korea to provide as much air cover as we could. November's cold winds and snow came down out of Manchuria, and the Yellow Sea was an inhospitable place. There was snow and ice on the flight deck each morning, and footing was tricky. The ever-watchful and agile flight deck handling crews did superb jobs in spotting for launches and recoveries. The brown-shirted plane captains and the yellow- and blue-shirted flight deck crewmen responsible for the safe tie-down and movement of the airplanes were just as cold as everyone else, but they did a superb job under some trying conditions.

We heard tales of MiGs in the air, and although we looked and looked, we were not fortunate enough to see any. We flew support for our F4Us and ADs on November 7 and 8. Lieutenant Commander Doug Hodson's AD-1 was hit by AA, but he managed to make it to the coastline and water before he crash landed. He was rescued by one of the destroyers and was back on board the next day and in the air again the day after that. We lost another F9F-3 to a deck-landing crash when Lieutenant Junior Grade Zeke Zuelhke returned with combat damage. He was uninjured in the mishap.

On November 9 airplanes from *Valley Forge* and *Philippine Sea* attacked the highway and rail bridges across the Yalu River, which formed the border between North Korea and Manchuria. General MacArthur ordered those attacks to stem the flow of supplies and equipment from China, but we were severely cautioned not to fly over Manchuria in the process. That presented a great challenge to the attack pilots because if you are going to hit a bridge, it is far better to make your attack along its axis rather than to try to pinpoint a bomb across its width. The Chinese had an untold number of AA guns on their side of the Yalu River shooting at us quite accurately. But under the rules laid down, we could not retaliate or do anything other than try to evade. At times the sky at high altitude would almost be black from the bursts of the large-caliber AA aimed at us from Manchuria.

The MiGs came out—at least a few of them did. Lieutenant Commander Tom Amen of VF-111 shot down a MiG-15, and Lieutenant Commander Bill Lamb of VF-52 shared a kill of a MiG-15 with another pilot. As hard as we looked, our division never saw them, but after the attack was well under way, and there was no need for further high cover, we dropped down to strafe along the Yalu River with the F4Us and ADs. Here I employed the same maneuver that I had used years before after diving on the Japanese fleet in 1944. On the strafing run, I led my section of two airplanes down the middle of the Yalu River for 20 miles at less than 100 feet. The North Koreans on the south bank were shooting, and the Chinese on the north bank were shooting, and I could see their tracers behind us. My satisfaction came from the fact that even though we could not attack the Chinese, by shooting at us they and the North Koreans were also shooting at each other!

We were settling into our routine for another month when just as suddenly as the war began for us, our part of the war stopped. *Valley Forge* was ordered to Yokosuka, Japan, where we off-loaded all aircraft to be barged to storage as spares. We were not sure what would happen to our F9F-3s because no other squadrons had them. (Later they would be modified to be F9F-2s.) At 0300 on November 19 we received a message that directed our detachment from Seventh Fleet to proceed directly to San Diego by the great circle route. *Valley Forge* departed Yokosuka at 0330, November 19, 1950, and headed east at 25 knots for a nonstop transit to San Diego. Our part in the Korean War had ended, at least for a while.

For naval aviation in the Pacific Fleet 1950 was a full year. We took jet fighters to sea and made jet air operations a regular occurrence. We made the first night jet carrier landings, devised new tactical doctrine, and developed new procedures. We operated in the western Pacific as the first fully deployed air group with jet aircraft, and we pioneered Navy jet air combat operations and shot down the first airplanes in Navy jet combat, along with conducting continuous jet combat operations against an aggressor nation. It was not easy, and some of the local command operating policies were less than clear and restrictive enough to hinder full use of these new airplanes. The knowledge of the potential of the jet airplane was minimal within our carriers in the beginning, but through perseverance and good operating principles VF-51 and VF-52 successfully showed the way. By the end of 1950 three carriers were deployed in the Pacific with jet fighters operating from their decks. More would come.

USS *Valley Forge* and Air Group 5 arrived in San Diego on December 4 to a tumultuous civic and family welcome. Unfortunately, while *Valley Forge* was en route, the Chinese had made deep inroads into United Nations–held territory and the position of those forces was in jeopardy. As a result, within hours of arrival, *Valley Forge* was ordered to return to Korea with a different air group. This time the air group would deploy with only propeller-driven airplanes to provide greater emphasis on close air support. *Valley Forge* deployed December 23, just two days before Christmas. That was hard to take for the fine crew in *Valley Forge*.

Months before our return to the United States, the system had started to prepare for the follow-on to our VF-51. New officers were ordered to AIRPAC for further assignment. Commander Earnest Beauchamp was ordered as the prospective commanding officer. His executive officer and department heads were selected from those ordered to AIRPAC for further assignment. Some of the officers waiting to join VF-51 were Lieutenant Dick Wenzel (to be operations officer), Lieutenant Forrest Petersen, Lieutenant Junior Grade Bob Rostine, and Ensigns Bob Rassmusen and Neil Armstrong (who later would be first to step on the Moon). Those were just a few of the twenty officers who were to join VF-51. It would be larger this time, so that it could operate more effectively in sustained combat.

The Navy still used the World War II system of replacing the entire officer personnel complement of squadrons at the end of a long cruise. Most of those returning with the old squadron moved on to new duty stations. A few young pilot retreads stayed for a second deployment to provide tactical continuity and to share their recent knowledge. The new officers and petty officers brought fresh views and new ideas. The new commanding officer would have his chance to imprint his style of leadership and tactical knowledge on his organization. Also, a natural selection process took place. Those naval aviators who did not have the stomach for tactical flying and long family separation gravitated to other pursuits in the Navy or resigned. Those that had tactical flying in their blood could and did come back time and time again until advancing rank or age forced them into other pursuits.

Most of the Air Group 5 officers left for new duty stations. Harvey Lanham went to the Naval Air Test Center at Patuxent River, Maryland, as did Dave Pollock. Others were ordered to the training command to be instructors or to staffs ashore. A number of the lieutenants junior grade and I were ordered to the U.S. Naval General Line School, Monterey, California. It was time for us highly specialized aviators to broaden ourselves if we were to advance our careers as line officers of the Navy.

I joined Mary, who had moved to Pasadena, California, during our deployment to be closer to family support. We bought a Ford station wagon, our second new car, and in January 1951 we moved north to Monterey, California, for what we hoped would be a year together in a delightful community.

7. TEST AND TEST AGAIN
JANUARY 1951 TO DECEMBER 1953

President Truman relieved General MacArthur of command in Japan and Korea, the draft age was lowered to 18½, the North Koreans again captured Seoul, and TF 77 continued air attacks in Korea. A P2V Neptune from VP-6 was shot down by the Soviets off the Siberian coast, Eisenhower was elected president, and King George VI died. The Mau Mau terrorists rose up in Kenya, UFOs were reported across the skies of the United States, the Soviet Union's first thermonuclear bomb was detonated, and TF 77 stepped up attacks to position forces for a Korean cease-fire. Ian Fleming published his first James Bond novel, Edmund Hillary and Tensing Norgay climbed Mount Everest, and Queen Elizabeth II was crowned.

There were 15,774 pilots, 129,412 aviation ratings, and 33 aircraft carriers of all types in the Navy. The first transcontinental TV broadcast was made from San Francisco, VF-191 flew the F9F-2B as the first Navy jet fighter-bomber, a contract was let for the XF2Y-1 Sea Dart, the XF3H-1 first flew, and Douglas test pilot Bill Bridgeman set a new speed record in the D-558-2 Skyrocket. An SNJ was the first airplane to land on USS Antietam's *angled deck. Soon angled decks and steam catapults were authorized for eight* Essex *class carriers. The Sidewinder missile was first fired. Air Development Squadron 4 was commissioned at Point Mugu, Lieutenant Colonel Marion Carl set a new altitude record in the D-558-2, and the F4D-1 was first flown by Douglas test pilot Bob Rahn.*

The U.S. Naval General Line School recently had been moved from Newport, Rhode Island, to what was previously the Naval Preflight School, Monterey, California. The relatively small complex, located inside the city limits of the small town, was centered on the former Del Monte Hotel, a 1920s building whose architecture and ambiance were impressive. The intent for the school was to create a better understanding among the many naval officers who had ente. ˘d the Navy in World War II of the differing warfare specialties—submarines, surface, and aviation. Students studied naval engineering, history, international law, and tactics (specializing in Allied tactical publications and communications) along with other relevant courses.

Mary and I arranged by telephone to rent a three-bedroom house in Monterey before we departed Pasadena in January 1951. On arrival we were pleased to find our house on a wooded hill above the small city and broad Monterey Bay. The children were placed in new schools, and we met our neighbors, fellow student Lieutenant Commander John Gullett and his wife, Nancy, and line school naval engineering instructor Commander Eli Vinock and his wife, Barbara.

Four of us from VF-51 were asked by the line school public affairs officer to meet with the local press as the first returnees from the Korean War. We were interviewed and photographed for a story in the evening paper. That story and photograph were published the night before school began. I noticed that Lieutenant Junior Grade Len Plog's hat was tipped back at a jaunty angle, but it was a good picture, and I thought we looked presentable.

The next day the General Line School class of 1951 was gathered in the cavernous ballroom of the former Del Monte Hotel to hear the commanding officer set the tone for the coming year. As we sat erect and attentive in folding metal chairs, the captain began to speak. It was obvious that something was bothering him, and it did not take us long to learn that the picture in the paper the previous night was the reason for his visible ire. He advised all officers in direct terms that naval officers did not wear their hats on the back of their heads like those pilots on the front page of last night's newspaper and proceeded to give a lecture on the proper wearing of the uniform. We four, Plog, Gortney, Klindworth, and I, sank down into our seats as our fellow students smiled and began to enjoy our obvious discomfort. I thought to myself, "Well, this is going to be some other kind of a year!"

The class of 1951 was parceled into sections of about twenty-five officers each. I was assigned to section B-2 with twenty-three other officer students along with two old friends, Lieutenant Commander Ray Swanson from my Point Mugu days and Lieutenant Junior Grade Bill Gortney. Thirteen of us were aviators, and eleven were "black shoes" (nonaviators—aviators wore brown shoes with their khaki uniforms, while all other officers wore black shoes), all below the rank of lieutenant commander. Lieutenant Commander Frank Bragg, a patrol pilot, was our section leader and suffered quietly the diverse natures and makeup of section B-2. Lieutenant Commander Joe Sahaj was our only submariner and took good-natured ribbing until we all went to sea in a diesel submarine during the course of instruction. Then we gave him much greater respect. Lieutenant Commander Al Blair was the senior black shoe and was a fine proponent for his warfare specialty. None of us changed our warfare designations, but we did learn to appreciate the challenges that the others faced.

Two other classmates were lieutenants from the Atlantic Fleet, whom I had not previously met, but who had backgrounds similar to mine. Lieutenants Bob Hoppe and John Darden came from VF-171 at Cecil Field, Florida, where they flew F2H-1 Banshees. Together, we all suffered through hours of boredom brought on by instruction in the more mundane aspects of naval life.

The year at Monterey was therapeutic after the rigors of war and family separation. Mary and I had a lot of fun with our children. We bought a pet descented skunk, which lived under the refrigerator in our kitchen. Mary gave the children swimming lessons at the Del Monte Hotel's ornate, tiled outdoor pool, which was surrounded by a large collection of anatomically correct statuary hidden among the many trees and bushes. Once the children stopped pointing and laughing at the statuary, they concentrated on their swimming in the ice-cold water. When they left the pool, their little bodies were blue, but they learned to swim well.

The year at line school passed quickly, and the course accomplished what it was designed to do: to give naval officers a broader understanding of our Navy. In early December 1951 we received our orders. Bill Gortney went to NAS St. Louis; Bob Hoppe went to the Naval Air Test Center at Patuxent River; John Darden went to Naval Ordnance Test Station China Lake, where he was killed the next year when the leading edge of one wing failed while he was flying at high speed and the plane immediately disintegrated. I was ordered to the Naval Industrial Reserve Plant, Grand Prairie, Texas, to the office of the Bureau of Aeronautics representative, which was located at the Chance Vought Aircraft factory. The industrial reserve plant oversaw three different companies: Chance Vought, newly moved from Connecticut to Texas; Texas Engineering and Manufacturing Company (TEMCO), a post–World War II aviation company; and Bell Helicopter, newly moved from New York. I was to be a Navy test pilot at Vought and TEMCO.

We left Monterey in mid-December with no idea where we might live once we arrived in Dallas. We visited Pasadena and then drove on to Dallas, arriving on New Year's Day, 1952, concurrently with a full-blown ice storm. We had previously thought of Texas as being hot and dusty. We found a house in Arlington, then a small town of 7,000, located between Fort Worth and Dallas: When settled, with the packing boxes inside the house, I went to work, while Mary took on the chore of enrolling children in schools and establishing ourselves in the community.

The office of the Bureau of Aeronautics representative, or BAR, as it was known, had a small staff of naval officers and civilians headed by Captain A. C. Olney. We worked mostly with the Vought and TEMCO management and engineers to provide on-site representation for the Navy. Vought was beginning production on a new version of the F4U, the F4U-6, for the Marine Corps in Korea, and was completing a contract for twelve of the radical, tail-less F7U-1 Cutlass jet fighters while developing the follow-on F7U-3. Vought had recently completed the delivery of a few F6U Pirates, an airplane so disastrously disappointing in its performance that some said that the afterburner was needed to taxi. The F6U was part of that first generation of new jet airplanes all designed in the mid-to-late 1940s and, like the others, suffered from slow engine design development. The F9F-1, Grumman's first jet fighter, was even initially designed to have four jet engines because each had such low thrust. TEMCO, next to Vought on the west side of NAS Dallas, was remanufacturing P-47s for Air Force military support of South American countries. Bell was just setting up its new plant to manufacture helicopters and seemed more busily engaged with hiring engineers than with manufacturing something to go out the door.

Lieutenant Commander John Ryan, a Texan and proud of it, was the flight test officer. Lieutenants Bob Shexsneyder, Paul Bugg, Norm Beree, and I worked for John, providing military production test pilot acceptance of every aircraft that was completed. I started flying production test flights of P-47Ds and Ns for TEMCO on January 15, 1952. The propeller-driven P-47 Thunderbolt, large for a World War II fighter, weighing about 13,500 pounds, and carrying 305 gallons of aviation gasoline internally, was a lot like the F6F. It had a Pratt & Whitney R-2800 radial engine and a very stubby fuselage. The principal differences between the D and the N models were the clipped outer-wing panels of the N. TEMCO was keeping its costs to a minimum and only fueled those airplanes with 100 gallons of gas for our test flights, thus placing a limit on the time for each test flight.

Our goal in test flying was to be sure the airplane controls were rigged properly, that the engine, all electric and hydraulic actuated devices, and avionics worked, and that all the dials and switches were functioning satisfactorily. Anytime that an airplane is remanufactured, there is always an opportunity for mischance. Also, those airplanes, manufactured during World War II, had been sitting idle at Davis-Monthan AFB, near Tucson, for four or five years. When we finished our acceptance flight and bought the airplane, we would park it near the fence on the airfield until an Air Force pilot would come along and ferry it to South America.

Vought's F4U-6 was a Marine Corps ground attack airplane that rectified many of those things that the Marine and Navy pilots found wrong in their F4U-4s in Korea. The F4U-6 was soon designated the AU-1 and had additional armor plate beneath the pilot for protection from rifle fire, a single- rather than dual-stage supercharger, a redesigned oil cooler bypass, and additional racks for bombs and rockets. Paul Thayer, former naval aviator and company test pilot for Chance Vought, had become director of sales at Vought as I arrived. John McGuyrt was chief test pilot and did the principal company development flying on the F7U series, aided by Jack Walton. Don Schulz was the test pilot flying most of the development and demonstration flights on the AU-1, and he also did the spin demonstrations.

Every naval aircraft must undergo rigorous flight testing and demonstration during development. Much of that flying is drudgery, but some of it was not unlike the old moving pictures of test pilots diving at terminal velocity and pulling out with large amounts of g's. Those of us at the BAR were the formal witnesses for many of those tests.

In March 1952 it fell to me to witness the Vought demonstration of maximum rates of sink for landing in the F4U-6. The goal for demonstration pilot Don Schulz was to achieve a maximum sink rate of 21 feet per second while landing, which would then certify the airplane for carrier operations. I might add that civilian test pilots were paid at a rate commensurate with the risk involved, and there was always a lot of backroom haggling over bonuses to which we Navy pilots were not privy.

I flew a loose chase wing position on Don Schulz in another F4U as he flew around the landing pattern. My presence had two purposes: first to witness the fact that he completed the test and second to give him another pair of eyes for safety. Don had difficulty in reaching the desired rate of sink. It was more a matter of technique than anything else, and he was hitting 18 and 19 feet per second but not the required 21 feet per second. Even so, those 18 and 19 feet per second touchdowns seemed to me to be more controlled crashes than landings. I am sure they felt much worse to Don. Having tried many times without achieving his goal, Don determinedly approached the touchdown point in the landing configuration one more time. At about 100 feet above the ground, he chopped the throttle, held the stick back in his gut, and down he came. The airplane hit the ground in a perfect three-point attitude, whereupon both main landing gear abruptly collapsed, the propeller stopped as it hit the concrete runway in a shower of sparks, and the F4U slid about 50 feet and stopped. Don Schulz walked away in disgust. He had achieved a sink rate of 26 feet per second. The engineers took the figures and by interpolation and extrapolation, those things that engineers do so well, managed to show that had Don been at 21 feet per second he would have successfully accomplished the test, and we, not wanting to go through another tortuous series of landings—and another airplane—agreed the test showed the airplane could meet the criteria. There was more than one way to skin a cat.

The French navy ordered 100 F4Us for its two carrier air groups. Those were designated the F4U-7 but were essentially upgraded F4U-4s that were delivered beginning in September 1952. The principal difference between the F4U-7 and the AU-1 was the F4U-7's supercharged engine. The AU-1 was strictly a low-altitude ground attack airplane. Paul Bugg and I each flew 50 of the 100 airplanes purchased. The F4U-7 was a delight to fly and was operational in the French navy for many years.

The Buggs lived near us in Arlington, Texas. Because neither Paul nor I could afford two cars, we bought a 1934 Ford coupe between us and alternated our driving to and from work so our wives could use the family cars. One day, while testing a newly refurbished P-47N, I flew over our house on the outskirts of Arlington at about 3,000 feet. As I looked down, I saw that Mary had clearly cut my initials in our overgrown front lawn. On occasion the grass would grow quite long—much to my discomfort and Mary's vocal admonishments. I flew lower to look, and sure enough, the initials were precisely cut in the grass. By then, Mary, hearing a P-47 overhead, was standing on the front porch looking up and shaking her fist at me.

I thought, "What have I done or not done?" Suddenly it struck me. I had failed to leave our only set of car keys with Mary before I left. We flew dressed in our uniform trousers and shirts with flight jackets. I reached under the seat belt and around the parachute leg strap to—yes—discover the keys in my right pants pocket. I made a wide turn while dropping down to about 75 feet over the open fields to the east of our house. Then I rolled the canopy open to fly up our street towards our house in a classic message drop pass, which we had used in World War II to drop a bean bag with a written message in it to a destroyer or cruiser. As I approached our house, I banked left and threw the keys out just aft of the left wing and watched as they sparkled in the sun, tumbling to land in the grass of the front lawn. I climbed quickly to not raise the ire of our neighbors unduly and watched Mary retrieve the bundle of car keys. That night I mowed the grass.

On April 6 I attended a two-week flight test school run by the Flight Test Division of the Naval Air Test Center. That short course in flying qualities and performance, given at Patuxent River, was designed to give officers of the various BAR offices a basis for measuring contractor test pilots and engineers in their demonstration roles. It was basically a quick introductory primer to test flying. While at the test center I had the opportunity to visit with Harvey

Lanham, Dave Pollock, Bob Elder, Bud Sickle, and many other friends and, just as important, to fly the F9F-5 that was modified with an experimental in-flight refueling probe. Bob Elder and the Service Test Division had just completed a project that used this new Royal Air Force (RAF) designed probe-and-drogue method for in-flight refueling. In two weeks I completed the course and returned to Dallas, even more dedicated to becoming an active engineering test pilot.

On April 5 I had my long-awaited first flight in the F7U-1 Cutlass. The F7U-1 was powered by two Westinghouse J-34 engines with afterburners and was an aerodynamic step up, but it was still underpowered. It was also the first airplane in the world designed with all-powered hydraulic flight controls, which made it interesting, to say the least. On the ground the airplane had a perpetual pool of hydraulic fluid under it. In the air you could not see the fluid leaking from the hydraulic system, but it was. The fact that I had my second flight in the F7U-1 five months later conveys the complexity of the airplane and the fact that we did not fly it much.

The F7U-3, the follow-on to the F7U-1, was an entirely new, much larger, and much more complicated airplane. Initially powered by two J-35 engines, while waiting the final development of the J-46 engines for which the airplane was designed, it was another underpowered airplane. In late summer of 1952 the Naval Air Test Center sent a Navy preliminary evaluation (NPE) team to Dallas to evaluate the F7U-3. Lieutenant Commander Bert Hendricks from the Flight Test Division was a member of that team, and Mary and I happened to drive by the north end of runway 18 at the airfield one afternoon as he took off. We watched as Bert accelerated slowly in the summer heat and tried to pull the airplane off the ground at about midfield. It rose 10 feet, then sank, hit the runway on its nose gear and main landing gear, and began a divergent porpoising action. The airplane bounced higher each time after hitting the ground, until it ran out of runway and dove into the large lake at the far end of runway 18. Bert was killed, and we lost the only currently flyable F7U-3. The NPE was canceled.

The accident investigation team determined that Bert attempted to take off with his leading-edge slats retracted. Those lift devices were newly designed to provide increased lift at substantially lower airspeeds. Because these slats were not extended, each time Bert flew above 10 or 15 feet out of the ground effect, the large wing of the tail-less F7U-3 would stall, and the airplane would fall back on the runway. Bert tried to power the airplane out of the predicament instead of retarding the throttles and accepting the fact that he might ignominiously get his feet wet in the lake. Instead, he was killed.

I flew the last production AU-1 on September 23 and the first F4U-7 to be manufactured on September 26, and at the end of October I set out to fly one of the F7U-1s to Point Mugu for missile test work there, which became an epic trip. Not only was the F7U-1 underpowered, but also it carried very little fuel, so I planned flight legs of no more than 500 miles via Amarillo AFB; Bulkley Field in Denver (to participate in an air show); then on to Kirtland AFB, Albuquerque; NAS El Centro, California; and finally to Point Mugu. Everything that could go wrong did go wrong. The airplane broke at every field where I stopped, and Chance Vought sent a representative to fix the airplane each time. It took seven days to deliver the airplane to Point Mugu, and it never flew again. Eventually, it was mounted on a pedestal at the main gate for all to see as a tribute to aeronautical progress.

My tardy return created a hardship for Mary. Before I left, she asked me to be back in Arlington for the city's Halloween parade because she was in charge of organizing it and needed help. I assured her that I would be back long before the parade day came. Needless to say, I missed it, and she has never forgiven me. At that parade she learned why parade organizers never put the horses in front of the marching bands.

In November 1952 Captain Charles M. Jett relieved Captain Olney and became the Bureau of Aeronautics representative. Shortly afterwards Captain Jett and I flew our Twin Beech JRB to NAS Anacostia to discuss technical matters at the Bureau of Aeronautics in Washington. He was going to discuss, and I to fly. The bureau was located in large, wooden temporary World War I buildings on the Mall, where the Vietnam Veterans Memorial is now. I took the opportunity to stop by the Pentagon, across the Potomac River, to visit the officer detailer section, and was surprised to learn that Commander Bill Pittman, formerly commanding officer of VF-53, was responsible for aviation lieutenant orders and was my personnel detailer. Officer detailers are important and powerful people, and over time I learned to approach them with deep respect and great suspicion, unless I knew them well. I told Bill that I wanted to go back to a jet-fighter squadron on the West Coast so that I could fight in Korea. He looked me in the eye, laughed, and said that he would send every naval aviator to Korea once before he would start sending his friends back for a second tour of combat. Needless to say, I got nowhere. We exchanged pleasantries, and I left to fly back to Dallas with Captain Jett, not thinking much about the conversation.

Ten days later Mary called me at work to say that she had just received in the mail a directive for her to go to the nearest passport office to get passports for herself and the children. She was not told where she was going or when she was to leave, but she informed me that she hoped that I would have a nice life; she was on her way to becoming a world traveler and had no qualms about leaving me behind. Neither she nor I had an inkling about what that cryptic directive meant. It was too late in the day to call Washington, but the next day I did call Bill Pittman to find out what was going on. He told me that I was being sent on exchange duty to the United Kingdom as one of two U.S. Navy officers to attend the year-long flying course at the Empire Test Pilots School at Farnborough, Hampshire, England, and we would be leaving after the Christmas holidays. Needless to say, I was ecstatic.

Captain Jett was particularly nice to Mary and me while we prepared for departure. We had some administrative cliff-hangers with respect to diplomatic clearances and travel because there was not a brisk trade in overseas travel originating from Texas in those days, and not too many people knew how to process passports or even where to get the process started. But we succeeded, just in time.

Captain Jett even arranged two flights in the F7U-3 so I could see the new state-of-the-art flight control systems and later comparatively evaluate other such systems in the United Kingdom. I worked hard and enjoyed those two flights in the new F7U-3, which at that stage of my flying career seemed to be a fine airplane. The F7U-3 smelled new and performed better than the F7U-1.

We spent Christmas at our home in Arlington, filled with anticipation of our upcoming journey to England. The children particularly looked forward to the new adventure. We stored all but a few of our household effects, sold our Ford station wagon, and on January 11, 1953, flew to Washington, DC, for the obligatory technical briefings on our state of aviation development, before we continued on to New York City to board SS *United States* for our passage to Southampton, England.

On Saturday morning, January 31, loaded with luggage, we cleared customs and boarded the newest, finest, and fastest passenger liner afloat. *United States* was an imposing sight with a black hull topped with broad red and white stripes, a white superstructure, and two red, white, and blue raked stacks. Since I was on orders to England and the Navy was funding our passage, we did not go first class, but we had a nice cabin class double stateroom for the five of us.

Our departure at high noon was festive, with telegrams and flowers from friends. Settling in, we almost missed seeing the Statue of Liberty; however, we were able to look back, and I caught Mary watching it solemnly. In fact, we were both silent, each wondering how the next year would go for us. It would be different in many ways.

We crossed the Atlantic to Southampton at a fast 35 knots. The children spent the time exploring the ship from top to bottom. The meals were enjoyable, the crew members were especially nice to our family, and in a little over three days, we arrived in Southampton during an unusual winter channel snowstorm. It was bitterly cold. We cleared His Majesty George VI Customs to be met by a chief petty officer from the staff of Commander in Chief Northeastern Atlantic and Mediterranean (CINCNELM), who expressed great surprise that Lieutenant Engen had a wife and even more surprise that we also had brought three children. No one, and especially he, expected that! After convincing him that they were indeed real and that we were together, I agreed to accompany him to London using the single train ticket that he had brought. Mary and the children took refuge with our good friends Lieutenant Tom Mix and his wife, Billie, in nearby Bognor Regis after Billie thoughtfully had met the ship on our arrival. Tom had been LSO in Air Group 5 and was on exchange with a Royal Navy jet attack squadron at the Royal Naval Air Station (RNAS) Ford, near Southampton.

London in January 1953 was gray, dingy, and cold and looked as if World War II were still in progress. The CINCNELM headquarters building on Grosvenor Square previously had been General Eisenhower's headquarters for planning the invasion of Europe. Many bombed buildings in London stood starkly empty, and there were gaping holes in the ground where Nazi bombs had fallen more than seven years ago. The building directly across North Audley Street from the headquarters was nothing more than a shell and still showed the pastel painted inner walls of apartments. Food rationing was still in force, and meals in the Royal Hotel, where I was staying, looked like a dietitian's minimum caloric intake, prepared with absolutely no zest.

I found my principal U.S. Navy interface for the next year, Commander Malcom W. (Chris) Cagle, on the fourth floor, which, to my way of thinking, was really the fifth floor. The commander in chief was Admiral Jerauld Wright, whom lieutenants never met. One of Chris Cagle's many responsibilities was to keep track of the ten naval officers on exchange throughout Great Britain at different Royal Navy and Royal Air Force units. Chris informed me that, other than checking in from time to time, I should now consider myself detached and proceed to Farnborough, where I would be on my own to find a place to live and report to the Empire Test Pilots School (ETPS), located at the Royal Aircraft Establishment. With Chris's help, I did buy a new English Ford Consul sedan, for the princely sum of $1,382. I also learned that my compatriot and fellow ETPS student, Lieutenant Commander Albert C. Koplewski USN, was a bachelor and was already in Farnborough.

Mary and I rendezvoused and found temporary family lodging at the Kings Clear Hotel in Camberley near Sandhurst. We also found two other ETPS classmates and their families living at the same hotel, while they also searched for places to live. Captain Jesse P. (Jake) Jacobs USAF, his wife, Pat, and three children and Captain Paul Bryce USAF, his wife, and three children seemed to be in the same culture shock that we were. Jake Jacobs located the U.S. Air Force commissary at Ruislip, and through him we surreptitiously supplied the chef at the hotel with American canned vegetables to replace the ever-present brussels sprouts that not one of us liked.

Mary and I found a two-story, four-bedroom house in Ash Vale, a very small and relatively poor but nice community not far from Aldershot and Farnborough. The house was owned by a nice English spinster lady, who had been raised in Kenya. She rented the house for the equivalent of $70 per month. We moved into the furnished house on February 19. Heat was supplied by individual coal fires in each room, and our hot water depended on a coal-burning boiler, which had to be fired up each morning. It then had to be stoked throughout the day. There was no refrigeration, and Mary learned how to keep food fresh in a naturally cooled larder, which was no mean feat. The house was near a large common used for field training for the Royal Army, and Mary became quite adept at instructing wandering lost recruits in full battle regalia how to read their maps.

Our three children attended the South Farnborough Preparatory School and wore uniforms of scratchy, rough, gray wool; knee-length socks; short gray pants or gray skirts; white shirts; blue ties; and scratchy gray sweaters. Mary went to the local ration board and registered for ration books for each of us. Shoes and most clothes were still rationed, as were all food stuffs except fresh vegetables and eggs. The eggs might as well have been rationed because each egg tasted like the fish meal the chickens were fed. We lived totally on the English economy, except for the occasional emergency trip to the U.S. Air Force commissary at Ruislip, where we found life-saving American meat and canned goods. As the only Americans in Ash Vale, we were simply known as the Americans and were soon accepted.

Also on February 19, having more or less solved the initial logistic challenges of living in a foreign country, and leaving the remaining and lion's share of those challenges to Mary, I chose the coward's tack and reported to ETPS. The school was begun in 1943 at Boscombe Down to train pilots to be test pilots. The many airplanes needed during World War II provided challenges, and quick solutions or fixes were needed for combat airplanes. The school was officially named the Empire Test Pilots School in 1944 and moved to Royal Air Force Field, Cranfield, in October 1945, and then again moved in 1947 to Farnborough to become part of the Royal Aircraft Establishment (RAE). ETPS was the premier test pilot school in the world at the time, and superior pilots from some fifteen nations came there to study the art and science of flight testing.

The RAE was organizationally under the Ministry of Supply and was the center of the British Empire's aviation knowledge. It was the principal aeronautics testing facility for the Royal Air Force and Royal Navy. A single old dead tree was carefully preserved near the main gate of the RAE. It was to that tree that American aeronautical experimenter S. F. Cody had tied his man-carrying kites around the turn of the century. It seemed odd that the British, who thought of all Americans as upstarts, honored those turn-of-the-century American efforts toward the genesis of aviation in England.

In 1953 the ETPS was well known and revered. Two U.S. Army Air Forces officers had attended the number 2 course in 1944, and in 1945 Lieutenant

Commander Jim Davidson and Lieutenant Mark Davenport were the first two American naval officers to attend course number 3. Generally, one or two U.S. naval aviators attended the course each year. Lieutenant Commander Joe Smith, briefly my commanding officer in VF-19 at Alameda in 1945, attended the number 8 course in 1949 and subsequently improved and formalized the curriculum of the U.S. Navy Test Pilot School at Patuxent River.

The small ETPS complex was located on the southeast corner of the airfield at Farnborough just inside Queens Gate and across the street from the Queens Hotel. Several World War II–style, one-story, drab, gray, stuccoed-concrete-block buildings contained classrooms, a BOQ, and officers mess. All sat on a low hill overlooking the airfield. Down the hill on the airfield's level was a large, arched, metal hangar painted black with a concrete ramp upon which the diverse aircraft used for instruction were parked.

Course number 12 convened on February 22, 1952. In our class of twenty-four were twenty-three serving military officers and one pilot from Faireys, an English aviation manufacturer. Besides Royal Air Force and Royal Navy pilots, there were pilots from Australia, Canada, France, Italy, Sweden, and the United States. The biggest single challenge that each of us foreigners had was learning the English language as it was spoken in the classroom. That, along with the terms and nomenclature used in the technical papers, initially seemed daunting because the only spelling or pronunciation allowed was true and proper English.

Each of us had achieved just by getting to ETPS. Each of us had been carefully screened to meet rigid standards of flight experience, character, courage, and integrity. Each of us loved to fly. Each of us was highly competitive with ourselves and others and strived to better what we had been able to accomplish before. This was an unusual group.

The school regimen was to attend academic courses in the morning and to fly in the afternoon, which permitted the perpetual low stratus clouds and fog over England to burn off for our test flying maneuvers. There were eighteen types of aircraft assigned, ranging from gliders, to jet fighters, to four-engine bombers and transport airplanes. We pilots were issued the necessary personal flying equipment of soft leather helmet, goggles, Mae West life jacket, oxygen mask, gloves, flight suit, and a set of pilot's notes for each of the eighteen kinds of aircraft. Each of us was given a permanent radio call sign for the year, which consisted of the word *sailor* and a number from one to twenty-four based on the alphabetical order of our last name. We were handed our pilot's notes one day and were scheduled to fly the next afternoon.

Our flying schedule and the assigned aircraft were posted on the blackboard in the pilot's operations room. On that first afternoon I found the airplane name *Oxford* printed behind my name for an area indoctrination flight. I had no idea what an Oxford was, let alone what it looked like, but by matching a line drawing of the airplane on the cover of my Oxford pilot's notes with an airplane on the flight line, I found the Oxford. It was an antiquated twin-piston engine airplane not unlike a Twin Beech. I walked around it, looking at the external appendages, and then worked my way through the cabin to sit in the pilot's seat and read the starting procedures. The propellers on British aircraft rotated to the right instead of the left, which created the need for left rudder trim to achieve balanced flight at low speed and high power instead of right rudder trim, as was necessary in all American airplanes. The Oxford was venerable, but still it was thrilling to get airborne in an airplane that I had never seen or flown before and to fly as a single pilot to explore a different country's countryside. We were scheduled and flew our airplanes in this offhanded manner for the rest of the year.

The purpose of ETPS was to teach pilots to respect the design and operation of many different kinds of airplanes and to be able to walk up to a new airplane, fly it capably, and reliably give an accurate assessment of it and its flying qualities. There are many pitfalls in flying, and the test pilot must be aware of all of them. The good test pilot does not blindly fly into danger but develops a sense or awareness when things begin to not go his way. He stops his test, or in England his programme, when he finds key indicators that all is not well in the aircraft that he is testing. The fledgling test pilot must learn those indicators above all else. Occasionally, the warning cues are too subtle, or a pilot moves too rapidly into a new regime of flight. Then his skill at flying is tested as never before, and all too often the test pilot can find that he is along for the ride. Occasionally, such rides can lead to disaster.

The English developed their airplane wheel-braking systems using pressurized air instead of hydraulic fluid to provide the energy needed to compress the friction disks of a brake. Tactical British aircraft had a lever on the control stick grip or wheel that, when squeezed, would meter compressed air to both wheel brakes from an air accumulator supplied by an engine-driven brake pump. As long as the engine ran and the pump continued to work, the pilot had main wheel brakes. Should the engine fail, the accumulator stored another six or seven brake applications. The pilot achieved increased braking by squeezing harder and differential braking by pushing one or the other rudder pedals forward while squeezing the brake lever. With each application, one could hear the compressed air being expended in a *pshhh* sound. American pilots initially flying in a British airplane could always be identified by the jerky movements of the airplane on the ground accompanied by the *pshhhing*. The Brits accused us Americans of looking like cowboys who had just mounted new horses. Using compressed-air brakes was a little like driving on the left side of the road or having torque applied backwards. The brakes took some getting used to, but we learned rapidly and soon were quite adept.

The studies were much more difficult for some than for others. I felt sorry for Captains Jacques Houlier, our French air force pilot, and Umberto Bernardini, our Italian air force pilot. They did not understand English well, and both had to listen to English, translate to French or Italian to think, and then retranslate to English to answer or to hold a discourse. Our Swedish classmate, Bengt Fryklund, spoke English as a second language and was more precise than any of us. Our Australian compatriot and a great man, Flight Lieutenant Tom Berry, murdered the King's English. Over time all of us became quite adept at speaking English.

On one occasion Jacques Houlier, flying our four-engine Lincoln bomber, passed over Cody's tree and touched down heavily on his main wheels as he landed at Farnborough, whereupon he bounced back into the air. That bouncing became divergent as he tried to get the airplane to stay on the ground. He was behind the power curve and was adding and retarding his four throttles while pushing and pulling on the control wheel, each action out of synchronization with what the airplane was doing. After the third or fourth bounce, as he passed the control tower in midair, the English tower operator came on the radio with a laconic "I say, Sailor 14, are you having difficulty?" Jacques's rapid and voluble response in pure French told the story. He finally salvaged the situation by adding full power and going around to make the landing again.

We progressed through the different testing periods together. For example, we all did weight and balance and center-of-gravity determination at the same time. Since judging flying qualities is the essence of being a good test pilot, we spent much of our time assessing different airplanes in various flight regimes, always writing reports and comparing our findings. We were critically judged on our flying techniques by Commander Ken Hickson RN, our chief technical flying instructor, and his three RAF squadron leader subordinates, Colin MacFee, I. D. (Tich) Crozier, and D. J. (Spud) Murphy. We were assessed on the accuracy of our technical assumptions in our reports by Wayson Turner, the chief ground technical instructor.

The manner of flight testing airplanes in 1953 was still relatively simple and much like it had been in the 1930s and 1940s, except that there was a developing deeper knowledge of aerodynamics and everything was happening much faster. We used pilots' knee pads on which to write all data taken from our stop watches, strain gauges, and cockpit gauges and to record our observations. We learned the basics extremely well by keeping the testing process simple and direct and by forcing ourselves to understand exactly what was going on, regardless of whether the airplane was upside down or right side up.

We flew the larger airplanes to assess flying qualities with differing centers of gravity; we did that by flying in pairs so that one pilot could go aft in the cabin and move lead shot bags to change the center of gravity while the other flew. The danger in changing the center of gravity, of course, was in placing too much lead shot too far aft or too far forward, causing loss of longitudinal control of the airplane. But it was exactly in the farthest forward or aft regions of the center-of-gravity travel that we most wanted to evaluate the flying qualities. It was there that they were altered appreciably and became much more critical and, of course, interesting to the test pilot. We made a game of seeing who could fly the airplanes at the most forward or most aft center of gravity. We then would compare what was said about the flying qualities in our respective reports, which were kept on file and available for anyone who cared to read them. From such comparisons, we measured each other informally to see who was best, and reputations were gradually built among us.

During one period we did spins—evaluating the entry, the fully developed spin, and the various spin recovery techniques. We did spins in a variety of airplanes and at different centers of gravity. Our flying area for those spins was just to the southeast of Farnborough and over the Aldershot common next to Ash Vale. One time, to my surprise, during one of our frequent weekend parties, Mary regaled us with her story on spins. She was used to the sound of airplanes and did not give them much thought. But once she had gone out to hang sheets on the clothesline and had heard a totally different sound. She looked up and saw seven to ten airplanes in the sky, big ones and little ones, all spinning toward the ground. As she watched, each pilot would recover to climb again to about 10,000 feet and start anew. She said that it was the best spin show that she had ever seen.

Being a good test pilot and living are not necessarily synonymous. Over time many of my friends were killed. One of the purposes of the course at ETPS was to build knowledge and character so that when you saw that your options were diminishing, or that the test was not going as planned, you knew enough and had the sense to stop and investigate on the ground. Then you could go up again to renew your quest. The flying instructors at ETPS were superb at imparting their judgment in those matters to us students, and no one in my class was killed while we were under instruction.

We were encouraged to try different things in the air, and I particularly enjoyed flying the Gloster Meteor jet fighter, except for the fact that the rpm gauges read in numbers of rpm and not in the more simple percent of rpm as in American aircraft. It was much more cumbersome to read 12,800 rpm on each engine gauge than a simple 100 percent. I tried and tried to master a maneuver performed in the Meteor by Squadron Leader J. Zurakowski of the Polish air force and a graduate of the number 2 course at ETPS. In that maneuver the pilot climbed vertically until he ran out of airspeed, and then at that critical moment he added full power on one engine while using idle power on the other. If the maneuver was done properly, the airplane would rotate nose over tail horizontally in place one-half turn, and the pilot would retrace the vertical flight path in the other direction. I fell out of that maneuver right side up and upside down. I did whip stalls and hammerhead stalls. I tried the maneuver at different altitudes. I regret that I ran out of time on the course and access to the Meteor before I mastered that maneuver.

Those who work hard frequently play hard. Aside from the many parties we had, we played golf to relax. We Americans even met an interclass challenge at cricket with some small success. To us Americans, cricket was the world's most boring game, sort of like watching grass grow. The return match for softball produced a much more uneven score, and then the Brits in their turn termed baseball a stupid game.

When we had first arrived at ETPS, the commandant, Group Captain C. E. Clouston RAF, had his foot encased in a plaster cast. He had broken his foot and was rendered hors de combat during the fun and games at the final formal dining-in for ETPS course 11. He walked with difficulty using a cane. Dining-in was a new term to us foreigners. It had originated long before in the officers messes on board ships of the Royal Navy to relieve the boredom of being at sea. It was subsequently adopted, but not necessarily refined, by the Royal Air Force.

Dining-in, a stag, formal evening procedure with participants in full mess dress uniform, would take place about once a month. There would be a short reception before dinner to honor a visiting dignitary, who later would speak. At a precise time all members of the mess would file into the mess for a formal dinner, elegantly served at long banquet tables. The mess president, the commandant, and the guest dignitary, frequently a government minister or member of the royal family, would sit at a head table facing all the mess members, resplendent in their formal dress uniforms. The mess chef, who during the week served sliced beef or lamb cut, we swore, with a micrometer, attempted to outdo himself for each dining-in and would be given recognition at the close of the proper formal meal. Port, Madeira, and cigars would be passed around after coffee and savory had been served, and the guest would speak on a topic that never seemed to be interesting.

After the meal and the appropriate toasts and responses, the mess president would bang his gavel on the table to signify the end of the formal activities, and all hell would break loose. Rolls or oranges, discreetly saved from the table, would fly through the air toward the guest or the commandant or a fellow mess member. Perhaps a giant salute firecracker would explode under one of the tables and deafen all, or on occasion a ceremonial cannon would be fired with all the formality necessary to replicate Waterloo or the battle of Trafalgar. Attendees would then repair to the bar and drink beer or whiskey until a football (rugby) game could be arranged in the hall. Those games would go on until the last person tired or the last person left the bar, usually about 0300. The local tailors and menders became quite wealthy repairing dress uniforms after

dining-ins. Skinned knuckles, barked shins, and black eyes adorned the cele-
brants for days after. I was always amazed at the process. At that time we had
nothing like it in the U.S. military forces.

Mary and I took the children to London on occasion. Those trips allowed me
to talk to Chris Cagle and to find out what might be going on in the U.S. Navy,
but Mary and the children had a more basic need. With rationing still in full
swing, they craved good American food. I would get a little beef in the mess at
each noon meal, but the children and Mary suffered from lack of good meat
and too much chicken that tasted of fish meal. Occasionally, on a Saturday, we
would leave Farnborough early and drive our car the 31 miles to London to arrive before noon. First we would go to the American embassy, then located on
the opposite side of Grosvenor Square from where it is today, and eat at the snack
bar. The hamburgers were absolutely delicious. We then would go to the English
cinema to see the newest American films and return late to Farnborough.

By spring the members of course 12 of the ETPS and our wives were fast
friends. Al Koplewski and I compared notes and helped each other in our studies. Al came to dinner frequently, and we would study together in the evening
or just talk. We both helped Umberto and Jacques continue to try to master the
English language. Bengt Fryklund's sister, Maryanne, arrived on holiday from
Sweden, and Mary and I and she and Bengt went to London to the theater. Pat
Jacobs and Mary would visit during the day and compare notes on the challenge of family living in England.

The coronation of Queen Elizabeth II was a world event in May 1953. We
even had three days off from school during the grand festivities. Subsequently,
on June 10 and 11, we were given our two, four-hour, written midterm examinations and then had a midterm break. We took our family vacation on the con-
tinent and visited Paris and Amsterdam to give the children a chance to see
those cities.

After our return Jake and Pat Jacobs gave a Fourth of July party for the entire class in their garden. In the late afternoon we had an English-style reception and lawn party, which culminated in American hamburgers and hot dogs
near sundown. Our British ETPS friends made a few remarks about upstart
colonials, but they came and participated, and we all had a great time. English
neighbors also joined in, after the noise and laughter indicated the party was
good. The Jacobs's local bobby occasionally rode his bike up and down the
street peering over the front hedge as a friendly check. Asked in, he politely declined the invitation. We were not sure if he was interested in keeping us in or
keeping others out. When it came time for the fireworks that we Americans had
brought, the British called it the American's Guy Fawkes Day, after Guy
Fawkes, who tried to blow up Parliament in the early 1600s.

The English seemed to be very offhanded about everything that they did or saw. One day while taxiing a de Havilland Vampire jet fighter back to the ETPS line after landing, my right brake failed. Rather than foul the taxiway for others, I used my left brake to turn onto the smooth grass between the taxiway and the runway and coasted to a stop. I called the tower to send a tow and shut down the engine to wait. It was a sunny, warm day. I took off my helmet and relaxed in the cockpit, enjoying the infrequent sunshine. In the distance an airfield worker on a tractor was towing the mowers that kept the beautiful green airfield turf so pristine. He mowed methodically back and forth across the grass between the taxiway and the runway and slowly came closer. The sun was warm, and I dozed until I realized with a start that the mower had stopped right in front of my Vampire. The airfield keepers were used to strange doings on the field at Farnborough; this gent sat on his tractor studying me and my airplane, which was blocking his progress. He contemplated the scene for a moment and then looked at me in the cockpit and said, "I say, are you going to be here long?" Between the two of us, we got the line crew to retrieve me and the airplane, and he was able to complete his mowing.

Our flying and schooling became more intense as the summer wore on. Each hour of flight time generated the need to write a report, which took two to three hours. We easily ran out of time in the day to study, and I was always writing until late at night. The course was demanding, and I am afraid that Mary and the children did not see much of me because I was totally wrapped up in the flying and the studies. I had been flying now for eleven years and had fought in two wars, but there in England I really learned about flying. I was developing the ability to assess flying qualities of individual airplanes and to become more a part of the machine that I was flying. I fully thought about and understood why the airplane was behaving as it did instead of accepting what the airplane handbook told me it would do. I was beginning to develop the ability to solve some of the more vexing airplane traits. My joy in flying increased immeasurably, and I felt that I had total command of the airplane in which I was flying. I had always tried to fly smoothly, but now I flew even more smoothly and understood what those nibbles at the ailerons meant and how the increasing pressure on the control stick communicated to the pilot just where he was in relation to the longitudinal design capabilities of that airplane. I had great confidence in my ability as a pilot, but I realized that you must accept and fly the limitations of your airplane.

By August we were evaluating the critical Mach numbers of airplanes. We flew Meteors, Vampires, and Venoms (another de Havilland jet fighter) to and beyond their established limits to investigate the effects on flying qualities. The critical Mach number defines for the pilot the high-speed end of the operating envelope of his combat airplane. A number of parameters help define the critical Mach number, but for a straight-winged airplane, it is the ability to maintain longitudinal control. An aircraft wing is designed to provide lift across the broad spectrum of flight, and its design is nothing more than a compromise between high and low airspeed. That compromise establishes the flying parameters for that airplane. The critical Mach number is that Mach number at which the distance between the centers of pressure and lift changes in such a way that the available aerodynamic power of the horizontal tail will no longer permit the pilot to control his horizontal flight. Most straight-winged airplanes will tend to pitch up; others can tuck nose down.

I drew the Meteor for a series of flights to measure the longitudinal forces in an untrimmed dive. One day, and after climbing to 37,000 feet, I trimmed the airplane for an indicated Mach number (IMN) of .79, some .03 below the critical Mach number, and rolled inverted to pull through and accelerate while diving vertically at the ground. I set the throttles to maximum thrust as I held a strain gauge to the stick with my left hand to measure stick force required in pounds of push and recorded the IMN and stick force on a knee pad on my right leg with my right hand. The push force was building as my speed increased from .80 to .81, .82, and .83.

At .84 and about .02 above the critical Mach number, the push force required caused my long-ago-injured and now-weakened left wrist to collapse. The stick slammed back into the aft travel stop. That Meteor began a series of snap rolls the likes of which I had never experienced before. I was passing through 29,000 feet, and I estimate that I must have done seven snap rolls before I could drop my pencil, grab the stick, and retard the throttles. The airplane immediately slowed up, and I once again had control. The structural strength of the Meteor and the less dense air at that altitude prevented the airplane from coming apart. I repeated the test, and having satisfied myself, I returned to write my report.

The Society of British Aircraft Companies (SBAC) began a series of air shows in England in 1932. That annual air show was moved from airfield to airfield until 1948, when the RAE permitted the SBAC to rent the airfield facilities at Farnborough. SBAC Week became a world-class aviation event and now is known internationally as the Farnborough Air Show. There were booths, static displays, and magnificent flying demonstrations of the current British and foreign aircraft. By 1953 it was becoming quite the international show. The year before a tragic accident occurred during the flying display when a de Havilland DH-110 flown by test pilot John Derry made a cross-runway, high-speed pass toward the south and the crowds gathered on the hill near the ETPS mess. The DH-110's design was descended from the Vampire, and it was capable of high subsonic and supersonic flight. As John Derry made his high-speed pass across the airfield, his airplane was upset by turbulence. Just as John Darden's airplane had done at the Naval Ordnance Test Station

China Lake in 1952, the leading edge of one wing failed and peeled back, followed by the immediate and abrupt total disintegration of the DH-110.

The heavy engines, turning at thousands of rpm, came out of the airplane and flew into the crowd. All the other pieces of wings, fuselage, and tails became missiles hurtling at near supersonic speed into the crowd of spectators on the hill just below the ETPS mess. Nearly seventy people, including John Derry, were killed, and many more were burned and badly injured. From that tragedy, air show rules were refined around the world to ensure increased safety for spectators. Today the biennial Farnborough Air Show remains one of the best air shows in the world. In 1953 it was a festive time for us budding test pilots as we met and talked to famous test pilots.

A number of innovative and successful concepts for aircraft carriers were thought of and designed by Royal Navy engineers, derisively called plumbers by their line officer counterparts. Those engineers conceived and designed the steam catapult to provide safer and better naval airplane launches. They devised the canted deck as a means of providing a clear way to take off again should the airplane's arresting hook not engage. This Royal Navy concept became the angled deck, first built by the U.S. Navy in USS *Antietam*, and was demonstrated to the Royal Navy in 1953. Subsequently the angled deck has revolutionized carrier aviation.

One man, Commander Nicholas Goodhart RN, was instrumental in developing many of those innovative designs. In 1951 Nick Goodhart wrote a paper on an optical landing system that would project an approach path in the sky for aircraft to follow to land precisely at the same point each time. That paper and Nick's concept came from his typical ingenuity. One day, in his office in London's Whitehall, he borrowed his secretary's pocket mirror and rested it on the desk at a fixed angle. He then took her lipstick, extended the red tip to just show, and set it on the desk before the mirror. As Nick held the mirror, his secretary walked around the desk, keeping the red lipstick's tip in the center of the mirror. Each time, as she approached the desk, her chin would always touch it at the same spot. In 1952 Commander Dennis Campbell, a member of the United Kingdom Naval Aeronautical Research Committee, placed Nick's idea before the committee after which the RAE was asked to build and carry out trials on the system in 1953.

Our Navy's Bureau of Aeronautics in Washington, through the U.S. naval attaché for air in London, followed that development with interest, and when the visual glide slope system was to be given trials in late November 1953, Al Koplewski and I were asked to evaluate the system at Farnborough. The mirror, as it was called, was highly polished cast aluminum formed to a cylindrically concave shape with a 10-foot radius. It was five feet six inches wide and four feet high. Two banks of green reference lights were placed at midheight on either side of the mirror, and an image light source was formed from a bank of eight 240-watt amber lights placed 160 feet in front of the mirror. Those amber lights were focused to provide a single reflected blob of light. Later, Lieutenant Lucky Finch and other pilots at Air Development Squadron 3 dubbed it the meatball because of its similarity to the Japanese aircraft emblem.

From our ETPS stable of aircraft, Al and I chose the Sea Vampire, Mark XXI, as the airplane to fly and laid out a comprehensive test program. We began our flying evaluation on November 10 without any LSO and flew our repetitive carrier landing patterns at 550 feet, some 350 feet higher than a conventional paddles approach, around and over the town of Farnborough. I must say that the British in Farnborough were most tolerant of noise. In fact, people did not even look up as we flew down city streets at about 500 feet. We completed our field landing trials on November 14, and the mirror was transported to Southampton to be placed on the flight deck of Royal Navy aircraft carrier HMS *Illustrious* for our shipboard evaluation. On November 19 I flew the Sea Vampire to *Illustrious* and completed my evaluation in two days with a total of seventeen carrier landings, still without an LSO. I wrote my report for the U.S. Navy and gave the mirror glowing praise. Al flew second but never completed his report, for reasons that I will explain later.

The mirror provided a means of carrier landing descent control that we had never had before. The mirror approach was easier to fly than a paddles approach and would be safer at night because it was flown higher. I particularly liked it because the pilot flew what he saw and did not have to rely on the judgment of an LSO. From a ladies' pocket mirror and lipstick and the inventive mind of a Royal Navy plumber came a concept that would revolutionize carrier landing operations in the years to come. In my report to the CNO, I recommended that the Navy procure the mirror immediately. It was a perfect companion for the angled deck.

By the end of November I completed my assigned final test flying assessment of the Meteor, Mark IX, to measure my skills at general evaluation of an airplane. At that time the U.S. Navy asked me to do another evaluation: an assessment of still another British concept, the flex deck.

It is common aeronautical engineering knowledge that there is an approximate 25 percent weight penalty for an airplane just to have landing gear. That weight is in the gear itself, the attendant hydraulic and electrical systems, and the load carry-through structure in the fuselage necessary to support the weight of the airplane. In naval aircraft that penalty is exacerbated because of the need for greater strength for carrier landings. A British engineer reasoned that if we could just get rid of the landing gear, then the airplane could have a greatly increased range and armament capability. The idea was first to see if a jet airplane could be operated without landing gear.

The pilots of Lieutenant Bill McBride's division standing in front of an SB2C-3 at NAS Kahului, Maui, May 1944: *(top row, left to right)* Al Emig, me, Roy Majors, and John Evatt; *(bottom row)* Emil Stella, McBride, and Bill Wright. (Courtesy of the author)

Ensign Jack Scott (in service dress blue uniform) and I (in aviation wintergreen uniform) shortly after completing operational flight training, Pasadena, Calif., August 1943. (Courtesy of the author)

Commander Dick McGowan, commanding officer of VB-19, in the cockpit of an SB2C-3, on the flight deck of USS *Lexington* in October 1944, shortly before he died. (Courtesy of the U.S. Navy)

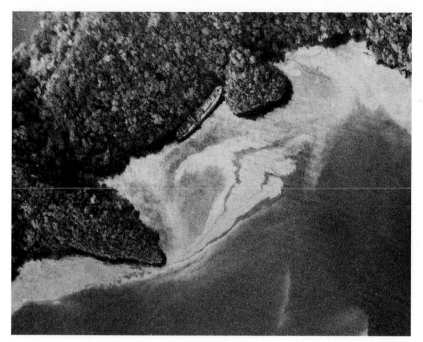

A Japanese cargo ship nestled beside a small island in Palau, August 1944. Such tactics were exposed by F6F photo reconnaissance airplanes. (Courtesy of the U.S. Navy)

Officers of VB-19 and VF-19 relax at Ulithi fleet anchorage during a rare time ashore during August 1944. I am seated on a coconut log on the far right. (Courtesy of the author)

VB-19 Ready Room 2 in USS *Lexington* before a combat launch, September 1944;
seated in the front row are *(left to right)* pilots Don Banker, Lou Heilman, and I.
(Courtesy of the U.S. Navy)

A Japanese carrier under attack, photographed by a gunner in an SB2C-3 at the battle
for Leyte Gulf, October 25, 1944. Note that all ships are maneuvering independently
to avoid being hit. (Courtesy of the U.S. Navy)

Respotting for the next launch on USS *Lexington*'s flight deck, October 1944. On the right is Primary Fly, where the air officer controlled the flight deck and landing pattern. The blackboard in foreground will have last-minute navigation data for departing pilots. (Courtesy of the U.S. Navy)

Japanese carrier *Zuikaku* and other ships maneuver during attack at the battle for Leyte Gulf, October 25, 1944. (Courtesy of the U.S. Navy)

Japanese carrier *Zuikaku*, as seen in 1942, without the full complement of eighty airplanes. The ship led the attack on Pearl Harbor. (Courtesy of the National Archives)

Japanese carrier *Zuikaku*, as seen from directly overhead during the attack on October 25, 1944. The ship sank shortly afterward. (Courtesy of the U.S. Navy)

Pilots of VBF-19, Lieutenant Bill DeVaughn's division, standing in front of an F4U-4 at NAS Santa Rosa, Calif., April 1945: *(left to right)* Harry West, me, DeVaughn, and Nick Nichols. (Courtesy of the author)

VBF-19 assembled before an F4U-4 at NAS Santa Rosa, Calif., May 1945. Note the ratio of enlisted crew to officers. (Courtesy of the author)

USS *Valley Forge* departs San Diego Bay, Calif., for the first full deployment of Navy jet airplanes to the western Pacific, April 1950. F9F-3s of VF-51 and VF-52 are visible on deck. (Courtesy of Mary Engen)

I flew the newly built Vought AU-1 Marine Corsair during production test flights near Dallas, July 1952. (Courtesy of the author)

To enter the cockpit of the first F7U-3 Cutlass took a good climb; I climb toward the cockpit at the Vought plant, Grand Prairie, Tex., October 1952. (Courtesy of the U.S. Navy)

British, Swedish, French, Italian, and American students from class 12 of the Empire Test Pilots School tour an aircraft plant near Coventry, England, April 1953 (I am third from the right). (Courtesy of the author)

On January 21, 1955, I ended one flight hung up in the flight deck barricade of the then straight deck carrier USS *Ticonderoga*. The tail hook broke off the airplane as the F9F-8 engaged the arresting wire. (Courtesy of the U.S. Navy)

A pilot's view before landing on the straight deck of USS *Midway*, April 1954. Note the high barricade and the LSO *(bottom left)*, showing a high dip signal. (Courtesy of the U.S. Navy)

I start down in a loop while flying a North American FJ-3 in February 1955. The Navy used a dark blue paint scheme for aircraft then. (Courtesy of the author)

Commanding officer Commander Max Harnish *(right)* and I walk the flight deck of USS *Forrestal* during the shakedown cruise near Guantánamo Bay, Cuba, February 1956. Note the new light gray paint scheme for FJ-3s. (Courtesy of North American Aviation)

I explain a maneuver to Secretary of the Navy Charles S. Thomas as fellow Gray Ghost acrobatic team pilots Tom Cassidy, John Wolmers, and Jo Humes judge the description, March 1956. (Courtesy of the U.S. Navy)

I prepare to fly the new Crusader III from the Vought test facility at Edwards AFB in November 1958. The inspection plate *(upper right)* will be replaced before the flight. (Courtesy of Vought Aeronautics)

The newer, larger F8U-3, parked beside the older F8U-2, illustrates the differences in the two planes, January 1959. (Courtesy of Vought Aeronautics)

The landing gear retracts as the F8U-3 Crusader III lifts off the runway at Edwards AFB for a test flight in January 1959. (Courtesy of Vought Aeronautics)

I climb into the cockpit of the F4H-1 for an altitude record attempt in September 1959. My pressure suit is necessary because of the loss of cabin pressure when I purposefully shut down both engines. (Courtesy of McDonnell Aircraft Corporation)

McDonnell test pilot Zeke Huelsbeck *(right)* greets me after one of my high-altitude flight attempts in September 1959. (Courtesy of McDonnell Aircraft Corporation)

Sitting in the F4H-1 cockpit, I give a thumbs up after a test flight in September 1959. The second seat was never used during early test flights. (Courtesy of McDonnell Aircraft Corporation)

Commander W. R. Eason leads as we review the squadron during the VF-21 change of command ceremony at NAS Alameda, Calif., April 1960. (Courtesy of the U.S. Navy)

An F3H-2 from VF-21 on the flight deck of USS *Midway*, April 1961. Note the ever-present movie camera *(far left)* to record all landings. (Courtesy of the U.S. Navy)

USS *Kitty Hawk* steams in the mid Pacific while overhead two VF-114 F4H-1s and one VAW-11 WF-2 await a clear deck for landing, July 1962. (Courtesy of the U.S. Navy)

Air Group 11 squadron and detachment commanders assembled on the flight deck of USS *Kitty Hawk* in November 1962: *(top row, left to right)* Commanders Jim Kirklighter, Bob Moore, me, and Bob Osterholm and Lieutenant John Vreeland; *(bottom row)* Commanders Garrett White, Hap Chandler, and Charles Bowen and Lieutenant Commander Jack Eckstein. (Courtesy of the U.S. Navy)

The left main landing gear broke off this VF-151 F-8D Crusader as I caught the number 3 wire on USS *Coral Sea*'s flight deck in the mid Pacific in April 1963. (Courtesy of the U.S. Navy)

USS *Mount Katmai*, with a new helicopter flight deck and fresh from overhaul, steams up the Sacramento River to Concord, Calif., in August 1964. (Courtesy of the U.S. Navy)

USS *Oriskany*, USS *Mount Katmai*, and a fast frigate conduct underway replenishment operations in the Pacific, March 1965. (Courtesy of the U.S. Navy)

I watch from USS *Mount Katmai* as USS *Bon Homme Richard* completes the approach alongside to rearm at Yankee Station in the South China Sea in May 1965. (Courtesy of the author)

I watch from the bridge while a carrier alongside USS *Mount Katmai* is concurrently conducting flight operations and rearming at Yankee station in the South China Sea, May 1965. (Courtesy of the author)

Captain Jesse Naylor and I sit in the captain's cabin in USS *Mount Katmai* before our change of command at Subic Bay in July 1965. (Courtesy of the U.S. Navy)

I relieve Captain Lawrence Heyworth *(left)* as commanding officer of USS *America* at the Portsmouth Naval Shipyard in January 1966. (Courtesy of the U.S. Navy)

Two of USS *America*'s four ship's wheels, photographed while the ship was in dry dock at the Portsmouth Naval Shipyard in July 1966. Compare the size of the wheels with the man and the large crane standing on the bottom of the dry dock. (Courtesy of the U.S. Navy)

I hold the Battle E plaque, which Vice Admiral C. T. Booth *(seated, far left)* just presented to USS *America* for being the best all-round carrier in the Atlantic Fleet, April 1967. (Courtesy of the U.S. Navy)

Lieutenant Junior Grade K. W. Leuffen tries to look nonchalant while awaiting rescue after his brakes failed and his A-4C Skyhawk taxied off the forward flight deck of USS *America* on December 7, 1966. (Courtesy of the U.S. Navy)

USS *America* begins an approach to USS *Marias* for underway refueling in the Mediterranean in May 1967. (Courtesy of the U.S. Navy)

A rubber and pneumatic flexible deck was designed to make a soft arrested landing area for the airplane. That deck was nothing more than six packages of twelve inflated cylindrical rubber tubes, each 24 inches in diameter and 60 feet long. Each group of twelve tubes was wrapped in a large sheet of neoprene rubber. Altogether, those made a soft rubber landing surface that was 60 feet wide by 144 feet long. The flex deck was constructed on the north side of runway 24 at Farnborough near a stand of trees but well clear of the runway. At the approach end of the mat was placed a single standard naval arresting-gear engine with its cross-deck pendant, or wire, supported so that it was about two feet six inches off the ground. The intent was to fly the Sea Vampire toward the wire and the rubber deck at an approach speed of 105 knots with the landing gear up and the tail hook about 18 inches off the ground. The airplane's tail hook would engage the wire, and the airplane would be stopped on the mat. A heavy hook was mounted on the nose of the Sea Vampire with which to pull the airplane to the forward edge of the flex deck. There it would be raised by a waiting crane, using straps under the wings, and swung to the side until the pilot could lower the landing gear and be set upon the ground again. It worked that way, sort of. I chose the same Sea Vampire, Mark XXI, that Al and I had used in the mirror trials. The airplane was light and carried a light fuel load so that we could keep the total arresting energy much lower than we would have with a heavier airplane.

After four flights to become adjusted to line up and approach to the deck and the arresting wire while flying the Sea Vampire some three feet off the ground, I began and completed the trials on December 4, 1953. I made six five-minute flights with one landing on each. The first and fifth flights were the most interesting.

On the first flight I did not know what to expect after catching the wire. The Sea Vampire was flying in ground effect as I flew just above the grass and parallel to runway 24. We did not want any people near the deck, so I received no visual signaling to help me establish my height or line up. I dropped down until I thought I could feel the hook hit the ground and then climbed a few inches. The precision required was far greater than I had imagined. I definitely did not want to hit the twin boomed tail of the Vampire on the ground and be slammed down short and then into the rubber deck. The thought of sliding on the ground into that deck at near eye level and at well over 100 knots was not at all appetizing. I was flying at 104 knots, which was 3 or 4 knots over the stall speed for the airplane at that weight. As I approached the flex deck and lost sight of the forward edge, I felt the hook snag the wire, and the airplane was slammed down onto the rubber bolsters and stopped about 40 feet short of the forward end of the deck.

The arrestment of the forward motion of the airplane was not unlike a normal carrier landing. The cushioning of the rubber bolsters was gentle enough, but I was thrown around in the cockpit even though I was wearing a seat belt and shoulder strap. I immediately shut down the engine to not burn the rubber mat. A little man in a black jumpsuit appeared from over the forward edge of the deck and bounced more than ran toward me. He placed the bull nose of a wire over the hook on the nose of the airplane, and I was gently winched forward on the deck. The rubber had been liberally doused with distilled water for lubrication before the landing. Once I had been winched forward, a mobile crane appeared, straps were placed below each wing, and the airplane and I were raised to about 10 feet above the ground and were swung off the mat and over the ground. I was given the wheels down signal, and I lowered the landing gear to be set gently back on the ground.

I was given the engine turn up signal and started the engine to taxi to make another flight and landing. The next three landings were the same as the first, and as I gained experience with flying low to the ground, it became more comfortable. The fifth landing was an anomaly. I approached the wire and the mat as I had before, but just as the tail hook caught the wire, I allowed the Sea Vampire to climb very slightly. With upward movement instead of no vertical movement, the Sea Vampire flew out until the wire stopped it in midair, and I was thrown down into the flex deck, which then did its thing. It threw the Sea Vampire back into the air in a series of bounces of decreasing amplitude to be stopped in the same position on the mat as on previous landings. I shut down the engine. My body had literally flailed about the cockpit. My head had been whipped around like a yo-yo and ached, and my wrist hurt from my old injury. During the bounces, a series of sharp pains coursed through my spine as it was compressed into the old Martin Baker seat injury. I felt like a wet rag, with the pain bringing sweat to my forehead.

But things settled down, and a quick appraisal of my moving parts showed that everything still worked. The Sea Vampire and I were lifted into the air, and I dropped the landing gear, started the engine, and took off for the planned final landing of the trials. The sixth landing, like the first four, was relatively uneventful. Those tests were most interesting. I was not sure just how practical the concept of building airplanes without landing gear would be. The ground-handling challenge would be enormous, but we had catapults that could launch us. I made my report to the U.S. Navy without the ringing endorsement that I had given the mirror, but still, new concepts have to be evaluated, and we had learned a great deal about that one. I had made seven wheels up landings—six of them intentionally.

That last landing of the flex deck trials completed my flying at ETPS, so my last landing in England was made wheels up. Each student's grades were assessed, and it was announced that Captain Bengt Fryklund of the Swedish air force had won the first prize McKenna trophy. In one sense Al and I were disappointed because each of us thought that one of us had a chance to win it, but our thoughts were only fleeting, and we were glad for Bengt. My congratulations to him were honest and sincere. He was a good test pilot and a close personal friend. Unfortunately, he was killed the following year while test flying the Saab Lancen in Sweden.

Without a doubt, the course at ETPS was a tremendous aviation gift to me. I had thought I knew all about flying, but now I had an appreciation for how and why airplanes did what they did as I had never had before. Flying airplanes of another nation, designed to different standards and criteria, was one of the opportunities that I enjoyed most. I had been flying for eleven years and had accumulated 2,500 hours of total Navy flight time. I could articulate an improved understanding of airplanes to others, and when I flew, I would do so with greater confidence, appreciation, understanding, and interest.

Mary and I and the children prepared to return to the United States for Christmas. In the last month I received my orders to Air Development Squadron 3 (VX-3) at NAS Atlantic City, New Jersey. Al Koplewski had orders to a Pacific Fleet fighter squadron but was staying behind for one last flight to evaluate the Wyvern, a Royal Navy turboprop attack airplane. After that evaluation he planned to spend Christmas with his family in Michigan before reporting to his squadron.

Mary and I said our good-byes to fellow students, staff, wives, and the many friends we had made in the United Kingdom. Al Koplewski came to Southampton to bid us good-bye as we boarded SS *United States*, and then he went on to RNAS Ford to fly the Wyvern. We returned to the United States as we had come, cabin class, and arrived before Christmas. Within days after our arrival in the United States, I was notified that Al Koplewski had been killed while flying the Wyvern. Al had entered into a deep aerodynamic stall while maneuvering at low altitude in simulated combat with an RAF Meteor. He did not recover from the stall and died doing what he liked to do. His death was a great loss to his many friends and family. Over the years following the graduation of ETPS course number 12, test flying accidents claimed the lives of many of our class of twenty-four pilots, until today I believe only twelve of us remain.

Mary and I went on to Atlantic City where I joined Air Development Squadron 3 to enter a new realm of tactical testing of procedures and equipment.

8. TACTICAL DEVELOPMENT
JANUARY 1954 TO JULY 1955

The years 1954 and 1955 were a time for positioning U.S. military forces after the Korean War as the nation strived to meet the expanding threat of the Soviet Union. USS Nautilus, *the first nuclear submarine, was launched. The Senate censured Senator Joseph McCarthy for his slanderous attacks, and four Puerto Rican dissidents shot at members in the U.S. House of Representatives. A P2V Neptune airplane from VP-19 was shot down off the Siberian coast by two Soviet MiGs. The Vietminh forces defeated the French at Dien Bien Phu, North Vietnam. Gamal Nasser seized power in Egypt. Two hurricanes, Carol and Edna, smashed into the East Coast, and the National Hurricane Center was established in Miami. British aviator Walter Gibb set an altitude record of 65,876 feet in a Canberra bomber.*

There were 16,722 pilots, 125,102 aviation ratings, and a total of 30 aircraft carriers of all types in the U.S. Navy. The Navy's initial steam catapult trials were conducted in USS Hancock. *Lieutenant Commander Bill Manby, flying a North American FJ-3, set an unofficial time-to-climb record from a standing start to 10,000 feet in 73.2 seconds, and that record was beaten by 2.2 seconds by McDonnell pilot C. V. Braun in an F3H-1N, who in turn was beaten by Douglas pilot Bob Rahn, flying an F4D-1, with a record of 56 seconds. The XF8U-1 with Vought pilot John Konrad at the controls exceeded the speed of sound on its first flight at Edwards AFB. The Bureau of Aeronautics issued new aircraft paint instructions to be phased in within two years. The mirror-landing system was adopted, and in-flight refueling systems were ordered for all new Navy fighter airplanes.*

Much had changed in the year that we had lived in England. The Korean War had ended, and many of the airplanes developed for that war had become available for active duty and reserve squadrons. The numbers of jet squadrons grew appreciably. The Navy pilot-training pipeline, which had been stepped up for war production, no longer had the interminable delays of the post–World War II years. Bright young enlisted men and officers were coming into the fleet in numbers. There was a new breed of naval aviator, one trained to become a jet pilot. Jet airplanes were now proven in combat, and new and more efficient jet engines were being developed. The Douglas F3D Skynight, while certainly not a high-performance airplane, had gained a role as a night fighter. The single-seated McDonnell F2H-3 and -4 carried improved air-intercept radars, making them more valuable as night fighters. The improved detection ranges of air-intercept radar made day visual intercepts even better. The sturdy, straight-wing Grumman F9F Panther was supplanted by the swept-wing, transonic F9F-6 Cougar. The F7U-3 Cutlass, with its more powerful J-46 engines, was just around the corner, and North American Aviation, Columbus Division, was perfecting the FJ-3 for fleet introduction in late 1954.

Mary and I and the children spent Christmas 1953 with Mary's sister and family in Excelsior, Minnesota, after which I returned to Atlantic City to begin the ritual of looking for a place to live. I found an old, white frame house on Ryon Avenue in Pleasantville, New Jersey. Mary and the children flew to Atlantic City, and we put down roots in a new town.

NAS Atlantic City was a World War II air station located midway on the flat, marshy New Jersey seacoast. It hosted two entirely different squadrons: Fleet Composite Squadron 4 (VC-4) and Air Development Squadron 3 (VX-3). The activities of those two squadrons filled the air around the clock. VC-4 fielded small teams of night-fighter pilots, who were also qualified in nuclear-weapon delivery tactics to augment the standard air group squadrons. The four-airplane detachment teams formed and trained to deploy in the Atlantic and Mediterranean. It was a nomadic and tough life for those naval aviators and crews as they came and went. VC-3, a sister squadron at NAS Moffett Field, California, provided the same kinds of services in the Pacific Fleet.

VX-3 was one of four air development squadrons under the administrative and operational control of Commander Operational Test and Evaluation Force (COMOPTEVFOR). COMOPTEVFOR coordinated all fleet testing of new ship and aircraft equipment and tactics in the fleet environment and was located some 350 miles south in Norfolk, Virginia. VX-3 had been established in

September 1946 at NAS New York to introduce the helicopter into fleet operations. In 1954, at the height of its tactical evaluation role, VX-3 conducted many projects, and many experienced pilots were assigned to it.

Fleet air development squadrons were an outgrowth of early aircraft development at NAS Anacostia in the 1930s and the need to have fleet acceptance of those aircraft being developed. It was a way to satisfy the customer. VX-1 at Key West developed ASW tactics and the tactics of lighter-than-air airships and helicopters; VX-3 at Atlantic City developed attack carrier warfare tactics; VX-4 at Point Mugu developed missile delivery tactics; and VX-5 at Kirtland AFB, Albuquerque, developed special weapon delivery tactics. In January 1955 VX-6 was commissioned to provide services for TF 43 in Antarctic operations.

I reported to VX-3 on January 13, 1954, just as Captain Noel Gayler was relinquishing command to Commander Hawley (Monk) Russell. Monk had carved a name for himself in carrier aviation during World War II in early night fighters and had a wealth of aviation experience. He could create great enthusiasm among his pilots, and we all enjoyed working for him. Commander Bill Leonard, a quiet and very experienced pilot, was executive officer, and Lieutenant Commander E. L. (Whitey) Feightner was chief projects officer. Whitey had flown with the then-new Navy flight demonstration team, the Blue Angels. Lieutenant Commander T. J. (Tom) Gallagher was the maintenance officer and subsequently became the operations officer. The thirty other pilots, from both the Navy and the Marine Corps, ranged from ensign to lieutenant commander or major and doubled as project development officers. There were two exchange officers from the United Kingdom, Lieutenant R. J. (Dickie) Reynolds RN, renowned for his ability to consume vast quantities of whiskey without showing any effect, and Flight Lieutenant Angus Fawcett RAF. The entire motley crew was close knit in flying and in socializing.

Development projects were assigned by COMOPTEVFOR at the direction of the Navy staff in Washington, and the management of each project was the responsibility of a single project officer. The diverse experience in the squadron also led to projects being created within the squadron; we had many inventive minds. A prospective project officer could sell his idea for a particular project to COMOPTEVFOR. That sales pitch usually took a large amount of tact and diplomacy before you could get the COMOPTEVFOR staff to tell you to go ahead and do what you wanted to do, but the system worked well. As I joined VX-3, the major projects were the evaluation of tactical air navigation (TACAN), an entirely new concept in navigation developed by ITT and the forerunner of our present-day, ground-based civil air-navigation system; the use of very low level flying to navigate undetected in a radar environment; and the evaluations of new fleet airplanes before they went to fleet squadrons. There were other projects, of course, and we had a stable of airplanes to fly that made any red-blooded pilot jealous. Because of the diversity of those airplanes, it was a real challenge for the maintenance crews to maintain them, and we seemed to be searching perennially for parts.

The Adcock range was being phased out for aerial navigation, and the CAA was installing VHF Omni-directional Ranges (VORs) for civil aviation, but the Navy had no VOR equipment in its tactical airplanes because there were no VORs on ships. The advent of TACAN for the armed services was absolutely mind boggling. Here was a system that provided the pilot with exact bearing and distance in relation to a station on the surface of Earth. More importantly, TACAN could be mounted on a ship! The TACAN signal was also in the VHF range, and we transmitted and received by line of sight. Depending upon the airplane's altitude, we could receive a TACAN signal out to the maximum range of 200 miles. Never before had we had anything that approached this capability. That was the good news. The bad news was that there was only one TACAN station in the world, and it happened to be at Atlantic City. Since the fighter airplanes that we flew only had room for one navigation black box, we stayed within 200 miles of Atlantic City. Whenever we flew beyond the 200-mile range of the TACAN, the needle and distance-measuring counter would spin aimlessly, indicating no reception, and we felt as though we were falling off the edge of Earth. Lieutenant H. H. (Speed) Moreland was the project officer, but all VX-3 pilots flew on the TACAN project.

Eventually, the Air Force installed the second TACAN station—at Elmendorf AFB near Anchorage. While that station was of absolutely no help to us in Atlantic City, we were comforted to know that someday there would be TACAN stations in between. We experimented with TACAN instrument approaches to landings and became very adept at flying approaches in the heavy fog of coastal New Jersey. In the name of development, we flew to weather minimums that were not allowed any place else in the United States. Eventually, the CAA installed combined civil VOR and military TACAN (VORTAC) stations that benefited both civil and military aircraft, and distance measuring became possible for all. However, at that time no civil jet airplanes were flying in the United States—not until the late 1950s, for that matter—and we continued to have the entire airspace above 25,000 feet to ourselves. Slowly, one, then two, and then five naval air stations and Air Force bases received their TACAN stations. By 1955 we could navigate in selected parts of the United States in TACAN-only equipped airplanes.

TACAN had great tactical significance for carrier air warfare. No longer did we need the vectors of an intercept controller. We knew where we were in relation to the ship. If only we had the position of the aircraft to be intercepted, we could navigate to intercept without voice communications. A separate project was established called broadcast control, and we began to make our own intercepts based upon bogey information broadcast in the blind by a ship's combat information center. That project and other TACAN projects culminated in an at-sea trial in October 1954 when the first TACAN antenna was installed in USS *Midway*.

The Navy had done nothing more with the in-flight refueling tests conducted at Patuxent in 1951–52, and there seemed to be nothing going on in the Air Force either. I set out to start an in-flight refueling project, and in February of 1954 I met with the managers of the English In Flight Refueling Company to discuss the use of their patented fuel-transfer package, which contained the all-important fuel drogue, to be towed behind the refueling airplane. In April a single event helped raise more interest. Three pilots from VF-21 at Oceana, Virginia, led by Lieutenant Commander F. X. Brady, arranged to use one of those English in-flight refueling packages in a North American AJ bomber and rounded up some of the old probes from the 1952 Patuxent River trials. Grumman installed the probes on three F9F-6s, enabling them to fly from San Diego to Floyd Bennett Field, with one airborne refueling over NAS Hutchinson, Kansas. They became the first group of airplanes to cross the United States in less than four hours, and Brady's time was three hours and forty-five minutes. I worked in isolation of their efforts, but their flight lent great impetus to further development of the concept.

Within thirty days of my proposal to COMOPTEVFOR, I sold the project to evaluate the tactical effectiveness of in-flight refueling and to culminate with trials at sea. COMOPTEVFOR Project V168 was the title. We could now get a tanker assigned for the evaluation and new probes built for our fighters. Grumman Engineering Aircraft Corporation was of inestimable help in doing that and did many things off-the-cuff to make the project a success. That close Navy-industry cooperation enabled many things to be done in a short time frame. The in-flight refueling tanker packages were old, the hoses brittle, and the fueling baskets into which we plugged our probes were rickety and beat up. At times it was discouraging, but gradually we piled up reason upon reason why in-flight refueling was not only tactically useful but also absolutely needed.

In late May 1954 three others and I flew to the Vought plant in Dallas to pick up four of the early models of the F7U-3 Cutlass. Those airplanes still had the interim J-35 engines because the J-46 engine had not yet fully met its design criteria. We returned with those airplanes to Atlantic City and modified them for in-flight refueling. That modification led to an interesting episode.

Monk Russell was to fly a broadcast control flight in the F7U-3 and to complete an air-refueling evaluation as well. He had not flown an air-refueling flight previously so I gave him a procedures briefing. After flying his broadcast control flight, Monk rendezvoused with the AJ-1 tanker at 20,000 feet. As he slid his F7U-3 in behind the tanker to receive fuel, the tanker pilot dutifully streamed the drogue. Monk concentrated on positioning his nose refueling probe so as to plug into the drogue basket on his first attempt. This took concentration and coordination. We found the best method was simply to line up a few feet behind the drogue with a three-to-four-knot speed differential and just drive the probe into the drogue, which seemed to stop pilots from chasing the drogue and missing. The take-up reel in the drogue package reduced the shock of impact and prevented the 50 feet of hose between the drogue and the tanker from behaving like a limp piece of spaghetti. Monk was concentrating so hard that he failed to see that the old, brittle fuel hose had parted just forward of the drogue, and the drogue was hanging by a single, thin hose-support wire. Monk, concentrating intently on the basket, plugged in and then looked in wonder at that small wire. He later said that he could not comprehend how he was to get fuel through something as small as that. In fact, if any fuel had been given, he would have had a full bath of it, and one or both engines probably would have exploded.

Monk quickly realized that all was not right and backed away from the tanker. When he did, the wire parted, leaving the drogue on the front of his probe. The F7U-3 had an airstream sensing vane on the left side of the nose that provided attitude information to the flight control system. Monk was not aware of that vane, and in the process of evaluating the flying qualities of his "modified" F7U-3, he slowed up the airplane to test it, fortunately at altitude. As he slowed to 135 knots, the F7U-3 performed a quick snap roll and scared Monk to death. Monk was often a voluble man, and he let go with a string of invectives that would have curled the hair of any sailor and greatly enlivened the VHF communications channel he was using. By the time he got back to Atlantic City to land, Monk had us all up in the tower to watch. It was a tribute to his flying ability that he got the airplane on the ground. Monk never tired of telling the story, which became more dramatic each time he told it.

It takes time and effort to integrate a new airplane into the fleet. Each new airplane brings new technology and improved equipment. Those upgrades drive the need for change or new tactics and often have a direct safety impact. That is why caution and good sense are stressed so strongly in tactical procedures investigation and integration and why experienced pilots are sought to do this job. Sometimes even that is not enough. In the late summer one of VX-3's Marine officers, Captain Vince Marzello, returned to NAS Atlantic City from an indoctrination flight and proceeded to make a touch-and-go landing in his F7U-3. After landing he added power and took off again and raised the landing gear. As he did so and turned downwind at 500 feet, his F7U-3 suddenly did a half snap roll to the left and dove directly into the ground. He was killed instantly.

With the aid of Vought, VX-3 sifted through the wreckage for clues as to why such an abrupt maneuver would occur in the F7U-3. Reconstruction of complex airplanes that have undergone massive destruction is complex in itself, but no stone was left unturned. After weeks of investigation, it was found that when the landing gear was retracted, through a design error the nose wheel steering mechanism was not disengaged as it should have been. Vince used left rudder in his turn downwind, and the nose wheel turned in the nose wheel well. As it turned, it impinged directly on a connecting rod that led to one of the power actuators for an elevon, or combined aileron and elevator, on the tail-less F7U-3. The airplane snap rolled because of that erroneous control input, and Vince was so low in the landing pattern that he had no time to escape. The design for the nose wheel was changed, and that never happened again.

Unfortunately, on occasion early models of an airplane can exhibit such problems, though much less often today than then. More recently, some relatives of military pilots killed in accidents have sought legal recourse and restitution from the airplane manufacturer. I find that most regrettable. Pilots and aircraft manufacturers do the very best that they can. We pilots know the risk, and, in fact, that risk makes flying more interesting to some. Going to the civil courts to press a claim against a manufacturer for things that went wrong in design was not even a consideration in the 1950s

The development of personal flight equipment was greatly needed in the very early 1950s. In the spring of 1954 fellow VX-3 squadron mate Lieutenant Tom Turnbull was flying an F2H-3 Banshee when he flamed out over the Atlantic while conducting broadcast control intercepts. Unable to relight either engine and being far out at sea, Tom ejected from his airplane and descended safely to the supercold waters of the Atlantic only to drown because he could not undo his parachute fittings and slip free of the parachute. Pilots can drown in their parachutes in calm weather, and they can also drown by being dragged through the seas in high winds when they cannot undo their buckles—a more violent death. Tom's accident led to the design of better quick-release fittings for our parachutes. Tom's accidental death and many others led to great interest and improvements in personal survival equipment. This was not just a VX-3 initiative; it was Navy and Air Force wide, and many pilots pursued this new interest. Pilots' helmets were improved and made lighter so they would not unduly stress the neck, while still effectively protecting the pilot's head in a survivable accident. Flying boots were designed with steel toe inserts to prevent the loss of toes on the forward canopy rim when ejecting. Special knives were designed so that pilots could snag and sever parachute risers if quick-release fittings could not be reached, and small handheld signal flares were devised for emergency signaling. Pilot equipment design was foremost in our minds as the new and more powerful jet airplanes came into the fleet, and many companies were created to meet this interest, while flight surgeons championed the need. One such person, in particular, was Lieutenant Frank Austin of the Medical

Corps, who was both a flight surgeon and a naval aviator. Frank graduated from flight training at Pensacola after returning from a tour with the Marines in Korea. He joined us in VX-3 and made up for his initial inexperience with his enthusiasm and drive to improve aviator equipment. He became a leading light in developing better survival equipment.

In 1954 many more senior and experienced naval aviators still had not transitioned to jet airplanes, and it fell to some of us in VX-3 to create our own jet pilots for projects. We transitioned prop pilots to jets in the F9F-7 and -8 because they were aerodynamically honest and easy to fly. Most made the transition easily, some more easily than others.

One transitioning pilot was Commander Saxe Perry Gants, a gentleman and a good naval officer. He had flown blimps for years and, of course, had mastered airplanes as well. Saxe arrived at VX-3 as next senior to Monk Russell, and as such, Monk was obligated to make him executive officer. Monk asked me to check out Saxe in jets as a way to work him into the squadron's flying. Saxe was a good thinker, and he studied diligently.

The day came when Saxe knew all the systems in the F9F-7, and he should fly. He manned his airplane, and we went over the cockpit one last time. Then I manned mine, and we taxied out together. Saxe took off and climbed to altitude to feel out the airplane by doing stalls and other basic maneuvers, and I stayed in a loose wing position. After some time it became clear to me that he was about twenty seconds behind the airplane and just never seemed to catch up. Still later it became clearer that, although Saxe was probably an accomplished blimp pilot, the F9F-7 was flying him rather than the other way around. We returned to the airfield at Atlantic City for him to make a few obligatory touch-and-go landings and takeoffs before ending the flight.

Saxe was in the lead, and I was still flying a loose wing position. He put his wheels and flaps down and made a long final approach to the landing runway. That runway was 6,000 feet long with a GCA trailer parked off its left side about 2,000 feet from the approach end. Saxe landed on the runway at a higher than normal speed—but seemed all right. Then suddenly he veered left off the runway onto the dirt and grass between the runway and a parallel taxiway. He stirred up a great cloud of dust as he went around the GCA trailer, just missing it, and careened back onto the runway to take off again. The radar crewmen spilled out of the GCA trailer like ants coming from an anthill. I have never seen anything like it before or since, and the airplane made one of the nicest recoveries that I have ever seen from a potentially disastrous, pilot-caused event.

Saxe eventually landed safely. Later Monk gave him an AD-5W and told him to go on a long cross-country flight to gain more fixed-wing experience and to check in by telephone every week or so. The GCA crewmen were eventually talked into remanning their trailer. Saxe just could not make the transition to jet flying, and orders to Washington and a desk job were waiting for him when he returned from his six-week cross-country trip.

Aviation safety is highly dependent upon remaining current in the airplanes that you fly, and it is safer to fly more rather than less. Air Force Atlantic Fleet (AIRLANT) recognized that fact; it encouraged pilots to meet a required minimum amount of flying and also authorized flying on cross-country flights on weekends as a way for pilots to build additional experience. Also, we were required to fly our new airplanes a certain number of hours to see what might break first and to determine how the airplanes held up under rigorous flying schedules. Cross-country flights were one way to put a large number of flight hours on an airplane in a relatively short time.

When the F9F-7 was introduced to the fleet, we set about to put as much flying time on the six assigned airplanes as we could. Many of us flew on cross-country flights on the weekends. Lieutenant Ed Morgan and I planned such a cross-country flight from Atlantic City to the El Toro, California, Marine Corps air station and back on one weekend in mid-June 1954. Ed and I had known each other in Pasadena where Ed had attended South Pasadena High School while I had attended Pasadena Junior College. Ed entered the Naval Academy the year after I tried and failed and graduated in 1946. After the obligatory two years of service in surface ships following his graduation, Ed applied for flight training and received his wings. He was one of our project officers as well as the administrative officer of the squadron.

We left Atlantic City about noon on Friday and planned the flight to stop for fuel at Craig AFB, Alabama; NAS Dallas, Texas; and El Paso International Airport—noted for a good, fast civil contract fueling capability. The flight was uneventful, and we flew in a two-plane formation, alternating the lead and stopping as planned. We refueled in El Paso in the late afternoon where it was clear, warm, and dry. Density altitude (the combination of an airfield's altitude above sea level and temperature, which can adversely affect aircraft performance) is an element of flying that pilots frequently do not take fully into consideration. However, we discussed the performance penalty that came with high temperatures and high altitude, particularly at El Paso.

We grabbed a quick sandwich and took off at 1900 local time for the flight to El Toro. I was going to lead this leg of the flight, and we agreed that we would make individual takeoffs because of the high density altitude and rendezvous as we flew west from El Paso. The F9F-7 was known as a gutless wonder because of its relatively low thrust and high gross weight. I took off and cleared the field boundary to climb west on course at reduced power, so that Ed could catch up. When he did not show up, I called El Paso's tower to see if he had taken off. The tower informed me that his airplane was burning at the end of the runway. I immediately reversed course and flew back to El Paso to find that the tower controller had made a gross understatement. Ed's airplane had crashed along a street extending from the runway, and a number of cars and what was left of his airplane were now burning about one-half mile from the field.

It was readily apparent that Ed had been killed instantly. His airplane was destroyed as it slammed to the ground and slid down the street, hitting about fifteen automobiles. Miraculously, no one else was hurt or killed. All the children and their parents had been inside their homes at dinner, and no one had been on the street. As I walked back along the path of his airplane, I saw that Ed's right wing had clipped the top of a telephone pole at the end of the 10,000-foot runway. That impact must have tripped the airplane and thrown it into the ground, where it then careered up the street on fire. The 9,000 pounds of jet fuel on board had fed the blaze.

It is one thing to deal with the many issues created by an accident with the help of others, and it is an entirely different thing to do that as an individual far from support. I called the squadron and, with Monk's concurrence, asked Mary to notify Anne, Ed wife. I called my father, waiting for us at El Toro, and he in turn notified Ed's father in South Pasadena. I made sure that the accident wreckage was preserved for the accident board to be convened later in El Paso and that the mortuary in El Paso prepared Ed's remains for shipment to Pasadena, where Anne wanted him to be buried. I flew to El Toro, met the casket at Los Angeles International Airport, and sent it to the mortuary in Pasadena. The next day I met Anne on her arrival in Southern California and spent time with her and Ed's father before the funeral to help them do the many things that must be done. I arranged for local naval representation at the graveside ceremony, and it was I who handed Anne the carefully folded flag that had covered Ed's coffin at the graveside and expressed the nation's gratitude to Anne for Ed's service to his country before he was buried. Those events were some of the hardest with which I have had to cope. I returned to Atlantic City alone in my F9F-7.

An interesting event that typified our flight operations at VX-3 occurred two months later when Lieutenant Junior Grade Bob Basso and I were to fly two F9F-8s to Cleveland to participate in the National Air Races on September 4, 5, and 6. We made a two-airplane section-formation takeoff from Atlantic City on September 3. During takeoff Bob's right wheel tire blew out, causing him to abort, while I continued my takeoff—as the safest thing to do. Bob's airplane careered onto the dirt midfield at the side of the runway, creating a large cloud of dust and doing some damage to his airplane before he came to a stop upright and otherwise unhurt. I orbited overhead, watching as things were sorted out on the ground. Monk Russell also saw the event and rushed flight surgeon

Frank Austin to the scene to see if Bob was hurt. Frank assessed Bob physically and mentally on the spot and asked how he felt, to which Bob replied, "Fine." Then, with Bob's concurrence, he and his luggage were rushed to another F9F-8, and within minutes he taxied out to take off and join me overhead. We proceeded to the Cleveland Air Races where we flew a two-airplane acrobatic demonstration on each of the three days before the crowds. Major John Glenn, then at Patuxent River, also was on the program and did an impressive solo acrobatic demonstration in an FJ-2.

We frequently took our projects to sea in any available aircraft carrier. That fall pilot carrier qualifications in USS *Bennington*, TACAN and air-to-air refueling projects in USS *Midway*, steam catapult trials in *Ticonderoga*—the second U.S. carrier to have the steam catapult after *Hancock*—and new arresting gear trials in USS *Lake Champlain* all made interesting and challenging flying in many different kinds of airplanes.

Lieutenant Commander Marvin Franger was the project officer for the low-level-navigation concept project, and before him the project officer had been Lieutenant Randall Prothro. Marv had had a great deal of experience fighting in World War II, and in VX-3 he was flying the Douglas AD-4 Skyraider single-engine, single-seat attack aircraft for uncommonly long flights. He frequently flew for ten hours and occasionally for up to twelve hours at altitudes of less than 100 feet. That is a long time for a single-pilot airplane and created great physiological and mental challenges. That kind of flying was very demanding as he and his project pilots determined what was feasible and what was not. Much of what they did set the operating procedures for Navy attack-aircraft navigation and delivery of nuclear weapons for the rest of the 1950s and 1960s. The public and the CAA tolerated those low-level-navigation flights, but I think that was because Marv and his pilots rarely flew the same route, and in any case, in those days the public was less apt to complain.

Lieutenant Commander Whitey Feightner wanted to see how that low-level navigation translated to jet flying and to find out if a pilot not trained in low-level navigation might be able to fly such a flight for a great distance. He reasoned that the answer to that question might significantly affect training efforts. I volunteered to be the guinea pig to try to fly at 50 feet and 300 knots in an F2H-2P photo airplane from Atlantic City over a planned route to a dam in central Ohio.

I prepared for the flight using many aeronautical sectional charts and marked my path along the way using easily recognizable points, such as a bridge over a river, a prominent hill or cliff, the confluence of two rivers, or a major highway intersection. The test rules said that I could use no radio or electronic navigation equipment. The entire flight had to be visual, and for obvious reasons I purposefully avoided large cities or big airports. There was no way that we were going to tell the CAA what we were doing because they would not have sanctioned it anyway.

On the appointed day I launched with my charts all folded sequentially in the cockpit. I dropped down to 50 feet to clear the low scrub trees of New Jersey and navigated across the Garden State without seeing too much. I crossed the Delaware River north of Philadelphia and struck off across Pennsylvania, staying at less than 50 feet and keeping my speed at about 300 knots. Up the hills and down the other side, following the contour of the ground, I carefully identified my first navigation points and, using my pencil and knee pad, tried to record time and checkpoints without flying into wires, trees, or houses. The checkpoints were much harder to identify than I had thought, and I began to think that Whitey might be justified in questioning whether low-level navigation could be done without additional training.

I flew over one backyard in which a lady was hanging out her sheets to dry and caught her pinning the second of two clothespins on a sheet as she looked up with her mouth open in amazement. I whipped over her and was gone before she could change her expression. I passed rural garages and gas stations where motorists and attendants did not have time to look up before I was gone. I never saw those swimming pools or sunbathers the helicopter pilots all talk about, and slowly I began to miss an occasional checkpoint as I passed north of Pittsburgh.

The concentration required to go over or under wires and fly around tall trees and towers was consuming all my attention at 300 knots. I did not have time to record my arrival times at the checkpoints as I had planned. The novelty of low flying wore off, and I became more aware of how hard it is to identify things at 50 feet while flying at high speed. It was an entirely different perspective. Finally, north of Appleton, Ohio, and after almost two hours of flying, I could no longer identify my checkpoints. I was not going to find my target, and I had to admit I was lost. I climbed to altitude to see just where I was and then returned to Atlantic City disappointed in my performance.

I wrote my flight report, detailing what had occurred. Low-level-navigation route training is a must, and we should plan to have routes and syllabi that will enable our pilots to train adequately. Such flying cannot be a one shot affair. My hat is off to the thousands of Navy, Army, and Air Force pilots who subsequently trained in low-level navigation. It requires finesse and experience to be done successfully.

Aircraft paint schemes in the Navy have varied widely over the years. In the 30s all carrier aircraft were painted light gray-blue with vivid identification markings of red, yellow, or blue. Also, yellow wings enhanced visibility. For a time rudders were painted with red and white stripes, and the national insignia was a blue roundel with a white star and red dot in the center. When World War II started, those easily distinguished markings were immediately muted, and our national insignia was standardized without the red dot in the center of the star, so it would not be confused with the Japanese meatball. Gone were the individual and squadron markings. Toward the end of the war, the undersides of aircraft were painted a dull off-white or light gray to blend with clouds when viewed from below. Light blue-gray on tops of the wings and fuselage was used to blend into the water below when viewed from above. There were variations, but generally naval aircraft conformed to that scheme until late in World War II when some aircraft were painted black for night missions.

Following World War II all naval aircraft were painted dark blue, and gradually individual squadron colors began to show up again on vertical fin or wing tips for easy recognition of that squadron's aircraft. Red denoted the first fighter squadron; yellow denoted the second fighter squadron; and blue, green and orange were used sequentially for the other three squadrons. The basic color of Navy airplanes continued to change periodically in the postwar years. Slowly, after the Korean War, individual squadron paint schemes crept back as squadrons experimented and quietly tested the authority of the Navy's Air Force Atlantic and Pacific Fleet commands. Many squadron commanding officers held to the traditional no-frills standard paint scheme of World War II, but gradually red and white checkered tails and wide swatches of yellow, red, or blue showed up on squadron aircraft in the 1950s. By 1956 one Atlantic Fleet squadron under the command of Commander Cliff MacDougal even had the MacDougal tartan painted over the entire vertical fin and rudder until the Atlantic Fleet defined stricter guidelines.

Cockpit paint colors also changed. For a while black instrument panels were thought to set off the visual importance of certain instruments. Those panels gradually were changed to dark gray and then light gray to enhance the pilot's vision when he looked into the far reaches of his cockpit to see the levers and switches that always seemed to be placed in the far left or right and aft panels. In 1955 some stalwart aviation physiologist decided light green was a good color for the cockpit of the FJ-3. When I asked what the purpose of such color was, I was told that it was neutral and soothing to the pilot! That operating room green was the most bilious color imaginable, but eventually we became used to it—just about the time that it was done away with.

In the same way that color changed in aircraft, cockpit lighting changed too. Over the years the Navy had a love-hate relationship with red and white lighting. We moved back and forth depending on which psychological design camp held power in naval aviation. The reds eventually won, but not before we vacillated back and forth over the years from 1940 to 1955. For a while we had soft white backlighting from behind the instrument panel. Then we had post lighting reflected back at the instruments and then red backlighting of panels and instruments. By 1955 we seemed to settle on small reddish white flective post lighting for the instrument panel and etched side panels backlit with bright red for switch identification or text.

By 1955 we also progressed to red-lit rectangular cockpit warning indicators. Those were placed strategically about the cockpit near the gauge, indicator, or lever and were meant to provide quick recognition for any change of status. The pilot was never quite sure where to look for those warnings, and so your gaze would sweep the cockpit panels frequently to stay abreast of the current airplane condition. *HYD1* and *HYD2* for hydraulic systems were good attention getters. *FIRE* could always get the adrenaline going. But then there could be different kinds of fire, so the indicators evolved to *ELECT FIRE* for electrical fire as opposed to *FIRE* for one in the engine bay or plenum chamber. It was a truism that a malfunction in any warning system would most likely be in the fire warning system. A flickering *FIRE* warning light can focus a pilot's attention as no other light can. Eventually, the warning lights were gathered into one convenient warning master light panel that eased the pilot's scan challenge.

Every pilot has a favorite aircraft. The degree of enthusiasm for that aircraft is directly related to its handling qualities. Some airplanes are more complex than others, and some fly better than others, but each is interesting in its own right. The North American FJ-3 Fury, a distant relative of the FJ-1 and a follow-on to its progenitor, the underpowered FJ-2, was such an airplane. For me it was love at first flight.

The FJ-3, with its J-65 engine of 6,600 pounds of thrust, was nimble to fly and light to the touch. Visibility was excellent, and the cockpit was organized in a simple, straightforward manner. Of all the airplanes that I had flown up to that time, the FJ-3 had the best flying qualities. When you strapped it on and took off, you and the airplane became one. That feeling is difficult to achieve, and I place great credit for it with two fine test pilots, Jim Pearce, chief test pilot at North American Aviation, Columbus Division, and his deputy, Dick Wenzel. Both Jim and Dick were former Navy fighter pilots, and they created the flying qualities of the FJ-3. Dick, of course, had joined VF-51 in 1951 after our first Korean War cruise and subsequently left the Navy to work for North American. Jim Pearce had previously lost one of his lower legs to cancer and had an artificial foot, on the heel of which he taped a felt pad for leverage so he could use his right brake when taxiing. There were no limits to his great ability.

Living near us on Ryon Avenue were two other Navy families. Two doors up the street were Commander Ralph and Ida Lois Werner and their five daughters. Ralph, the operations officer of VC-4, was another early night fighter in the Atlantic Fleet. Our daughter, Candace, and the Werner girls were inseparable. Ralph was a great leader of men. In the next block were Lieutenant B. B. (Bud) and Sally Gear and their two daughters and two sons. Bud and I were matched in rank, experience, and views of tactics and formed a strong friendship. We respected each other. Neither of us was a social lion, and when we were home, we spent time with our families, trying to make up for the time that we were away. Ida Lois Werner and Sally Gear were strong Navy wives like Mary. They took life as it was, raised their families, and became good friends.

Early in 1955 Bud Gear left VX-3 to become executive officer in an F2H-4 Banshee squadron in Jacksonville. I inherited the FJ-3 den and became responsible for fleet tactical development of the airplane. We conducted the air-refueling project, TACAN work for instrument approaches and for broadcast control intercepts, and the evaluation of the Sidewinder missile—just then coming to the fleet. The FJ-3 was fuel limited, just as all high-performance jet airplanes seemed to be. It carried only enough fuel internally for about one hour of flight, but two external fuel drop tanks gave the airplane an easy two hours in the air, depending on throttle use and the altitude at which you flew. The weight and drag penalty of the tanks was not onerous, but it was noticeable.

One Saturday morning in early 1955, while flying alone and without external tanks, I climbed to 54,000 feet over Atlantic City. The clear, crisp morning sky was a deep blue, and I could see from upstate New York to southern Virginia. CAA flight plans for our local flights were unknown, and I was free to do what I wished, particularly at that altitude. With my evaluation tasks completed, I decided on the spur of the moment to shut down the engine and see how long it would take me to glide down to 10,000 feet, where I planned to restart the engine and return to the field. That was not one of the more brilliant decisions that I ever made in an airplane because I immediately lost all cabin pressurization. I watched with considerable interest and concern as the cabin altimeter unwound like a clock gone amok. I found myself pressure breathing on oxygen at a cabin altitude of 54,000 feet, just as on our B-36 intercepts years earlier, only this time it was of more concern. Back then we had had service ceilings at or below 45,000 feet. In 1955 we were admonished not to fly at cabin altitudes over 50,000 feet because at some magical altitude, if you were not wearing a pressure suit, your blood would boil, and you would die. I could not recall what that altitude was, but obviously it was not 54,000 feet because although my lungs filled under pressure every time that I opened my mouth, I remained conscious. My blood did not boil, so I decided to make the best of the situation and to glide at the airplane's best glide speed of 205 knots and trade altitude for time and distance. It took sixteen minutes to reach 10,000 feet, where I relit the engine to return to NAS Atlantic City. I never chose to do that again.

In April 1955 I received my orders to be executive officer of Fighter Squadron 21 (VF-21), then at NAS Oceana, Virginia, but I would not detach from VX-3 until July. VF-21 was receiving the newest FJ-3s later that summer.

Meanwhile we continued to evaluate the FJ-3 carrying Sidewinders and firing the 20mm cannon. We flew the airplanes on board USS *Lake Champlain* on May 31 to carrier qualify our FJ-3 pilots. At the same time, the Carrier Suitability Branch of Patuxent's Flight Test Division was evaluating the next iteration of arresting gear engines for aircraft carriers. The FJ-3 passed its carrier trials with flying colors and continued to please all the pilots who flew it.

In mid-June I was invited to Columbus to fly the newest version of the FJ-3, the FJ-3M. The 1950s were a time of great aerodynamic experimentation and continual improvement. New means of drag reduction were found, and airplane wings were modified to make them more effective across the broad spectrum of flight. Instead of the movable slats of the FJ-3, the wings of the FJ-3M had fixed, fully cambered leading edges. Previously, the FJ-3 could build up a dangerous amount of ice at mid and low altitudes. Now, hot air from the engine's sixth-stage compressor could be routed through the leading edge of the wing to prevent icing buildup. The airplane also had a new rudder, called a splitter rudder, that improved its effectiveness while reducing drag. This was nothing more than a rudder with a flat plate of aluminum beginning at about midchord, strengthened by about ten aluminum ribs. A permanent in-flight refueling probe was placed under the left wing inboard of the left drop tank as well. The airplane flew like a dream at both low and high speeds, and I was again impressed by its handling qualities. The Air Force F-86H also used the cambered leading-edge wing.

In December 1954 COMOPTEVFOR Project V98 was established to evaluate landing aids and, particularly, the same British mirror that I had evaluated and recommended earlier. Our Navy purchased three mirrors from the British for trials while the design challenge for stabilization was being met. Quite coincidentally, its designer, Lieutenant Commander Nick Goodhart RN, was now assigned to Her Majesty's embassy in Washington. On January 31 I flew the first flight to use the mirror. It was the same mirror, still not stabilized for the ship's pitch and roll, but it was rewarding for me to see how well it worked and to hear the other pilots' enthusiasm for the system. We used the mirror for every landing and gained experience on each flight. Someone in VX-3, either Lieutenant Ken Sharp or Lieutenant Lucky Finch, likened the reflected image in the mirror to the round, red insignias of the Japanese in World War II—the meatball—and it was reported in flight that way. *Meatball* was shortened to *ball* and is used to this day.

Procedures, set in motion over time, are very difficult to change. We found this to be particularly true in attempting to alter the role of the LSO in view of the capabilities of the mirror. The duties and responsibilities of the LSO were ingrained into every ship-based naval aviator. Senior officers and LSOs particularly were dedicated to that thinking. No pilot ever argued with the LSO when he critiqued that pilot's landing pass. The LSO's word was law. For the first time the mirror gave the pilot a means to know exactly where he was on the glide path—a better way. That knowledge challenged the LSO's authority. Then began some mighty arguments throughout the Navy about the LSO's authority. The deciding factor became the need to maintain safety on the flight deck and to ensure airspeed control. The LSO was retained as the person to have the authority to accept or to deny a landing.

Strict rules have been developed over many years of flight deck operation to control closely what should and should not be done during flight operations. The air officer is responsible for seeing that all flight operations from, onto, and around the flight deck are conducted expeditiously and safely. He delegates a great deal of authority to the LSOs and catapult officers so that in the press of operations safety will be foremost. On the flight deck trust and confidence are absolute requirements, and each person who works on or flies off the flight deck places his or her life in the hands of others who must do their jobs with precision.

The LSO and the air officer work extremely closely. Before World War II and until 1945, the LSO was assigned to the ship's air department. In fact, during World War II some LSOs were not pilots. That did not work well. In the post–World War II years, because air groups were ashore for much of their training time, the LSOs were assigned to the air groups. Initially, and until well into the 1950s, they were assigned to the air group staff, and then gradually their assistants became squadron pilots under training to become LSOs. Today the LSO hierarchy is more complex. Each fleet has a short LSO school, and there are different grades of LSOs from squadron, to air wing, to staff LSO. While I respect LSOs, I think we could do much better. LSOs are not unlike air traffic controllers—they tend to be self-perpetuating.

Into that broad argument about what the LSO should and should not do came Lieutenant K. H. (Ken) Sharp, VX-3's LSO. He was a fellow pilot and project officer, and it fell to him to ensure the mirror was rigged at the proper angle and aligned with respect to the runway. As most LSOs do, Ken had a hard shell and quick tongue, and he could give as much as he could take. In fact, Ken gave much more than he received. The pilots in VX-3 were quick to realize that the mirror gave them greater independence from the LSO, and the standing joke was to present Ken with a clean rag and to tell him to go polish his mirror whenever he became too full of himself.

Underneath all that, Ken was smart enough to see that there was a philosophical challenge to the previously unquestioned authority of the LSO. That could have great safety ramifications in our carrier operations. Ken sought support from AIRLANT, and there were a number of conferences to discuss the philosophy of the LSO's authority.

At that time we still had many piston-engine-powered airplanes that required a cut signal to retard the throttle to land on the deck. Most carriers were still straight deck carriers. The timing of the cut determined how far down the flight deck the pilot would touch down. One obvious possibility was to retain the authority of the LSO and provide him with cut and wave off lights on the mirror. Those lights were added, and the LSO was, indeed, kept in the decision loop for carrier landings. The strong authority relationship between the LSO and the air officer was maintained.

After my departure from VX-3 on August 22, 1955, Commander R. G. Dosé and others flew on board *Bennington* using the mirror, and in September the Navy announced that the mirror would be procured for all carriers. So, again, an experiment with a ladies' pocket mirror by a Royal Navy officer in 1951 and some trials of a prototype by two U.S. naval aviators flying Royal Navy jets onto a Royal Navy carrier in 1953 led to the VX-3 trials and U.S. Navy acceptance in 1955 of a landing aid that would revolutionize and make eminently more safe our carrier operations. Also, in September of 1955 the Navy announced that all fighter aircraft in production would be fitted with the in-flight refueling capability. I felt very proud and satisfied as I ended my tour in VX-3.

As we approached the mid-1950s, naval aviation was entering a golden age of airplanes. Many new fighter and attack airplanes were being developed for the Navy by Douglas, McDonnell, North American, and Grumman, and those planes were rolling off production lines. There was a great diversity of carrier airplanes in the fleet. Many of those airplanes were only in the fleet for one to two years before their performance was eclipsed, and they were phased out. Each new model brought new improvements as we leapfrogged ahead.

Mary, the children, and I left Atlantic City in mid-July 1955 in a confused state. According to my orders to VF-21, I was to go first to the University of Southern California for a six-week-long aviation safety course and then to return to the East Coast to NAS Oceana, Virginia, to report as executive officer.

Things did not work out quite that way. Commander Max Harnish, commanding officer of VF-21, had my orders changed at the last moment as I was leaving Atlantic City. The family already had made plans for the trip to California, but Max felt that it was more important that I be on board to help with the planned squadron transition from the F9F-6 to the FJ-3. The change of orders did not sit well with either Mary or the children and created a severe family morale problem. Eventually that was sorted out. We drove to Minnesota for a fifteen-day family vacation. Then Mary and Candace flew to California for a visit, while our two boys attended six weeks of summer camp in Virginia. I went on to Oceana alone to find a place for us to live.

9. RETURN TO THE FLEET
JULY 1955 TO MAY 1957

Boeing began building the B707 jet airplane. Nikita Khrushchev denounced Joseph Stalin, and an anticommunist revolution in Hungary was brutally put down by the Soviets, raising the ire of Western nations. Gamal Nasser, new president of Egypt, nationalized the Suez Canal, and Britain and France retaliated by attacking Egypt to keep the canal open to all nations. The U.S. Sixth Fleet evacuated U.S. nationals in the Middle East. Dwight Eisenhower was reelected president and proposed a doctrine to provide aid to Middle Eastern countries. In 1957 he sent federal troops to Arkansas to enforce desegregation while Congress enacted civil rights legislation. And, in 1957, the Soviet Union and China kept pressure on the United States in the Far East by increasing deployment of their submarine forces along with increased air activity at sea.

There were 17,457 pilots, 135,600 aviation ratings, and 30 aircraft carriers of all types in the U.S. Navy. Airborne Early Warning Wing Pacific was formed at Barbers Point on Oahu. The McDonnell F3H-1 Demon jet fighter joined the Atlantic Fleet, and the first Douglas A3D-1 Sky Warrior was delivered to VAH-1 at Patuxent River. Top fleet gunnery honors went to VF-112 of AIRPAC and to VF-43 of AIRLANT. The last scheduled flight for the Martin Mars flying boats ended at Alameda, and the last AD-7 Sky Raider was delivered to the Navy at Douglas El Segundo. Two Vought F8U-1 Crusader jet fighters and two A3D-1s were flown nonstop from USS Bon Homme Richard *on the West Coast to USS* Saratoga *off the East Coast, and John Glenn broke the transcontinental speed record in an F8U-1.*

In July I left Mary and Candace in Minnesota, and I drove to Virginia Beach, Virginia, to report to VF-21, based at NAS Oceana. Subsequently, I found the reason for my being in VF-21 was due in large part to Commander Ralph Werner, our former neighbor in Pleasantville, New Jersey, who had preceded me to Oceana to take command of Air Task Group (ATG) 181. He picked me as his ace in the hole for VF-21 because he was concerned about the low experience level in the squadron.

ATG 181 was composed of VF-21, flying FJ-3s and commanded by Commander W. M. (Max) Harnish; VF-41, flying F2H-4s and commanded by Lieutenant Commander W. H. (Tag) Livingston; VA-86, flying F7U-3s and commanded by Commander Pearly Gates; and finally VA-42, flying AD-6s and commanded by Commander L. H. (Lew) Squires.

Air task groups were the Navy's way to create greater flexibility in air group deployments. They were intended to provide better deployment rotation for shorter family separations as well as improved Navy combat potential. The numbers of Navy air groups were authorized annually by Congress in the Navy budget. But the Navy could take one squadron from each authorized air group and then combine them into air task groups.

VF-21, the day-fighter squadron of the group, was an interesting mix of the old and the new in experience. Max Harnish, the commanding officer, had flown last in an AD squadron and was just transitioning to jets. Max was a bright naval officer with a Germanic disposition and little sense of humor. As executive officer, I provided the greatest amount of jet experience. Lieutenant Commander Jo Humes, a tall, lanky Naval Academy graduate, had a bit of jet experience. Jo had an easygoing, wry wit and seemed able to identify well with the squadron pilots. There were four lieutenants with varied squadron and jet flying experience, followed by six lieutenants junior grade, three of whom had made the previous deployment in VF-21. There were eleven ensigns newly graduated from flight training and the product of the newly integrated jet transitional training. The squadron experience level was about normal for the mid-1950s transition to jet flying in the Navy. Each pilot was pleased to be there and looked forward to the training cycle and subsequent deployment. Except for me, no one had flown the FJ-3 before.

I found a nice, four-bedroom brick house about 200 yards from the ocean on the corner of 45th Street and Atlantic Boulevard in Virginia Beach. A hurricane was forecast to hit the coast as I reported, and shortly after I joined the squadron, we flew our FJ-3 airplanes to Columbus, Ohio, for a brief stay until the hurricane had moved north of Oceana. After we returned, I moved our household effects from temporary storage into our house, hoping that I had the right things in the right rooms. In mid-August Mary and Candace arrived in Virginia Beach about the time the boys' summer camp was over, and the family spent the rest of the summer on the beach. That vacation atmosphere of Virginia Beach helped make up for the big change in our orders. The house was ideally suited for the family and for squadron parties on the beach. However, Mary never forgave Max Harnish for the abrupt change of our plans, and it clouded her relationship with him from then on.

The routine in AIRLANT had been that air groups would deploy to the Mediterranean for six months, after which they would return, and the officer personnel complement would disband while new officers coming from previous shore duty would re-form the squadron. The cycles seemed repetitive and lasted roughly eighteen to twenty-four months. The enlisted complement of squadrons rotated based upon the individual's length of time in the command, and the senior petty officers provided a continuum of technical maintenance talent. There was a decided difference in mien and tempo between the Atlantic and Pacific Fleets. In the Atlantic Fleet distances between countries were shorter, leading to briefer at-sea periods, thus shorter operating periods.

The squadron commanding officer was responsible for developing a training syllabus to qualify all new pilots in the weapons delivery capability for their particular airplanes. When that training syllabus was completed, usually in twelve to eighteen months, the squadrons would deploy as units of an air group. AIRLANT scheduled training and set the timing for group deployments. In August 1955 it was obvious to me that VF-21 had a great deal of training to conduct in the FJ-3 and its many systems. The FJ-3 with the 7,400-pound thrust J-65 engine was still not out of the maintenance problem stage. Lots of new things broke or needed to be fixed.

The squadron commanding officer was also responsible for morale, good order, and discipline, and he set the operational tone for the squadron. As executive officer, I was responsible to the commanding officer for the administration of the squadron. That essentially entailed ensuring that all housekeeping needs were seen to, that all reports and correspondence were correct and timely, and that the officers and men productively worked at their respective duties and obeyed all orders. The commanding officer did the fun stuff and was supposed to be the good guy; the executive officer did the grunt work and was supposed to be the bad guy. Almost immediately it became apparent to me, and I think to Max, that he was operationally in over his head. By unstated mutual agreement we slowly reversed our roles as best we could until months later when Max gained more jet experience. He was a superb administrator with an eye for detail, but he remained aloof from his squadron officers. Somebody has to be the good guy, or it would be a hell of a squadron, so I assumed that role and began cementing personal relationships together in the organization. The squadron officers used our house for parties, particularly weekend beach parties. Max and I danced around each other in this unsettled command relationship, and I was always careful to not undercut him as commanding officer. Eventually, we worked relatively well together, but not before I came close to being fired a few times, but by then he would not have done that because Ralph Werner would not have allowed that.

The squadron trained intensively during September, October, and November 1955. Intercept training, division offensive and defensive tactics, navigation, and FCLP were high on our list. I flew with every pilot, and it was clear that some were better than others, but the majority of the pilots responded aggressively to our training regimen and made good progress. Jo Humes and I worked hard to hone the flying skills of the others, and our wives became close friends as well. Max remained more distant, but he too threw himself into his job.

Naval aviators' lives depend on being totally professional with honor while developing the tactical skills necessary to fly their airplanes to the fullest. Some pilots can develop the necessary tactical skills. Some cannot. There is no place for lone eagles in any tactical organization. Such loners soon separate themselves from the team to their own and the squadron's detriment. Pilots are expected to conform, and if they do not, they soon find themselves on the outside looking in. To be sure, there is competition, and one must always try to be the best in the squadron, but the best squadrons depend on achieving professionalism through teamwork. A healthy spirit of competition exists between squadrons as well. No matter how good a sister squadron may be, it is always the second-best squadron.

Captain John Wolmers USAF was an exchange pilot from the Air Force's Air Defense Command and was assigned to VF-21. John had previously flown F-94Cs and F-86Ds, and he worked hard to merit the trust and confidence of his Navy compatriots in VF-21. He was a pilot perfectionist and brought a great deal of tactical skill and professionalism to the squadron as well. I always enjoyed flying with John because he understood his airplane's limitations and capabilities and he was not afraid to go anywhere. I could count on him to be on my wing regardless of our maneuver. He learned to do his ground job as well, that being a new concept to him. In Air Force squadrons, a pilot still had no responsibilities other than flying airplanes.

On December 20, 1955, we began to exchange our FJ-3s for even newer and more capable FJ-3Ms. They were equipped with the newly mandated air-refueling probes and new cambered leading-edge wings that dramatically improved the high-speed maneuvering and handling qualities of the airplane. Most importantly, the new airplanes could carry the new Sidewinder missile. One of the first things that I checked was to see if the airplane still had the FJ-3 tendency to drop the left wing as you flew through .92 or .93 Mach number. It did, but that was more of an aerodynamic oddity than a limitation. I believed the trait probably came from the jig in which the FJ-3 wing was manufactured. North American test pilot Jim Pearce had shown me how to keep the wing from dropping simply by bending it in the air. By slapping the stick to the left at low altitude and high speed, the pilot could literally put a set in the wings, just enough so that the next time you dived transonically you could accelerate to supersonic speed without the wing drop. That procedure certainly was more academic than useful because the next ham-fisted pilot to fly the airplane could cancel the set and the left wing would drop again.

We gave the new airplanes a flashy paint job with the squadron's assigned color, yellow. But we picked bright lemon yellow, almost an iridescent yellow. We reasoned that as long as yellow was our color we might as well make the most of it. Our sister, and night-fighter, squadron, VF-41, was assigned the color red. North American Aviation, Columbus Division, designed for us a yellow speed line that ran down each side of the fuselage, and we also put a broad yellow band on the tail. The Pacific Fleet squadrons were painting up their airplanes more than Atlantic Fleet squadrons were, but we livened up the East Coast. Also, I was pleased that the sickly operating room green cockpit paint was gone. Instead we had neutral gray panels that enhanced visibility inside the cockpit, particularly at altitude.

On October 1, 1955, USS *Forrestal*, the first of this new class of large aircraft carriers, was commissioned at the Newport News dry dock and shipbuilding facilities. Captain Roy L. Johnson became the commanding officer, and the ship was magnificently large and impressive. ATG 181 was selected to be the air group on board for the shakedown and training for USS *Forrestal*, and that was a great plum. We had not had a new aircraft carrier class in the Navy since the 1940s, and here was an opportunity to breathe aviation life into a new ship. The key officers and petty officers in the ship had come from other carriers and were experienced, but 90 percent of the crew were untrained, and *Forrestal* had never operated aircraft—the carrier had no corporate memory. It would be like moving into an entirely new city that had never had cars on its roads or used its fire department before. In such a case, there are procedures, but no one has ever practiced them, and launching or landing airplanes under those conditions can become sporty at times. We had about sixty days, including the Christmas leave, in which to get our own act together in VF-21 before deployment in *Forrestal* to Guantánamo Bay, Cuba, for this shakedown cruise.

In early November Ralph Werner and Max Harnish flew out to make the first carrier landings in *Forrestal*. Through a misunderstanding on the part of Commander Schwab, the air officer, Ralph was waved off at the last instant, and Max was allowed to make the first carrier landing in *Forrestal*. Ralph never forgave Commander Schwab, and of course Max was greatly pleased, but Ralph was too big a person to think about it for long.

ATG 181's squadrons were based at NAS Oceana, so it was a simple thing to prepare for the shakedown at Guantánamo. On the appointed day in January 1957, the airplanes were flown from NAS Oceana to NAS Norfolk and were loaded on board *Forrestal* at the naval operating base. The officers and crews of the squadrons boarded the night before we were to sail, and at the appointed time Captain Johnson had all the tugs made up for the ship to depart. But that was not to be, at least on this day. Winds of 20 knots were setting the ship down on the pier so hard that the ship literally could not leave, and we had to delay our departure for one day and sail for Cuba on Friday, January 27, for the shakedown of this great new aircraft carrier.

Forrestal looked and smelled new—everywhere. For the first time there were two officers' wardrooms instead of one. The enlisted messes were numerous and strategically placed. The hangar deck, always the main or first deck in aircraft carriers, was cavernous. There were three deck levels instead of two between the hangar and flight decks, which increased storage space for the squadrons. It was the first time that I had ever gone to sea in a carrier in which every squadron had room to stow all its equipment. The officers' staterooms, air operations areas, combat information center, and the many squadron offices were all located on the 03 level, just below the armored flight deck, which was magnificently large and offered great flexibility with its Royal Navy canted deck. The island structure rose above the flight deck to the 09 level, meaning this domain of the signal gang was nine decks above the hangar deck.

We in VF-21 and the other squadrons would have to forego some of our own needed training time to help the ship become a professional unit. Our job was to be as supportive as we could, while still trying to fly and train too. There is nothing more complex or beautiful than a working aircraft carrier; however, a lot must be done before you get to the working status. A new ship must first master its own functions before the air group can fly, and to make that happen, an incredible amount of talent must be mustered and training given down to the lowest seaman. That is particularly true for the critical flight deck crew, and now *Forrestal* had three catapults with new jet blast deflectors along with what was to be called the angled deck.

On January 28 *Forrestal* was just south of Cuba when the air group was first launched. We had not flown while en route because Captain Johnson wanted his crew to have the wisdom and training of the fleet training group at Guantánamo first. The three jet squadrons were launched and flew to the naval air facility at Leeward Point, on the west side of Guantánamo Bay. The ADs of VA-42 flew to McCalla Field, with its shorter runways, located on the east side of the bay. That evening *Forrestal* entered Guantánamo Bay and anchored to receive briefings from the fleet training group's refresher training team before beginning sixty days of intensive damage control and engineering plant training exercises and flying. The professional fleet training group knew how to provide just enough pressure and challenge without inundating the green crew. *Forrestal*'s crew members would slowly build their ability to handle the many functions of their city-sized ship.

Each morning *Forrestal* was made ready to sortie through simulated mine-fields with the crew in full battle dress and at general quarters stations. The ship's crew spent the busy day at sea conducting many intensive drills and each evening would navigate the ship back into port to anchor for the night. For five days a week this went on. On Saturdays and Sundays there was continued ship's work to address the many deficiencies noted the week before, while the fleet training group had time ashore with their families. Also, there were occasional weekend social functions and ship's company division picnics ashore.

Critical to the mission of any aircraft carrier is the ability to launch, recover, and handle the many different kinds of aircraft flying from the flight deck. The reason ATG 181 was deployed to Guantánamo Bay in *Forrestal* was to provide the necessary airplanes to land, take off, and move about the flight and hangar decks for training both the flight and hangar deck crews. The fleet training group monitored how aircraft were moved, spotted on the deck, and tied down; how the catapult teams functioned; and how the arresting gear crews functioned on deck and in the machinery spaces as well. Slowly, more and more aircraft were positioned on deck and more complex fire and crash drills were held until the fleet training group observers felt that the ship's crew were performing satisfactorily.

The four squadrons of ATG 181 had their own training to do as well, and it was sandwiched in between the required services for *Forrestal*. VF-21 and VF-41 provided training for the fighter directors in the ship's CIC. We would launch from Leeward Point and fly to the vicinity of the ship to provide the services required, all the while continuing to build our own individual and squadron tactical skills.

Utility Squadron 10 (VU-10) provided towing services for gunnery training for VF-21 at 15,000 and 25,000 feet. In the clear blue skies south of Cuba, divisions of four airplanes fired their four 20mm cannon at a 6-by-24-foot banner towed by twin-engine Douglas JD-1 airplanes. Frequently, at the end of a flight, there was time to put my division in trail or in tight formation and fly mild acrobatics such as loops, rolls, and Immelmanns. Soon my pilots felt comfortable flying in formation whether right side up or upside down.

One day at Leeward Point I mentioned to Max that I would like to form a squadron acrobatic team, and he quickly agreed. I named Lieutenant Junior Grade Tom Cassidy to fly left wing, Captain John Wolmers to fly right wing, and Lieutenant Commander Jo Humes to fly in the slot. We began by practicing when time was available so as not to interfere with the more important squadron training. We flew on Saturdays and Sundays and practiced over the Hicacal bombing target on the mudflats of Guantánamo Bay. We worked up a routine of maneuvers consisting of formation rolls, Immelmanns, Cuban eights, vertical fleur-de-lis breakups, and diamond-formation double Immelmanns. The team became very sharp at maintaining fixed position with only a foot or two of separation between airplanes, and we built great trust in each other's abilities. Skills learned in acrobatics are always important to fighter pilots.

We had one or two thrills as we trained. On one occasion we practiced our vertical fleur-de-lis break from which the four individual airplanes would depart to return over the same spot from four different directions. We did that, but we failed to talk about who would go high or low. The four opposing airplanes closed simultaneously at a relative speed of 1,000 knots and almost produced a fiery end to our team 50 feet above the ground. With that thrill behind us, we worked out who would go high or low and right or left. When we were good enough, we moved the practice to the runway at Leeward Point, and the ground crews and other pilots enjoyed the shows.

Lieutenant Jack Robinson was one of the pilots who had transitioned from the previous cruise in VF-21. One day in February his engine flamed out, and he managed to relight the engine and return to the field. Jack was a thorough but cautious pilot, who tried hard to be good but who lacked the natural grace of the excellent pilot. The maintenance crews could not duplicate his flameout on the ground no matter how hard they tried. Finally, not wanting that particular airplane to have an unknown problem, I took the airplane up late one afternoon to try to duplicate Jack's flameout. I had the entire sky to myself, since all the air group pilots had stopped flying for the day and were mustered at the Leeward Point BOQ outdoor patio bar.

I climbed directly to 42,000 feet and rolled inverted to point the nose of the FJ-3 at the Leeward Point BOQ below. The airplane quickly accelerated through Mach 1 as I dove intentionally to produce a sonic boom, knowing that the aerodynamic shock waves formed on the airplane would travel straight to the ground once I pulled out at 25,000 feet. The boom hit squarely on target, and having my compatriots' attention, I proceeded to wring out the airplane down to ground level with every maneuver that I knew, all the while seeing if I could duplicate Jack Robinson's flameout. I could not, and I put on a continuous thirty-minute effort that culminated in a double Immelmann executed from runway level. My goal was to show the VF-21 pilots that the airplane would not flame out because of a pilot-induced maneuver so as to build their confidence in the airplane. I landed and went to the BOQ patio, where my friends applauded. But I noted a warning glance from Ralph Werner, who seemed torn between chewing me out and patting me on the back. But he threw me a half-smile/half-frown and never said a word.

Placing a boom accurately did not always work. One night in February I was flying by myself at 45,000 feet after doing some night intercept training. Having completed the intercepts, I turned toward Leeward Point and looked down to see the field far below, beautifully outlined in red, blue, and green lights, shining like jewels. It was one of those clear, black, moonless tropical nights, and in exuberance more than anything else, I rolled over onto my back and pulled through to aim the airplane straight down at where I thought the control tower was, while I accelerated through Mach 1. I held supersonic speed until about 25,000 feet and then pulled out so as to throw the boom at the control tower. Later, completing the flight, I landed and taxied to the chocks. No one said anything. I was not about to ask anyone if they had heard anything, but I did wonder why no one mentioned the boom.

I found out why the next evening at a social function at the Guantánamo Bay officers club. As I arrived at the bar, I heard a lot of talk by the ship's officers about a mysterious explosion that had occurred the night before. It seemed that the officer of the deck had just called away Captain Johnson's gig from the aft boat boom to come to the officers' accommodation ladder and pick up the captain to take him ashore when this explosion shook the entire ship so badly that the officer of the deck thought the gig had blown up. No one knew what caused the explosion, and there was considerable speculation as to what it had been. I never said a word to anybody, but now I knew why no one at the field had heard my boom, and I mentally cataloged the need to be much more accurate in the future.

There was not much to do in Guantánamo Bay. A few of the squadron officers might take one weekend in Montego Bay, Jamaica, but mostly the officers and men stayed at Guantánamo. Caimanera, the Cuban town just outside the main gate, definitely was not known for good clean liberty. This lack of things to do led some of the naval air facility officers at Leeward Point to offer sailors an overnight ride to Santiago de Cuba, about 150 miles to the west. They set up a daily flight of a Twin Beech airplane to Santiago and would take five or six sailors down one day and bring them back the next.

The trip to Santiago became so popular that our sailors were standing in line for the next flight, and "Leeward Air Lines" was making the trip every day. Castro was fighting in the hills behind Santiago to overthrow Batista, and safety in the town was of some concern. I decided to see what the big attraction was for all those young, single sailors and became the pilot for the next flight. We flew to Santiago and landed on a grass strip just to the west of Morro Castle, an old fort on the coast outside Santiago. Obviously by prior arrangement, the ebullient liberty party was met by a cab that would later bring the previous liberty party to the airplane for the return flight to Leeward Point.

It took about twenty minutes to make the round trip into town to switch liberty parties, and the old group showed up at the airplane looking considerably more docile than those we had just brought. On the return trip I learned that the big attraction was a certain house in town where for $5 a sailor could get a bottle of whiskey, a bed, and female companionship for the night. Max and I had visions of the mothers of those young men accusing VF-21 and the Navy of aiding and abetting their sons' moral decline, but it took a lot of diplomacy and a few more trips before we could wind down the operation in a way that did not incite mutiny.

Personalities make the world go 'round, and that is certainly true in the Navy. Early in the refresher training period, Commander Schwab, the air officer, made a few caustic comments about the air group in the executive officer's cabin during the nightly department head meeting. Because he had already committed the monumental goof of allowing Max to make the first landing on *Forrestal*, his comments almost led to blows between him and Ralph Werner. After their run-in and for much of the remainder of refresher training, neither Commander Werner nor Commander Schwab spoke directly to the other. But because they were required to sit by rank at the head table in the wardroom for evening meals when we were on board, that placed them side by side. I laughed as I watched Ralph lean behind Commander Schwab to ask the operations officer to pass the salt. But time heals, and by the end of the ship's training, both were on speaking terms again.

Ralph Werner arranged to have one of the three landing mirrors in the Navy placed on loan to *Forrestal* and ATG 181. That mirror was mounted on wheels and could be moved all over the flight deck to determine which positions, port or starboard, offered the best presentation to the pilot. Consensus still placed the best position on the port side. Lieutenant Francis (Fran) Babineau, the air group's LSO, viewed the mirror as a competitor, but he seemed to tolerate it. Lieutenant Hal Marr, earlier of VC-4 in Atlantic City, was the AIRLANT staff LSO and was in charge of all LSO training in the Atlantic Fleet. He visited *Forrestal* a great deal to monitor the use of the mirror and to observe the evaluation. Some pilots were a bit reluctant to accept this new landing aid over the abilities of the LSO, but eventually all agreed that the mirror provided better and faster visual cues to the pilot

Landing weight in airplanes is critical knowledge to those who must set the arresting gear engine tolerances before each airplane touches down. The airplane's speed is critical because the square of the speed times the weight determines momentum and thus the energy that must be dissipated on arrestment. Thus, it is vital to the pilot, as well as to the ship, that the arresting gear be set correctly. During and after World War II, the relative landing speeds of our airplanes were low, and so there was not wide disparity in engaging speeds as long as the ship could maintain the correct wind across the deck and the pilots flew the correct speed. With the advent of jet airplanes, our relative landing speeds doubled from 50 knots to 100 knots. We carried much more fuel, and that in turn created greater variability in the weight of the airplane during a flight. That variability led to the requirement for the pilot to declare his fuel weight before landing so that the arresting gear could be set properly. Initially, that information was radioed as the flight entered the pattern to break, but confusion often resulted as to which airplane was next to land, and too many wrong arresting gear settings caused the fuel declaration to be moved closer to the landing so the arresting gear could be set properly. The procedure was established to give the fuel weight on the radio when the pilot had the mirror and meatball in sight, and hence came the procedure for the pilot to say "ball, 2,100," meaning that the pilot was approaching, could see the ball for visual reference, and had 2,100 pounds of fuel remaining. The LSO knew the plane's speed by its attitude, and later radar refined that estimated speed to a very accurate figure.

Weekend evenings were occasionally festive at Guantánamo Bay. There would be receptions at the officers club where we would congregate on the verandahs overlooking the bay to discuss the past week, or the next week, or flying, or anything else that moved us. The wives of those officers permanently based in Guantánamo came as well, and a good time was had by all. In the evenings the broad salt flats of the bay provided a fertile field for a phenomenon of the Caribbean islands—infinitely small flying insects. They commonly came out after sunset and were appropriately named the no-see-'ems or, more aptly, the flying teeth. They were the scourge of the officers club terraces. Warm evenings brought them out by the tens of thousands, and it was funny to see officers in their dress whites and ladies in their cocktail dresses continuously moving and slapping at exposed skin, all to the dulcet melodies of a Caribbean steel band. Everyone was susceptible to them, and eventually everyone gravitated inside to escape.

USS *Forrestal* drew many visitors from Washington. On March 13 Admiral Arleigh Burke, then CNO, visited *Forrestal*, and ATG 181 put on an air show. The other squadrons dropped bombs and strafed, and the VF-21 acrobatic team performed last. We used different routines for our shows, and in this particular routine we used the vertical fleur-de-lis break to return to the ship individually and low to end our show. Tom Cassidy, flying my left wing, was to fly down the flight deck on the port side of the island from bow to stern, and Captain John Wolmers was to fly up the starboard side from stern to bow, while I flew in from the port side, and Jo Humes flew in from the starboard side. We had it timed to arrive at the ship at the same time, but it just so happened on this day that Cassidy was a few seconds slow pulling through at the top of his loop. As a result, he arrived back at the ship five or six seconds after the rest of us had passed over the ship and were moving away. Admiral Burke, having seen the three of us fly by, was standing on the flight deck looking aft when Tom came hurtling down the deck from bow to stern at 500 knots about 10 feet above the spectators' heads. The noise and blast from Tom's airplane startled Admiral Burke so much that he dropped to his knees. Tom is the only lieutenant junior grade that I am aware of who has knocked the CNO to his knees and gotten away with it.

We put on our show for the secretary of the Navy on March 23, and he was impressed enough to be waiting in the ready room on our return to congratulate us. Our routine had become quite polished, and we had honed the show down to fifteen minutes and culminated it with either a diamond-formation double Immelmann or a vertical overhead break.

As the end of March approached, the crews of *Forrestal* and the air task group became adept in their drills, and the members of the fleet training group no longer had dour looks on their faces or spoke quite as disparagingly of our efforts at the battle drills as before. The engineering drills ran more smoothly. The flight deck crew could rig the emergency barricade in the standard time of less than sixty seconds. Damage control teams could dewater compartments, and the ship could be steered from secondary control. *Forrestal* was beginning to show every sign that the ship would be ready to join the fleet. Ralph Werner ran a good air group. He knew what was going on, even more so than some of the squadron commanding officers, simply because he listened to what was being said by the pilots and maintenance men. Ralph had great qualities of leadership. He no longer flew as much as he had in earlier years, but he was smooth on the controls, and he flew each type of airplane in the air group. He was a hard taskmaster but had a heart of gold and drew the respect of all.

Now we learned we would not be deploying in *Forrestal*. Ralph Werner called us all together and informed us that we would be making a western Pacific deployment later in the year in USS *Bennington*, a Pacific Fleet 27C class aircraft carrier. I was disappointed because, after fighting two wars in the Pacific, I was looking forward to seeing some of the sights and scenes in the Atlantic and Mediterranean, and the large deck and great capability of *Forrestal* were awfully nice. But it was not to be.

USS *Forrestal* completed training, and on Monday, March 26, 1956, we started north to return to Norfolk. We were to have one more operating period in *Forrestal*, so when we arrived back in Norfolk on April 3, the air group left its airplanes on board. After a week with our families, *Forrestal* sortied from Norfolk to join the ships of five nations for a NATO exercise off the Virginia capes.

On April 12, the first day of air operations, my division and Jo Humes's division flew on the second launch to provide intercept services for the assembled NATO ships. Returning to *Forrestal* to land, Jo's division entered the break first. We were no longer using the mirror, but rather paddles approaches, and he received a wave off on his first pass. I delayed my division break just long enough for Jo to turn downwind again, which placed me next to land, close behind him. As he rolled out of his final turn to land on board, I watched him closely to control my own landing interval. I saw his FJ-3 touch down in the area of the arresting wires and suddenly do a snap roll to the left. Something terrible had gone wrong with an arresting gear wire. In a flash his airplane was smashed down on the flight deck inverted, after which it slid up the angle in a shower of sparks and smoke, went off the angled deck, hit the water in a terrific splash of spray and steam, and disappeared. Jo was killed instantly.

I continued my approach but was given a wave off as the flight deck crew swarmed out onto the flight deck to check the wire and to look for other damage. Subsequently, my division was recovered on board several minutes after the accident. Had Jo not been given a wave off initially, it would have been me that was flipped on landing, but if you dwell on such things, you can go bonkers.

We sent the word to Mary by ship-to-shore telephone, and she went to Twinks Humes to inform her and to stay with her. When an accident such as Jo's occurs and a person as important to the organization as the operations officer is killed, it leaves a big hole in the squadron. There was much we would have to do later. Jo had named me to inventory his things, which I did. Because of the complexity of flying airplanes from an aircraft carrier and the need to rely on catapults and arresting gear, it is vital that each pilot maintain trust in the ship's equipment. Captain Johnson knew that well. He stopped all air operations, and *Forrestal* summarily left the exercise to return to port to determine just why the cross-deck pendant had failed. We held Jo's memorial service several days later at NAS Oceana.

From the preliminary accident review, it appeared that Jo's airplane caught the number 2 cross-deck pendant in a normal manner and that as the arresting wire paid out it broke. The pendant then wrapped around the tail hook, causing the airplane to snap roll to the left and hit the deck inverted. The Carrier Suitability Branch of the Flight Test Division at the Naval Air Test Center at Patuxent River was called on to investigate why the accident occurred, and Commander John T. Shepherd of Carrier Suitability headed a team of flight test engineers to investigate the arresting gear system. On April 21, off Virginia Beach, Lieutenant Robert S. McMahon of Carrier Suitability, flying an FJ-3, duplicated Jo Humes's accident—exactly. He caught the number 2 wire. The wire broke. The airplane snap rolled to the left. McMahon's FJ-3 hit the deck inverted, he was killed, and the airplane was lost after it slid off the edge of the angled deck in a shower of sparks and fire. Now we had two deaths, and Carrier Suitability had to go through the same administrative ritual of notification of next of kin.

The flight test engineers burrowed into their data. High-speed Mitchell instrumentation cameras and strain gauges installed for the investigation enabled them to learn that one of the two cross-deck pendant attachment fittings failed from slamming into the armored flight deck when the FJ-3 hook engaged the cross-deck pendant. The dynamics of the arrestment and the height of the FJ-3 tail hook combined to create a sine wave in the wire that caused the two cross-deck pendant connecting fittings to pound on the deck. After some undetermined number of hits, the fitting failed, and the cross-deck pendant wrapped around the tail hook, causing extreme side loads to flip the airplane inverted. The fix was to place on the flight deck a 3-by-5-foot pad of a gelatinous rubberlike substance so that on arrestment the swedged fittings would first strike that pad. To this day all steel-decked U.S. aircraft carriers have those pads forward of the arresting wire deck-edge sheaves. Jo Humes and Bob McMahon died, but their accidents enabled safer carrier flight operations today. It is in just this manner that our procedures and equipment have been developed in aircraft carriers. Like rules for handling ammunition, flight deck procedures have been written in blood. There is a reason for each procedure and for the design of each piece of flight deck equipment in our carriers.

Back at Oceana we continued our intensified training before a planned September-October deployment. The personnel changed as officers and men were shuffled or left the squadron. Max Harnish made Jack Robinson operations officer over my objections. We were now flying thirty to forty hours per month and making good progress in our remaining training.

It is difficult to convey in writing the exhilaration that comes with flying. But on early mornings, when the skies are clear blue and you climb into your airplane to fly with fellow pilots whom you trust, flying enjoyment can be complete. Strapping into your harness and seat, fitting the oxygen mask over your face in preparation to taxi, and feeling the cool oxygen course through your lungs all seem to help clear the cobwebs from your mind and focus you on the task at hand. In tactical squadrons, takeoffs and rendezvous of airplanes are accomplished without a word being spoken on the radio. Hand signals and the aspect of the airplanes suffice for all communications between pilots. The thrill of a good gunnery flight or successful intercept, the nearness of your wingman or leader, and the challenge of doing the difficult all blend together and bring satisfaction and pride.

Returning to Oceana at the end of a flight was always fun. By good planning I could set my throttle for the pattern break while still some 20 miles out and leave it untouched until I arrived over the runway at 500 knots. The lack of throttle movement made it easy for my wingman or my entire division to lock into close formation. By a simple flick of my control stick I would drop the right wing almost imperceptibly to signal my wingman and section leader to slide into a tight parade right echelon, and we would break the formation over the runway numbers to land alternately on left and right sides of the runway so that all four airplanes of a division were rolling out on the runway at one time.

Flying fighters in the fleet was the epitome of flying. Flying the FJ-3 was a true joy, and VF-21 was now well trained!

In August we prepared ourselves for deployment by starting our FCLP again using paddles because *Bennington* did not have the mirror yet. We did our FCLP at Fentress Field a few miles south of Oceana, usually in the early morning to avoid summer turbulence later in the day. Fentress was remote enough from Oceana that we had the field to ourselves, and we did not always adhere to established procedures. On one day Lieutenant Junior Grade Tom Cassidy and I flew down to Fentress in a section of two for FCLP or bounce. Instead of breaking high, we dropped down to fly at 460 knots 50 feet over the heads of LSOs Fran Babineau and George Hafner and then pulled up into a section loop. We completed the loop, again at 50 feet above the ground, and broke the formation to turn downwind for six FCLPs. On the last carrier pattern touch and go after liftoff, I sucked up the landing gear, held the FJ-3 just above the runway to accelerate to 210 knots, and did an Immelmann, ending up on a northerly course at 3,200 feet, to fly back to Oceana.

On September 11 and 12 ATG 181 flew out to *Forrestal* to refresh our carrier landings. We each made four day and four night carrier landings on that magnificent, broad flight deck. That final good-bye to *Forrestal* would serve to accentuate the much smaller size of USS *Bennington*'s flight deck the next month.

It was time to say good-bye to my family again. Our year together at Virginia Beach had been one of the best. The three children lived on the beach and were brown as berries. We had surfed together and spent our weekends in family fun. Mary and I both worked in support of Max to make VF-21 a good squadron, even though at times that seemed hard. Mary wanted to spend the cruise time in La Jolla or Del Mar, but her loyalty to the squadron's wives and our children's schooling compelled her to stay in Virginia Beach. Mark Harnish returned to her home in the Midwest, and we moved a mile north along the beach to an apartment next to Margaret and Tag Livingston, so the two families without dads could support one another. Margaret was due to have twins in a few months, and Ida Lois Werner lived not far away.

On October 7, 1956, we left Oceana and flew west, stopping at NAS Memphis and the air force base at Clovis, New Mexico, for refueling. VF-41 and VA-42 flew by their own routes. VA-86 could not deploy in its F7U-3s because the airplane was a nightmare to maintain and because its commanding officer, Commander Gates, had been killed in a recent accident. So we had a new Grumman F9F-8 fighter squadron, VF-174 from Cecil Field, Florida, with Commander Charles Schroeder commanding. All the maintenance crews and the tons of squadron gear and special handling equipment for the different airplanes were flown west by contract civil airplanes. The four squadrons of ATG

181 all arrived at NAS North Island between October 7 and 9 and were stuffed into *Bennington* to depart San Diego on October 12.

I say stuffed. *Bennington* was an *Essex* class project 27C or conversion carrier. In addition to the angled deck and H-8 hydraulic catapults, the ready rooms were located below the armored hangar deck with escalators to carry the pilots more rapidly to the flight deck. Of great importance, all *Essex* class attack carriers were now configured to carry jet fuel. Gone were the dual five-inch mounts on the starboard flight deck, and the open fo'c'sle was now enclosed in a hurricane bow. We had to fight hard to fit ourselves and our gear into nooks and crannies in the ship. But we succeeded.

We left San Diego, with Carrier Division 5 embarked, and went directly to Hawaii to begin the critical process of melding the ship and air group into one fighting unit. This was difficult, and Ralph Werner had many a battle in front of executive officer Commander John Parks, as he wrestled Commanders Warner (ship's operations officer), Knight (air officer), and Beyer (supply officer) for spaces. Those department heads were full of good intentions, but the ship's company had spread out while there was no air group on board, and now they needed to make room for others, which was difficult.

The mid-to-late 1950s produced another period of Navy personnel policy change. The personnel system said, "If you are an aviator, particularly one who has not deployed previously in a carrier, you should get experience at sea in a carrier." Many patrol airplane pilots were being ordered to the carriers. Many of those more senior officers lacked jet carrier experience, which was a detriment to good operations, particularly until all had gained recent experience together. Ralph Werner had his work cut out!

Added to the mind-set of the senior officers, the disparate Pacific and Atlantic Fleet backgrounds made the marriage of an East Coast air group summarily embarked in a West Coast aircraft carrier a difficult one. Most admirals and captains were operationally timid about jet airplanes and still seemed to believe that if you did not fly them, they would not have accidents. Unfortunately, our deployment and subsequent carrier deployments continued to show that flying jet airplanes from converted *Essex* class carriers was not as forgiving as flying from the larger *Midway* and particularly the much larger *Forrestal* classes. Aircraft were flown from converted *Essex* class carriers until the 1980s, but never as successfully over a variety of sea conditions as from the much larger decks.

Our two weeks of refresher training from October 16 to 30 in the Hawaiian operating areas went rapidly. On the afternoon of October 18, Lieutenant Jack Robinson was killed when his FJ-3 stalled after a normal catapult shot and crashed into the sea forward of the ship. There is something very final about the sudden and final stop of engine noise as an airplane crashes into the sea. Nothing of Jack's airplane remained afloat but two drop tanks, and those passed silently down the starboard side as we watched in vain for a pilot's head to bob to the surface. Jack was gone. The subsequent investigation came to the conclusion that his engine was not developing full power—but for unknown reasons. Jack's death set in motion calls to Mary in Virginia Beach to inform his wife, Barbara. Mary and the other wives rallied in support and did the best they could to help.

We continued our training, but with one less airplane and one less pilot, and Lieutenant M. D. (Shorty) Short became operations officer. Shorty and I roomed together in a two-officer room on the 02 deck just under the forward part of the angled deck. There could be no sleeping during flight quarters, but then neither he nor I ever had that opportunity anyway.

On several occasions during our ship's refresher training, *Bennington* broke the routine at sea to tie up at the carrier piers at Ford Island in Pearl Harbor. That offered all hands an opportunity to go ashore. On one such evening the ship and air group officers gathered at the nearest watering hole, the officers club on Ford Island. What happened there set the tone for the upcoming cruise in *Bennington* for Lieutenant Junior Grade Tom Cassidy. Tom was standing at the bar socializing with some officers when he found himself near Captain R. C. Jones, commanding officer of *Bennington*. They exchanged pleasantries, and one topic led to another until Tom proceeded to impress upon Captain Jones that he, Tom, was the best fighter pilot in the Pacific Fleet. Not only was he best, but he or any carrier pilot could easily conn an aircraft carrier because pilots were used to high speeds and high relative motion, and carriers moved so slowly! At that point in Tom's evening, this was eminently clear to him.

The next morning, as *Bennington* prepared to get under way, Tom was catching a few extra winks in his stateroom before sauntering to the squadron ready room for the day's events. There was a firm knock on his door followed by the announcement that "I am the captain's Marine orderly and have come to escort the lieutenant to the bridge, at the captain's request. Sir!" Tom dressed hurriedly, and the two went to the bridge where Tom was told to observe the finer points of maneuvering a large ship in some very narrow waters.

For the remainder of that cruise, every time we would get under way, the captain's orderly would bang on Tom's stateroom door to escort him to the bridge for instruction. Tom came to dread that knock and tried to get me to intercede, but Captain Jones had informed me early on with a twinkle in his eye what he was doing with Tom, so Tom would not be missed at the flight deck parade muster for getting under way. Tom also tried to hide, but the Marine orderly knew the ship better than Tom did and always found him.

With credit to all concerned, finally Tom was given the opportunity to conn

Bennington out of Buckner Bay at Okinawa on February 23, 1957, by himself. But Captain Jones continued to see that Tom was on the bridge for every sortie and in the process won Tom's respect. I did notice that Tom was not quite so large when ashore after that night at Ford Island. When *Bennington* left the Wooloomooloo dock in Sydney, Australia, seven months later and sortied from Sydney harbor, the captain's orderly found Tom in ample time for him to stand by Captain Jones on the bridge.

Our refresher training period culminated in the standard battle problem and operational readiness inspection (ORI) given on November 1 by the fleet training group from Pearl Harbor. ATG 181 and *Bennington* did not excel in their ORI, but they certainly passed well enough to earn the right to continue their deployment westward.

Rear Admiral A. P. Storrs, Commander Carrier Division 5 (COMCARDIV 5), was embarked in *Bennington*. His chief of staff, Captain Magruder Tuttle, and operations officer, Captain J. P. (Blackie) Wienel, gave COMCARDIV 5 a decided operational flair, but the tempo of operations for our flying in *Bennington* was far too conservative for our liking. Blackie Wienel, an old friend from my *Valley Forge* days, was always a great help during the cruise. We departed Pearl Harbor on November 2 and flew for only two days as we passed Midway en route to Yokosuka, Japan. The political unrest in the Middle East, which lead to outright combat between Egypt and Britain and France over the Suez Canal, and the Soviet march into Hungary to quell the uprising there caused a general increase in the readiness of the Pacific Fleet. For a time five carriers were deployed, but gradually we returned to the then-normal deployment of three carriers. After USS *Lexington* and USS *Bon Homme Richard* returned to the States in December, the deployed carriers were USS *Bennington*, USS *Shangri-La*, and USS *Hornet*. Still, the operating tempo was low—each pilot was flying ten to twelve hours per month—and that came to be of great concern to the senior officers in ATG 181.

Bennington visited Yokosuka for in-port upkeep from November 12 to 20 and then moved south to Okinawa and then farther south to Manila. On December 12 we had another FJ-3 accident off Luzon. Lieutenant Junior Grade Jack Jester received a wave off as he tried to land on the 0700 recovery. Taking the wave off, he flew up the angled deck but did not seem to add full power as he should have. His airplane drifted to the right and settled such that his right wing tip hit the flight deck, and the airplane abruptly rolled farther right to hit the flight deck inverted along the number 2 or port catapult track. Jack was killed instantly, and his airplane slid forward and off the flight deck into the sea. Luckily, nothing was parked forward, and no one was injured on deck. Jack was not married; we made the necessary notification to his parents by telegram, and I carefully wrote a letter for Max to send to his parents. VF-21 now had fourteen airplanes and fourteen pilots. Lieutenant George Hafner, the air group's LSO, began to fly with VF-21 to help make up for our shortage of pilots.

In December Ralph Werner requested that VF-21's acrobatic team participate in a major air show at Manila International Airport. Ensign Lane Hubbard had joined our team earlier, when John Wolmers left the squadron. He took the right wing position, with Tom Cassidy still on my left wing and M. D. Short filling the slot. Before *Bennington* anchored in Subic Bay, we put a few of our airplanes ashore on the airfield at Cubi Point to polish our routine. The airfield was not much more than a bare airstrip at that time, and we lived on board ship. But it was clear that Cubi Point soon would become a magnificent facility. Almost twice as much earth was moved to build that airfield than to build the entire Panama Canal.

The day of the Manila air show came, and teams representing the Royal Air Force, the Royal Australian Air Force, the Chinese Nationalist air force, and the U.S. Navy and Air Force gave flight demonstrations. The air show was well attended, and the Gray Ghosts, as we were known, were given kudos as one of the best teams.

On December 19 *Bennington* departed Subic Bay for a Christmas port visit in Hong Kong. One of the highlights was the Christmas Eve service in Saint Andrews Church in Kowloon. The melodies were the same, but the words to Christmas songs used in the Church of England were far different from those in the Episcopal Church in the United States. Afterwards, as we walked down Nathan Road toward the boat landing to return to *Bennington*, it was most unusual for us to hear Chinese carolers singing English Christmas carols in Chinese. We left Hong Kong on December 29 to conduct flight operations.

In January *Bennington* moved north to Yokosuka while we flew along the way and then went to Sasebo for some ship's repair. A compounding factor in the small amount of flight time that we were getting in the FJ-3 was our difficulty in maintaining the airplanes on board ship. While the FJ-3 was a delight to fly, it was not a rugged airplane like the Grumman F9F-8. Its J-65 engine, the English Sapphire engine, was built under license for the Navy and Air Force by Curtiss Wright. Our two technical representatives, Carl Marohn of North American Aviation, Columbus Division, and Floyd Swope of Curtiss Wright, were instrumental in the upkeep of the FJ-3. Those civilian technicians could do wonders and were also a good communications bridge back to the company to keep its engineers informed on the quality of the product. Carl and Floyd literally joined VF-21 and were included in all social events. They went on liberty with the officers and spent a lot of valuable time working with our maintenance men.

Before we arrived in Sasebo, we were well into our fourth month of deployment. Long cruises breed boredom, and boredom breeds recreational high jinks, such as crossing the equator ceremonies. In World War II a U.S. Navy officer from a destroyer escort liberated a *Life* magazine cover picture of Olympic swimming star Esther Williams from an Australian destroyer wardroom while in Darwin, Australia. Over time that picture was captured as a prize, always by officers of other U.S. ships. By the 1950s the dog-eared picture was encased between two pieces of clear plastic with cork fitted around the periphery, should it be thrown in the water, which it frequently was. An accompanying battered logbook recorded the adventures of the capture or attempted capture and dutifully noted the heinous abuse of officers who tried and failed. The ship that retained custody was required to fly continuously a motheaten, stained, yellow quarantine flag from its signal halyard to identify that ship as the custodian of the Esther Williams picture.

The junior officers of VF-21 learned that "Esther" was in the possession of USS *Sea Fox*, a diesel submarine then nested alongside the sub tender stationed in Sasebo. The officers of *Sea Fox* had taken the picture from the officers of *Lexington* through some elaborate scheme, and nothing would do except to get it back. We organized, and I was elected the leader. Two big Marine officers from the ship, knowledgeable in hand-to-hand combat, volunteered to help, as did others. In fact, we had more than we needed, and I had to be selective. Detailed briefings were held in our ready room over several days to instruct each officer about entry into the sail, to assign hatches to be locked open, to plan entry into the wardroom, and to learn various dos and don'ts in submarines and in *Sea Fox* in particular. We did not want to sink it. Our plan came together, and with the support of *Bennington*'s executive officer, Commander John Parks, we were given an officers' launch to use for transportation to and from *Bennington* and the sub tender. Of vital importance, the officers in the sub tender agreed not to hinder us. We arranged for the wardroom officers of *Sea Fox* to be invited to a cocktail reception given by several female civilian schoolteachers in Sasebo. The date was January 19. We knew that only two *Sea Fox* officers remained on board, and the trap was set.

Using the sub tender as a base, we attacked *Sea Fox* after dark and executed an elaborate plan to gain surprise entry through the sail. All went well except that during an initial scuffle to force our way into the submarine's sail one of our officers accidentally kicked the boat's general alarm switch and sent the crew of *Sea Fox* to general quarters. We boarded the submarine as the crew ran to their stations, closing hatches while we tried to lock key hatches open with chains and padlocks. The executive officer of *Sea Fox*, Lieutenant Commander Robert Murrill, ran to the wardroom, and the crew pressurized the hull so that the hatch to the wardroom could not be opened without some key knowledge that we aviators did not have. Our team could only look through the quartz window of the wardroom hatch at a grinning Bob Murrill holding "Esther" and taunting us. We departed without the picture but had given a noble try. Subsequently, the commanding officer of *Sea Fox* paid a visit to *Bennington* to rub it in and to inform the airedales (aviators) that their best efforts were not good enough—as, indeed, in this case they were not. Subsequently, Commander in Chief Pacific Fleet (CINCPACFLEET) ordered an end to the antics before someone was hurt badly. I do not know where "Esther" is today, but I would lay odds that she resides in some retired officer's den and provides the backdrop for some tall tales and humorous memories.

By February 1957 the increased readiness posture brought on by the Soviets' reaction to the Hungarian revolution was relaxed. The normal three carriers of the Seventh Fleet were again rotating between areas in the north, south, and central western Pacific. Since the Korean War had ended in 1953, China and the Soviet Union maintained an aggressive posture toward the Seventh Fleet's presence in the western Pacific, and occasionally the Seventh Fleet would conduct special operations (SpecOps) to monitor those countries' military electronic capabilities, as well as their response times, and other factors that reflect the will of a nation's military forces.

En route north to Buckner Bay in February, Carrier Division 5 conducted one of those SpecOps off the coast of China. It was a cat and mouse game, highly classified, and conducted with appropriate safeguards to prevent escalation into incidents—but there was always risk. I was to be the mouse and to fly a single FJ-3 in a manner to get a response. Two divisions of VF-21's FJ-3s stationed farther off shore in radio silence would be my added protection. The electronic warfare airplanes of VC-33 would monitor the electronic order of battle of the Chinese as the effort progressed, and a few U.S. land-based aircraft were coordinated into the exercise as well.

On February 24 the task group launched aircraft, and we flew to the preplanned locations in radio silence. This was to be a test of the Chinese ability to detect an incoming flight and their will to do something about it. On time, alone, and flying at 35,000 feet, I turned toward the coast of China west of Shanghai. I flew very fast directly at the Chinese coast to appear on Chinese radar as though my single airplane was going to penetrate the coastline, but as I crossed the beach, I turned hard to starboard and flew parallel to the coast. All the while the airborne electronic sponges soaked up the resulting communications and radar activity. Needless to say, I was not intercepted, nor did the Chinese seem to try, but we obtained the desired electronic signatures, and the task group moved farther north to visit Yokohama.

In early March VF-21 moved ashore to NAS Atsugi for some more much-needed flying. While there we discovered that the hydraulic fluid in our FJ-3s had mysteriously become contaminated with water, and as a result a comprehensive purging operation was required. That took time and much effort. Concurrently, there was a requirement for *Bennington* to participate in a major Pacific Fleet international exercise scheduled earlier as INTEX-57 or Exercise Beacon Hill. Max Harnish decided that I should take five of our fourteen airplanes, those that had already undergone hydraulic system purification, and five pilots to sea in *Bennington* to fulfill VF-21's role. He would stay ashore at Atsugi with most of airplanes and crew to complete the maintenance work. Thus, the five of us began an enjoyable three weeks at sea, as we flew to *Bennington* after the ship left port March 12.

Exercise Beacon Hill entailed Seventh Fleet forces working with Royal Navy, Chinese Nationalist, and Australian navy units according to some fictitious scenario. Its goal was to offset Chinese and Soviet operating initiatives in the western Pacific. Another Seventh Fleet task group with the carrier *Shangri-La* was to join us, and both air groups were to be pitted against designated enemy units. I moved my small detachment into VF-41's ready room, and we got along famously as we all worked together. Initially, VF-21 stood the daytime condition I combat air patrol (CAP) watches, and VF-41 stood the nighttime CAP watches. Condition I CAP was defined as the ability to be airborne in three minutes if required. That meant that we sat for two to four hours in the cockpits of our airplanes on the flight deck while spotted on each of the two catapults ready to launch. The sun beat down on our faces and arms, and our skin soon was peeling from the relentless tropical sun.

As the exercise progressed, we were launched on a number of occasions after bogey aircraft. When the mock war escalated, we flew more and more. That is, we flew until March 26 when Ralph Werner awoke to the fact that we would soon exceed our fuel cost budget for the fiscal quarter ending March 31. The squadrons were broke! The arbitrary and somewhat fictitious Navy requirement to expend only one fiscal quarter's worth of fuel and then stop operating was typical of the fiscal policy of the operating forces then. I believe the problem was solved through some creative bookkeeping, and after some operational cliff-hanging, we completed Exercise Beacon Hill.

In early April we headed north to Buckner Bay to attend postexercise debriefings and to compare notes with the other participants. It was a welcome break to sit down with old friends in *Shangri-La*, such as Commander Ralph Hanks and Lieutenant Commander Paul Bugg of VF-142, to trade information and swap sea stories. It was at this time that Rear Admiral Fitzhugh Lee came on board *Bennington* preparatory to relieving Rear Admiral Storrs as COMCARDIV 5. The debriefing completed, all ships got under way out of Buckner Bay, and *Shangri-La* headed south, while we headed north to Yokosuka. Max and our nine shore-based airplanes flew on board *Bennington* on April 5, and that afternoon Rear Admiral Storrs turned command of Carrier Division 5 over to Rear Admiral Lee in a brief change of command ceremony. *Bennington* went into Yokosuka for the last time for this cruise.

During this time my next duty station was being determined. Officers at the end of the line in the western Pacific were vulnerable to being ordered places without being able to express their desires. Distance made detailing an easier task for the personnel people because no one could complain, and I learned over time never to trust a personnel detailer—they will say anything and then never admit to it. I will say, though, their job is tough.

VF-21, at least as we knew it, was going to be disbanded on our return, and a new group of officers, under the command of Commander James Holbrook, was already being formed at Oceana to take over. They would fly the new Grumman F11F-1s. I wanted to use my test pilot training and go to the Flight Test Division of the Naval Air Test Center at Patuxent River, but someone in the Bureau of Aeronautics slated me to go to Washington to serve in the Ships Installations Division, probably because of my initial work on the mirror and rubber deck.

However, Captain Harvey Lanham, then director of the Flight Test Division at Patuxent River, interceded on my behalf, and by the time we left Yokosuka and headed south to Australia, I was the happy recipient of orders to the Flight Test Division. Ralph Werner and the squadron commanders were notified that they would be ordered to the Naval War College in Newport, Rhode Island.

The remainder of our cruise passed rapidly, and we did not fly very much. We departed Yokosuka on April 18 and headed south to Australia via Saipan, Guam, and the Caroline Islands. We crossed the equator on Tuesday, April 23, when Neptunus Rex boarded and made shellbacks of the lowly pollywogs on board, and we passed through the slot between Bougainville and Guadalcanal, famed for the many battles of World War II. *Bennington* passed directly over the spot where USS *Lexington* rests on the bottom as a result of Japanese attacks in the 1942 battle of the Coral Sea and, as the carrier did so, paused to hold a moving memorial service for *Lexington* and those lost in the battle. We arrived in Sydney early on April 30 to a tumultuous welcome and grand port visit, then departed eight days later on Tuesday, May 7. The Australians were strong and loyal allies in World War II, and that feeling continues.

En route to the United States, our flying was constrained for several reasons. We were intent on getting home as early as possible; since we were proceeding without escorts, the carrier was vulnerable in conducting flight operations, particularly if an airplane were to go down; and the ship was fuel constrained by the vast distances to be traveled. We stopped briefly in Pearl Harbor for fuel on May 16 and continued on for San Diego and home.

On May 21 the airplanes of ATG 181 flew off *Bennington* to NAS Miramar to complete the long cruise. Both ship and air group had done well, given the constraints, and had operated well considering how they were thrust together. Both jet and propeller airplanes were still being flown from our carriers in 1957, but by then the early ratio of 25 percent jets to 75 percent props had been reversed. The fourteen pilots of VF-21 flew across country, stopping for the night of May 21 in Albuquerque, New Mexico, and arrived home in Oceana, Virginia, on May 22. The airlift of men and equipment was made in much the same way as when we had left some eight months before. The wives and families were waiting on the flight line at Oceana, and the welcome seemed worth the waiting for all concerned. We were a happy family, together again.

One week later, on my thirty-third birthday, I flew an FJ-3 to Patuxent River to call on Captain Harvey Lanham and to see what might be in store for me. After landing at the large test center airfield and taxiing down the hill to the flight test line area, facing the Patuxent River, I walked to his office. In a recent helicopter accident, Harvey had broken his right leg, which was encased in a large plaster cast. As I walked into his office, I could see that he was walking with the aid of a cane, which he kept near his desk. We exchanged pleasantries, and I thanked him for rescuing me from Washington.

Harvey told me that I was to go to the Flight Test Division's Carrier Suitability Branch. My heart sank on hearing that because I still had it in my mind that someday I might fly the X-15. While Carrier Suitability conducted important test work, it was not my vision of interesting flying. In fact, I was concerned that I would spend two years flying around aircraft carriers with my wheels and flaps down. I thanked Harvey for his consideration and told him that I would very much appreciate it if he would place me in the Carrier Branch—where I might fly higher and faster.

He seemed to ignore my comment, and we talked about the cruise in *Bennington*, events in the Pacific Fleet, and his accident. I waited a tactful length of time and then cautiously reaffirmed my desire to be in the Carrier Branch. Harvey said, "No, I have decided to put you in Carrier Suitability because of your experience." I caught the flash in his eyes from being challenged on a decision that he obviously had made, and I knew that I was treading on thin ice. I changed the subject, and we talked of other things.

Harvey was preparing for his own departure from the Flight Test Division, so we talked for a few more minutes, and I rose to leave, while thanking him again. As I walked toward the louvered swinging door between his and his secretary's office, I gave it one more shot and said, "I would really appreciate it if you would put me in the Carrier Branch." Harvey grabbed his cane, cocked it back over his head, and threw it at me as I ducked through the swinging door. The cane and I arrived simultaneously, but it missed me and sailed through the door to ricochet around the secretary's office. She had a most startled, questioning look on her face as I walked by, but I had a smile on mine, and I did not stop.

I returned to Oceana where I and several others conducted some cross-deck flying operations between USS *Saratoga* and the visiting HMS *Ark Royal* in our FJ-3s. The purpose was to ensure that our respective flight decks could support the other nation's airplanes if needed and was an enjoyable last flying experience before I left VF-21 in June. My family spent some time at the beach, and then we moved north to Patuxent River.

When I reported to Flight Test several weeks later, Harvey had already departed for his next duty station, but he had left me a present: I went to the Carrier Branch.

10. THE MACH 2.4 BARRIER
JUNE 1957 TO SEPTEMBER 1959

The U.S. civil aviation structure was redesigned for the new jet civil transport airplanes. Egypt and Syria formed the United Arab Republic, and Iraq became its own "republic" when a military group overthrew the government. The Chinese Communists shelled Quemoy Island after cease-fire negotiations with the Chinese Nationalists failed. Sputnik *and then America's first satellite,* Explorer 1, *were launched. Khrushchev visited the United States, and the Saint Lawrence Seaway was opened. Two monkeys, Able and Baker, were rocketed skyward to a height of 300 miles, and NASA selected seven astronauts in 1959.*

There were 18,446 pilots, 134,212 aviation ratings, and a total of 26 aircraft carriers of all types in the Navy. The last CVL, USS Saipan, *was decommissioned. The CNO approved a reorganization of carrier aviation to standardize the size of air groups and their assignment to specific carriers. Commander Slim Russell USN and others developed a new training concept for replacement air groups. Lieutenant Commander George Watkins set a new world altitude record of 76,939 feet in the F11F-1F at Edwards AFB, a record that soon fell to the Soviets, and Major E. N. LeFaivre USMC set time-to-climb records to five altitudes in the F4D-1 at NAS Point Mugu. In a period of great aircraft development, the Lockheed P3V-1 patrol airplane, the North American T2J trainer and A3J-1 attack airplanes, the TEMCO TT-1 trainer, the McDonnell F4H-1, and the Vought F8U-3 fighters made first flights. The Bureau of Aeronautics and the Bureau of Ordnance were disestablished to form the Bureau of*

Naval Weapons. The bow wave of newly developed jet airplanes was reaching its crest.

Mary and I, with our children, left Virginia Beach for NAS Patuxent River in July 1957. I checked in to be placed on a list for housing on the base, and we moved temporarily to a base Quonset hut while waiting for our quarters to come available. I went to work.

The commander of the Naval Air Test Center (NATC) was Rear Admiral C. H. (Dutch) Duerfeldt. He and his staff interfaced with the Bureau of Aeronautics and set policy for the Flight Test, Service Test, Armament Test, and Electronics Test Divisions and the Navy Test Pilot School. In reality, the test divisions worked with the offices in the Bureau of Aeronautics on a daily basis. The Navy Board of Inspection and Survey (BIS) had been created long ago to monitor development of new equipment and to conduct trials of new ships and aircraft. The aviation portion of BIS was at Patuxent River, and Captain S. R. Ours was president of the board there. Commander Charles Fritz was his principal deputy.

Captain Filmore Gilkeson was director of the Flight Test Division. Commander John Kilner was the deputy director, and Commander Paul Stevens was the flight test coordinator. There were 35 officers, 145 civilians, and 230 enlisted petty officers and nonrated men in Flight Test, and the organization was undergoing change after successfully fighting a move to be colocated with the Air Force at Edwards AFB. The Carrier Branch, one of four branches in the Flight Test Division, was being renamed the Flying Qualities and Performance Branch (FQ&P). The other branches were Carrier Suitability, Rotary Wing, and Patrol. Commander Larry Flint had just taken over FQ&P from Commander T. H. Gallagher, and Lieutenant Commander George Watkins was his deputy. There were nine officers and as many engineers, plus a few secretaries, in FQ&P.

To my thinking FQ&P was what test flying was all about, and determining and evaluating the flying qualities of an airplane were what I had studied in England. I noted that the pilots in FQ&P stood high in their respective test pilot school classes, and generally they were highly talented pilots. The FQ&P Branch was small, considering its responsibilities. John A. (Jack) Nial was the senior flight test engineer, and Theron W. (Tee) Davison was the senior performance engineer. There were five or six civilian aeronautical engineers and three naval officer engineers. Lieutenant Commander Archie Stockebrand, a fellow officer in 1952 at BAR Dallas, was the senior aeronautical engineering duty officer (AEDO) and as such was the principal engineering deputy to Larry Flint. The seven project pilots were each assigned two or more projects and along with our engineers were kept quite busy.

The Navy test pilots at Flight Test exhibited an entirely different mind-set than they would have in the fleet. Flight Test pilots rarely flew tactically and almost always flew singly. Flight Test pilots needed to unlearn much of what they did in the fleet and to use their aviation knowledge and test pilot training to the maximum extent possible. They had to determine the risk of a program or flight and not allow others to get them into trouble—a not infrequent occurrence. The personalities of the individual test pilots in FQ&P varied widely, and one or two were extreme. We flew eighteen to twenty-five hours a month, and that required almost three times as much time in writing reports.

Also, being a Navy test pilot was in large measure different from being a civil or company test pilot. Company test pilots often had flights with higher risk, because they frequently flew in airplanes that had not been flown extensively. Company test pilots were salaried and then paid additional bonuses based on risk—provided they were smart enough to call it to their employers' attention beforehand. Risk could draw big rewards, and some company test pilots were highly paid; most were just paid well. That pay could have been a bone of contention between military and company test pilots, but it was an unwritten law that we never talked money with our civilian counterparts. Anyhow, they probably would not have told us how much they were being paid. It is fair to say that the mortality rate among company test pilots was higher than among military test pilots. Amazingly, those that flew the X airplanes seemed not to have the most accidents, and I felt that was a direct correlation to the amount of extra care, engineering time, dedication, and money invested in the programs. Of course, they also flew far fewer flights.

The risk for Navy test pilots seemed highest in record attempts, one-off projects that explored new regions of flight, aerodynamic investigations, and NPEs. In the latter category Navy test pilots frequently found things that the manufacturers had not yet discovered or, worse yet, had known about but failed to pass on. Almost all company test pilots on Navy programs were former Navy test pilots who left the service to specialize in test flying. There were exceptions such as John Konrad of the Vought Division of Ling-TEMCO-Vought (LTV) and Bob Little and Bill Ross of McDonnell, all of whom were former Air Force officers.

Not all activity at NATC was test flying. Lieutenant Commander Al Shepherd left Service Test at Patuxent for a squadron in the Pacific Fleet about the time that I arrived, and when he left, I fell heir to his responsibility to serve on courts-martial boards at NATC. I would gladly have let Al keep that duty, but I am sure he was glad to give it up.

In August our quarters at the Naval Ordnance Laboratory, Solomons, Maryland, became available, and we moved into a detached, white, three-bedroom frame house facing the Patuxent River. Solomons Island, at the confluence of the Patuxent River and the Chesapeake Bay, was remote, to say the least. A causeway had bridged the distance to the small island long ago, but it still retained its name. A Navy ferry ran on an hourly schedule back and forth to NATC from 0600 to 2200 each day, and crash boats could be used in medical emergencies, which seemed to occur regularly.

There were some family decisions to be made in living in Solomons. For schools the choice of class and academic content was small. The Our Lady Star of the Sea parochial school was light-years ahead of the public school in that area. Although we were not Catholic, our children went to the parochial school through the good offices of Father Cole and Sister John-Martin. The following year Travis was packed off to grandparents in Pasadena, California, to study there. We bought a small boat for local transportation and water skiing.

On August 6 Larry Flint and I flew to McDonnell in St. Louis for a program review for the new and soon-to-fly F4H-1. That airplane was initially designed as an attack airplane but was underpowered. With the advent of new and much more powerful General Electric engines, it showed great promise as a new fighter. We flight test pilots would be evaluating that airplane late in 1958 after its first flight.

As the summer wore on, I drew flying assignments to support some of the pilots in the branch. Lieutenant J. D. (Jake) Ward was doing some performance testing on the FJ-4B airplane to develop data for one of Tee Davison's hand-held fuel calculators, to be issued in the fleet. I was grateful, until I realized Jake was probably bored doing it himself. Performance testing could be a little like watching grass grow because of the repetitive requirements to record exact fuel flows at different power settings. However, Jake also had a flight test program in the F4D-1 to investigate its interesting transonic longitudinal trim change. The F4D was a single-seat, bat-winged airplane with no horizontal stabilizer that employed a trim-change compensator, an automatic device, to allow it to fly smoothly through the transonic realm. The trim-change compensator worked frequently, but not all the time. Lieutenant Bill Lawrence shared a few performance flights with me in his A4D-1 program, as well. Captain Hal Vincent USMC, a gung ho test pilot, also kindly shared some of his flying chores with me.

One of my first assignments was to explore the flying qualities and performance of one of two North American FJ-4Fs. Those modified FJ-4 Fury fighters were being built at the North American Aviation, Columbus Division, plant, and each would have a Rocketdyne AR-1 rocket motor installed above the tailpipe of the standard J-65 engine. The AR-1 weighed 36 pounds and used liquid hydrogen peroxide as the oxidizer and JP fuel to provide some 5,000 pounds of rocket thrust augmentation for slightly over two minutes. I was to be the principal pilot at the Flight Test Division on the FJ-4F project when we started flying the airplane, and Larry Flint would provide backup. Major Roy Gray, of the Service Test Division, would fly the other airplane. We were to investigate the value of that extra rocket thrust and to explore the flying qualities of the airplane at the much higher altitudes and Mach numbers that would be possible.

On September 16 Larry Flint and I flew to NAS Norfolk to the aviation physiological unit to receive personally fitted partial pressure suits in which to fly. The partial pressure suit was designed to provide the body with skintight protection to prevent one's blood from boiling at altitudes above 60,000 feet. It had an integral soft helmet and heated faceplate, which we had been advised could cause vertigo because of the minuscule vertical heating wires formed into the faceplate itself. Our suits were issued and fitted; we took a proving flight in the altitude chamber and returned to Patuxent River the next day.

Contractor pilots frequently came to Patuxent to demonstrate contractual points on their company aircraft, just as Don Schulz had done in 1952. It was FQ&P that principally witnessed those flight test demonstrations. One of my first chase assignments was to witness the contractor's spin demonstration of Lockheed's T2V-1, a new trainer that grew out of the TV-1 or Air Force T-33. Skip Crandall, the Lockheed test pilot, had done his workups over Palmdale, California, before he arrived. Skip flew those spin flights on October 8, 9, and 10, 1957, and I chased him to help him correlate what the airplane was doing as he made his demonstration points. But there was another even more important reason. A test pilot can sometimes overly concentrate on the task at hand and miss the larger picture, and the chase pilot is there to watch out for him and to be a second set of eyes if things become too hazardous.

The T2V-1 did wind up into a pretty good spin, but it recovered nicely. The inverted spin was what I would class as a real beauty. Months later, while doing some buildup spins in the T2V-1 to catalog my own body's responses for a spin program in a different airplane, I did ten inverted spins one day. I went home tired but happy. The next day, when I awoke, I looked into the mirror to shave and saw that the whites of my eyes were blood red. I had broken blood vessels in both eyes from the negative g's. However, my vision remained good, and I chocked that up as another learning point on the curve of experience in aviation.

In October 1957 I flew to Buffalo, New York, to visit the Bell Aircraft and Cornell University laboratories. My visit was connected with the development of a variable stability airplane intended to examine flight in stability conditions hitherto thought to be less than satisfactory, as well as for test pilot instruction. Such a variable stability research airplane was needed to establish criteria for the newly developing fly-by-wire concept of aircraft control and to teach test pilots how airplanes with less than ideal flying qualities behave. Fly-by-wire was a control concept in which there is no direct mechanical linkage from cockpit to control surfaces. All pilot inputs to fly the airplane would be sent by wire to an electronic box, which then would send signals by wire to the control surface actuators to control the airplane. Bell Aircraft and Cornell were developing such an airplane to meet Navy requirements, and we were very interested for ourselves and the test pilots school. Later, such an airplane was developed and flown under contract by CalSpan at both the Navy and Air Force test pilot schools.

On October 13 I joined a Service Test team that went to Douglas's El Segundo, California, plants and then on to the Douglas test facility at Edwards AFB to evaluate a new concept for in-flight refueling, which would give the Douglas A4D attack airplane and eventually other airplanes the capability to be either a tanker or a bomber. This was a buddy store system developed by E. H. Heinemann, now chief engineer of Douglas, El Segundo. Quite simply, this buddy store, a fuel tank carried under a wing or fuselage, transferred fuel through a hose and drogue that could be extended or retracted by an air-driven impeller on the nose of the tank. The beauty of the idea was that any tactical airplane could have the capability to be a tanker. Aircraft carriers would not have to carry tactically expensive, dedicated tanker aircraft. My chore was to evaluate the flying qualities of the married store and airplane, and my test pilot compatriots from Service Test were the prime movers for the engineering design and tactics of air refueling. I drew great pleasure in remembering my efforts to revive in-flight refueling some three years before and how fast it had been embraced by both the Navy and Air Force. Also, at Edwards AFB, I met company test pilots George Jansen and Cal Shoemaker. From them I learned of the efforts of Max Stanley of Northrop and ten or fifteen other civilian test pilots from aircraft companies in Southern California to form a Society of Experimental Test Pilots for the betterment of flight test safety and procedures. Initially, those efforts were viewed by aircraft companies as a threat of unionization, but subsequently the test pilots made high marks in their efforts to bring professional ethics and improved safety to test flying.

We had a fatal accident in FQ&P in the summer of 1957 when the J-65 engine failed in Lieutenant Bev Randolph's F11F-1 while he was doing test work over the Chesapeake Bay. Bev chose to stay with the airplane, which glided like a rock, and tried to reach one of the runways at Patuxent River. Unfortunately, he ran out of altitude before he arrived at the field and was forced to put the airplane into a large stand of pine trees near the naval air station. As strong and sturdy as the F11F-1 was, it was not strong enough in this case, and Bev was killed. Bev was an interesting example of a test pilot. He had graduated from the Naval Academy and had flown one tour in a squadron before being nominated for and attending the Navy Test Pilot School. He was a capable but not an aggressive pilot and seemed something of an anomaly in test flying. Bev was not decisive in the air, and in the test flying game decisiveness can mean the difference between life and death. Frequently, timing is everything.

In December a severe ice storm brought freezing temperatures to southern Maryland and the Chesapeake Bay. The upper Chesapeake Bay and the Patuxent River froze solid, and there could be no boat transportation between NAS Patuxent River and Solomons for a week. All the families living in Solomons were forced to stay home until a Navy fleet tug came up the bay to break up the ice, allowing us to resume commuting by ferry between home and work.

I continued to pursue my quest to learn more about the flight testing of spins in airplanes. In addition to going to the aerodynamics laboratory at the National Air and Space Administration (NASA) station at Langley, Virginia, and talking to the engineers and those who operated the spin tunnel, I endeavored to start our own spin program. The Navy had lost and was continuing to lose airplanes in the fleet because of spins. Mostly those losses occurred in the fleet introduction program at VC-3 at Moffett Field, where pilots were flying into unusual corners of the flight envelope. Two contractor pilots also had to leave their airplanes precipitously while demonstrating spins at NATC. For obvious reasons, some companies wanted to abolish the requirement for spin testing. I resisted that. I was convinced that we needed to renew our knowledge and to learn more about our current airplanes in the spinning mode and more about spin testing. There were other factors. A spin was a dynamic maneuver. Not much had been done recently in defining spins in our new breeds of airplanes, and aerodynamicists had not covered themselves with glory in predicting spin characteristics. Spins were one of the last flight test areas where only the test pilot could investigate and influence the outcome. To me it was a last frontier for test pilots. The Navy historically tested for spins in the 1930s and 1940s, but the advent of the F4U, and others like it, and its proclivity to spin when mistreated had steered pilots away from examining spins, particularly those you were apt not to recover from. Preliminary to starting such a program, I began spinning various airplanes to learn more.

In mid-December I asked George Watkins to chase me while I flew an FJ-3 to attempt some inverted spins from a vertical entry. I knew the FJ-3 would spin upright in a straightforward manner, but company test pilot Dick Wenzel had gotten into trouble once because of asymmetric external stores and fuel tanks in an FJ-4B. The two airplanes were different, but not that much so. We briefed beforehand, and I told George what I was going to do. He agreed that he would orbit at 35,000 feet and watch me approach vertically from directly below to apply prospin controls so that the airplane would enter an inverted spin at about 35,000 feet. I would hold in prospin controls for a five-turn inverted spin and then recover. He would circle and descend with me to record what the airplane was doing. All went according to plan. I approached vertically from below, and as the airplane slowed to my intended speed of 1.2 times its stall speed, I pushed full forward stick, kicked hard right rudder, then put in full left aileron—and nothing happened, at least at first. The airplane continued to slow while rising vertically, then suddenly tucked to fall nose over tail twice in a most unusual movement, and then whipped off into an inverted spin. I completed the spin and recovery and called the taciturn George on the radio. "George, did you see that?" George replied laconically, "Yeah. Do it again!" With that lighthearted comment, he took the edge off any excitement that I might have felt and put me back on the planet. Test piloting can bring out a lot of humor; humor is a way of relaxing.

After the holiday season, on January 12, Commander Ward Miller, head of the Carrier Suitability Branch, and I flew to Columbus to attend a program review for the entirely new A3J-1 Vigilante. That airplane was being built by North American Aviation, Columbus Division, and would have its first flight in about one year. George Gherkins, chief engineer for North American Aviation, Columbus Division, was proud of his team's new design. The airplane was to be a supersonic nuclear attack and reconnaissance airplane and would be the first ever to fly by wire.

After completing the A3J-1 program review, I flew one of two newly completed FJ-4Fs from Columbus to Patuxent to begin its trials. Major Roy Gray and I would share our information to write a joint final report on this interesting one-off kind of an airplane. To my knowledge, it was the first hybrid jet and rocket motor airplane, and with it we could look forward to some interesting flying. By the end of January I had done some zoom climb buildup work in an F11F-1 to simulate what we would do in the FJ-4F, and then both Roy and I flew the FJ-4F to peg the airplane's flying qualities without the rocket motor. Those qualities were basically good.

In February two members of the graduating class of the Navy Test Pilot School, Lieutenant M. D. (Shorty) Short and Lieutenant R. F. (Dick) Gordon, joined FQ&P. Shorty and I started a broad program to catalog the requirements and specifications for rate of roll in all airplanes. Engineer Jack Nial had long been interested in upgrading the Navy specification, then SR-38E, which dealt with flying qualities of airplanes, and rate of roll was a good starting point. He assigned Harry Down as our engineer. So began a project that would last several years and create opportunities to fly and to evaluate many Air Force and Navy airplanes before it ended. To begin with, we evaluated our own airplanes currently assigned to FQ&P.

Harry and I configured an F4D-1 so that we could achieve accurate and repeatable aileron deflections. Using a bathtub stopper chain from the local hardware store that was fastened to the side of the canopy track and to the top of the stick, we intended to catalog one-quarter-, one-half-, three-quarters-, and full-aileron-deflection rates of roll, principally at slow speeds, the regime in which we were most interested. The F4D-1 was particularly interesting because it was a tail-less fighter that used its elevons as combined elevators and ailerons. Harry and I did a workup flight to assess the smaller values of deflection and resulting rates of roll, because we both reasoned that the tail-less F4D might prove to be interesting. We were prescient. Increasing aileron deflection was giving us increased adverse yaw (the tendency of the aircraft's nose to yaw away from the direction of the roll), not a tendency that a pilot likes. I prepared to do a flight to investigate full deflection rolls at 1.2 times the stall speed of the airplane in the landing configuration. Harry Down's test card called for flying at 6,000 feet. I must admit that an inner warning light came on in my brain, and I added 4,000 more feet of altitude for Mary and the kids.

Climbing to 10,000 feet, I slowed to the correct speed and dropped my landing gear; the F4D had no flaps. The planned full deflection throw would not require the chain because all I had to do was to bang the stick into the normal full stops, which I did. An enormous amount of adverse yaw kicked in, and within a fraction of a second, I was on my back, and the airplane was in a fully developed inverted spin, passing through 9,500 feet and going down rapidly. We have a policy for high-performance airplanes in the Navy: if you are out of control at or below 10,000 feet, you leave the airplane—NOW!—because there is not enough altitude in which to recover before you hit the ground. I could not leave just yet. Summoning all I knew, I stopped the inverted spin, and as the airplane recovered and fell nose down at 5,000 feet, I gingerly pulled through so as to not enter an accelerated stall, which was a precursor to an upright spin. I flew out of the evolution at 2,500 feet and proceeded back to Patuxent where Harry and I had a major discussion about the responsibilities of engineers and pilots. I will say that Harry was just as shaken as I. He did not have the engineer's philosophy that test pilots are expendable and only worth $10 dollars for flowers.

Returning again to fly the hybrid jet/rocket-powered FJ-4F, I made three flights in February 1958. The 250 gallons of liquid hydrogen peroxide rocket fuel was burning out at between two minutes and fifteen seconds and two minutes and twenty-one seconds. The AR-1 rocket motor seemed to be performing well. The partial pressure suit was not particularly restrictive, and I became used to the sun playing havoc with my sense of balance as it played across the fine heating wires in my helmet's faceplate. On one of the flights I reached an indicated Mach number of 1.16 and on another an altitude of 61,000 feet—pretty good for an airplane that could only fly subsonic while straight and level. On the third flight I zoomed to 65,000 feet where the J-65 engine was about maxed out and idle rpm was 102 percent.

Perhaps the most interesting phenomenon was the liquid hydrogen peroxide itself. Directly beneath the pilot's seat North American had installed a thermoslike 250-gallon tank for this liquid. Mounted on the left side of the pilot's glare shield was a single, three-inch-diameter temperature gauge that gave a direct readout of the temperature in the upper part of the tank. The instructions to the pilot were to eject if the temperature ever reached 76°F because an explosion would be imminent. I found that during a flight, in my perception, the temperature gauge increased dramatically in size until it seemed to be the biggest instrument in the cockpit. I think Roy Gray agreed with me. The few flights we had in the FJ-4F reflected the complexity of the rocket system, and early in March 1958 I flew the airplane to Columbus to have the system reworked for further tests.

In March 1958 Lieutenant Commanders Ted Dankworth, George Watkins, L. H. (Tiny) Granning, and I were promoted to commander. We would be promoted on different but relatively close dates because the date of promotion depended on our position on the lineal list of officers in the Navy. Ted and I gave a joint wetting down celebration party at the officers club at Patuxent River. Soon George Watkins would return to a fleet squadron in the summer, and I would become Larry Flint's deputy branch head at FQ&P. There were more trips to Buffalo as we helped to define the variable stability airplane, which was approaching reality, while our rate-of-roll project was moving into high gear.

Sputnik was launched by the Soviets, creating quite a stir in the world. Our entire family gathered on the lawn to watch it one evening outside our quarters as it passed rapidly overhead, and we were impressed. About this time the word went out from NASA that the agency was looking for volunteer applicants for positions as astronauts. Spaceflight was around the corner. The word spread rapidly, and we test pilots talked about Able and Baker, the monkeys that were sent into space. Writer Tom Wolfe later accurately captured the attitude of most of us in *The Right Stuff*. It seemed to us that NASA engineers and managers were looking for monkeys.

Those at NASA were really of a mind-set that astronauts would be passengers in space vehicles controlled from Earth, and that assumption completely turned off many potential astronauts. For that reason alone, I would not have volunteered. But the clincher for me was the height limitation of 5 feet 11 inches—they were looking for shorter monkeys. At 6 feet 2 inches, I could not and would not scrunch down that low. I thought back to 1948 and Charlie Muckenthaler's kind efforts to keep me in fighters when the Navy tried to levy the same height restriction. The same physiologist must have worked on Navy fighter pilot and astronaut criteria. It is a great credit to the original seven astronauts that they persevered, did maintain human control in the spacecraft, and demonstrated over and over again that the pilot is an essential part of spaceflight success. The whole astronaut corps has gone on to prove the importance of the human, and those NASA engineers and managers who initially may have thought otherwise have either learned or been replaced. But in the late 1950s the physical rigors of the selection process and training of astronauts seemed to reaffirm that NASA was indeed looking for man-monkeys to ride in space capsules.

April 1958 was a typical test flying month; I flew twenty-one flights and logged twenty hours of flight time. There was a wide variety of flying, including A4D-2 spins, vertical entry spins in the T2V-1, and rate-of-roll flights. Of my twenty-one flights, eight were in the FJ-4F with the AR-1 rocket motor firings lasting from two minutes and twenty seconds to two minutes and twenty-four seconds. We completed our FJ-4F flying with a maximum altitude for the project of 67,500 feet. In the final analysis, the short duration of rocket time and the very sensitive liquid hydrogen peroxide as an oxidizer caused the concept to fail. The Navy could not store and handle the unstable hydrogen peroxide at sea in a safe manner. It may have been a good idea for high-performance thrust augmentation, but the practicality of the concept caused it to fail. A number of projects in the 1950s were like that: they were not bad ideas; they failed from their own complexity. We were just reaching out. I flew the FJ-4F to North American Aviation, Columbus Division, to have its AR-1 rocket engine and hydrogen peroxide tank removed so it could be reconfigured as a straight FJ-4.

On May 2, 1958, now Lieutenant Commander Shorty Short and I flew to Edwards AFB to conduct evaluations of various Air Force airplanes in our rate-of-roll project. Our hosts were Captains Gordon Cooper (later a Project Mercury astronaut), Bob Rushworth, and Bob White. They would come to Patuxent later, at our invitation, to fly Navy airplanes. On this trip we each evaluated roll parameters of the Boeing KC-135, Cessna T-37A, Martin B-57E, Douglas C-133A, and North American F-100C. It was most interesting to move from one airplane to another and to analyze the different responses to aileron input. We were beginning to see the need and reason for updating our roll specifications. I returned to Patuxent to evaluate the YTT-1, a small primary trainer candidate built by TEMCO, and to continue evaluating inverted spins in the T2V-1.

Occasionally I would talk to George Spangenberg and Hal Andrews in the Bureau of Aeronautics. The X-15 program, which I had been following closely, was moving toward its first flight, to be conducted by North American pilot Scott Crossfield. Navy participation would be coming soon. Because of my long interest, I wanted the commander of NATC to assign me as pilot. However, a move was made by Commander Butch Satterfield, then director of the Navy Test Pilot School, to write the specifications for the supposed selection. He had a reason for doing this, I believed. Lieutenant Commander Forrest

(Pete) Peterson was a personal friend of Satterfield and was then the chief flying instructor at the test pilot school. Pete Peterson was not long on actual test flying experience, but he had graduated from the Naval Academy, had a master's degree in aeronautical engineering, and had done well at test pilot school—three of the stated requirements. Butch wrote the specifications to match Pete's background, and, wonder of wonders, Pete was selected to be the Navy pilot to fly the X-15. I was temporarily shattered, having thought about that opportunity for the previous four years. I think it was the way that Satterfield aced me out that bothered me the most. I did not hold it against Pete. But life goes on, and there were more projects and airplanes to fly. I continued my test flying with renewed dedication and vigor, and as is often the case, things worked out better for me in the long run.

In the summer of 1958 my spin project was gathering momentum, and our capability to gather qualitative data was growing. Douglas test pilot Knick Knickerbocker came to Patuxent to demonstrate spins and spin recovery for the A4D-2 with stores. Knick had a most interesting ride during one of his previous demonstrations at Patuxent River. To demonstrate the airplane's ability to recover from an erect spin after five turns with an airplane aft center of gravity, Knick entered the spin at about 38,000 feet. After the obligatory five turns, he initiated recovery controls, and nothing happened, except the airplane continued to spin with the chase pilot counting the turns for Knick. He tried to rock the airplane with elevator. He tried both prospin and antispin controls, while the chase pilot counted "fourteen, fifteen, sixteen" turns. Finally, as he was passing 12,000 feet, Knick felt the airplane beginning to respond to his repetitive control inputs. Probably the controls were becoming more effective in the denser air. The chase pilot dutifully continued to count, but with trepidation in his voice: "twenty, twenty-one, twenty-two" turns. The airplane rather sloppily flew out of the spin well below 10,000 feet after some twenty-three turns, much to Knick's great relief. Douglas had a lot riding on that spin demonstration, and so did Knick.

On August 8, late in the evening, Mary gave birth to our fourth child, Charles. Ordinarily such an event entails driving to the hospital, but at Solomons there was the mandatory boat ride. As the time drew near, we called the duty corpsman at the Naval Ordnance Laboratory, and he in turn called the crash boat to come pick up Mary. We all met at the boat landing on the warm evening of August 7. As Mary professed that things were progressing rapidly, the corpsman said, "Have a nice trip. I will call the doctor to have an ambulance waiting for you on the other side." I looked at the crash boat coxswain, and he looked at me, and I recognized someone else who had never delivered a baby. So I grabbed the corpsman, and we all departed on the same boat.

Fortunately, everything worked out well, and Mary arrived in time for Lieutenant Patrick McNulty to deliver our third son in a normal fashion at the naval hospital. On the next morning our second son, Chris, ended up in the same hospital after falling out of a tree and breaking his arm, and Mary expressed a desire to not come home for a while. It was not to be, though, and Mary and the baby made the return boat trip to Solomons four days after his birth. She and Chris recovered at home. Interestingly, seven other wives at Solomons also delivered babies within days. We began to think that it was the water we were drinking until someone wisely observed that it had been exactly nine months since the Patuxent River had frozen, keeping us all home from work for a week.

Captain Bob Elder relieved Captain Fil Gilkeson as director of the Flight Test Division, and Fil ascended to the commander's staff at NATC as deputy commander. As good as Fil was as director, and he was good, morale in the division soared even further with Bob because he had such a great grasp and reputation in naval aviation. He was and is a great leader, a genuinely nice man, and an outstanding pilot with a wealth of flying experience.

The summer weather was upon us, and we of Solomons started a boat pool and took turns driving our boats to work. We would tie them up by an old seaplane ramp, work all day, and then motor home to our doorsteps. Captain Hal Vincent, our Solomons neighbor and a good friend, and I attended happy hour one Friday evening, after which we returned to the ramp where I had left my boat. Hal said, "I think I will ski home." We always carried one set of water skis, and while I readied the boat, Hal stepped out of his shoes and socks and handed them to me. He carefully rolled up his freshly pressed dress khaki trousers exactly two turns, tucked his tie into his shirt, and made sure his Marine dress cap was on tight. He looked mighty sharp as he stepped into the water skis on the seaplane ramp sloping to the water and I tossed him the towline handle. We both were all set for the trip home, so when he said "hit it," I applied full throttle, and Hal easily slid off the ramp and onto the water like a pro. He was up on the skis without getting a drop on his trousers—until the outboard engine quit. I had forgotten to hook up the fuel line to the gas tank and had just enough fuel to make the start. I watched helplessly as Hal slowly sank into the Patuxent River, at first distress showing on his face, until finally all that was visible was his head and cap. For a moment I thought I saw a bit of pure hate play on his face; then only his cap showed. I will say Hal had a lot of color. He subsequently did ski home in his uniform, totally wet. So much for happy hour. We are still good friends today.

In August both McDonnell and the Vought Division of LTV readied their two airplanes, the F4H-1 Phantom II and F8U-3 Crusader III, for first flight. The NPE would follow in September, and we set about to define the two teams that would compose the evaluation. Larry Flint and I named Lieutenant Dick Gordon as the F4H-1 project officer and Lieutenant Bill Lawrence as the F8U-3 project officer. From NASA Dryden Neil Armstrong was named to fly the F4H, and from NASA Ames Bob Ennis was named to fly the F8U. Both were former naval aviators. From Carrier Suitability Lieutenant Commander Bill Nichols would fly the F4H, and Lieutenant Commander A. C. O'Neil would fly the F8U. Captain Bob Elder would lead the joint team, and with Larry Flint and me, we would fly both airplanes to provide comparative qualitative analyses.

The entire team went to Norfolk to be fitted and indoctrinated in the use of the new full-pressure suit because we would need it for our very high altitude flying in those two high-performance airplanes. The full-pressure suit was the Navy's answer to the Air Force's partial-pressure suit. With its removable helmet and faceplate and its metal ring joints at the upper arms, neck, and legs, it supposedly provided more mobility and a much better environment in which to fly. A great deal of effort was going into the development of life sciences equipment in the late 1950s, and the Navy led much of the progress.

The pressure suit was a necessary evil. It was a way of being able to operate at the very high altitudes that our new airplanes could achieve and would provide safety should the cabin pressurization fail. Our indoctrination was pretty straightforward. I was fitted one day and came back the next to get the indoctrination, which involved lectures and a pressure chamber run to test the integrity of the suit in a way that would give a pilot confidence in it. That run was made singly because of the restrictive size of the pressure chamber. We were seated individually in a small 6-by-6-by-4-foot chamber and, wearing our pressure suits, were taken to 35,000 feet while an adjacent, larger chamber was taken to 125,000 feet. A glass of water was placed on a shelf on the side of the chamber in front of my faceplate to demonstrate what could happen to unprotected liquids, including my blood, under explosive decompression. Doctors peered at me through small quartz windows. The whole scene seemed to me to be reminiscent of a gas chamber at some state penitentiary. At a signal, some unseen object punctured some unseen diaphragm between the two chambers, and the sole participant—me—was explosively decompressed to 75,000 feet. At that instant the water blew out of the glass to disappear, dramatically demonstrating what would happen to my blood were I not pressurized. The suit seemed to blow up to full inflation to place the pilot—me—in an involuntary spread-eagle position. The faces at the window burst into laughter at my predicament as the suit suddenly and fully extended. I answered their jocularity with a one-fingered salute to show that I could still move my digits. The suits were an improvement in capability, but they did not provide as much freedom as their designers liked to think they would. However, armed with our suits and a piece of parchment proclaiming our new skill, we returned to Patuxent and flew in a specially configured F8U-1, which Dr. Frank Austin, now a qualified test pilot at Service Test, was using for his pressure suit experiments.

Frank made many new contributions to life support systems and aeromedicine after being the first flight surgeon–naval aviator to graduate from the Navy Test Pilot School in 1957.

The NPE team for the F4H and F8U was to complete the most complex evaluation to that time. Each aircraft company had conducted the first flights of the airplanes and done preliminary data gathering, accumulating about twenty to thirty flight hours. McDonnell pilot Bob Little made the first flight in the F4H-1. Vought pilot John Konrad made the first flight in the F8U-3. The plan was that the Navy would evaluate each airplane on its own merits and then compare the two. This was to be a shoot-out NPE competition, winner take all, and megabucks rode on the outcome. The Navy team departed Patuxent on September 7, 1958, and proceeded to St. Louis for ground indoctrination in the F4H-1. NASA pilots Neil Armstrong and Bob Ennis joined us there. Then we proceeded to Dallas and Vought for the weekend, followed by two days of ground indoctrination in the F8U-3. On September 13 we flew to Los Angeles and drove to Edwards AFB, the scene for our NPE flying.

The team spent the next twenty-six days flying and working at Edwards AFB. Bob Elder flew the F4H-1 first, and I flew it second. Larry Flint flew the F8U-3 first, and I flew it second. We all shared our flying duties so that we could amass equal times in the airplanes to provide meaningful comparisons. My first impression of the F4H-1 was that it flew like a truck. The stick forces seemed inordinately high—particularly the elevator forces—but the two General Electic J-79 engines with afterburner were something else. The 13,000 pounds of thrust each engine provided made the airplane a superperformer. The F8U-3 was another story. The single seater had the nicest flying qualities of any airplane that I had flown to date. It was a true Cadillac, and with its afterburner-equipped Pratt & Whitney J-75 engine, that airplane also was a real superperformer. This was going to be some kind of a competition. Early on, we all thought that the Navy should buy both airplanes, but that was not to be.

We settled into a routine of flying, and Bob, Larry, and I rotated between McDonnell and Vought facilities at Edwards. The project officers executed the test programs and ensured equal opportunity for all to fly. The F4H-1 had two seats, although we never carried another person. It had two engines, with a variety of hard points under each wing to carry various external stores, integrally mounted missiles in wells under the fuselage, and eventually an air-intercept radar to be used by a naval flight officer. The F8U-3 had one seat, no hard points on the wings, integrally mounted missiles under the fuselage, and, eventually, an air-intercept radar. It was truly an interceptor. The F4H-1 J-79 engines had a ten-hour limit before they had to be changed. The F8U-3 J-75 engine was more robust and farther along in its development. They were very different airplanes, but each was special in its own right.

Each test pilot had specific flying experiences, good and not so good, as the test programs unfolded, and slowly we formed differing opinions of each airplane. We had philosophical discussions among ourselves late in the day after flying stopped as we sat around the data tables. I thought the project officers did a great job in guiding the team to explore fully all the performance and flying qualities parameters. Each of us had our thrills.

On September 24 I thought I saw Dick Gordon give me a slight insider's smirk as he handed me my data card for a time-to-climb performance-measuring flight. As I read the short test card that I must fulfill, I saw that after a maximum performance climb to 45,000 feet, my next point was to fly at a speed of 995 knots indicated airspeed (kias) at 10,000 feet. In 1958 no one had ever flown that fast, that low, at least to my knowledge. Having lost more than a few friends in the past to high speed and high dynamic pressure, or Q, I had a deep respect for high-speed, low-altitude flight. But the point was valid, and Dick Gordon needed it. I accepted the card without saying a word.

To get the high-speed point that Dick wanted, I was going to have to work hard, and I made my plan accordingly. After taking off and completing the high-performance climb to 45,000 feet, which was recorded by onboard instrumentation in the F4H-1, I rolled inverted and pulled through to dive for the ground with full afterburner on both engines. As altitude decreased, my indicated airspeed built up, and I concentrated totally on making the speed of 995 kias, exactly, at 10,000 feet. It was still early morning and calm. I knew that any external turbulence might upset me at that speed and could start a self-destructive chain of events for the airplane.

I made the data point, and with no small amount of internal relief for being still in one piece, I came out of burner to look down to see with great alarm the bright red low-fuel warning light. The fuel gauges confirmed in no uncertain terms that I had a total of 800 pounds of fuel left, that the current rate of fuel flow was in excess of 20,000 pounds an hour, and that I was some 100 miles from Edwards, up north near China Lake. In my concentration to make the one test point, I had allowed the high thrust of the engines to guzzle almost 7,000 pounds of fuel in the few minutes it took me to descend to 10,000 feet, and I was in no way guaranteed that I could make it back. Coming back to idle power to conserve what fuel I had, I traded speed for altitude, zoomed to 24,000 feet while the speed bled off, and then headed for Edwards. Fortunately, that tradeoff provided the difference between making it and not making it, and I completed the flight forty minutes after taking off with a few pounds of fuel still indicated on the gauges. I made as nonchalant a report to Dick Gordon as I could to match his demeanor in assigning the task. There were other flights like that.

On October 7, while flying the F4H-1, I was accelerating through a Mach number of 1.35 when the right engine literally blew up. The damage was contained within the engine casing, but for just a moment I was confronted with the need for some quick decisions. It turned out that the engine starter had failed to disengage after start, and there was no way that I could have known that. When the starter failed, its ball bearings were propelled back into and through the engine to catastrophically take out most of the turbine blades. The immediate slewing yaw and engine fire warning light provided a good thrill at supersonic speed, but the airplane was rugged. The fire went out, and I made a single-engine landing at Edwards, proving the value of the designers' twin-engine concept, but the starter problem ended our F4H-1 flying for that NPE.

Flying the F8U-3 continued to be a pure delight. On investigating its ability to accelerate, I found the airplane to be accelerating at 2.2 IMN just as fast as it did at 1.7 IMN. We were speed limited at 2.2 IMN by the strength of the forward windscreens of both the F4H-1 and the F8U-3, but I felt sure that the F8U-3 could accelerate out to 3.0 IMN. We were never able to try that. One time, returning from completing one of Bill Lawrence's test cards, I was flying across the desert floor at 3,000 feet. In pure exhilaration I pulled up and did a loop, perhaps the first for the F8U-3. I entered the pattern at Edwards, landed, and taxied to the flight line. As I stopped the airplane, John Konrad approached, slowly shaking a shaming finger at me and smiling. I had forgotten that our every move in the F8U-3 was being monitored by telemetry. Test pilots were now living with big brother!

The F8U-3 was not without its problems. Early on we found that occasionally, at moderate supersonic speeds, the air moving through the throat of the intake duct could become critical, causing a shock wave to form. You could first hear that occurring as a low duct rumble and then feel and hear the shock move farther aft in the duct until it was right below you. At that point the duct would unload, and flame would shoot out of the front of the airplane while great compressor stalls would go bang, bang, bang! It sounded as if you had a 40mm gun between your legs. Dust would fly throughout the cockpit, and you did not know what to let go of first—the stick or the throttle. It was impressive and clearly limiting. It would have to be fixed.

We terminated our phase I NPE flying on October 10. We had a great amount of data that needed to be analyzed. Each airplane had problems that needed to be fixed. Clearly, the F8U-3 had the major problem with its duct criticality. The F4H-1 had an almost equally vexing problem with high stick forces and the starter disconnect. We agreed that we would return to complete phase I of the NPE in mid-November after each company had worked to improve its product, and the team then disbanded. There was a great amount of interest in the NPE results and the two airplanes, almost too great. So, in fairness to all concerned, we agreed to maintain complete silence as to our feelings and opinions of the two airplanes, and we did just that.

The NPE team returned to Edwards AFB on November 18 to complete the

evaluation of the two airplanes. McDonnell had fully rectified the high longi-
tudinal-feel-force problem by adjusting the spring feel in the F4H-1. We found
that chief aerodynamicist Conrad Lau of Vought had worked miracles and redesigned the F8U-3 duct, thus making possible a series of high-speed flight
comparisons in the two airplanes. On one flight I took the F4H to 2.0 IMN at
35,000 feet. In a comparative flight I took the F8U-3 to 2.2 IMN and 790 kias
at 35,000 feet. Other team members did similar tests. The F8U-3 was the
fastest of the two. During that time we became aware of the tremendous energy
and power in the sonic booms that we were generating. Not only did we become more aware, but others were finding this vexing by-product of speed to
be troublesome. A Canadian F-104, on a low-altitude flyby to open a new Canadian civil air terminal, broke every window in the glass-encased terminal! I
was informed that on one flight of mine over Santa Barbara I had dropped a
lady's dining room chandelier, the point of which stuck in her dining room
table. Sonic booms were a big topic as the NPE team completed its data gathering for the two great new airplanes and headed back to Patuxent and Washington. It was decision time, and a decision was being forced early.

Time was of the essence for contractors' cost and for politics. Each airplane
program was important, not only to the economy of the country, but also to the
local economies of Dallas and St. Louis. The team again agreed that, if possible, we would like to buy both airplanes; we felt we were in a win-win situation. If buying both was not possible, the F4H-1 offered the greatest growth potential because of its two engines, its space for two crew, its planned radar
system, and its flexibility for carrying external stores. The F4H-1 would have
less speed than the F8U-3 and the second-best flying qualities. Bob Elder, Dick
Gordon, and Bill Lawrence went to Washington to brief Vice Admiral R. B.
Pirie, deputy chief of naval operations (air), and Vice Admiral Murr Arnold,
then chief of the Bureau of Aeronautics. The final decision was made at that
level, but not before the secretary of defense and President Eisenhower were
briefed on the implications of the contract award. Then the decision was announced. It would be the F4H-1.

Subsequently, the one flying F8U-3 went to NASA Dryden to become a
high-speed test bed. The second F8U-3 and the partially completed third airplane were used for spare parts. I wrote Vice Admiral Pirie a personal letter to
tell him of the tremendous thrust in both airplanes and their capability to make
many records for the United States. That letter would play a part in the future.
McDonnell set about to prepare for phase II of the NPE, some months ahead,
and for the obligatory contractor demonstrations.

Occasionally, very occasionally, some pilots do things that are not quite in
the regulations. I think the statute of limitations for one such action in 1958 has
fully expired by now. An Engen family crisis occurred in mid-December. Our

oldest son, Travis, then fourteen years old, was coming home for the holidays from his studies at his paternal grandparents' home in Pasadena. He was flying across country by himself on United Airlines when a general strike was called on December 17 by all airline pilots. The strike call was abrupt, and Travis was caught in Columbus, Ohio, between flights. I did not quite know how to salvage what looked like a disaster, but I called Dick Wenzel of North American and asked him to meet Travis and hold on to him. I flew an AD-5W, one of our flight test airplanes, to Columbus to collect Travis and brought an extra helmet and flight suit for him to wear. After thanking Dick, we set off across country in a blowing snowstorm for Patuxent River, Travis sitting in the right seat of the AD-5W in the crewman's position. The flight was noteworthy only for the lack of trouble we had while flying instrument flight rules (IFR) en route, and in two and one-half hours we arrived back at the flight test line. As the propeller wound down, I told Travis to get out of the airplane, say nothing to anybody, and walk straight to our car, parked near the hangar, which he did. As I signed the yellow sheet after the flight, the lineman said to me, "That was the youngest sailor I have ever seen!" I responded, "They seem to be getting younger and younger." The family, with all four kids at home, had a great Christmas, with ice skating on the ponds. Travis returned to California legally after the pilots' strike ended.

Early in 1959 I was selected to address 600 insurance adjusters on the topic of sonic booms. I think this duty was payment for my transgressions in the F4H and F8U-3 during the phase I NPE. Someone must have heard from that lady in Santa Barbara. The insurance adjusters were meeting in Chicago, and I stopped there on February 12, en route to Palmdale, California, for the A3J-1 NPE and a continuation of the rate-of-roll project flying various Air Force airplanes.

Lieutenant Commander Bill Whalen had joined FQ&P and was the A3J-1 NPE project officer. My participation—to fly a few flying-qualities evaluation flights—was minimal. The A3J-1 was a large and sleek carrier airplane with two J-79 engines with afterburners. Extra fuel tanks and/or bombs were carried in an internal centerline space between the engines, and the bombs were to be ejected aft out of the airplane for delivery. It was novel. As I recall, the airplane weighed about 72,000 pounds fully loaded. Even more noteworthy was the fact that its fly-by-wire complexity made it the first airplane in the history of man to cost more than its weight in gold. (Gold then was fixed at $35 per ounce.)

In February 1959 we flew from North American's new large facility at the Palmdale airport, some 27 miles southwest of Edwards AFB. The A3J-1 flying qualities proved to be as good as the engineers said they would be, with one exception. I found the control force harmony to be good; the ratio was about one (aileron) to two (elevator) to four (rudder). I also did the first slow roll in the airplane, and when I rolled past the vertical to be inverted, the airplane kicked in a –1 g. That surprised me so much that I did it again, and as soon as I was inverted, the kick was repeated. I went back and told the engineers, who scratched their heads until someone figured out they had put the wrong value in the airplane's computer for positive g inverted flight. That was about my only noteworthy contribution to the A3J program. It turned out to be a better reconnaissance airplane than bomber, but all who flew it liked it. Unfortunately, my old and dear friend Bud Gear from VX-3 days was later killed in one when his A3J hit the ramp on *Saratoga* one dark night.

Leaving Palmdale after a day or two, I went to the Flight Test Directorate at Edwards to fly the F-100F, F-104A, TF-102, and F-101A, all Air Force fighters, to record their lateral response to fixed amounts of aileron deflection. Those data were additional to the data needed in our efforts to rewrite the roll parameters for the design specification SR-38E. It was readily apparent to me that there were different philosophies in the design of Navy and Air Force tactical airplanes. Those design philosophies seemed arcanely rooted in past beliefs, as well as warfare roles and missions. I could not understand why the Air Force would design a new fighter and then limit the pilot's use of its full potential. Air Force roll design parameters seemed comparable to those of the Navy, but then the Air Force added the stick limiter or stick kicker in the longitudinal control system. The Air Force used those in such airplanes as the F-101 and F-104 fighters to keep the airplane from being overstressed or to prevent the pilot from entering an aerodynamic stall. The Navy philosophy was to give pilots full authority for control of the airplane and train them to fly the airplane so as to not overstress it or to not fly it into the stall inadvertently. In the case of the F-104, there was some validity to the Air Force reasoning because it lacked adequate stall warning, but I still maintained that enough potential maneuvering capability was forfeited by the stick limiter to be the difference in some tactical situations between a win and a loss.

At this time, on the East Coast, Navy and Air Force pilots who belonged to the Society of Experimental Test Pilots (SETP) were trying to start our own chapter of the society. I could count ten of us, including Lieutenant Colonel Eugene Deatrick USAF, then in the Pentagon, but the headquarters of the SETP in Lancaster, California, told me that a minimum of twelve was required to start a new chapter. Completing my flying at Edwards, I returned to Patuxent to search for two test pilots who could qualify under the stringent requirements for SETP membership and get them to sign up. Gene Deatrick came up with the additional potential members from the Air Force so we could start the chapter, and he and I formed a friendship that lasts till today. Bob Elder was elected to be the first chairman of the East Coast section.

In the spring our spin program had a windfall. The Bureau of Aeronautics let us use Vought's spin demonstrator, the XF8U-1, which could be configured with strakes under the aft fuselage to be an F8U-2 as well. We were in need of a high-performance airplane that exhibited squirrelly spin characteristics, and we found one. A number of fleet pilots had gotten into trouble with incipient spins in enough different airplanes that we wanted to examine the post-stall and early spin phases to see what we could learn about those dynamics with a view to designing them out of airplanes. The XF8U-1 had most interesting post-stall characteristics and for spin demonstration purposes had been configured with not only a lap belt but also a chest belt and a pilot's head restraint—plus a spin chute.

I launched into a vigorous test program specifically to examine the early or incipient phase of the spin. Airplanes do not encounter accelerated stalls under high g loads while flying supersonic, but they do as soon as they slip subsonic. We began our investigation in that area, and I must admit that some of the rides were absolutely mind boggling in terms of the gyrations of the airplane and the forces placed on the pilot's body. It is difficult to break an airplane at the lower air densities above 35,000 feet, and it was there that we worked. Using a supersonic windup turn maneuver under 3- to 4-g loads, I would allow the F8U to slip subsonic. When it did, I would enter an accelerated stall, and the gyration would begin. To the uninitiated, the maneuver could be most confusing as the airplane bucked and rolled, yawed and pitched, for some ten to twenty seconds until it would begin to settle into an oscillatory spin, which in itself could be disorienting. We were able to catalog and analyze all phases of spins for both the F8U-1 and F8U-2 by reconfiguring with the aerodynamic ventral strakes. We did vertical-entry inverted spins and found that if held long enough the airplane would eventually right itself to spin upright in a highly oscillatory manner. A credit to Vought, the airplane never broke.

Even though you can be thoroughly familiar with an airplane's spin characteristics, the maneuver can be so violent that occasionally you can become disoriented. On one occasion, I was to investigate the effect of prospin controls on the steady-state oscillatory upright spin, with Dick Gordon as my safety chase pilot. I entered the spin at 40,000 feet with Dick circling around me as I descended, each turn becoming more oscillatory. The nose of the airplane would rise to the horizon and then snatch-fall to be inverted as the airplane whipped around, only to slow, nose rise, and fall again in a wicked repetitive spin. Each turn took three to five seconds, but I could count them as Dick provided a continuing backup turn count on the radio. I became confused in moving from using prospin to using antispin controls, and the spin continued past the intended five turns. As Dick counted "ten, eleven, twelve," his voice became a little more anxious. Finally, as I worked to right myself, Dick called "pull the chute!" I was then on turns eighteen and nineteen and passing 15,000 feet, and I did pull the chute. It worked as advertised, throwing the nose of the F8U directly down at Earth—the airplane seemed to hang in the chute. I released the chute and pulled out. Later, we sent a helicopter to recover the chute. I think that flight contained a lesson about overconfidence. It does not hurt a test pilot to have his ego pricked now and then.

By that time I was head of FQ&P, and Larry Flint moved up to relieve Commander Bert Earnest as chief projects officer. Bob Elder continued as director of the Flight Test Division. Spring and summer project flying was hot and heavy with spins in the F8U, F11F, and A4D-2; an NPE at the Douglas facility at Edwards AFB flying the A3D-2Q; and an evaluation of the F4H-1 air-refueling probe position. On one flight in May I made forty plug-ins in an hour. I was so intent on being successful at that latter effort that I held the stick grip very tightly and after landing I found I had lost the feeling in my right index finger, which lasted for several days. We conducted the phase II NPE for the F4H-1 at Patuxent from July 28 to August 12 and gave the clear go-ahead for serial production.

In August my orders arrived to detach from Patuxent River in September and to take command of a fighter squadron, VF-64, in Alameda, California, after going through the new replacement air group training in the McDonnell F3H-2 Demon at NAS Miramar, California. I finished out the summer in project flying and report writing and passed on my active projects to other pilots in the branch. At the last moment Vice Admiral Pirie directed that I go to Edwards AFB and make an attempt at establishing the world's altitude record for airplanes before I took command of the squadron.

We said good-bye to our many friends in Solomons and at NAS Patuxent, and Mary and I drove our two cars to California. We spiced up the trip for the children by having a musical chairs game in the two cars with different children for the different legs of the trip, and they had a lot of fun. The bottom line is that it is work for a family of six to drive two cars across the United States, particularly when you have been used to crossing the country alone and in four hours at 40,000 feet. We arrived at Del Mar and rented two adjoining apartments on the beach for the twelve weeks of training. The off-season rental gave us the ocean for our front yard and four bedrooms, two kitchens, two living rooms, and four bathrooms. Mary put the kids in school and settled in for some temporary living, and I left immediately for Edwards AFB and the McDonnell facility there.

McDonnell pilots Bob Little and Zeke Huelsbeck and I had theorized previously about how to make the altitude record attempt in the F4H-1. So, as Mary and I drove across country, they were preparing for the attempt by arranging the necessary theodolite camera coverage and radar positive control for the pattern, pull-up, and recovery. The flight would be a zoom climb using as much speed as possible to provide the energy to gain the altitude. The principle was similar to throwing a stone into the air as high as possible. They also knew late summer was the best time of the year because climatological conditions offered the seasonal desert high pressure and a standing temperature inversion to enhance thrust. We wanted at least −60°C at our planned run-in altitude of about 45,000 feet. We felt that we could get at least 2.4 IMN at that outside air temperature, while using full afterburner and some supertweaking of the J-79 engines. I would accelerate at a lower or higher altitude depending on which had the coldest temperature for that day. Once reaching the maximum Mach number attainable, which was planned to occur at or near Palmdale, California, I was to pull the nose up at a constant 2.2 g's to 43 degrees above the horizon at 53,000 feet and hold that trajectory until the airplane quit flying. I then would have some 94,000 feet in which to recover and return and land if the airplane did funny things. We also considered the effect that winds at altitude and the rotation of Earth could have, and we planned to make the runs from west to east for any boost that might give. Last, but certainly not least, was the sporting license. To achieve any record, you first must declare what you intend to do. The Federation Aeronautique Internationale (FAI) is the keeper of all aviation records and sets the rules by which you must play, and you must play by its rules if you want a record.

The endeavor involved a certain amount of risk because much of what we were doing had never been done before and I would be flying at speeds where any control failure could destroy the airplane. The death of Air Force pilot Captain Mel Apt in the X-2 research plane came to mind. His experimental airplane departed normal flight, tumbled, and destructed. I did not relish that thought, but also I did not dwell on it. Each flight would be a pressure suit flight. We were seeking to eclipse the current Soviet-held altitude record of 93,769 feet, which had been set on July 14, 1959, by Vladimir Iljiuchin, flying from Podmoskovnoye airfield in a T-431 airplane. According to FAI rules, we would have to beat that record by 3 percent, or achieve 96,583 feet, to gain the record. We had to start someplace so we made the first attempt on September 14, at least to give ourselves a capability benchmark. We were not sure how high we might get.

On that bright, clear morning over the California desert, I launched in the F4H-1, alone, with no safety chase airplane; we would rely totally on voice communications. I flew the preplanned route, climbing to the west to 40,000 feet to coast out over Point Mugu and there begin the supersonic acceleration. I turned northwest over the Anacapa Islands at full power to parallel the California coastline, while accelerating to 1.5 IMN, and made a sweeping turn to the right above Santa Barbara to head east for Palmdale, accelerating all the way while allowing the airplane to climb slightly to our target altitude of 43,500 feet. The pattern seemed too small, and the distance really clicked by at that speed. I arrived at the pull-up point almost too soon at 2.41 IMN. I advised all concerned on the radio that I was commencing my pull-up, and the response was a laconic "roger, you are marking well." In that connotation *marking* meant I had a heavy contrail strung out far behind me in that clear, deep-blue desert sky.

I reached and held an attitude of 43 degrees of climb, although this was hard to tell accurately, and I was on my way through an altitude of 55,000 feet. As I passed 73,000 feet, both afterburners on the J-79 engines blew out—there was not enough oxygen to sustain them. Passing 80,000 feet, I watched with great interest as the Kollsman barometric altimeter just quit, with both needles aimlessly pointing down at the six o'clock position. The airspeed indicator concurrently quit and read zero. I had no way to tell how high I was from then on or how fast I was going. But, more importantly, I had been gradually pulling the engine throttles back to keep an engine speed at 100 percent rpm. The throttles were on the aft stops, and the rpm was increasing through 104 percent. If I did not do something fast, the engines would burn up, so I shut them both down. My pressure suit immediately filled with life-saving pressure as the cabin altitude dumped to match the unknown outside altitude, and the suit distended, making my arm movements difficult.

Ground control said something to me on the radio, and I responded, and that was the last I heard on the radio for the remainder of the flight. It just seemed to quit. Still going up and entering 0-g flight as the airplane's parabolic path was reaching its zenith, I saw that the sky was a dark blue-black. As I looked ahead, I could see the curvature of Earth clearly. It was a terrific sight, but there was not much time to enjoy it. I held the controls loosely in a fixed neutral position. An Eberhard Faber yellow wooden pencil, then a hex nut, and then a Phillips-head screw, in that order, slowly floated from the cockpit floor up before my faceplate and then disappeared somewhere up forward of the cockpit glare shield. The airplane reached its zenith; still upright, the nose slowly fell through the horizon like an arrow shot into the air, and I was on my way back to Earth. I was over Edwards AFB.

The airplane accelerated downward, and as I returned through 80,000 feet, the altimeter and airspeed indicator both began to work again. I relit the left and then the right engine at about 46,000 feet and returned to land at Edwards with my dead radio. I had used all but 1,000 pounds of my fuel, and it had been a good effort. I had been in the air for forty-five minutes. Shutting down the engines, I asked the line crew to vacuum the cockpit for the pencil, nut, and screw. We learned the radio had burned up, perhaps because of lack of pressurization, and decided that I would turn it off at 70,000 feet in the future. Bob Little, Zeke Huelsbeck, and I agreed that we had a good flight pattern, but we extended the run-in leg a few more miles. The theodolite and radar data showed that we had reached 93,820 feet in the maneuver, and we agreed to try a 45-

degree climb the next time. The engineers told us that the loss of airspeed (energy) in the pull-up nullified the advantage of pulling harder to attain a higher angle of climb. We would have to stay somewhere between 43 and 47 degrees.

Not flying on some days and flying two flights on others, we settled into a routine on each of the eight days we flew over the succeeding fifteen days. Rise before dawn, launch in the cool morning by 0730, fly the profile, make the zoom, and return to analyze our effort, prepare the airplane for the next flight, and sit around and critique the previous flight with the engineers to modify the next one slightly. The altitudes that I achieved ranged between 91,900 and 94,837 feet, and we exceeded the Soviet record, but not by the required 3 percent. It was clear that the 2.41–2.43 IMN that we could achieve was our limiting factor. We needed more speed—not much, but still more speed.

Each flight was distinctive in its own way. Various little things happened, but on every flight the mysterious pencil, hex nut, and screw slowly passed before my faceplate in that same order as I went through 0 g at the top. No matter how hard the ground crew looked, they could never find them. I finally accepted them as mysterious crewmates and indications that I was at the top and about to start down. My morning wake-up sonic booms were becoming an irritant along my flight path over Point Mugu and Santa Barbara. On the recoveries I attempted engine relights at varying altitudes on the way down and obtained one engine relight as high as 67,000 feet. After the pull-up and once I had passed 65,000 feet, I felt that I had little control over the airplane—that no matter what I did with the stick the airplane was on its way and would go to an altitude predetermined by the initial angle of climb and speed of the airplane. On the tenth and last flight, I pulled to a higher angle of climb, and as I shut down the engines at about 80,000 feet, the airplane rolled 180 degrees and slowly spun 180 degrees so that I was going up tail first and upside down. I had quite a view and quite a ride! The maximum altitude achieved was 94,837 feet.

We gleaned a great many bits of valuable information for future use of the airplane and for flying at extreme altitudes, which we shared with the whole test flying community. On the tenth flight, one of the engine bleed-air doors malfunctioned as I made my dash for speed and pull-up. There was no indication in the cockpit, but when I returned to the line, the entire right milled-titanium stabilator (a tail control surface, consisting of the combined horizontal stabilizer and elevator) was badly scorched by hot gases and had to be changed, no small undertaking. Bob, Zeke, and I scratched our heads as to why it had malfunctioned and agreed that this was an appropriate time to stop this series of attempts. I called Larry Flint and told him of our agreement to terminate the altitude record effort and expressed my belief that the airplane could still take the record but that we needed more thrust to get to about 2.45 IMN to reach the required 3 percent increase over the Soviets. I said that I must move on to my squadron but that I hoped that he would come take the airplane to greater heights after thrust could be augmented through the use of water injection or some other means. I left Edwards for Miramar, frustrated, but still knowing that I had just completed some of the most interesting flying that I had ever done.

I returned to Miramar to start my training at Replacement Air Group 12. The F3H-2 Demon was a comedown after flying the best of the best, but there were things to be learned and new challenges of command to be faced.

Ten days after I left Edwards, and after the stabilator on the F4H-1 had been changed, Zeke Huelsbeck suited up in his pressure suit to explore flying the pattern for the altitude record with slightly upgraded thrust, in preparation for Larry Flint to come out for a try. As Zeke hurtled through the sky, headed east from Santa Barbara to Palmdale, the bleed door problem cropped up again, and hot gases burned through the hydraulic control lines to the new stabilator. The stabilator abruptly moved to full leading edge down, giving an instantaneous maximum airplane nose-up control input, and the Phantom disintegrated at 40,000 feet, killing Zeke instantly. Pieces of the airplane were spread over miles, and we lost a great test pilot and friend. Subsequently, in December, Larry Flint did come to Edwards and did fly another F4H-1 with improved thrust and did gain the world's altitude record of 98,560 feet for the United States.

The F4H-1, the first of a new breed of tactical airplanes, went on to be used for many record attempts in 1960 and 1961. Other pilots sought and blazed records in the F4H-1, an airplane that typified the golden age of naval aviation development of the 1950s. In that decade major improvements in airplane design proved the wisdom of a Navy aircraft development system that was founded in the 1920s and 1930s, expanded in the 1940s, and burst forth in the 1950s.

Aviation records are statements of ability and resolve. They show the potential of an airplane and the individual abilities of the pilots who are lucky enough to fly them. The F4H went on to be the principal fighter in the Navy, the Air Force, and the armed forces of many foreign nations and was flown for over thirty years until the 1990s—a tribute to the airplane's designers and manufacturers and the Navy.

PART THREE
HEADED FAIR

11. ALL-WEATHER DEMON
OCTOBER 1959 TO OCTOBER 1961

Alaska and Hawaii gained statehood, and Castro toppled the Batista govern-
ment in Cuba. John F. Kennedy was elected president, U-2 pilot Francis Gary
Powers was shot down over the Soviet Union, and the Vietcong, with support
of the North Vietnamese, established the National Front for the Liberation of
South Vietnam. A U.S. RB-47 was shot down by the Soviet Union with the loss
of the aircrew, and in 1961 the United States broke off diplomatic relations
with Cuba, after which the Cuban missile crisis developed. In Southeast Asia
Pathet Lao rebel forces threatened the royal Laotian army. The nations of the
South East Asia Treaty Organization (SEATO) met, forces were deployed, and
then the Pathet Lao agreed to a cease-fire. Yuri Gagarin became the first man
to orbit Earth in Vostok 1.

There were 17,214 pilots, 121,985 aviation ratings, and 24 aircraft carriers
of all types in the Navy. Lighter-than-air training ceased. Commander L. E.
Flint set the world altitude record of 98,560 feet on December 6, 1959, in an
F4H-1 Phantom II. In 1960 the first Navy Transit navigation satellites were
placed in orbit, and the first carrier onboard delivery squadron was estab-
lished as VRC-40. Lieutenant Colonel T. H. Miller set a 500-kilometer closed-
course speed record of 1,216 mph, and Commander J. F. Davis set a 100-
kilometer record of 1,390 mph, both also in the F4H-1. Commander Alan B.
Shepard became the first American to go into space, and Lieutenant R. F. Gor-
don flew from Los Angeles to New York in two hours and forty-seven minutes
in the F4H-1. USS Kitty Hawk *was commissioned. Lieutenant Huntington*

Hardisty flew an F4H-1 over a three-kilometer course for a new low-altitude speed record of 903 mph.

At the time that I returned to sea duty in 1959, naval aviation was moving to a new concept: level readiness. Everyone agreed there was a need to do away with the swings in aviation unit readiness caused by deployment cycles. Captain R. G. Dosé in Jacksonville, Commander Allard (Slim) Russell, and others in the office of the deputy chief of naval operations (air) in the Pentagon, as well as training officers in the fleets, championed that concept. First, there was the need to define and to establish more precisely the standards for training, and all agreed there was the need to develop the means to train the individual pilots of both fleets to the same standards, similar to the operational training first developed for naval aviation in 1917–18 and then again in 1942–44.

Two replacement air groups (RAGs) were formed in 1958, one for the Pacific Fleet at NAS Miramar, under Captain R. H. Dale, and one for the Atlantic Fleet at NAS Cecil Field, under Captain R. G. Dosé. Day and all-weather fighter, light attack, heavy attack, and instrument-training squadrons were formed in each fleet from existing air group squadrons and placed under those new air group commanders. The initial challenge was to identify and then to gather and organize the proper tactical talent to provide the best possible weapons training. The word went out, and pilots volunteered for the duty. The next challenge was to establish the pipeline for fleet replacement pilot training. The replacement air groups were beginning to function by the end of 1958.

The year 1959 was the transitional time for RAG training. Eventually, it was hoped, there would be an even flow of trained replacement pilots and the then-new naval flight officers (NFOs, non-pilot-trained bombardier/navigators) to provide level readiness in each fleet squadron and air group. I personally had concerns about the level readiness concept because in standardizing, while bringing the less aggressive performers up to some established norm, you can also constrain the tactical innovators and superachievers. It was a good concept if you were on a staff, looking down at the fleet, but I questioned how it would work in the squadrons. I felt that excellence, not standard performance, should be our goal and that sometimes rigid procedures could inhibit the development of new tactics. But we were on our way; we had to start someplace.

In October 1959 Captain Monk Russell was commander of Carrier Air Group 12, and Commander Paul Stevens was his chief of staff. The Pacific Fleet RAG squadrons were then training cadres of pilots much in the same manner as squadrons had completed their own training before. In October 1959 fourteen pilots destined for VF-21 in the Pacific Fleet came together in VF-121, the all-weather training squadron of Replacement Air Group 12 to train in the

F3H-2 Demon airplane. In a major realignment of squadrons and air groups in 1959, VF-64 had become VF-21. I was now the prospective commanding officer of VF-21, and Lieutenant Commander C. C. Buck was the prospective executive officer. We, along with a few lieutenants, lieutenants junior grade, and ensigns, reported for duty to be trained and made ready to join Air Group 2 when it returned from deployment in the early spring of 1960. We would replace those VF-21 pilots returning from deployment, who would then move on to other duties.

NAS Miramar had not grown much since I had last seen it two years before. The base was constrained to the north by Highway 395 and on the south by the relentless approach of suburbia. Even a hospital was being built three miles south on the main runway departure centerline. The lack of community planning would some day negate the use of the naval air station. VF-121 was situated in a large hangar, surrounded by some thirty-five F3H-2s in an aura of orderly chaos. Commander John Thomas was commanding officer, and Commander D. S. (Diz) Laird was executive officer. I spent the month of October and much of November just preparing to fly the F3H-2 and taking the obligatory tests levied by the checkout process in the new RAG. This was a far different and slower process than I had been used to before, but I did as bid and filled in the training squares. Fleet replacement pilots (FRPs) were treated like second-class citizens by overburdened and busy instructors, and there were too many airplanes to maintain and too few to fly.

I was greatly pleased to be commanding officer of a fighter squadron, but the airplane we would be flying was certainly not my choice. I had assiduously avoided the F3H at Patuxent River. The Demon was a big, slow fighter, certainly so by comparison with the F8U and F4H. The F3H had a rocky beginning when its first engine, the Westinghouse J-40, never produced the desired amount of thrust, and several test pilots were killed flying it. The first forty airplanes were sent down the Mississippi River by barge from St. Louis to New Orleans and then on to oblivion. The F3H-2 now had the Allison J-71 engine and still seemed underpowered. There were severe turbine-blade-rubbing problems while flying in heavy rain, and the fix was to increase the clearance between the turbine blades and the shroud each time that problem occurred, which in turn decreased the available thrust. Pilots called it the great converter—it converted jet fuel to smoke and noise. The F3H-2 Demon sat on the ground like a great praying mantis with its cockpit some 10 feet in the air. Pilots had broken legs and arms when they accidentally fell while attempting to get into or out of the cockpit, and many pilots jokingly said they should get flight pay just to sit in it. The airplane was not really terrible; it just did not have charisma. Its saving grace was its superb weapons system. With its

APG-53A radar, Sidewinder missiles, and two Sparrow III missiles, the airplane was a formidable night fighter, the Navy's best at the time, albeit slow by my standards and difficult to maintain.

Commander Billie Spell and Lieutenant Commander Pat Working ran the operations and training departments in VF-121 and had one year's RAG training experience under their belts. The challenge to gaining flight time was the F3H itself, because of the already-mentioned complexity. While undergoing RAG training, we FRPs destined for VF-21 trained as individuals and not as a tactical unit. We would begin our tactical flying together later.

After four months of VF-121 hurry-up-and-wait training, I had flown some sixty hours in the airplane, and the commanding officer, Commander John Thomas, led a group of us to carrier qualify in USS *Oriskany* during the first week of February 1960. Over seven days I made thirty-four day and night carrier landings in the F3H-2. All things considered, that carrier qualification was more efficient and better than making qualification landings later when the squadron would deploy in its assigned ship.

Escape and evasion training (E and E) was provided under the administrative mantle of the Fleet Airborne Electronics Training Unit Pacific at North Island, San Diego. The E and E school grew out of the experiences of U.S. POWs during the Korean War and U.S. servicemen's first confrontations with Communist "retraining." The fighting man's code, developed under President Eisenhower's administration, basically was designed to give those who were unfortunate enough to become POWs something to hang onto and to survive with when in the hands of the enemy. Experience in Vietnam in the late 1960s and early 1970s would cause some to view that code in a different light, but in 1959 the policy was to provide captors only name, rank, and serial number and totally resist compromising any information thought to be of value to the enemy. That survival school helped give fantastic patriotic and moral stamina to POWs Everett Alvarez, James Stockdale, John McCain, and many others. The E and E school entailed a brief day of water survival in the Pacific Ocean, culminating in a helicopter pickup, and then four days in the mountains east of San Diego near Warner Springs to experience survival in the mountains and to learn to evade those who were attempting to capture you. Finally, there were thirty-six hours in a prison camp run by some well-qualified and, in our view, mean suckers, who tried to break you.

On Sunday, March 6, we began our E and E training, and I, as a commander and the senior officer, was frequently singled out to be an example. The five VF-21 officers in the fifty-nine-person class included me, Lieutenant Commander Cal Buck, Lieutenant T. B. Green, and Lieutenants Junior Grade R. E. Graber and R. A. Anderson. All on the course were flying aircrew members. We were given nothing to eat and subsisted on weeds and bugs for several days, while we navigated from A to B across valleys and over mountains and evaded capture. By the time we were all "captured" later, we were weak from lack of food and perfect bait for the prison "guards" to play with for a day and a half.

Two fellow VF-21 officers not on the course took it upon themselves to help us out. On the day following our capture, Lieutenants Junior Grade John Newlin and Ron Fidell flew two airplanes directly over the camp and showered the stockade with hundreds of leaflets proclaiming that the five officers from VF-21 were special catches for the enemy force. The falling sheets of paper called attention to the fact that previously we five had had access to special military secrets. Needless to say, we received additional special attention from our captors! I am proud to say that everyone of the fifty-nine aircrew took it and walked out with their heads held high, albeit some 10 to 15 pounds lighter.

We VF-21 officers completed our flying RAG training and were detached March 14, 1960, to proceed to Alameda, home port of VF-21 and Air Group 2. Mary, the children, and I packed up our two cars and moved north where, at the end of March, USS *Midway* and Air Group 2 returned from deployment. The commander of Carrier Air Group 2, Commander Ed Holley, was relieved by Commander R. J. (Bob) Selmer at the air group's hangar at NAS Alameda in early April. On April 8 I relieved Commander W. R. Eason as commanding officer of VF-21, and Commanders Jack Kendall, Sam Gorseline, Bill Emerson, and Bill Hertig took command of their respective squadrons—VA-22, VA-23, VF-24, and VA-25. Our heavy attack squadron, VAH-8, was commanded by Commander Cyrus Fitton and was based at Whidbey Island in Washington. Cy would be relieved later by Commander J. T. Cockrill. Captain Ralph Cousins was commanding officer of USS *Midway*, which then underwent repairs at the Hunters Point Naval Shipyard.

Lieutenant Commander J. D. (Jake) Ward was operations officer in the returning VF-21, and because of our previous friendship as fellow test pilots at Patuxent River, I asked Jake to stay on for another tour as operations officer in VF-21. I was deeply grateful that he said yes because I respected and valued his flying experience. To Jake's credit, he did a masterful job, as did his wife, Janelle, too, because his agreement to stay brought another long cruise and more family separation for them.

During the month of April the returning crew of VF-21 was given much-needed leave and relaxation. I was ordered by Commander Naval Air Force Pacific Fleet (COMNAVAIRPAC) to USS *Oriskany* for several days in April to observe an F3H missile shoot at sea. On my return and during the month of May VF-21 worked and flew from 1800 to 0800 the next morning for six days a week and literally turned night into day. This was not without challenge, however, because Alameda is a large bedroom community on San Francisco

Bay. The city fathers of Alameda were besieged with complaints about the nighttime noise we were making, but they held their ground and supported us while we finished the month's flying. After that, we still flew at night, but not all night, every night.

We flew and trained with the Air Force ground controlled intercept (GCI) sites along the California coast and worked hard at polishing our intercept procedures. The Air Force needed the business, and we needed the training. The night-fighter pilot has to develop skills to work alone and to function as a single air-combat unit. We also maintained our squadron tactical organization and flew by twos and fours but stressed the importance of establishing each individual pilot's ability to fly and shoot missiles. I wanted to be sure that each pilot was good because his life would depend on that when we deployed. I selected Lieutenant Junior Grade R. A. (Dick) Anderson to be my wingman, and we flew together from then on.

Radar is the night-fighter pilot's right arm, his tool of choice. Our radar in the Demon allowed us to search 100 miles forward of the airplane. We could detect and intercept other airplanes, or we could fly in-trail formations, maintaining safe separation. To navigate, we could map the contours of the coastline or San Francisco Bay, and we could detect ships at sea. Each pilot was required to develop his skills until he felt entirely independent and capable of flying in the void of black nights at sea. Self-reliance is developed over time and is a measure of training and experience. It develops slowly, but when it is there, the pilot and his commanding officer know it. The ability to fly and fight at night and in all weather has improved immeasurably over time. The airplane, its radar, and its weapons are key, of course, but the process of building reliability in the pilot or crew through training is the most important ingredient.

The GCI sites were developed in the 1950s on the same concept as the carrier radar environment at sea. Those sites were located strategically about 400 miles apart around the periphery of the United States and in the central United States as well. They provided continuous radar coverage and early warning for the defense of the United States in the Cold War. Those GCI sites also provided positive air traffic control for Air Force and Navy airplanes long before civil aviation had any capability to do so and were the precursors of the en route air traffic control centers that we have today. Many a lost fighter pilot has called for a "practice" steer to identify his position. When, subsequently, the Federal Aviation Administration (FAA) developed its own civil ground-based radar system, those GCI sites were gradually disbanded, and the line of air defense moved to more remote sites along what became known as the defense early warning or DEW line. But in 1959 the Air Force GCI controllers needed training just as we needed radar intercepts for our training, and the GCI site near Santa Cruz, California, was a godsend for both. We worked well together.

Air Group 2 deployed to NAS Fallon, Nevada, from June 4 to 17 for integrated training between squadrons. Because of the RAG training each pilot had received previously, the Air Group 2 squadrons were much further along in their training cycles than would have been the case in previous years. I had to admit the RAG training was paying off. Flying at a remote naval air station like Fallon with the entire air group is much like deploying in a ship and lets the units integrate their tactics and procedures.

Early on during our night flying at Fallon, some of VF-21's junior officers discovered that their takeoff path for one particular runway would take them near the BOQ. After several VF-21 pilots lit their afterburners just as they were passing the BOQ early in the morning, an undeclared psychological war broke out between the VF-21 Demon pilots and the VF-24 Crusader pilots. In the Demon, when the afterburner lit, there was a bright yellow flash over the entire area with a resounding explosion as the raw jet fuel was forced into the tailpipe of the J-71 engine and lighted explosively. For those in the BOQ, sleep was out of the question. However, it did not take long for VF-24 to provide burner checks during the day for the benefit of the sleeping night-fighter pilots. Nobody was getting any sleep, the commanding officer of the naval air station was mad, and Bob Selmer intervened to force an afterburner truce about the time we returned to Alameda.

The F3H-2 proved to be a very difficult airplane to operate and maintain. Lieutenant W. W. (Smokey) Stovall was the squadron maintenance officer and did a very fine job, as did those senior petty officers who knew and maintained the airplane. Because of the adversity of trying to keep this complex airplane flying, it became a rallying point for high squadron morale. Also, Smokey Stovall was one of the pilots who fell from the cockpit of the Demon; luckily, he only broke his arm, but he was grounded for weeks before he could fly again.

In July all squadrons in the air group flew to USS *Lexington* off Monterey Bay to retain carrier landing qualification, and each pilot in VF-21 made eight day and eight night landings. In August we split our flight time fifty/fifty between day and night, and in September we again deployed to Fallon for concentrated air group flying training. I flew fifty-four hours that month, the most I ever flew in one month in the F3H. Also, by now each VF-21 pilot was quite skilled, and so it came as a surprise when Lieutenant Junior Grade Ray Graber was killed one night while making an instrument approach up the bay to NAS Alameda.

Ray flew into one of the fog-shrouded foothills just east of Hayward when he failed to maintain sufficient altitude during an approach to landing. Today called controlled flight into terrain (CFIT), this remains a killer in aviation. Ray Graber's wife and children lived nearby, and the entire squadron rallied to support them. After Ray's funeral and the completion of the accident investigation, the squadron continued its heavy flying schedule, rededicated to not letting that type of accident happen again.

The proof of the pudding for any fighter pilot is his skills in the use of his weapons system. VF-21 deployed to Point Mugu in mid-October for seven days to fire Sparrow III missiles under a free-play but still controlled scenario on the Pacific Missile Range. Each pilot fired at least one Sparrow III at remotely controlled BQM jet target drones in head-on presentations, which gave the challenge of high relative speeds and the necessity for quick decisions. The Sparrow III missiles with semiactive seeker heads were deadly weapons—when they worked.

The APG-53A radar enabled the pilot to detect a large unidentified airplane, or bogey, beyond 100 miles but normally was effective inside 100 miles at between 80 and 40 miles. We were happy to achieve detection in that range. The hardest firing solution was the head-on, down-the-throat shot, and in that type of run, the pilot would lock on his target as soon as it was at about a 20-mile range on the radar screen. He locked on by using his left cockpit console radar control to slew a small acquisition ring out to encompass the radar blip. The radar would then lock on, and the automatic fire-control solution would begin to unfold on the pilot's radar screen. First, the range marks and target blip would be replaced by a steering dot for the pilot to follow. Second, a large speed ring would appear, indicating closure rate by a gap in the periphery: three o'clock for 300 knots, nine o'clock for 900 knots, up to twelve o'clock for 1,200 knots. There were minimum and maximum ranges for missile firing, and the pilot knew what he must do to be within those parameters as soon as he locked on. Next, missile selection and arming switches were placed on. Inside 20 miles the speed ring would begin to shrink towards the center with decreasing range. The pilot would fire his missile by pressing a button on the control stick grip before reaching minimum range—provided he had set all his switches properly. The missile would leave the airplane and track automatically to the target on reflected radar energy. A proximity fuse would explode a charge in the warhead and cause an expanding ring of shrapnel to cut the target in half. The radarscope's speed ring would continue to get smaller, indicating impending collision, until at the minimum range a large breakaway X would be displayed to tell the pilot a collision was imminent. He must break off the attack with a fast roll, either right or left, to then pull down and away. If all had gone well, the missile would have done its job.

When we returned, "victorious," to Alameda from our missile shoot at Point Mugu, we flew en masse in our fourteen Demons down San Francisco Bay toward Alameda for all the crew and families to see. They watched for our return and could see the black exhaust plumes of our airplanes long before they could see the airplanes. The J-71 engine certainly was distinctive. I figured with a signature like that it probably was lucky that we were night fighters.

The missile system of the F3H made it formidable as a night fighter, and it was a pleasant airplane to fly and honest in the sense that the airplane told you all you needed to know to fly it well. But still it was gutless. It would go supersonic if pointed down, but not in level flight, even in afterburner. Without its weapon system, it was a docile and unspectacular airplane.

Captain Ralph Cousins was seemingly from the old school. He was taciturn, very regulation oriented, and cool to subordinates, almost to the point of being cold. Ralph was an experienced aviator and at one time commanded Air Group 11. He was typical of the new, experienced breed of operators who were taking command of our carriers. *Midway* was Air Group 2's assigned ship and in October completed refresher training to return to Alameda. Bob Selmer arranged through Ralph Cousins and NAVAIRPAC to take the air group to sea in the first week of November for our initial operations. This was my first seagoing experience in a *Midway* class ship, although I would subsequently serve in the other two ships of the class. They all were rollers rather than pitchers, and the deck motion could be unsettling to pilots on black nights. We had a good at-sea period with many landings, both day and night.

Truly, we were operating and flying more in 1960 than we had been in earlier years, and the Navy had progressed a long way from the four-hours-a-month flying that we had done just ten years before. It was clear to all of us that this increased operating tempo was creating a better and safer atmosphere for flying jets in the fleet. At this time, in the early 1960s, we still had one propeller-driven AD-6 squadron in the air group.

There was one alarming lack of development in *Midway*. The carrier air traffic control center (CATCC) procedures were outdated and uncoordinated, although the people responsible for the procedures thought them adequate enough. As the principal all-weather pilot on board, I may have realized this first, but other squadron skippers realized it as well. Bob Selmer was concerned that we were so close to deployment and the CATCC was still not good enough to create confidence among his pilots. At this fortuitous time, USS *Ranger* returned to Alameda with Lieutenant Commander Clyde H. Tuomela as CATCC officer. Clyde had been a night-fighter pilot in VF-41 with Tag Livingston during our 1957 *Bennington* cruise. Now, as CATCC officer in *Ranger*, he had set about to devise new and better all-weather procedures. I learned of those procedures while embarked in *Ranger* for a short time and was impressed with what Clyde had done. He created order out of disorder and made the process of flying on board ship in all weather easy. Bob Selmer and I began to try to adopt Clyde's procedures in *Midway*. Also, I became Clyde's salesman and touted his procedures through all of my night-fighter friends flying from other ships. The *Ranger* procedures using TACAN, radar, and time were the best we had ever had and eventually became the standard for the Navy. Still, in *Midway* we were having trouble adopting *Ranger*'s procedures.

We finished 1960 with another short at-sea period in *Midway* during the second week of December. In January, before we had our last training period before deployment, Lieutenant Junior Grade Ron Fidell experienced an unexplained engine failure at night over San Francisco Bay. In light of the heavily populated areas around the bay, as well as our responsibilities as pilots, we had discussed that unpleasant scenario many times in the ready room. Following squadron procedures and not wanting to eject because of the many communities nearby, Ron chose to ride his airplane in and landed in the bay just west of Alameda. He did a good job and was not hurt other than perhaps swallowing too much salt water, and we recovered the airplane from the bottom of the bay. But that accident exacerbated a deep fear that Ron had concerning flying over water. One thing led to another, and I was forced to leave him behind when we deployed. He was reassigned to an East Coast squadron for another chance to fight that fear, but eventually he left the Navy. Squadron pilot Lieutenant Commander Jack Dunn also chose to resign from the Navy because of a personal business opportunity about the same time, so we would deploy with seventeen officers and fourteen airplanes.

In January we began preparing in earnest for our February 15 deployment. The commander of Carrier Division 3, Rear Admiral Frank Miller, and his staff came on board, and *Midway* went to sea for a major exercise with many other ships and units from January 16 to February 2. Ralph Cousins was fully cognizant of *Midway*'s characteristic roll in the Pacific Ocean swells that constantly swept in from Hawaii and cautioned the air group to tie down all aircraft that were not moving on deck. Each of us commanding officers, in turn, lectured our troops and established procedures with the air officer, Commander Bob Witmer. Standard practice was to have at least three tie-down chains on any aircraft the minute it stopped moving and six tie-down chains at other times. If the airplane was not going to be moved in less than twenty minutes, we put nine tie-downs on the airplane.

Wonder of wonders, my squadron was caught short. While moving a Demon, the young plane captain (the enlisted man responsible for that particular airplane) climbed down to secure it when the sailor on deck left without making the obligatory three-point tie-down. Before he could tie down the Demon, the ship rolled, and the airplane began to move on its own. The airplane disappeared smartly over the port side of the flight deck near the number 2 elevator and did not float for ten seconds. The ship proceeded to conduct the man overboard muster, and we gratefully found no one missing. But as soon as that was finished, I was summoned to the bridge to face one irate Captain Ralph Cousins, who waited my arrival while building a cold fury. There can be no excuse for losing a multimillion dollar airplane over the side, no matter what, and I took the full barrage from the captain. As air officer, Commander Bob Witmer came in for his fair share too, and it looked like Captain Cousins was going to name Engen and Witmer as parties to a formal investigation. We both could see visions of a long, green judicial tablecloth in our futures. As it turned out, Bob Selmer and Commander Joe Frossard, *Midway* operations officer, persuaded Ralph Cousins not to crucify us. The investigation was completed with appropriate responsibilities being assigned, and my troops felt bad that they had let me down. But that was not half as bad as I felt, and it did not get the airplane back.

Departure time came, and that evolution certainly had not become easier! On the foggy morning of February 15, Mary dropped me at the forward brow of *Midway* and drove away immediately. I saw others endure their private good-bye turmoil and remembered the wife of a *Lexington* sailor during World War II who, with tears clouding her eyes after saying good-bye, backed her car off that very same pier. She was rescued immediately, but the car stayed on the bottom. I stood on the flight deck as we moved slowly under the Bay Bridge and then picked up speed past Alcatraz, Fort Mason, and the San Francisco Yacht Club and then under the Golden Gate Bridge to meet the first long swells of the Pacific. Then I went below. We would be back in seven or eight months.

I had asked Bob Selmer to borrow Clyde Tuomela from *Ranger* to help our CATCC procedures during our transit to Hawaii and our ORI. We did manage to imprint many of the good *Ranger* procedures on the *Midway* CATCC crew, but still the process entailed removing some people who could not seem to embrace the new procedures. By the time we left Pearl Harbor on Sunday, February 26, we had the all-weather flying procedures for carrier approaches firmly in place and would polish them during the ensuing cruise. Clyde Tuomela returned to *Ranger* with my everlasting thanks.

Before we left Hawaii, on the night of February 21, Hank Halleland landed wheels up at Barbers Point in his F3H. I am sure he felt as bad as I did about the needless accident. Hank was maintenance officer and talked COMFAIRHAWAII into letting us take the moderately damaged airplane to Japan to be fixed while we flew with thirteen Demons for some time. Also, Lieutenant Whitey Varner of VF-24 lost the left main wheel of his Crusader as he landed on board *Midway* on February 24. The wheel flew up the deck, struck one of my F3Hs in the folded outer wing panel, and then caromed into the back of a flight deck crewman, who was seriously injured. Unfortunately, despite what flight surgeon Art Holmboe and *Midway*'s senior medical officer could do, he died. We then flew with twelve Demons until we exchanged the outer wing panel with one from Hank's previously damaged airplane.

The obligatory ORI, held under the watchful eyes of COMFAIRHAWAII, went reasonably well. Each squadron attained grades at about the 90 percent, or low excellent, level, and the ship received an 80 percent. The inspectors always seemed to grade the carriers harder than the air groups and squadrons. During that busy period I saw the value of Jake Ward and wished I had fourteen other officers as good as he was in all that he did. Lieutenants Bob Lewis, Cody Sherar, Hank Halleland, and Tom Green were stalwarts, as well.

We sortied from Pearl Harbor on Sunday, February 26, and headed for Guam. No matter how many times you enter or leave Pearl Harbor, flight deck parade evokes emotions in the crew at that historic place. That sortie was no different from the others. However, one thing was different for me that time. I had just received my orders in the mail from Washington. I was selected for an air group and would take command of Carrier Air Group 11 in Miramar upon our return at the end of September. My selection was a real plum because only two opportunities arose each year to take command of an air group in the Pacific Fleet. I left Pearl Harbor with a song in my heart, until a sailor driving a forklift on the hangar deck ran into one of the F3Hs. Then we had eleven to fly.

We crossed the Pacific swiftly as we headed for Guam. The boats to be used for crew liberty in foreign ports were nested in twos on the hangar deck. Those boats, a compromise for crew morale, used up valuable space. Also, each tractor, each jet starting unit, each oxygen cart, and anything that took up square footage and deck space compromised our ability to conduct flight operations. The footprint of the small Douglas A4D attack aircraft was called the basic unit, or deck multiple, of 1. Deck multiple was a new term in 1960, certainly for me. A Demon's multiple was 2.13. Every movable object on the flight and hangar deck had its own deck multiple. Added together, the ship's total deck multiple determined the flexibility for carrier operations. *Midway* was carrying too high a deck multiple and was in danger of having a locked deck. There is just so much space on board a carrier, and the required landing area accidentally can become unusable due to too many aircraft on the flight deck. A locked deck is what every air officer dreads. So we did not fly unless absolutely necessary on our transit west. Everyone was concerned, but Captain Cousins had to live with that concern for the ensuing cruise. We planned to alleviate the problem later by putting five F3Hs and seven F8Us ashore temporarily.

The ship moved rapidly by Wake Island, and we had a day's stop in Guam. After dodging a distant typhoon, which produced some very high seas, we launched aircraft on March 12 and put them ashore at Cubi Point in the Philippines. Before we had been deployed for one month, the new level readiness became an issue. Cal Buck learned that he would be detached in the summer, earlier than we expected, and I learned that Lieutenant Cody Sherar was applying for limited duty as an aerological officer and that Lieutenant George Reith would be leaving as well. I was alarmed. Subsequently, I was informed we were to receive two fresh new lieutenants junior grade and a senior lieutenant commander to replace the three officers who were leaving. This was an entirely new ball game for me and promised to make the cruise more of a training cruise than one during which we could meet every challenge. It appeared to me that the Bureau of Naval Personnel was using level readiness as an excuse to provide personnel flexibility at the cost of readiness in the deployed fleet and that COMNAVAIRPAC was rolling over as it agreed. I shared my concerns with Bob Selmer.

On March 19 our detachment of Demons and Crusaders temporarily at Cubi Point flew back on board, and *Midway* entered the harbor at Hong Kong for a port visit on March 21. We were there for two days, just long enough for the ship's company to purchase some $16,000 worth of personal merchandise, when the ship was summarily ordered by the commander of the Seventh Fleet to get under way on two hours notice and head south. Every Navy ship has an emergency recall plan for just such circumstances, and we were able to roust out all VF-21 officers and men, except for Lee Webster, our Allison representative. We left Lee behind as we sortied early March 23 to meet a developing threat in Southeast Asia: a rebel Laotian force supported by the Soviet Union, China, and North Vietnam was moving south to conquer the royal Laotian army. SEATO was considering intervention. There was grave concern that if Laos fell, South Vietnam would be next. *Midway*, *Coral Sea*, *Lexington*, and *Bennington*, with their respective task groups, were positioned in the South China Sea in early April for possible action.

The schedules of *Midway* and the other ships were disrupted for the next forty-five days until the Pathet Lao signed a cease-fire agreement. During that time a Marine F8U squadron, VMF-311, with my old friend Lieutenant Colonel Dick Rash from VX-3 days, initially flew on board to replace VF-24. The plan was that the Marines could more easily fly off and operate from airfields in Laos or South Vietnam, if necessary, while *Midway* retained its own group at full strength. Those Marine F8Us were later replaced by an Iwakuni-based Marine A4D squadron commanded by Lieutenant Colonel Rushlow, after *Midway* moved north to Yokosuka briefly to pick them up and put VF-24 ashore at Atsugi, Japan. At this same time Captain R. G. (Bob) Dosé came on board to relieve Ralph Cousins as commanding officer. The change of command was held in Yokosuka on April 21, and then *Midway* returned to the South China Sea. When the Pathet Lao signed the cease-fire under the threat of escalation on May 4, the Seventh Fleet returned to normally scheduled operations, and VF-24 returned on board. The flexibility of the aircraft carriers and their ability to provide air power where it was needed was proved once again.

We all had deep respect for Captain Ralph Cousins. He was a good carrier commanding officer. With his departure, executive officer Commander K. E. (Doc) Gulledge also left, and Commander C. F. (Joe) Frossard, formerly the operations officer, became executive officer. We noted almost immediately that

Captain Bob Dosé brought with him a relaxed but good operating credo. As spring progressed, we seemed to fly more with less effort. He quickly won the hearts of the pilots.

Flying the Demon at night was also particularly satisfying to me now. Moonless nights in the western Pacific can be absolutely pitch black; there is no difference to the pilot between the sea and the sky—it is all one black hole. Near Japan we found not only black nights but also poor weather; still, on any given night launch we would keep two to four Demons airborne. After an hour of intercepting targets or, if there were no targets, bumping heads (a flight leader or wingman taking turns intercepting the other for training) with our squadron mates, we would then regroup to return to be in the proper sequence for our landings. *Midway*'s CATCC procedures had improved, and the ship would be into the wind and ready to receive us when we arrived. Landing on board ship is not hard; in fact, it can be easy. The Demon was so stable that it practically landed itself. In the daytime I could catch any numbered wire that I wanted. At night it was a little harder to pick your wire, but not much.

I always enjoyed landing on board ship at night because it is challenging and fun. The hard part comes after you land. VF-21 was always the first down the slot to land on board, and as the VF-21 flight leader, I was always the first to land. After the arresting gear crew disengaged the hook, the flight deck crew would taxi me forward to the number 1 spot on the port bow. The procedure was for the fly one director to taxi you across the foul line and pass you forward to another director, who would put your left wheel about two inches from the port flight deck scupper and carefully inch you forward until you were as far forward as possible. Your nose wheel would be just inches from going over the forward deck edge or round down of the flight deck. After a hold-your-right-brake signal, the director would spin you. The tail of the airplane would swing out over the edge of the flight deck, and you would be in an absolute black hole at the most forward part of the flight deck. The ship's island and the seeming safety of its red moon glow lighting seemed miles behind you. If your canopy was open, or if you opened it after being parked, the wind blowing across the deck at 35 to 40 knots would vacuum the cockpit of any papers not firmly fastened down. You could hear the water rushing by just 65 feet below your left wing. Then you had to climb out of the cockpit to inch your way back toward the safety of the left wing while reaching for two goat steps that, you hoped, had popped out of the fuselage when you lowered your landing gear. One false step and you would fall over the side into the black water. That is the most hairy feeling in the world and surpasses any thrill of a carrier landing. Those who have been first on board on a black night and taxied to the number 1 spot on the port bow never forget the sensation.

Midway stopped in Buckner Bay, Okinawa, on the return trip north and hosted the change of command for CTF 77. This subordinate Seventh Fleet command for the carriers was rotated between carrier division commanders to give each an opportunity to operate the larger force of three task groups. Rear Admiral Frank Miller relieved the carrier division commander embarked in *Lexington* as CTF 77 in a very brief ceremony on board *Midway*, and we subsequently were under way to hold exercises with the Air Force squadrons stationed at Kadena AFB, Okinawa. Lieutenants Sherar and Reith received their orders to depart in July, and Lieutenant Commander Cal Buck would leave at the same time. I felt bad about losing him, but his orders would give him a command on the East Coast. I was told by COMNAVAIRPAC that the new pilots would arrive in the same time frame, but trading three experienced hands for three unknowns bothered me a great deal. More than ever, I suspected level readiness was an excuse for the personnel people to move people around in the name of improved fleet capability.

Mary and I made a big family decision for the month of June. She would fly at our own expense to Japan for a visit. We had never done this before, but we had heard of many wives flying to the Mediterranean to visit their husbands. June seemed to be a good time in the cruise from a scheduling standpoint, and for my part the money would be well spent. We each needed a lift in our morale. Our three youngest children went to visit my mother and father in Pasadena, and Mary flew to Tokyo with Peg Selmer and Louise Barton, wife of carrier air group operations officer Commander Frank Barton. They arrived at Tokyo International Airport as planned, and Mary and I stayed at the Imperial Hotel in Tokyo. Over the course of her three-week visit, she and I were able to see a lot of Japan, albeit mostly the island of Honshu. Her visit was a lifesaver for both of us, and when she left, we both knew that we could take the remaining few months of separation in our strides.

By June 8 two new pilots reported on board: Lieutenants Junior Grade Robert Hendershott and Don Hanna. To my knowledge those two were the first replacement pilots to be sent to a deployed Pacific Fleet squadron since perhaps the Korean War and certainly the first since the fleet replacement pilot program began in 1958. After they arrived and we made them feel at home, each pilot flew under closely controlled and observed conditions during the day. We sent them to Atsugi to fly shore based to build up recent experience and flight time. Hendershott seemed to be a bit rough around the edges but capable. But Don Hanna was a solid citizen and did well. I watched Hendershott closely and continued to give him an opportunity to fly.

Midway left Yokosuka on June 30, and we planned for Hanna and Hendershott to fly and complete requalification landings on the night of July 1. After both pilots had flown during the day, we began to run them through the deck (a series of landings and catapult shots) at night. Hanna did very well. Hendershott was having problems in landing on board and was not consistent; in fact, he was so inconsistent in his flying that he could not land on board, and we bingoed him, or directed him to proceed, to Atsugi when he reached his minimum fuel mark.

Fuel is the single most important operating limitation for every jet airplane. Carrier operation cycle times and developing emergency situations revolve around the amount of fuel carried in the airplanes. In a carrier qualification situation such as Hendershott's, fuel on board is foremost in everyone's mind. Any decision that is made on his behalf must take into account the fuel that he has. Consequently, if he reached a specified minimum fuel state without being able to land on board, Hendershott would be bingoed to his divert field, in this case NAS Atsugi. A gravy factor was cranked into the fuel reserve in case everything did not go exactly as planned. *Midway* was operating 100 miles east of Atsugi. When Lieutenant Junior Grade Hendershott reported that he had reached the predetermined minimum fuel remaining and he still had not landed on board, that triggered the decision to send him to Atsugi. It would take him forty minutes to get there.

Hendershott flew to Atsugi and approached the field to land, but his airspeed was far too fast for an approach to a landing. Even so, he tried to salvage the landing without going around again. As a result, he was fast, and his nose landing gear touched the runway first, instead of his main landing gear. From his voice transmissions to Atsugi tower, he quite obviously was agitated and not thinking straight. Because of its speed, the airplane set up a porpoise maneuver that became increasingly divergent each time the wheels hit the runway. At midfield, bouncing higher with each succeeding contact, he was in extremis and chose to eject from his F3H. Because he was on the way down in one of the porpoise cycles, there was not sufficient time or altitude for his parachute to open fully, and he was killed when he hit the ground. His airplane, now pilotless, touched down, sheared the landing gear, and slid to a stop on the runway with very little damage in the cockpit area. If he had stayed with the airplane, he would have lived.

I was shattered, disappointed in my decision to fly him at night, and mad. Lieutenant Junior Grade Hendershott had been sent to the fleet as a fully qualified night-fighter pilot. If he was not ready, then someone in the RAG squadron must have known that. You do not fly with someone in training for sixty or seventy hours without knowing how good, or how bad, he is. He was sent to the fleet to fly in one of the most demanding environments in aviation with the certification that he was capable—and he was killed. Someone had not done his job properly. At first I blamed myself and reviewed how we had introduced him to flying in the fleet, but he had been given a relatively easy and controlled opportunity to begin flying. I was concerned that level readiness was not working in the fleet as some had envisioned it would.

On the other hand, Don Hanna did well and was soon flying as a member of the VF-21 team. His capabilities were what were expected of a fleet replacement pilot. By late July Lieutenant Tom Drumm, an experienced night-fighter pilot, arrived to take Hendershott's place. Maybe the level readiness people had the message and were thinking more clearly.

On July 27 a *Midway* flight deck crewman inadvertently walked behind an F3H that was being turned up at high power and was immediately blown overboard. Just being blown from your footing is surprise enough, but then to fall 65 feet into cold seawater moving by at 25 knots really adds to the surprise. The crewman was rescued by the helicopter in four minutes and in another four minutes was back on board, uninjured—proving again that the life of a flight deck crewman is a tough one. He works in conditions that are beyond description where the wind can blow 45 knots, noise can rise above the threshold of pain, and rain, ice, or snow can fall day or night. One false step and he can get sucked into a jet intake or blown overboard, or he can walk into a whirling propeller.

The flight deck is the domain of the aviation boatswain mates. A special breed, they have learned to live on the flight deck and thrive on the physically demanding conditions. My hat is off to all aviation boatswain mates; they are the cream of the crop. Wearing the easily identifiable yellow shirts, they control the movement of aircraft on the flight and hangar decks, working at the direction of the flight or hangar deck officers, who in turn work for the air officer. Over time, the yellow shirts get to know the pilots, and the pilots get to know the yellow shirts. Each respects the other, provided their actions merit it. Some pilots are known as nervous nellies, some as cool cats. All are treated accordingly when being taxied for launch or recovery. The interaction between yellow shirts and pilots becomes up close and personal through eye contact, and both know who is who. The yellow shirts will on occasion adjust their signals and demeanor to match the pilots, and the pilots must have absolute trust in the yellow shirts, who control their every move while on deck. It has to be that way if you are to have a smoothly flowing flight deck operation so that no one will be killed. Trust, both ways, is of the essence if you are to maneuver with your wheel one or two inches from constant threat of disaster.

On August 18, 1961, I made my 500th carrier landing. It had taken me nineteen years of flying some 4,400 hours from twenty-three different aircraft carriers to do that. Today, our naval aviators can do that in three or four cruises from three or four aircraft carriers.

Events moved rapidly through the summer of 1961. Rear Admiral Sharp and his staff were now embarked in *Midway*, as CTF 77, and exhorted *Midway* and

Air Group 2 to fly more. On August 11 Hank Halleland was catapulted in a Demon and immediately had a loss of power so that by the time he was 2 miles ahead of the ship he ejected while still flying at about 200 feet. The ejection seat and parachute worked well; Hank was picked up by the helicopter and was back on board *Midway* shortly, but we had lost another airplane. Art Holmboe found that Hank had sustained the standard Martin-Baker-seat compressed-spinal-disk back injury. Over time the Martin Baker seat resulted in many compressed spinal disks, but the alternative made the risk acceptable. Hank was moved to the Naval Hospital at Yokosuka for evaluation and was subsequently airlifted to the States and Oak Knoll Naval Hospital for recuperation.

Spare carrier aircraft were kept in Japan to be used as required during deployments. As airplanes were lost during the *Midway* cruise, we were assigned additional ones, but by the end of August we had twelve airplanes and fifteen pilots. Other squadrons lost airplanes, as well, except for the A4D squadrons. The A4D was a tremendously successful airplane, both in its operational capability and its reliability and the resultant flying safety. By early September our planned time in the western Pacific was coming to a close, and in deference to our hasty departure from Hong Kong in March, *Midway* returned to Hong Kong on September 7. While we were in port, Hong Kong was brushed by a typhoon, but *Midway* held fast and rode out the storm. We were able to collect the things we had purchased some six months previously, and *Midway* departed for the United States on Monday, September 11.

Passing the Hawaiian Islands on September 22, we flew all the airplanes to exercise them. On September 26 we flew them off to return to Alameda. Captain Bob Dosé brought *Midway* into Alameda the next day, and one more cruise was brought to a conclusion.

Between 1958 and 1960, as level readiness was being introduced into the fleets, difficult situations arose from time to time, but the concept was beginning to work. Squadrons could be used more effectively without having to stand down for basic tactical training. Air groups were tactically more cohesive and operationally ready because the squadrons could spend more time in productive, coordinated training and more advanced operations. Naval aviation tactical operating procedures (NATOPS) were being written for all naval aircraft and even aircraft carriers. Lieutenant Commander Clyde Tuomela's work in USS *Ranger*'s CATCC eventually became the Navy-wide standard for all-weather approach and departure procedures.

In September our oldest son, Travis, entered MIT as a freshman, without much help from his father, I might add, at least in 1961. Mary and I, along with Candace, Chris, and Charles, prepared to move south, where I would take command of Air Group 11 at Miramar. But first VF-21 moved south to Miramar as part of the general base relocation that had been levied earlier by the CNO. All

Pacific Fleet fighter squadrons would be based at Miramar, all light attack squadrons would be at newly built NAS Lemoore near Fresno, California, and AD squadrons would be at Moffett Field. The heavy attack squadrons would remain at Whidbey Island in Washington. We flew our F3Hs to Miramar on October 2, and I relinquished command of VF-21 on October 3, 1961, to Commander Robert Kuntz. It would be his turn to take VF-21 onward. I returned to Alameda, and my family packed up and moved south to Miramar, where I would have new flying challenges.

12. CAG 11
OCTOBER 1961 TO DECEMBER 1962

The United States established the Military Assistance Command in South Vietnam and sent Army training missions to help the South Vietnamese. France and Algeria signed a truce after seven years of civil war. China invaded India, seized territory, and then announced a cease-fire. Many anti-racial-discrimination laws were enacted in the United States, and John F. Kennedy won the presidential election, defeating Richard Nixon. COMSAT was created to coordinate development of worldwide satellite communications. Soviet missile sites were discovered in Cuba, and President Kennedy imposed a quarantine on the island and froze all military personnel on active duty. Those actions were rescinded when the Soviets agreed to stop supplying missiles to Cuba. John Glenn orbited Earth three times in Friendship 7, *Scott Carpenter made three orbits later in* Aurora 7, *and still later Walter Shirra completed six orbits.*

There were 18,371 pilots, 135,453 aviation ratings, and 26 aircraft carriers of all types. Commander George Talley made the first landing on USS Enterprise *in a Crusader. The F4H-1 set a series of time-to-climb records to many altitudes. Naval Reserve units called up in 1961 were stood down in August 1962. Naval aviators James Lovell, John Young, and Charles Conrad were chosen as astronauts. On September 18, 1962, the Department of Defense (DOD) levied a joint Army–Navy–Air Force regulation establishing a uniform system of designating military aircraft along the lines of previous Air Force designations.*

By the end of October 1961 Mary and I had moved to Del Mar and into a house on the hill overlooking the Pacific Ocean. The children were sent off to new local schools. I reported to NAS Miramar for training at Carrier Air Group 12, where Captain John Sweeny was the commander and Commander Paul Stevens was his chief of staff. Commander M. M. (Mike) Casey was commanding officer of VF-121, the F4H squadron, and Commander Jeff McVey was commanding officer of VF-124, the F8U Crusader squadron. Commander W. C. (Baldy) Chapman was commanding officer of VA-126, the instrument training squadron. I would spend brief training times with those Miramar squadrons and much more time with VA-125, the A4D RAG squadron at Lemoore. Since I had already flown all five types of airplanes that were in the six squadrons of Carrier Air Group 11, I decided I would concentrate on flying the F8U and A4D because those airplanes were more easily maintained, and as the CAG, I would be less of a burden to the squadrons when I flew a lot— which I intended to do.

A major change was taking place in naval aviation during the fall of 1961. The procedures for flying aircraft were being standardized between the two fleets. Earlier in 1961 Vice Admiral Robert Pirie, deputy chief of naval operations (air), observed carrier qualifications on the East Coast, where some A4D pilots made their carrier landings with speed brakes out and some with them in. That puzzled Pirie, who was then told it was because some had trained in the Pacific Fleet and some in the Atlantic Fleet. That observation was the genesis for standardization between the Pacific and Atlantic Fleets in the Navy and the adoption of NATOPS.

Having observed the A4Ds, Vice Admiral Pirie asked Captain R. G. Dosé on his Navy staff in Washington to fix the problem. Captain Dosé sent Captain Allard (Slim) Russell and others to the Air Force's strategic air command and tactical air command staffs to see how they handled standardization. The results and subsequent deliberations were widely discussed in the Navy, and it is fair to say that there was not unanimity. There was a great deal of outright resistance, particularly on the part of the training officers of COMNAVAIRPAC and COMNAVAIRLANT, who felt that the central staff of the Navy in Washington was not the right place for operational responsibility to lie. That would be too centrally authoritative and restrictive.

Casting aside the Air Force procedures for strict central control for the disciplinary function of enforcing the standardization procedures, it was decided that the CNO staff would coordinate the NATOPS program, and both fleets would share in the responsibility for writing specific aircraft procedures and for enforcing those standards. The Navy launched its NATOPS program and thus began great improvement in tactical standardization between the fleets. It would still be some time before such standardization would be reality.

In November I flew briefly with VF-121 in the F4H-1, just for a refresher and to see how the airplane had developed since I had tested it at Edwards AFB. I flew the F8U with VF-124 for a flight or two, again to refresh myself, and took a quick instrument flying course in the F9F-8T of VA-126. On December 3, 1961, I reported to VA-125 at NAS Lemoore, where Commander Bill Dauphin was commanding officer. Mary kept the house going in Del Mar with the children in school while I stayed at the BOQ in Lemoore for my training. NAS Lemoore was brand new, and there was not much to occupy one's time, other than flying. Someday it would be a great base, but then its chief attributes were the two long runways and the great distances between the various activities on the air station.

I moved rapidly through the A4D flying syllabus and spent a fair amount of time absorbing the tactics of weapons delivery and learning the capabilities of the weapons themselves. The A4D was such a simple and honest airplane to fly that it was a work of art—a true tribute to Ed Heinemann. I mainly concentrated on FCLP both day and night and practiced the various bomb delivery tactics from dive/glide to over the shoulder. It was wintertime flying at Lemoore, and the heavy valley fogs near Fresno and Bakersfield frequently stopped all forms of transport. You could become lost just driving a car to the hangar. We flew at Marine Corps Auxiliary Air Station (MCAAS) Yuma, Arizona, when we could not fly at Lemoore.

I did a certain amount of fill-in-the-square mundane flying training early in December, and after a family Christmas in Del Mar, I returned to Lemoore to complete my attack training. My orders said to relieve as commander of Air Group 11 (CAG 11) in January, and I wanted to be ready to do that. On January 10 I was standing in the squadron ready room at Lemoore when the duty officer said, "We need to take an A4D part out to the VA-125 troops qualifying in USS *Midway* off Monterey, California." Because of my timing, I was going to carrier qualify in the A4D after I took over Air Group 11 but felt very competent in the airplane. I volunteered to take the part to the ship in an A4D. It would be my first carrier landing in the A4D, but I figured I might as well start my qualifications. My offer was accepted without question, and within a matter of minutes I was on my way to land on *Midway* again. Forty-five minutes after leaving Lemoore, I made my first A4D carrier landing. There were one or two raised eyebrows in *Midway*, including those of Commander Bill Dauphin, but I did not give anyone time to think up reasons why I should not be there and marched up to see Captain Bob Dosé on the bridge. We had a good chat, and then I was catapulted off to fly back to Lemoore. I thought someone might give me another carrier landing or two, but that was the only one I made in my RAG training. I would have a chance to do those later.

Two days after landing on *Midway*, I was in Yuma for weapons training in the A4D. We dropped practice bombs on various trucks and tanks on the Marine Corps ranges in the Chocolate Mountains, and finishing that, RAG instructor pilot Lieutenant Jim Seely and I flew as a section of two A4Ds to Miramar before returning to Lemoore. Therein lies a tale. I was flying lead, and a large winter storm was pounding the California coast, especially San Diego. We flew by instruments most of the way, and the weather was particularly bad at Miramar. The A4D sat on three tall, rather spindly landing gear to enable it to carry a wide variety of bombs and other stores under its wings. The height of the landing gear also created a general restriction to not land the airplane in over 19–20 knots of 90-degree crosswinds.

Jim Seely and I flew the short flight west from Yuma, across the Chocolate Mountains to San Diego, in very heavy rain; I mean really heavy rain. It was coming down in buckets and beat against the windscreens of those little A4Ds so hard I wondered how Jim could see to fly formation on me. I had more than casual concern for the amount of water that the engines were ingesting, harking back to the problems with the Demon. Everyone else in the San Diego area was smart enough not to be flying, and we had the air to ourselves as Miramar approach control passed the two of us off to the GCA unit. Our option was to return to Yuma, but our fuel was already too low for that, so we split up and began our individual approaches to a landing on runway 26. I monitored the crosswind reported by the GCA controller as it rose to become a steady, direct crosswind of 25 knots from the left. I continued my approach to break out at 200–300 feet in heavy rain and touched down on the water-soaked runway. There was so much water that it must have destroyed the lift of the airplane's wings after touchdown, and I rolled out straight down the runway, even with that high crosswind. Jim Seely landed two minutes behind me. As I was taxiing back, I could see the fantastic rooster tail of water that his airplane created and thought to myself that maybe we were not so smart after all. But we landed safely and later returned to Lemoore.

After completing my abbreviated attack training at Lemoore on January 23, I returned to Miramar, and on January 31, 1962, I relieved Commander Thad Coleman as commander of Air Group 11. In my view this was one of the best aviation commands in the Navy. I practically had to push Thad out of the way because he did not want to leave, and I did not blame him.

In the years since I had left Air Group 19 in 1945, the Navy had progressed from three squadrons of some thirty airplanes, to four squadrons of eighteen to twenty airplanes, to five squadrons of fourteen airplanes, and to six squadrons of fourteen airplanes in 1962. The various detachment airplanes for early warning, electronic warfare, and rescue helicopters were additive. The size of each air group was driven by the size of the aircraft carrier deck. Thus *Essex*, *Midway*, *Forrestal*, and *Kitty Hawk* classes each had a different group composition, all determined by the deck multiples permissible in each ship. That flexibility stood the Navy in good stead.

The six squadrons in Air Group 11 were VF-111, flying F8U-2Ns, commanded by Commander R. E. Moore; VA-112 and VA-113, flying A4D-2Ns, commanded, respectively, by Commanders James Kirklighter and Garrett (Whitey) White; VF-114, flying F4H-1s, commanded by Commander H. W. (Hap) Chandler; VA-115, flying AD-6s, commanded by Commander Charles Bowen; and VAH-13, flying A3D-2s, commanded by Commander Robert Osterholm. I had known most of those officers before and certainly knew their service reputations. Each was a good leader, but I could not take credit for choosing them because they were there when I arrived.

Our assigned ship was USS *Kitty Hawk*, the Navy's newest and finest aircraft carrier. Captain Bush Bringle was the first and current commanding officer, and Commander John Thomas, previously commanding officer of VF-121, was executive officer. *Kitty Hawk* had been built at the Philadelphia Naval Shipyard and commissioned in 1961, and the carrier had a stellar group of ship's officers. Part of Air Group 11 flew east to join *Kitty Hawk* for the ship's shakedown training at Guantánamo and made transit around Cape Horn to the assigned home port of San Diego. While *Kitty Hawk* looked similar to *Constellation*, the carrier was the first of a new class and had serious problems with the engineering equipment and steam generating plant. Because of those problems, *Kitty Hawk* had entered the Hunters Point Naval Shipyard for extensive voyage repairs, changes, and other fixes immediately after arriving on the West Coast and was still there. Captain Bringle, John Thomas, and several other officers had traveled from San Francisco to be present at my change of command ceremony at Miramar, and I made special efforts over the next several months to ensure that I reciprocated this marked goodwill.

The staff of the air group commander—seven officers and ten enlisted men—was small but dedicated. Lieutenant Commanders George Rothrock and Doug Mow were the principal officers, who, along with good yeomen and key maintenance officers and men, kept the air group administratively in line. Lieutenant Commander R. A. Geist was the staff LSO and in turn trained other LSOs from the squadrons. Clearly, my principal challenge was going to be the distance between squadrons; two were at Miramar, two at Lemoore, one at Moffett Field, and one at Whidbey Island, Washington. When we deployed later, there also would be detachments from early warning, helicopter, and electronic warfare squadrons that would join the air group.

I started flying the F8U-2N with VF-111 in mid-February 1962. It was really good to get back into the cockpit of the Crusader again. This Cadillac of an airplane was easy to fly and in my view would be reliable transportation as compared with the more complex F4H-1. Hap Chandler's squadron was the first

Pacific Fleet squadron to have the F4H-1, and he would be having fleet intro-duction challenges the other squadrons would not have. The complications of fleet introduction and the fact that the F4H-1 required an NFO made the F4H-1 less than attractive in terms of my transportation between squadrons. In mid-February I attended another nuclear weapons training course, this one on operational planning. The emphasis on nuclear warfare during this Cold War period was heavy.

On February 19 I flew a Crusader to Whidbey Island to spend time with Bob Osterholm and VAH-13. I wanted each commanding officer to know me and to enable them to unburden themselves easily in ways that I could be a help and not a hindrance. I planned to return to Miramar on February 20 and woke up early enough to watch the momentous first orbital space launch of John Glenn in his *Friendship 7* at Cape Canaveral. It was a stirring and beautiful sight, after which I proceeded to take off in my Crusader for Miramar some 1,400 miles to the south. As I flew south along the civil airways, under the control of the FAA's Seattle Center, I asked the air traffic controllers for news of John, and they, as well as the controllers at the Oakland Center, kept me informed. I appreciated their thoughtfulness. It was interesting that in the nearly three hours that I flew south, John Glenn was making almost one full orbit of Earth.

On March 1 and 2 VA-112 and -113 flew on board USS *Oriskany* for re-fresher landings, and I joined them for my day and night qualification landings in the A4D. On March 7 I flew an F8U to Alameda, then drove to *Kitty Hawk* at Hunters Point, south of San Francisco. It was time to begin the integration process for the air group and the ship, and I was all too familiar with how im-portant that can be. A thousand things have to be done, and if not tended to, they seem to cause ill will between the ship and air group. Captain Bringle was a prince of a gentleman and a great naval officer, whom I first had met when I was in VF-21 in *Forrestal*. Remembering Ralph Werner's travail in *Benning-ton*, I wanted to ensure that the air group spaces in *Kitty Hawk* were adequately reserved so that when we came on board later in the summer they still would be available.

In mid-March I flew to the Naval Ordnance Test Station China Lake to be-gin discussions on the possible drop of a tactical nuclear weapon by either VA-112 or VA-113 flying from *Kitty Hawk*. This plan was driven by the Atomic Energy Commission's need to detonate one of the newer weapons oc-casionally. COMNAVAIRPAC asked me to be prepared to assign one of the two VA squadrons to make that drop. Of course, the plan was subject to ap-proval at the highest levels of authority in the U.S. government, and many things would have to fall into place before such an event might come to pass, but the tactical feasibility study had to begin before such approval. Leaving China Lake, I went on to Yuma to spend the afternoon and fly an F4H-1 with

VF-114 as it trained on a weapons deployment. Hap Chandler had many good troops in his squadron, including my old Solomons neighbor and test pilot friend Dan McCormick and Lieutenants Hunt Hardisty and Peter Booth. Hap did a superb job instilling spirit in his squadron.

On March 27 I planned to fly to Moffett Field for VA-115's administrative material inspection and planned debrief later that day. Those inspections were a time-honored form of auditing a Navy squadron to measure the management effectiveness of each squadron, and as CAG I was expected to be there. I arrived at the hangar at Miramar about 0700. The weather on the Kearny Mesa was WOXOFF in aerological code. The ceiling and visibility were zero zero. In fact, it was so bad that automobile driving had almost come to a standstill. I navigated carefully, almost by sense, to the field operations building and filed an instrument flight plan for an F8U flight to Moffett Field. The weatherman looked at me incredulously as he gave me the zero-zero bit and dutifully recorded it on my flight plan so that when I crashed, he could say, "I told him so." Moving on to the operations duty officer, I found someone that did not want to clear me. I just looked at him and then showed him my green instrument card, which granted the holder the right to be his own clearing authority. I signed my flight plan in the pilot's space and in the clearing officer's space as well. I tore off his copy, looked him in the eyes, wordlessly handed it to him, and walked out to try to find my airplane.

I must admit the weather was bad. I could not see 50 feet, let alone 100 feet. After some fumbling around I found my F8U on VF-111's line, preflighted it, started it, and slowly taxied out. As low as I sat in the F8U cockpit, I still could see less from the cockpit than from the ground. Once or twice I thought I might wait for the weather to improve, just a little, but I had burned too many bridges in the process of getting that far. Ground control quickly asserted that it could not see me to give me taxi instructions—I am sure to get that on the magnetic tape for the accident board—and I slowly taxied one blue taxi light at a time to the duty runway using memory more than sight. Arriving at the head of the runway, I called for clearance for takeoff at 0750.

The tower informed me I was not in sight but subsequently cleared me for takeoff. I lined up on the runway in solid fog, held my brakes, and then released them to start rolling. This would be a true instrument takeoff. I could see only one dim white light at a time on the right side of the runway. I selected afterburner, felt the comforting soft push in the back as the afterburner lit, followed by quick acceleration, and shifted my gaze inside the cockpit to rely on my instruments. In a matter of seconds the F8U lifted off the runway, I raised the landing gear, lowered the wing to clean up the airplane, accelerated to break out on top of the fog at a ridiculously low 400 feet, and flew to Moffett Field. The weather at Miramar could be that way sometimes.

I returned to Miramar that afternoon and two days later drove my car the 200-plus miles to Lemoore to be there for an administrative material inspection for VA-113 on March 29. March had been a full month, and if it was any indicator of my future months, I was going to be one busy person. Those distributed commands were going to take much more effort than I had estimated initially, and I again questioned the wisdom of basing airplanes according to their mission. It may have been better for the supply officers, but it sure made it difficult for the air group commanders who would fight the wars.

One other duty cropped up in March. Our son Chris had taken a *San Diego Union* paper route in Del Mar. Any dad knows that when his son takes a paper route, the father also buys into the process somehow, and there will be occasional bad weather or sick days, usually discovered between 0430 and 0500, when his services will be required. On such rainy and cold days I frequently became the most senior paper "boy" in Del Mar as Chris and I made our rounds through that small community.

Hap Chandler took his squadron to Point Mugu in April 1962 for a missile-firing exercise and invited me to observe, which I did from April 9 through 12. The exercise was a first missile-firing opportunity for a fleet F4H squadron, and Hap's squadron did very well. Concurrently, VA-112 and -113 deployed to Fallon to conduct and to qualify in some competitive bombing exercises. They had invited VAH-13 to come along to provide the training wherewithal for night bombing.

The United States was putting great store in nuclear weapons delivery, and all kinds of delivery tactics were developed in both the Navy and the Air Force. The Navy developed the night buddy bombing mission as a means to place additional weapons on the required targets at night, as well as in the day. The procedure entailed one A4D pilot, or occasionally two A4D pilots, teaming up with an A3D pilot flying on his wing. The A3D with its radar-mapping capability would navigate to the target at night, following the topography of Earth at about 200 feet to minimize radar detection. The A3D pilot would line up the A4D pilot with his intended target based on the judgment of the A3D bombardier navigator. This was done in total radio silence using the wing lights of the A3D to signal preparation and breakaway for the A4D's drop. At the appropriate and exact time, the A3D would flash a break-off signal with his wing lights, and the A4D pilot, fully prepared with armament and bomb switches turned on, would pull up into a classic Immelmann-type loft maneuver, in which his weapon released automatically exactly when the A4D was vertical.

The A4D would continue the Immelmann and then descend to ground level as quickly as possible while the weapon continued up to 12,000 or 13,000 feet before it started down to fall on the intended target. The A3D would bank sharply to avoid the A4D pilot's target and fly on to his own assigned target.

Both airplanes must avoid the nuclear blast. At night that could become a somewhat dicey evolution, and Fallon, where we practiced, was famous for its high desert black nights. There was not much to see out there. Jim Kirklighter, Garrett White, Bob Osterholm, and their respective squadrons were practicing that maneuver when I arrived in my F8U at Fallon late in the afternoon on April 17.

Actually, I think that Whitey was having some fun with me and was trying to test my fighter pilot flying abilities in the attack field. The buddy bombing mission took a lot of coordination to get to the bomb release point and, I think, a lot of luck for the bomb to hit any target. Whatever Whitey thought, the challenge was there, and I planned to do my best. I made an afternoon flight on the wing of an A3D just to get the hang of what part of the A3D I should use for formation flying. It was a big airplane, and I settled on the recommended position—down and to the right of the wing-mounted number 2 engine pod in a position to look up at and see the bombardier navigator's eyes if he looked at me.

At about 0130 the next morning my turn came to fly the buddy bombing mission. The A3D pilot and I in my A4D took off together to begin our flight to the target. I would drop a single bomb. The A3D pilot was nice to me, making gentle turns along the preplanned path so as not to give me a bad case of vertigo. We dropped down to fly across the desert floor toward the target, flying at 200 feet. It was difficult to hang on to the A3D at night, but I knew others had done it. Sensing the approaching bombing run, I readied all my switches for the drop. I was tucked in close to the right engine nacelle in my little A4D and could feel us accelerating; a quick glance at my airspeed indicator confirmed that we were going from 420 to 460 knots. I knew the target was out there somewhere. Nothing was said between the two airplanes, but the A3D pilot had cleared the target for our run with the range control officer earlier. The A3D pilot flashed the be prepared light signal, and our countdown started so as to arrive at my precise pull-up point somewhere up ahead. The desert floor must have been flashing by, but it was unseen some 150 to 200 feet below us. This was one of those many special times in naval aviation when you placed your life in the hands of a fellow pilot. I relied totally on the A3D pilot. My whole loft maneuver was going to be done on instruments, and my bomb switches were set to release my practice bomb automatically at the precise point in the maneuver determined by the computer. I wondered if Whitey was enjoying my situation.

The A3D bombardier navigator flashed the wing lights again, the A3D began a turn to the left, and I was on my way! I pulled the stick back, and the dimly lit A3D abruptly disappeared below me. I was on my own, flying the loft angle bombing system (LABS) instrument directly in front of me on the instrument panel. It told me I was on the desired path and to keep pulling hard. I noted a steady 4.5 g's and no heading drift right or left. So far, so good. I kept pulling until at about 7,800 feet (the ground level at Fallon was about 3,900 feet above mean sea level) the practice bomb was automatically released to proceed on its own to the target now some five miles ahead in the black night. I kept pulling back on the stick to enter my escape maneuver. Within seconds I was on my back and headed back down at the ground to roll upright and then pull out at low altitude. This was the well-known lets-get-the-hell-out-of-here maneuver to be as far from the target as possible at simulated detonation. I could not see the unguided bomb, which was long gone and doing its own thing, continuing up until it reached apogee, and then beginning its free fall to the target with increasing speed.

The Fallon target range operator came on the radio, "Stinger 310, bull's-eye!" I smiled to myself as I flew back to Fallon. My bomb was the only bull's-eye that night. Whitey tried to get me to stay on and fly another buddy bombing run, but I nonchalantly told him I had already done it and must return to Miramar. No way was I going to try that crazy maneuver again and spoil a record like that! I knew success came from the skill of the A3D pilot's navigation, some luck, his radar, and the A4D's computer. So I rested on my laurels but did gain the respect of my bombing community, who labored on.

Requirements to do other things kept cropping up. On April 22 I boarded *Oriskany* to be the chief observer for a five-day squadron missile shoot under the auspices of the commander of Carrier Division 1. Such exercises were scheduled as weapons training exercises, this one being WEPTRAEX 2-62. Other fleet organizations were asked to provide the talent and manpower so that the exercise could be conducted safely and productively. It was also an opportunity for the observers to learn, which helped them evaluate their own air group or squadron.

On May 5 Captain Walter Curtiss relieved Captain Bush Bringle as commanding officer of *Kitty Hawk* at the Hunters Point Naval Shipyard. I flew up to Alameda in an F8U and motored across the Bay Bridge and down Highway 101 to Hunters Point. I had looked forward to being in *Kitty Hawk* with Bush Bringle. Captain Curtiss was an unknown entity to me just then. I did know that he was a former aviation cadet and as such he had entered the Navy in the 1930s to fly. It was a grand change of command ceremony on the hangar deck. All my squadron commanders were there as well.

I had arranged at COMNAVAIRPAC to take Air Group 11 to sea in another carrier for group refresher landings in May. We needed to maintain our currency because when *Kitty Hawk* came out of the yard, we would have to do some fast training to meet a proposed deployment departure date in September. All the squadrons moved their equipment, personnel, and airplanes to Alameda to board USS *Ranger* on May 10. It was our first time to operate together at sea, and over the period May 11–17 every pilot made enough landings to meet the carrier landing currency criteria. I flew the A4D for seven landings and the F8U for eighteen day and night landings. This was also our opportunity to fly and observe *Ranger*'s CATCC procedures. I wanted the pilots and, in particular, their commanding officers to see how a good CATCC operated. Within one week of our completing our at-sea period in *Ranger*, *Kitty Hawk* finished the yard period and sortied from San Francisco to return to San Diego.

I drew great satisfaction from the capabilities of each squadron after our period in *Ranger*. The commanding officers were doing their jobs well, and in addition the young pilots coming to the fleet were good. Air Group 11 was ready to go to work in *Kitty Hawk*. Additional training needs would arise, to be sure, but even if additional training was not forthcoming, the pilots and squadrons were capable of making a good deployment. On a larger Navy scale, I felt we were making good progress in individual pilot jet training, not only in the RAG, but also in the training command.

Kitty Hawk proceeded into refresher training with the fleet training group at San Diego, and during the second week in June we boarded and flew from *Kitty Hawk* to provide services for the ship's exercises. *Kitty Hawk* was still our newest carrier at the time, and everything about the carrier was spotless and shipshape, but there were some troubling signs in the air operations division. Its procedures were a little too loose for my liking. We would have to do much more training together. The remainder of June was spent preparing for a training cruise in Hawaiian waters. The air group assembled on June 28 and 29 at NAS North Island to be loaded on board *Kitty Hawk* at the carrier quay, and we sortied from San Diego on June 30 bound for Pearl Harbor and the Hawaiian area to begin joint training of the air group and ship with the goal of making all into one unit.

Commander Charles Curtis was *Kitty Hawk*'s operations officer. Charlie was a quiet naval officer who seemed to spend more time concerned with the ship than with the air group. That made life nice for me, but it also meant that he often was not on top of the air group–ship training status. We crossed the eastern Pacific to operate 100 miles west of Oahu and began flying on July 3. Almost immediately my concerns about air operations were confirmed. We did not have the aggressive leadership or direction that was needed. I went to Captain Walter Curtiss immediately and shared my concerns. I felt that if we did not rectify the lack of coordination in air ops, we were going to lose an airplane and pilot. He had noted that something was not going well, and we both agreed that we would try to rectify the situation as soon as possible. In the meantime we each would continue to monitor air ops progress because the air group depended on air operations for vital information and coordination. I alerted my commanding officers to keep their eyes open and to help the ship where they could.

Kitty Hawk, as magnificent as the ship was, also had serious engineering problems. Commander Jim Slaughter, the chief engineer, did his level best, but *Kitty Hawk* was the first of that class and had a newly designed 1,200-pounds-per-square-inch steam system, whereas previous carriers had had 600-pound systems. Things kept breaking. It was not unusual to have two rather than six boilers on the line providing not only steam for the ship's propulsion but also steam for catapults, for electric power to maintain the aircraft, and for fresh water for the crew—the list went on. The engineering challenges nearly drove Walter Curtiss mad. Several times we had to stop air operations and send airplanes to Barbers Point because the ship did not have sufficient power to put the needed wind across the deck to recover them. However, we flew as much as we could, and slowly the ship and air group came closer and closer together, except for air operations. For my part, I was able to fly with the squadrons, but my time was spent principally on the bridge or in air ops ensuring continued safe flight operations.

In two weeks we completed our mid-Pacific training cruise and returned to San Diego on July 16. On the return trip I talked to John Thomas and to Walter Curtiss about the air operations division. We would be deploying in less than sixty days, and in my view the issue was critical. Captain Curtiss asked me who in the San Diego area might be able to do the job, to which I replied, "Commander Mike Casey, CO of VF-121." I knew Mike relished his current job as commanding officer. He was a contemporary and personal friend and would have killed me if he had known I was throwing his name around. But *Kitty Hawk* needed help—badly.

Walter Curtiss had been in the Bureau of Naval Personnel and knew how to handle such personnel matters quickly. Mike Casey, stationed at Miramar, had his orders to *Kitty Hawk* before our next at-sea period in August. When Mike walked on board, the entire complexion of air operations changed in *Kitty Hawk*, and he and I, and everyone else, for that matter, worked together beautifully. I will always owe Mike one for what he did and for what I did to him. After his air operations job, Mike became operations officer in *Kitty Hawk*, made a number of cruises, and went on to his deep draft and major commands. I hope he will forgive me for his short tour in VF-121.

On July 23 I flew an F8U-2N to land at Andrews AFB near Washington, DC. It was an opportunity to visit my Navy friends, to share some of my recent Pacific Fleet experiences, and to learn just where naval aviation was going. It also gave me an opportunity to see if anyone was interested in my coming to Washington. I could not dodge it forever. Visiting the Bureau of Naval Personnel or the CNO's staff is a delicate matter. First, I was already in one of the most sought after jobs in the Navy, and I wanted to maintain low visibility in case the personnel staff had forgotten about me. But, second, I did not want to be sandbagged by some personnel officer, in whom I had little trust, and ordered to some second-class job. There were a lot of those in the Navy. I delicately threw my hat in the door and nosed around.

It turned out that someone indeed had asked for me. Bob Elder was en route to command USS *Coral Sea* and had asked for me to be ship's operations officer. Would I be interested? I knew that I could not parlay my CAG job for long—too many people wanted it. I had the greatest admiration for Bob Elder and would have gone anywhere to serve under him. It was also an honor to have a CAG job and a ship's operations officer job. There were not enough of those kinds of jobs to go around, and having two just was not done at the time. So I said, "OK, but leave me in my air group as long as you can." I returned to San Diego, flying across the United States at 51,000 feet, trying to think how to tell Mary tactfully that we would be going for another tour of sea duty after this one.

Rear Admiral Ralph Shifley, commander of Carrier Division 7, and his staff moved on board *Kitty Hawk* on July 31, and we went to sea off the Southern California coast for nine days in early August. Carrier Division 7 was the third and final tier of the *Kitty Hawk* deployment team of air group, ship, and carrier division. I found it to be a blessing for me to go to sea because that was the one time that my whole air group was in one place. I frequently still marveled at the rocket scientist who had decided to break up the air groups and base the various kinds of squadrons at different fields.

We went to sea again for several days at the end of August, and then *Kitty Hawk* held a family-day cruise for dependents and friends on September 1. Such cruises were normally scheduled just before deployment to show the families what dad, son, or brother did in the ship, and over time they have been great morale builders for the families. Also, about this time, the Navy was informed there would be no requirement for a tactical nuclear weapon test in the Pacific, at least in 1962. We were relieved of our planning and operational responsibility to drop a tactical nuclear weapon, which certainly would make the transit to the western Pacific less complicated.

The complex logistical challenge of bringing the 1,000 officers and men and 94 aircraft of Air Group 11 to San Diego from four widely separated bases and loading all the stores and personal gear into *Kitty Hawk* was solved over several days before we departed on September 13, 1962. Mary and I knew this would be a four-month cruise for me because I would have to return in January to report to *Coral Sea* as operations officer. Mary planned to move back to Alameda in early October to put the children in school, and I would join her there. Consequently, our good-byes were a bit easier this time. But still, that final moment comes when all lines are cast off and the ship slowly moves out and away from the quay and the water between you grows wider and wider. The reds, greens, blues, and yellows of the clothes worn by those on the quay stand out less and less as the distance grows, and all officers and sailors look to see their families or loved ones for that last time. Those on the quay have a harder time spotting their loved ones because the uniforms on deck quickly blend together. The old hands pick a gun mount or an airplane to highlight their positions longer. Regardless, it is not a happy time.

Kitty Hawk conducted flight operations off Hawaii from September 16 to 22 before entering Pearl Harbor on a Saturday. On the next Monday, September 24, we sortied for our final training with the fleet training group and for our battle problem, on which we would be graded. Even with the magnificent size of *Kitty Hawk*'s flight deck, I still had to send two F4Hs and four F8Us to Barbers Point to maintain the desired ship's operating deck multiple for the necessary flight deck flexibility. Poor Commander Jim Slaughter, the chief engineer, and Captain Curtiss still had real problems with *Kitty Hawk*'s engineering plant. The six boilers were going out of commission randomly with great frequency and rapidity. We frequently did not have enough steam to catapult the airplanes or to make the speed needed to recover them. The Philadelphia Naval Shipyard, *Kitty Hawk*'s builder, did not cover itself with glory in my book.

Our ORI, on Thursday, September 27, went reasonably well in spite of engineering problems. By that time I knew all the observers because of my previous ORIs in 1957 and 1960, and I was able to stay a step or two ahead of them as the air group and ship were given challenge after challenge. I purposefully did not fly during the ORI so that I could coordinate our efforts. It was a key decision because during our important nuclear launch sequence plan (LSP) exercise I was in the strike warfare room monitoring the movement of weapons and airplanes on the flight and hangar decks along with various squadron officers. For some reason, critically needed information was not being received in strike warfare and could not be passed on to the squadrons. The exercise was turning into a mess. I thought I knew what was wrong and ran up to flight deck control in the island to confirm that the ship's enlisted talker on the sound-powered phones there did not understand what he was seeing on the aircraft status boards and as a result was not sending the correct information. A quick word with the aircraft handling officer, and he replaced the talker with someone who knew the identities of the different airplanes. The complexion of the whole exercise changed almost immediately. There was a great deal of coordination and talent shown by the squadron loading crews and pilots. They were the main players. The graded result for that major exercise was the highest ever given to a ship and air group—98.4 percent. We cooled the exercise! Upon completion of the ORI, *Kitty Hawk* entered Pearl Harbor for the crew's well-deserved weekend.

At high noon on Monday, October 1, we left Pearl Harbor for the western Pacific. As usual, when you left a port other than your home port, only the duty line handlers were on the dock. When commanded they perfunctorily threw the lines from the dock, and we were under way without fanfare. The *Arizona* memorial looked fresh and starkly white in the noonday sun as *Kitty Hawk* glided by with the ship and crew at flight deck parade. We rendered the traditional honors as we passed silently. In stark contrast the rusting and oil-covered hull of the capsized USS *Utah* still rested where the ship was sunk on December 7, 1941. We left Pearl Harbor and headed west.

Kitty Hawk broke down and was dead in the water twice the next day. The reason for the second breakdown was a boiler that blew up, although miraculously no one was injured. Fire brick actually flew out of the stack and rained down on the flight deck. We were 360 miles west of Hawaii and had ten airplanes in the air at the time. Those were bingoed to Barbers Point and recovered when the ship could get under way again hours later. This promised to be some other kind of a cruise, but fortunately engineering reliability actually got better.

The next day I was flying an F8U-2N while conducting air-intercept training as we moved farther across the Pacific. The ship's radar picked up a fast moving bogey to the west, and I was vectored out to identify whether or not it was a Soviet Bear airplane. On occasion they were beginning to be seen in the Pacific. I intercepted the target easily and found a Pan Am Boeing 707, probably its Flight 1 from Tokyo to Honolulu. Having identified the airplane, I joined on the right wing and slid in to a distance of two or three feet from the number 4 engine to fly formation on it. I settled my Crusader in nicely, letting the nose of my airplane project forward enough to catch the eye of the copilot. All the shades were pulled down in the passenger cabin, and several minutes passed before the copilot actually noticed someone else in the air with them. I could see his startled face looking at me, and immediately I could see the pilot stand up in his seat and also look across the copilot at me. Then all the window shades started to rise; faces peered out the windows on the starboard side of the airplane. People started waving, and I waved back. After two or three minutes I added power, accelerated, and hit afterburner. I kissed off to the copilot and waggled my wings, flying up and away. You could not do that today, but then it was a friendly gesture in the middle of the Pacific Ocean, where those on the airliner had no idea anyone else might be with them, let alone a single-engine Navy jet fighter. I never heard a word about it.

It was a rough Pacific crossing because of typhoons Emma and Frieda, but *Kitty Hawk* moved north and then west of them as they churned the Pacific behind us. I found Rear Admiral Shifley to be easier to talk to than Walter Curtiss, who had a reserved New England personality. As it turned out, Captain Curtiss had spent a good deal of time on major staffs and had not been flying or operating at sea recently. Mike Casey and I held his hand a good deal. I spent an inordinate amount of time on the navigation bridge during flight operations because he expected it. He was a nice man and a fine officer. He just was not an aggressively operating captain initially. He got better. Admiral Shifley's chief of staff was another former aviation cadet, Captain John J. Lynch, former commanding officer of USS *Coral Sea* and a likable, unflappable, and supportive person.

On October 9, the day before we entered Yokosuka, we rendezvoused with *Midway* as the carrier left Japan to return to the States. Normally conducted in port, such meetings are important. They allow crews to exchange key operating information. Captain Gordon Hartley, staff operations officer, and I rode over by helicopter to see our counterparts. Mine were Commander Billie Holder, commander of Air Group 2, and Commander Bob Kuntz, commanding officer of VF-21. We stayed as long as we could, but *Midway* was going west at 25 knots and *Kitty Hawk* was going east at the same speed. We said goodbye as the distance between the two ships quickly grew; they continued east, and we continued west.

Our visit to Yokosuka, our first port of call, was to provide a platform for the change of command for the commander of the Seventh Fleet. Vice Admiral William Schoech was relieved by Vice Admiral Thomas H. Moorer on October 14 on board *Kitty Hawk* in an impressive ceremony. *Kitty Hawk* had dressed ship from stem to stern as never before. The list of guests read like a who's who in the Navy and naval aviation. Captain Paul Stevens, commander of Air Group 12, flew out from Miramar with Vice Admiral Ekstrom, commander of Naval Air Force Pacific Fleet. Paul and I sat together and marveled at the array of Navy talent. Paul would soon be relieved by Captain Larry Flint. Admiral Moorer took the time to talk to me, and I appreciated his thoughtfulness. He was always a strong supporter, and his younger brother, Joe, and I were close friends.

We finished out October in a flurry of flight operations south and east of Japan, and we flew and provided support to the Marines on Okinawa during the amphibious exercise Lone Eagle. We also did night operations in the straits south of Japan, where there can be hundreds of small fishing boats on any given night. This is not bad for the pilots, but it raises the ulcer level for every carrier skipper as he must thread his ship through the small white lights while conducting flight operations. The air group was well trained, and the professionalism of each squadron commanding officer and his pilots was about the best that I had seen. But there is always training to do. We operated in some poor weather day and night and flew into some strange fields, but nothing seemed to perturb those pilots. I had never seen such quality in any air group I had been in before, and it was not because it was mine. I taxed their abilities, albeit safely, and they always responded. They were good, which made me feel proud.

Irritants seemed to arise from outside, not inside, the command. DOD was populated by a new secretary of defense, Robert McNamara, along with his young and inexperienced but smart systems analysts, a la the Ford Motor Company. They were bright but woefully inexperienced in the military sense to be making defense policy decisions. I did not fully understand their impact on the Navy at the time, being so far away, but we were entering a trying decade of defense policy consolidation. Among other things, those mental giants did not understand the Navy's aircraft nomenclature and set about to change it. A joint Army–Navy–Air Force instruction was dutifully issued creating joint terminology, and we implemented it on November 1, 1962. The F8U-2N became the F-8D, the A3D-2 became the A-3B, the WF-2 became the E-1B, and for a while it was a mess. I personally found the idea reprehensible. The Navy's system of alpha-numeric aircraft identification told you what the aircraft mission was, what the sequential numeric type of that manufacturer was, who the manufacturer was, and what model of that type of aircraft it was. I made a strong mental note about political appointee wanna-bes.

Another issue that the DOD minions raised was the Navy air group and the Air Force wing. They asked, "Why should there be wings and groups in the different services?" They reasoned that the Navy should have wings too, like the Air Force, and subsequently changed that terminology as well. The Navy carrier air group became the carrier air wing (CAW). That so infuriated most of us that we retained the termed CAG for the commander of a wing, nee group, regardless. It is that way today. The services fought this DOD general drift toward joint procedures, but those head-strong young neophytes in defense issues did not understand how or why the services had developed procedures over time. They tried to drive the individual services closer and closer together, but not for the right reasons. The changes did not create a stronger military. But then I did not see anyone in the Navy stand up and really fight those changes either. We just rolled over.

Within two months of our departure date, we began experiencing personnel changes in the air group. First, on the CAG staff, as we deployed, Lieutenant Commander Henry Dibble reported as CAG operations officer and Lieutenant George Boaz as CAG weapons planning coordinator. In October Commander Warren O'Neil was named as my relief, and that in turn caused a flurry of plans for command changes because Commanders Osterholm, Chandler, Bowen, and Kirklighter were all junior to O'Neil. By that time executive officers of squadrons were being screened for subsequent command and were generally fleeting up to relieve in their current command. Navy level readiness appeared a little more reasonable than it had initially, and we received qualified replacement pilots for those who were rotating back to the States. The system seemed to work, but in Air Group 11 it seemed to me that was because of the quality and strength of the officers and strong unit cohesiveness. I wondered if that would continue.

I found that when we flew at night and in poor weather, it was much easier for me to do it than to sit and watch others do it. As I sat in air operations and the CATCC spaces late at night, or when I went aft to the LSO platform or stood by the captain on the bridge, my heart was continually in my throat as others came down the glide slope to land on board. It took considerable control for me to provide the outward appearance of calm when inside I was churning. Confidence in your troops is a quality that every good commander must evince. I did my best, and to my knowledge no one saw my inner turmoil. However, I am positive that those who preceded me and those who followed me felt the same way. It goes with the territory.

Mary wrote that Bob Elder was trying to speed up my arrival in *Coral Sea*, but I was content to hang on as air group commander as long as I could. In November we generally operated near and had port visits to Sasebo, Okinawa, and Manila. Our flying hours were correspondingly high, but an inordinate number of typhoons always seemed to be threatening operations yet never canceling port visits. Rear Admiral Shifley was asked to provide a firepower demonstration for the military representatives of SEATO. Air Group 11 began to prepare for that December event. We were also tapped to provide one-third of the military portion of the Philippine National Aviation Air Show in late November and practiced for both.

On the morning of November 13 *Kitty Hawk* had anchored in Buckner Bay to ride out the fringes of Typhoon Karen. I stood on the boat landing at Buckner Bay when one of our helicopters flew overhead, and I looked up, waved my arms, and stuck out my thumb for a ride. The helo circled around and landed in a nearby open field and picked me up to return to the ship. That afternoon *Kitty Hawk* was still anchored in Buckner Bay and was about to get under way to recover my airplanes, temporarily ashore at Naha, when I suggested that we do that at anchor as a better alternative. I am sure that this had been done before someplace, but not with jet airplanes, principally because other carriers did not have the arresting gear capability of *Kitty Hawk*. My idea of recovering jet airplanes at anchor took some selling on my part, not only to Captain Curtiss, but also to Admiral Shifley. I had an ally in Mike Casey. We had 20 knots of wind down the deck, and the ship quite naturally swung on its anchor to point into the wind. The wind across the deck was enough to recover all but the fighters and the A-3Bs, which we did. But I knew that if we had had an accident, I might just as well have walked over to the side of the flight deck and jumped off. We were under way at 0700 on November 14 to pick up the fighters and the A-3Bs. We continued to fly that afternoon and evening. On November 15 I flew an F-8D along with Lieutenant Dick Cavick of VF-111 to Clark Field and on to Manila to discuss our portion of the Philippine air show and then returned to Naha, Okinawa.

It has been said frequently that the four acres of a flight deck can be the most dangerous acreage in the world. That is true. When you pack eighty-plus jet and propeller airplanes and helicopters into that acreage and launch them at speeds up to 150 knots in 125 feet and arrest them in a similar distance from a relative approach speed of 110 knots and do that on a deck that rolls and pitches, any mistake can have disastrous results. When you add sailors and air-crew to the equation to work among the moving aircraft in winds up to 40 or 50 knots and at sound levels above the threshold of pain, there are even greater hazards. I have already expressed my admiration for those who work in that environment. *Kitty Hawk* and Air Group 11 had their share of broken toes, arms, and legs, along with occasional, more serious injuries.

I wanted to do something for those fine flight deck crewmen that I had lived with for my adult life. In November I sat down and wrote an official letter to the CNO to try to gain greater recognition and incentive for those officers and men. In the letter I recommended that they receive flight deck hazardous duty pay to compensate their efforts. I knew that there would be resistance to such a move from those who had not lived in that environment, so I sent the official letter via every carrier aviation command above me in the Pacific Fleet before it would arrive in the CNO's office. I put a great deal of myself into the letter to sell the concept. I would not hear anything of my effort for almost two years.

On November 23 *Oriskany* and *Kitty Hawk* steamed side by side while Rear Admiral Paul Masterton, commander of Carrier Division 5, came to *Kitty Hawk* to be relieved as CTF 77 by Rear Admiral Shifley. On November 24 the air group practiced for the SEATO firepower demonstration on the first launch and for the Philippine air show on the second launch. Those two launches, each requiring the participation of the majority of the air group, provided one of the most hectic days of my life. The seas were high, and the flight deck had a siz-able pitch with some side movement as well. With the help of the Fresnel lens (a more advanced landing aid than the mirror, using a lens that can only be seen from certain angles), instead of the older mirror, to provide accurate and stabi-lized glide slope information, each of the two recoveries were made with no accidents. Commander Lloyd Cooper even offered me the opportunity to make the 8,000th landing in *Kitty Hawk*, but that would have taken some contriving, and I chose to thank him and say that I would take my chances for a 1,000th landing in a ship with the others. Needless to say, I did not make that one, nor did I ever make a 1,000th landing.

On Sunday, November 25, we launched from *Kitty Hawk* to provide the Navy part of the Philippine National Aviation Air Show at the former Nielson Field, now the Philippine International Airport. After launching us, *Kitty Hawk* went into Manila Bay to anchor for a five-day port visit before moving north to Subic Bay. The timing for the air show flybys and demonstrations was exact, and the pilots did well. Afterwards we flew to Cubi Point to land and position the airplanes there. Lieutenant Dick Rich of VF-114, who announced the show, said the Navy portion easily impressed the crowd more than the others. That was borne out later at the interminably long awards ceremony and beauty judging contest that evening in Manila, when I accepted a plaque for the Navy effort on behalf of all pilots from Air Group 11. The applause was the loudest and longest for the Navy, and it was interesting that our Philippine friends still felt strong ties to the United States.

On December 3 *Kitty Hawk* sortied from Subic Bay, and we flew the SEATO demonstration flights flawlessly. I watched from the deck with the SEATO observers. The hits were good, the timing was spot on, and I was proud of each pilot. Vice Admiral Moorer was highly laudatory as he spoke to the gathered SEATO flag and general officers. Those military guests stayed on board for meetings until December 6 when they were flown off to return to Cubi Point. Also on December 6 Commander Harry O'Connor was relieved as air officer by his assistant, Commander Lloyd Cooper. Harry, a plank owner (one of the initial crew), flew off the ship to go to Albuquerque and VX-5 as commanding officer. We would serve together again years later in the Pentagon.

The character of this cruise, at least to this point, had been one of meeting the schedule while dodging typhoons. There had been no revolutions, no wars, and no political-military situations. Our role was principally one of showing the flag. After the wars and flaps of previous cruises, this one seemed docile, but that was the luck of the draw and probably good for our nation.

During this period in the South China Sea I had my first indication I was aging. A pilot relies the most on his eyes. I was thirty-nine years old and had been flying for twenty-one years. On a December night in the South China Sea I was flying an A-4B tanker as the duty aerial tanker in case some pilot needed fuel. It was a typical black night over the South China Sea, and I gave token fuel to two or three pilots for their in-flight refueling practice. There was an undercast below. We high flyers flew above it while we orbited, before starting the nightly daisy chain of instrument letdowns and approaches. My approach time came, and as I began my descent through the undercast, I glanced at my airspeed indicator to check my airspeed. To my complete surprise I could not clearly see the instrument or read my airspeed.

Knowing your airspeed in descent to maintain critical separation from other aircraft is highly desirable. Knowing your airspeed to fly the approach for a carrier landing is vital. I peered at the instrument again, adjusted the lights, and still could not read it. My eyes were playing tricks on me in the subdued red light. Fortunately, the Navy had pioneered the use of angle-of-attack information for accurate speed control during approach and landing. The beauty of this information was that, unlike indicated airspeed, it was impervious to the airplane's weight change caused by consumption of fuel. All Navy tactical airplanes had an angle-of-attack gauge on the instrument panel and a lighted indexer mounted above the left cockpit glare shield, easily in the pilot's line of sight as he flew the Fresnel lens. I could see the much brighter red angle-of-attack indexer and used that to make a normal approach and landing. That event was a rude awakening to me that age was taking its toll and I would need glasses to fly at night.

Kitty Hawk and the entire task group made a port visit to Hong Kong from December 10 to 16, and while there Commander Hap Chandler relinquished command of VF-114. I would miss him and our fun-loving good times. *Kitty Hawk* left Hong Kong to operate again in the South China Sea and then went into Subic Bay on December 26 for the last in-port period before my change of command. There were rounds of going away parties for me, Charlie Bowen, and Jim Kirklighter at the Cubi Point and Subic Bay officers clubs. The one at Cubi Point was especially fun. VA-112 arranged an "impromptu" skit during which they produced a swaybacked Philippine horse of some ancient vintage. The club's manager was concerned about his dance floor, so the troops carefully wrapped each hoof in a checkered napkin before they marched the horse in and put me on it to ride around the club. Afterwards, I tied the horse to a palm tree by the front door of the club, thinking that the horse and I could find our way back to the ship later. My plan was modified by the shore patrol, who arrived to investigate the report of a horse at the officers club. Of course, everyone played dumb, but all pointed at me as the culprit. It was my horse. The horse was carefully returned to its rightful owner without harm.

Commander Warren O'Neil arrived in the Philippines on December 29, and *Kitty Hawk* sortied from Subic Bay on January 1. Our change of command was held on January 3, at sea north of Luzon, just before *Kitty Hawk* and Carrier Division 7 began a carrier-versus-carrier exercise with *Ranger*. After the change of command, I mounted a waiting F-8D to fly ashore to Cubi Point. I had privately planned a departure salute to the many fine people in the ship and air group and asked Commander Lloyd Cooper to launch me last on the scheduled deck launch. Catapulted from the number 3 waist catapult, I raised the landing gear and lowered the wing while accelerating in afterburner just on top of the water and did an Immelmann. Rolling out of the Immelmann, I dived on the ship to pass down the port side low on the water and did four consecutive loops with quarter rolls in the vertical segments, so that on completing each I flew by the ship below flight deck level in a different direction. Finishing those four loops, I proceeded with an air show routine I had planned. I beat up the ship pretty badly, and I was sure that Captain Curtiss and Admiral Shifley might not be pleased, but this was my swan song to twenty-one years of active flying, we were in international air space, and I was going to go out with a bang! It was worth it to me. Completing the show, I flew on to Cubi Point and turned the airplane over to the waiting VF-111 pilot to fly it back to *Kitty Hawk*.

I returned to the States on an Air Force military airlift command (MAC) flight from Clark AFB, arrived at Travis AFB on January 6, and proceeded to Alameda for a reunion with Mary and the children, who had moved north in my absence. We had missed Christmas, but just coming home can be like Christmas. Already *Coral Sea* was beckoning, and there were training courses that I had to complete before being able to assume new responsibilities as operations officer later that month.

13. PENANCE FOR FLYING
JANUARY 1963 TO JANUARY 1964

Britain and the United States signed a treaty to conduct all nuclear tests un-
derground, and the Soviet Union launched Vostok *5 and 6 spacecraft. The*
Diem government was overthrown in South Vietnam, and the United States
provided aid to and recognized the new government in South Vietnam. Color
TV was relayed by satellite for the first time. A civil war broke out on Cyprus
between Greek and Turkish Cypriots. The United States and the Soviet Union
agreed to establish a hot line between Washington and Moscow, and two Soviet
reconnaissance airplanes flew over Alaska. Nineteen sixty-three was the cold-
est year since 1740 in England, and Gordon Cooper orbited Earth twenty-two
times in his spacecraft Faith *7. President Kennedy was assassinated in Dallas.*

There were 17,672 pilots, 132,538 aviation ratings, and 25 aircraft carriers
of all types in the Navy. The secretary of the Navy approved the recommenda-
tions of the Dillon Board, thus broadening his authority and responsibility in
the Navy Department. This made the chief of naval material directly responsi-
ble to him, not to the CNO. The Navy and NASA agreed on military-civilian
satellite responsibilities for the Transit navigation satellite system. Navy RAGs
were redesignated combat readiness air groups (CRAGs), and carrier air
groups were redesignated carrier air wings (CAWs). The Air Force was given
two squadrons of A-1E Skyraider airplanes to be used in Southeast Asia, and
the first fully automated carrier landings were made in USS Midway *by an*
F-4A and F-8D. Five new Navy and Marine aviator astronauts were selected,
and the secretary of defense approved flight pay for naval flight officers.

Captain R. M. Elder took command of USS *Coral Sea* while the aircraft carrier was in the Hunters Point Naval Shipyard for needed repairs and extensive work. Part of that work was to replace the number 3 deck-edge aircraft elevator, lost when the previous commanding officer, Captain M. F. (Mickey) Wiesner, had inadvertently dug it into a swell while pulling away from an underway replenishment ship, and the elevator had gone to the bottom of the Philippine Sea. Additionally, improvements were installed such as a new red moon glow lighting system high on the ship's mast for greater flight deck night visibility and safety, the first installation of the pilot landing aid television (PLAT) for carrier landing evaluation and safety, and the first shipboard installation of the new U.S. Navy Transit satellite navigation system. *Coral Sea* completed the yard period in December 1962 and sailed north to home port, Alameda, for the holidays.

Captain Elder was faced with an inordinately large turnover of his key officers. Commander J. F. Davis became executive officer, Commander Dickie Wieland became navigator, Commander L. R. Mix became air operations officer, and I was to be operations officer. A number of us had prior association with Bob Elder, and we had deep respect and loyalty for him.

Coral Sea departed for San Diego on January 2, 1963, and, once there, remained in port while the officers and men attended various training courses and schools. On Monday, January 14, *Coral Sea* put to sea for refresher training under the fleet training group, and on January 20 I reported to COMNAVAIR-PAC for shipboard schooling. Instead I found that I was to fly to *Coral Sea* that afternoon for temporary duty as the ship and crew completed training. Commander John Thompson, formerly the CIC officer, was currently operations officer in *Coral Sea* and was so busy organizing the ship's training schedule that we spent no time together. I dutifully followed him as he moved about the ship for two or three days, and then I went ashore to complete a required two-day emergency ship-handling course. Subsequently, I reported to *Coral Sea* for duty on Saturday, January 26. John Thompson left the ship on Tuesday, January 29, and I became operations officer. To say that this was rushed would be an understatement, but in retrospect my experience was typical of the way other senior officers were rotated into and out of jobs in *Coral Sea*, much to the consternation of Captain Elder.

We moved north on January 30 to return to Alameda while conducting carrier qualification landings for Replacement Air Group 12. On January 31 Captain Larry Flint, an old friend and now commander of the replacement air group, landed on board in an F-8D and caught a wire, only to have the left main landing gear break off and promptly depart the ship over the port side. As Larry sat on the deck, perplexed, those of us who knew him laughed, causing him great embarrassment. Larry, a good pilot, and had just landed a little harder than usual.

Coral Sea entered San Francisco Bay on February 2 at 0815. Harbor pilot Captain I. J. Tjaldeen came on board, and *Coral Sea* moved slowly by Alcatraz in heavy fog and then south under the Bay Bridge to make the turn east for Alameda. As the new operations officer, I was not yet fully cognizant of the navigation team's abilities, but I observed Captain Elder and Captain Tjaldeen discuss the situation while Tjaldeen, who was indecisive, I thought, conned the ship. *Coral Sea* moved slowly toward Alameda, and Captain Elder observed attentively from near the bridge radar repeater, which I learned later had failed. Radar information was being passed from CIC to the bridge by telephone talker.

At 0949 the starboard bow lookout advised the bridge that he had sighted the number 1 buoy to the Alameda channel close aboard to starboard, which meant that the ship had just missed the channel. The ship barely had way on. Captain Elder quickly assumed the conn and ordered all stop, followed by a backing bell. But before *Coral Sea* could respond, the ship was gently set down by the ebbing tide on the sandy bottom just left and north of the channel. At 0958 the ebbing tide left *Coral Sea* hard aground, and the ship's engineering plant was secured to prevent damage.

During the next seven hours divers were put over the side and reported no hull damage, and a fuel barge was brought alongside so that *Coral Sea*'s chief engineer, Commander Allan Barnes, could pump off 10,000 barrels of Navy special fuel oil in an effort to lighten the ship. Concurrently, the fog lifted for all to see *Coral Sea* aground in San Francisco Bay. The situation became the event du jour for San Francisco radio and TV stations, and civilian helicopters circled the ship at will. Their reporting frenzy exacerbated what was an embarrassing but not damaging event to the ship. That evening at 1854 *Coral Sea* floated clear of the sandbar on the flood tide. Captain Elder, aided by the harbor pilot and seven tugs, conned the ship into the channel and up to pier 3 at NAS Alameda. In retrospect, the short time the ship's navigation team had had to train and work together put an undue burden on themselves and certainly on the captain.

Over the weekend COMNAVAIRPAC appointed a three-officer investigation board. On Monday morning, February 4, the board convened in *Coral Sea* with Rear Admiral Paul Masterton, COMCARDIV 5, as president and members Captain K. E. Taylor, chief of staff, COMFAIRALAMEDA, and Captain L. E. Harris, commanding officer of *Midway*. The board deliberated for three days, adjourning on February 7. For reasons unknown to me, Captain Elder was denied the legal counsel of his choice by COMNAVAIRPAC. He was lauded by the board for the fact that no damage was done. However, based on the findings of the board, COMNAVAIRPAC made the decision to relieve Captain Elder of command. From the perspective of those who observed the proceedings, the results had the air of a kangaroo court. Those of us in *Coral Sea*

were heartsick about the entire event. Navigator Dickie Wieland and CIC officer Paul Ratte received nonpunitive letters of reprimand. As operations officer,
however new, I felt guilty.

Within five days Captain Charles E. Roemer was ordered to *Coral Sea*, and
on Wednesday, February 13, he relieved Captain Elder in a ceremony on *Coral
Sea*'s hangar deck. We officers and men, resplendent in full dress uniforms,
stood at attention in ranks, and there was not a dry eye in the lot. Bob Elder and
his lovely wife, Irene, stood tall and made the change with great dignity. Subsequently, Vice Admiral Smedburg, then chief of naval personnel, offered Captain Elder any command he chose in the Navy—except a command at sea.
Since that was his life, Captain Elder chose to retire from the Navy on November 1, 1963, and subsequently was employed by Northrop Aircraft Company. He worked there for many years and was instrumental in a number of
new aircraft programs for the Navy and the Air Force. Captain Charles Roemer
and his wife, Louise, stepped into trying roles for themselves, too. It was a difficult time for all and a credit to the Navy that it had such fine officers.

On the next day, February 14, Captain Roemer took *Coral Sea* to sea for carrier qualifications. At noon on February 15 RF-8A pilot Lieutenant Delmar
Young of VFP-63 was killed when his airplane flew into the water off the port
bow. Notwithstanding that, all the officers of *Coral Sea* rallied around Captain
Roemer to give him the best support we could on his first trip to sea in his new
ship. Captain Filmore Gilkeson, then chief of staff, COMCARDIV 3, and investigation board member Captain Leroy Harris both visited the ship to evaluate how we were operating. To my knowledge they gave Captain Roemer and
the ship a thumbs up because nothing changed. Commander J. S. Roth,
prospective air officer, reported on board on February 17, and we had just five
more weeks in which to ready the ship and air group for a long deployment.

We loaded our normally assigned Air Group 15 on board and departed
March 4 to participate in a major weapons training exercise in the Southern
California operating areas. As *Coral Sea* left Alameda, the wind was steady at
20 knots out of the west, and I told Jerry Roth to be ready to launch aircraft
early. Passing under the Bay Bridge, we manned flight quarters stations in full
view of downtown San Francisco, and as we passed Alcatraz, pilots manned
the airplanes on the flight deck for the first launch. The flight deck was its normal beehive of activity as we came up on the Golden Gate Bridge, and the
wind was right down the deck at a steady 30 knots. Cars were beginning to stop
on the bridge, and people looked down on the busy flight deck 200 feet below.
I stood by the captain on the port side of the navigation bridge and recommended that we launch aircraft. He looked at me and asked, "Do you always
operate this way?" He meant, are you always this aggressive, to which I
replied, "Yes sir." We launched aircraft as we came out from under the Golden

Gate Bridge, which by that time was lined with a few hundred people. We went to sea flying.

When we arrived in the Southern California operating area, Rear Admiral Dan Smith and his Carrier Division 3 staff flew on board to be the chief observers. Commander Spence Matthews, commander of Air Group 14, was the chief observer for the missile-firing exercises. The entire exercise was a bath of fire for me. We conducted underway replenishments, missile and gun firing, and heavy air operations with the destroyers *Marshal* and *Halsey Powell* in company as well. It all seemed to work, except for the time I scheduled a rendezvous for an underway replenishment but failed to have the two ships closer than 25 miles at the appointed rendezvous time. Captain Roemer was tolerant and that was sorted out. Later, I was able to fly with VA-153 and VA-155. We returned to Alameda at noon on March 15, and I could see that the next year was going to go fast, at least if the past ten days were an indication. The life of a ship's operations officer is based on little to no sleep. Nothing changed, and the year did go fast.

On Thursday, March 21, we held a one-day family cruise for our dependents and returned from that to have the ship's administrative material inspection the following Monday, conducted by officers from *Midway* and Carrier Division 3. My days and nights were filled with planning for our transit to Pearl Harbor and then on to Sydney, Australia. Mary and I also had a lot of planning to do. Our oldest son, Travis, was a freshman at MIT, Candace was a senior at Alameda High School, and our second son, Chris, was a freshman. Last son Charles, not yet in school, was a thorn in his mother's side. We planned to break our coming eight-month separation with a trip to preserve our own sanity. She would bring the two youngest to the western Pacific for the summer of 1963 and follow the ship at our own expense.

We loaded Commander Wayne Hammet's Air Group 15 on board, and on Wednesday, April 3, *Coral Sea* departed Alameda for Pearl Harbor for continued training. After that we would continue on to Sydney with Destroyer Division 152 to represent the U.S. Navy at the twentieth anniversary of the battle of the Coral Sea. Carrier Division 3 would join us later in Guam because Admiral Sides, commander in chief of the Pacific Fleet, would be the senior U.S. Navy representative for our visit in Australia. The burden for all planning for *Coral Sea* and six destroyers rested squarely on my shoulders, and Captain Bud Kobey, the commander of Destroyer Division (COMDESDIV) 152, and I spent a good deal of time together. I more than went out of my way to make the trip nice for the destroyers, and my effort paid off in goodwill later.

Favorable winds on the five-day transit to Pearl Harbor permitted two days of air operations. We entered Pearl Harbor to moor early in the morning on April 8. The air group had several minor and two not so minor accidents in

A-4s and F-3Bs while we flew and trained at a hurried pace. Still hanging over our heads was the workup for the air group and ship, the ORI, and 3,000 miles of open ocean. Time was our greatest challenge because April 29 was the date when we must be in Sydney.

On Monday, April 15, Rear Admiral C. H. Duerfeldt, commander of Fleet Air Hawaii, along with selected members of his staff and the fleet training group, boarded *Coral Sea*, and we were under way just after 0800 for our ORI. The obligatory navigation through the simulated minefield, the simulated torpedo attacks, and the many damage control and general quarters drills were firmly implanted in my mind from previous experience in *Midway* and *Kitty Hawk*. Jeff Davis and Al Barnes took care of the damage control exercises, and Jerry Roth had his hands full with simulated flight deck casualties, emergency rigging of the barricade, and simulated flight deck fires. My function as operations officer was to be in CIC and on the bridge providing coordination for all ship and air group fighting functions. I tried to visit as many different air group and ship hot spots as I could. Jeff Davis and I kept the captain informed and provided him information with which to make the necessary decisions. Wayne Hammet tried to do the same with air group information.

The professionalism and will to do well within the ship and air group were high. What was evident was that we had not been training and exercising together as much as we should. We completed all our drills, but I could feel a certain edge or roughness as we moved from drill to drill. The air group–ship launch sequence plan went well with Wayne Hammet and the ship's weapon coordinator, Commander Bob Hessom, working together, but the timing was just a little bit off. Chief of staff of COMNAVAIRPAC, Captain Sid Bottomley, and the staff air group training officer, Captain Jeep Streeper, flew out from San Diego to observe the ship, which indicated to me the continuing interest and concern for *Coral Sea*'s fast workup and accelerated schedule.

We finished the ORI on April 17, and *Coral Sea* tied up at Ford Island in Pearl Harbor that evening. In addition to preparing for the scheduled COM-FAIRHAWAII critique of our battle problem the next day, I found myself making sure that the chief engineer topped off with fuel, the supply officer had all the last-minute stores on board, the air group had its airplanes back from Barbers Point, all last-minute intelligence briefs were completed, the operations order for our transit to Sydney was published so that COMDESDIV 152 could have copies, and on and on. If it had not been for the operations administrative assistant, Lieutenant Junior Grade Don Zirkle, I don't know how we could have done it! The operations department yeomen really worked hard.

The ship, air group, and observers gathered in the wardroom the next day at 1300 for the critique of our ORI. Rear Admiral Duerfeldt assigned the ship and air group an overall grade of 78+ percent. It was not stellar, but given the time and training effort expended, I felt that we had done well enough to demonstrate our ability to operate well during the forthcoming cruise. I knew we would get better as we went along. The critique, like our training, was rushed, and all visitors were asked to leave the ship at 1515. We were under way for Australia at 1555 that afternoon. It was April 18, and I looked forward to our transit as an opportunity to settle down after the previous hectic weeks.

That transit would have to be businesslike and relatively rapid to meet our arrival date in Sydney of April 29. We were blessed by good winds from the west and conducted some air operations as we went along. Air operations knowledge resident in our aircraft carriers had improved vastly by then. Where carrier department heads in the early 1950s had had no knowledge of jet flight operations, there was now daily working experience. Because of that currency and jet operations knowledge, readiness in the fleets was infinitely better in 1963 than it had been earlier.

Charles Roemer had a great sense of history. He had been the LSO in *Lexington* when that ship was sunk in the battle of the Coral Sea, and I could see that he looked forward to this trip to Australia. We sortied from Pearl Harbor and rendered the customary honors as we passed the *Arizona* memorial. Captain Bud Kobey, with four of his six destroyers, left earlier to precede us in company with the oiler USS *Manatee*. Fuel was a major consideration on this long trip. We did not want to draw down *Coral Sea*'s fuel below 25 percent for many reasons, and so only two destroyers, USS *Somers* and USS *Buchanan*, accompanied *Coral Sea*. We planned to meet the slower USS *Manatee* several days before we reached Sydney.

Commander Henry Glindeman was commanding officer of VF-154. On April 20 I flew one of his F-8Ds to get some much-needed flight time and recurrent intercept training. Maintaining your aviator's qualifications becomes a personal goal, and I prided myself that I had been able to do that thus far, even with our hectic schedule. However, fate and a little sloppy flying on my part intervened, and I had an embarrassing deck landing accident, just as Larry Flint had earlier. *Coral Sea*, like *Midway*, was a roller, and the carrier would roll in the long swells of the Pacific Ocean, particularly when they were on the beam. The deck was moving appreciably when I returned from the intercept training flight to land on board. I touched down left wheel first as the port side of the flight deck came up to meet me. The arresting hook caught the number 3 wire, and the left main landing gear broke off the airplane as it came to a stop in the arresting gear. There was no one to blame but myself. The accident was the price for trying to keep current. Some would argue that I did not need to fly at this point in my career, but to them I would point out that current experience breeds respect and from that comes better performance. However, it pained me greatly to break Henry Glindeman's airplane, and I vowed to myself that in the future I would continue to fly with the air group when they were based on shore.

The four ships of Destroyer Division (DESDIV) 152 in company with *Manatee* crossed the Pacific ahead of us. We planned to meet *Manatee* on April 27 before entering Sydney harbor and already knew that we were going to be down to less than 28 percent fuel remaining. We planned to cross the equator at the 180th meridian, the international date line, for the time-honored initiation of some 3,200 pollywogs simultaneously into the domains of both Neptunus Rex, for crossing the equator, and the Golden Dragon, for crossing the international date line. That would make them a special category of shellback—a selective golden shellback. Logistically, this crossing-the-line ceremony was a tough one because there were so many pollywogs to initiate in *Coral Sea*. Davy Jones boarded the ship at midnight, Sunday, April 21, and because of the date line we skipped to April 23 as the day we crossed the equator. The day was dedicated to the initiation ceremonies, and we shellbacks maintained control through superstition, secrecy, and good crowd control on the flight deck. Using the deck-edge elevator, we brought up forty pollywogs at a time to be processed through the rites. They walked the plank, ran the gauntlet, and kissed the belly of the royal baby. Finally, covered with garbage and oil, they achieved the exalted status of shellback so they could get to the showers quickly. When the day was over, the old shellbacks were much more tired than the new shellbacks. We chopped (changed operational control) to the Seventh Fleet on that day and became TG 77.3.

On April 25 there was high drama in *Coral Sea*. Captain's mast is the principal form of administering nonjudicial punishment in the Navy, and while at sea Captain Roemer held mast on the starboard bridge wing. At mast those accused of sufficiently severe infractions of good order and discipline stand before the captain, who listens, judges, and either dismisses the charges or assigns a suitable punishment for the crime or infraction. On this day a nonrated sailor was assigned punishment for insubordination and was en route back down the ladders toward the brig, escorted by two Marine guards. The young sailor bolted and ran into the hangar deck to disappear. Commander Jeff Davis held muster on station for all hands, which brings everyone in the ship to their workplaces to be accounted for. This young sailor was missing. The ship was diligently searched and searched again. Every void and hiding place was opened and examined. The sailor was never found. During the captain's mast, *Coral Sea* had passed close by a South Pacific island by the name of Vanikoro. The island looked idyllic, with sharp, high, craggy mountains and lush, green growth that spilled down to white sandy beaches. When the sailor could not be found, it was surmised that he might have jumped over the side after he bolted from the Marines and tried to swim to the island. The three-ship task group returned along its track and diligently searched the sea but no trace of the man could be found. The distance that he would have had to swim made it questionable that he could have ever reached the island. After completing the sea search, the task group notified consular authorities by message and reluctantly continued on. The sailor was never found.

The standard navigation charts we used were actually charts first drawn by Captain Cook and others in the 1700s and updated over the years. The depths shown on the charts were limited to those recorded by oceanographic vessels that had passed that way. We planned that our transit would add new ocean depth knowledge and accuracy because of our satellite navigation capability, and Captain Roemer and Dickie Wieland were most interested in doing that. *Coral Sea* took bottom soundings as we crossed the Pacific in coordination with *Somers* and *Buchanan*, which frequently were deployed some 10,000 yards out on each side.

On the particularly black South Pacific night of April 27, at 0222, all three ships reported rapidly shoaling water where there was no previously reported land. The Fathometers showed readings that went from 670 fathoms, or some 4,080 feet, to just 90 feet in a mere one and a half nautical miles. Captain Roemer put the three ships into a column with *Buchanan* leading *Coral Sea* and *Somers* bringing up the rear. When *Buchanan* subsequently reported a depth of 60 feet, the column stopped, backed, and turned south until 200 fathoms was recorded on the Fathometer. Then the group resumed its southwestern course. Little was and still is known about ocean depths in these infrequently traveled areas. Sea mounts can rise because of volcanic action, and a particularly black night is not a good time to discover a new island, particularly if you go aground. Although we saw no surf, we dutifully recorded the spot for others to search in the light of day and moved on toward our rendezvous to refuel with *Manatee*, which we did that afternoon.

The destroyers of DESDIV 152 entered various ports along the southern, eastern, and northeastern coasts of Australia. We launched many of the air group airplanes to the Royal Australian Air Force (RAAF) station at Richmond, near Sydney, before we entered Sydney harbor so each squadron could fly and train while we were in port. I and my fellow ship's aviators could fly, too. *Coral Sea* entered Sydney harbor to moor on the afternoon of April 29. The visit was a tremendous success from all viewpoints. Admiral Sides arrived with the Pacific Fleet Marine Corps Drum and Bugle Corps, and 200,000 Australians visited *Coral Sea* over a fourteen-day port visit. Considering that Australia, the size of the United States, had a population of ten million people in 1963, that number of visitors was high. Each officer and man went out of his way to greet the Australians, and they, in turn, opened their homes and hearts to the visiting U.S. Navy. The drum and bugle corps was a major hit wherever it played.

We flew the ship's C-1A airplane to the outback one day for a visit to a sheep station. Commander Tom Mix and I flew Captain Roemer and five other officers from the ship and air group, plus one local Australian navigator, to the small community of Nyngan, 250 miles west of Sydney. We landed on a dirt airstrip and then motored to Bucking Guy, a sheep station. The day was a little like a visit to a Montana ranch or Nebraska farm, with home cooking and good old-fashioned family hospitality. I was struck by the thousands of kangaroos that we saw wherever we went. Returning to Sydney, we flew in our C-1A low across the flat, almost faceless land and scared up some emus that seemed to run like the wind.

Departing Sydney on May 13, we sortied from the harbor so that the air group could put on a flying display for civic and military officials. We reentered Sydney harbor and spun the ship while debarking the guests and then left to move north toward the equator and Guam, our next port. That trip north was a memory trip for the crew, particularly Captain Roemer. We sailed into the Coral Sea, where the ship's chaplain, Commander Bill Sodt, held memorial services directly over the spot where *Lexington* sank in 1942. We also found that our charts were not as accurate as we would have liked to believe they were. Our satellite navigation readouts showed some islands to be three miles from where the charts showed them. This new navigation technology was going to change a lot of things. We passed Bougainville, Guadalcanal, and Woleai Atoll, flying our airplanes as we went. I was struck, as I continue to be, with the power an aircraft carrier represents. This great ship, carrying the armed might of the United States, goes where it will and can provide presence or power for the United States wherever it goes.

We anchored in Apra Harbor, Guam, on May 22, and Rear Admiral Dan Smith and his COMCARDIV 3 staff came on board. At this juncture I gave up my major planning duties to put more time in as the ship's operations officer. We also became TG 77.6, with Rear Admiral Smith being commander of the task group and of TF 77, in tactical command of all carriers in the Seventh Fleet. No longer having the freedom to make our plans, I became acutely aware of the interface between the carrier division, its commander, and the ships of the task group under his control. It was a tough transition, but a good one.

Rear Admiral Smith had an enviable record in World War II as commander of Carrier Air Group 20 in *Enterprise* and then in *Lexington*. Mutual support is important in any naval operation, so Captain Blackie Kennedy, Commander Pete Deputy, and I tried our best. This worked—most of the time. Eventually, things smoothed out, and the ship and staff got along fine. Blackie Kennedy, the staff operations officer, was particularly good to work with. The CARDIV staff scheduled those days that we were under way, and the port visits were set by the commander of the Seventh Fleet. As operations officer, my job was to fill the allotted time at sea with meaningful training and operations.

The majority of the air group officers and men lived on the 02 deck level just below the flight deck. Generally, the enlisted men lived aft in berthing compartments, and the officers lived forward in one-, two-, or four-officer rooms. The enlisted men had the noise of the arresting gear engines and landing aircraft to contend with, and the officers had the catapults and launching aircraft. It was about a wash with respect to the level of noise. The idea was that everyone lived in proximity to their work. Jerry Roth and I each lived in one-officer staterooms next to each other on a thwart-ship passageway not far from flag country (the admiral's area) and the captain's in-port cabin. (His small sea cabin was in the island.) Our rooms were quite small and spartan, so we conducted our administrative business in our respective offices. While Jerry and I had not flown together in the past, our backgrounds were similar and we became good friends. He was a good air officer.

Coral Sea left Guam, and the task group conducted flight operations as we moved toward Subic Bay. The port visit after Subic Bay was to be Hong Kong, where Mary and the two boys would join me. I looked forward to that with great anticipation. En route to Subic Bay we completed Operation Glass Door, which was a standard carrier-versus-carrier air warfare exercise to help maintain the carriers at a high level of readiness. We flew against the attack carriers *Constellation*, *Ticonderoga*, and *Oriskany* and the antisubmarine warfare carrier *Yorktown* and then went into Subic Bay for two days on May 31. We arrived at the start of the monsoon season, and the rain came down in buckets, making it difficult for the air group to gain any training at Cubi Point.

Captain Roemer worked at qualifying Jeff Davis and me in ship handling. We made approaches to underway replenishment (UNREP) ships, conned while alongside, and made breakaways. We were given the opportunity to anchor the ship and get it under way. He was very good about this training, and once we were qualified, he also qualified other commanders from the ship and air group. The captain said, "I have had my fun. Now I must allow others to learn." I never forgot that.

Most aviators, who have bet their lives on their ability to assess relative motion in airplanes, develop an easy ability to maneuver a ship. A large ship, such as an aircraft carrier, with its four screws and two rudders, is very responsive to the ship handler. While the carrier is alongside another ship to replenish, two screws can be set at the same rpms, and the other two can be used to change any desired fore and aft relative motion quite precisely. A good steersman on the bridge can maintain a ship's heading within a half degree, and thus conning officers can have quite fine control. The key to being able to maintain position on another ship just 60 to 80 feet from bridge to bridge is not to have to use large changes of either rpm or rudder and to catch the relative motion early and firmly. We learned well under Captain Roemer's tutelage.

On June 10 we anchored in Hong Kong along with our two stalwart destroyers, *Somers* and *Buchanan*. There I found Mary with the two boys. Aside from suffering from the twelve-hour time difference between San Francisco and Hong Kong, she was ready to sightsee and shop. We proceeded to see it all, from the floating restaurants to the shops, the China Fleet Club, and the Tiger Balm Gardens. Her presence put an entirely new face on ports we visited, which made the cruise an entirely better experience for both of us. My duties in port, other than preparing for our next at-sea period and standing the command duty watch, were minimal, and we could enjoy each other's company, which the four of us did. *Coral Sea* spent ten days in Hong Kong and departed next for Manila Bay. Mary and the boys flew by commercial airliner to Manila to wait for our arrival at NAS Sangley Point.

Our at-sea periods settled down into flying days and steaming days. The period between Hong Kong and Manila was filled with rearming, getting stores, refueling from USS *Caliente*, and flying for the air group. On June 25 we entered Manila Bay with USS *Mauna Kea* and *Buchanan* and anchored off Sangley Point as we fired a twenty-gun salute to the Philippine government. I had the opportunity to show Mary around Manila, and then we drove to Subic Bay to see friends and the fabled sin city of Olongapo. The four of us made a trip to the Paxanon Falls south of Manila and shot the rapids in dugout canoes through steep canyons with vividly hued snakes and lizards in full view. The boys ate it up! This was an educational time for them, and they learned about countries and the people who lived on the Pacific Rim.

At the end of June Commander Wayne Hammet was relieved as CAG 15 by Commander W. R. (Bob) Bascom, and in July TG 77.6 moved north to Japan, operating along the way. The air group was now flying enough that they were good, and I tried my level best to give Bob Bascom and his air group as much flying time as possible. We had a few relatively minor accidents, such as the A-3B that lost its left wheel while landing and then boltered (that is, touched the deck, missed the wire, and took off again) to be sent to Atsugi where the pilot landed on the long runway and was stopped midfield by arresting gear. The airplane was repaired subsequently by the Japanese company Nippi, which was under contract to the U.S. Navy, and flew again.

On July 9 *Coral Sea* moored at Piedmont Pier in Yokosuka while the air group went to Atsugi for some concentrated flying ashore. That gave me the opportunity to fly the F-8D with VF-154, for which I was most grateful. This ability to fly with the air group continued to cement ship and air group working relations in 1963. Just six years previously, when we had deployed in *Bennington* in ATG 182, the ship's operations officer had never even flown a jet, let alone flown with one of the squadrons in the air group. Certainly, in *Coral*

Sea we had infused closer cooperation, support, and understanding between the two. I felt proud of that progress, and I believe we were embarking on even greater understanding.

During the July 15–22 at-sea operating period, Jeff Davis and I learned that we each had been selected for promotion to the rank of captain. The opportunity for promotion was not high—only 280 out of 700 were selected for promotion—so both Jeff and I were pleased. Commander Pete Deputy, air operations officer on the staff, also made captain. Each of us would pin on the eagles at different times later in 1963 and 1964 depending on the vacancies available and where we stood in the lineal list of those selected.

From the end of World War II until the 1970s the path for success in naval aviation changed little, at least for those who specialized in carrier aviation. Early in a career frequent deployments and time at sea in active flying billets were essential. A department-head billet in a squadron was next, and that would lead to the opportunity for squadron command. Along the way some dropped out because of fear of flying, some were killed, some chose to specialize in administrative jobs ashore, and some were shunted aside into other career channels by the luck of the draw and the personnel detailer. Squadron command and then succeeding tours as a department head on a carrier or major seagoing staff raised the opportunity for selection as captain. Once you became a captain, you needed a shore tour in Washington and a deep-draft ship command to open the opportunity for command of an aircraft carrier. At each succeeding level of responsibility, fewer and fewer officers were chosen to move along to the next level. The epitome of success for most of us was to command an aircraft carrier, and only a few were accorded that opportunity.

Once you reached the carrier command level of accomplishment, a new set of rules materialized for selection to flag rank. Those involved not only the previously stated seagoing aviation skills but also diplomacy and Navy political acumen as well. An officer's potential for higher flag rank and further command became more important. The entire progression was not set in concrete, nor was there any sure route to flag rank, but it was clear enough to my contemporaries—and to me—what we must do to succeed.

On the night of July 21 Lieutenant Junior Grade Smink of Commander T. B. Russell's VA-155 ejected from his A-4B while on the downwind portion of his landing pattern because his engine failed. He ejected so quickly that we did not know that he was in the water until we saw him fire three green flares from a handheld signaling flare gun after he was in the water. He was picked up by the *Chokai Maru*, a Japanese merchantman, and returned later. The next day we anchored in Sasebo.

Once anchored, I found my way ashore and found Mary and the boys ensconced in a Japanese inn with the tale of all tales about their trip from Tokyo.

They started the trip on a superstreamlined train and for the next twenty-four hours were gradually relegated to less and less sumptuous transport until they traveled the final miles in an open-windowed World War II–vintage passenger car pulled by a coal-burning steam engine. Between the soot that covered them and the changing accommodations, they had had a real adventure. Our son Chris also had climbed to the top of Mount Fuji by himself before they had left. We visited nearby Hiroshima and other places until the ship departed on July 29. The return trip to Yokosuka for Mary and the boys entailed two trains, one airplane, and five taxis, proving again that wives had to be resourceful when following a ship.

August found *Coral Sea* operating farther south and east, near Okinawa, to dodge a major storm, Typhoon Bess, which had targeted southern Japan. We were forced to cancel our port visit to Kōbe abruptly, surprising the now-considerable summer contingent of wives following the ship at their own expense. One of *Coral Sea*'s junior supply corps officers had been flown into Kōbe by the ship's C-1A to make the many arrangements needed when anchoring in a foreign port. He was left high and dry but found twenty-five American wives, each about to run out of money because they had not seen their husbands for several weeks. Being resourceful, he set up a card table in the lobby of the largest hotel in Kōbe and proceeded to advance each wife a few dollars from her husband's pay—dispensing the cash he had brought ashore for stores. I later learned that the line of American wives snaked around the lobby as they formed up to receive the needed cash. To the Japanese, who had different values and beliefs with respect to women, this had all the appearance of American camp followers being paid off. The wives later laughed about it.

The new secretary of the Navy, Paul H. Nitze, visited the Seventh Fleet in August and came on board *Coral Sea* on August 15, just before observing a major fleet replenishment on August 17. At this time Rear Admiral J. W. Gannon arrived to relieve Rear Admiral Dan Smith as COMCARDIV 3 and CTF 77. I would miss Dan Smith for a number of reasons, but one was that whenever we entered Yokosuka to moor, the CARDIV 3 band would strike up "The Yellow Rose of Texas" in honor of the admiral's wife, Ginny, who always met the ship. It was a festive and peppy tune that always brought smiles, both on and off the ship.

We rounded out August 1963 with a port visit to Beppu and then went to Iwakuni, where the Marines had their major air station in Japan. In September the operating tempo picked up because of heightened tensions between China and Taiwan. Such historic regional tugs and pulls determine in large part the positioning of our carrier forces and their operations at sea. CINCPAC would tell CINCPACFLEET, who in turn told COMSEVENTHFLEET, who told CTF 77 where the pressure was to be applied. CTF 77 directed the carrier task groups to provide the muscle, and those in Washington would assess its effect.

The sensitivity to positioning of the Chinese navy and air forces drove the tempo of the Seventh Fleet's operations at this time. The locus of operations kept us south of Japan and visible near Taiwan. Later we traded off duties with *Hancock*'s carrier group so that *Coral Sea* could go into Yokosuka on September 7. Mary was there, and we spent time at Atsugi, as well, while I flew training flights with the A-4 squadrons and with VF-154. Finally, *Coral Sea* deployed unexpectedly on September 21 because of the increasing Chinese operations, and we left 100 officers and men behind. Mary, Chris, and Charles returned by commercial airliner to Alameda to prepare for school as planned on September 22, but without much help from me. Her presence had made a vast difference in the cruise for us both, since we knew that there were only two more months to go and that I would be leaving the ship in January. After departing Yokosuka, the ship moved south to sight-relieve the *Hancock* group on patrol near Taiwan before *Coral Sea* put into Buckner Bay for a few hours on Friday, September 27, to pick up the 100 men that we had left behind in Yokosuka.

The air group fighter squadrons stood night and day condition III CAP watches at sea during the entire deployment whenever there were no flight operations. That preparedness provided a defensive posture to ensure that no aircraft would overfly the task group without first being intercepted. Tensions around Taiwan subsequently relaxed in October, and we moved north to prepare for the semiannual joint international exercise, Nightmare, with the South Koreans. We visited Sasebo on October 3, then sortied on October 7 to escape approaching Typhoon Kit, and remained at sea for the exercise.

Our last port visit for this cruise was to Yokosuka on October 19. Jeff Davis learned that he had been promoted to captain, which meant that I could not be far behind. Winter began early in Japan in 1963, and it was cold, damp, and rainy in Yokosuka. It was particularly cold on the higher plain some 40 miles south at Atsugi where I went to fly with VF-154. At this time the *Hancock* group was in the South China Sea, and *Oriskany* was visiting Beppu, but *Oriskany* shortly sortied to go south with *Hancock* to give visible strength to the South Vietnamese government, then under pressure from the North. Those ships took up positions in the Gulf of Tonkin, where in less than a year events would lead to greater U.S. involvement.

On October 29 we were under way from Yokosuka in heavy fog, and the weather seemed appropriate for the end of a cruise. I sensed from the captain on down within the ship and air group that everyone was ready to return to the States. The weather lifted as we went farther to sea so we could begin flying, and the task group moved south toward the Philippine Sea. *Coral Sea*'s relief in the western Pacific was USS *Kitty Hawk*, which deployed from Pearl Harbor on November 4.

On November 6 *Coral Sea* was refueling USS *Somers* when *Somers* collided with *Coral Sea*'s number 3 elevator. The elevator had been lowered to the hangar deck to facilitate the replenishment and stuck out from the ship's hull some 50 feet. It was a glancing blow, but glancing blow or not, a collision is a collision and is dreaded at sea. I had just left the navigation bridge for the flag bridge to discuss our schedule when Commander Vince Maynard, commanding officer of *Somers*, allowed his ship to move in dangerously close to *Coral Sea*. As I stood on the flag bridge, it seemed to me that *Somers*'s main mast was just five feet away from me and the ships still had not touched. I could look down on *Somers*'s main deck. I thought Vince had it made, until suddenly *Somers*'s bow sheared out and the destroyer's stern swung into *Coral Sea* so that *Somers*'s afterdeckhouse struck the underside of *Coral Sea*'s number 3 elevator. Hoses parted, black oil went everywhere, and *Somers*'s afterdeckhouse sustained a gaping hole. That seemed to be the sum total of the damage aside from some bent pride. We would have to check the operation of the number 3 elevator, but both ships responded well and continued operating. No one was hurt in what might have been a bad collision.

The next day, while attempting to land on board *Coral Sea*, Lieutenant S. A. Jackson of VF-154 approached low and struck the ramp with the underside of the fuselage of his F-8D. As was often the case in such accidents, he luckily flew away but was losing hydraulic fluid to his flight control system. As he turned downwind for another try at landing, his hydraulic pressure went to zero, and his flight controls froze. He was forced to eject within two minutes of the time he had hit the ramp. He was rescued by the helicopter and was back on board in short order, but we had lost an airplane.

On Tuesday, November 12, *Coral Sea* put into Buckner Bay to off-load CARDIV 3 for the staff's return to Alameda. Their presence was not required for our great circle, nonstop transit to the States. *Coral Sea* and *Kitty Hawk* would not have a sight relief because of the different tracks of the two ships. Since we would not make the normal stop in Pearl Harbor, at some point in our transit I was to fly into Barbers Point as a passenger in one of Commander Rufus Small's VAH-2 A-3Bs to debrief some classified matters with CINCPAC-FLEET, while the ship passed far north of Hawaii. Our cruise was ending like it started—in a rush. In the last mail to come on board I received news as to what I would be doing in Washington for my next duty. I would head a group of naval officers in long-range air warfare planning on the staff of the CNO.

With the staff's departure I was cast back into a planning role as operations officer. Our first concern in our transit to the States was the challenge of Soviet Bear bomber overflights. We would be proceeding as a single ship, without plane guard destroyers, and would provide our own helicopter as plane guard for any flying that we might do. The second concern was to be within proper distance of Pearl Harbor to launch the A-3B. Finally, our due date in Alameda was the primary concern because we had to be there at a certain time for many reasons, not the least of which was keeping faith with the crew and families—giving them a time to aim for.

We departed Buckner Bay on November 13 and met the refrigerator ship *Grafias* to receive some fresh stores for the thirteen-day trip home. We would have two days dated November 18 because we would recross the international date line. We launched and flew the E-1B early warning airplane at selected times for the first five days to watch for Soviet Bear airplanes. On Sunday afternoon, November 17, we had an indication of their approach and launched the ready CAP of two Demons from Commander Ed Herman's VF-151 to intercept, but the Bears did not materialize, and we then moved beyond their range capability. The North Pacific acted like the North Pacific in November with appropriately high seas, making for a rough crossing.

Early on Thursday morning, November 21, I boarded an A-3B and sat on the after cockpit floor cover for the downward escape hatch with my back braced against the aft bulkhead. The A-3B was not designed to carry passengers so I had no seat belt. I felt naked, but VAH-2 needed the three-man crew for the flight, and I, as the passenger interloper, took the risk of no restraint. *Coral Sea* was pounding bow first into heavy seas, and as luck would have it, the catapult officer chose to fire us just a little out of sync with the pitching movement of the deck. He fired us as the deck was going down, not up. At the end of the catapult stroke, the A-3B hit solid green water coming over the flight deck, but those J-57 engines kept running, and we flew to Barbers Point 600 miles to the southeast. *Coral Sea* continued on without me, which I guess says something about one person's importance.

At CINCPACFLEET that afternoon I expressed Captain Roemer's regrets for not being there and provided the necessary intelligence debrief to the staff. The next morning we launched in the A-3B from NAS Barbers Point on the continuing flight to Alameda. This time there was no green water on the launch, and in a matter of six and a half hours we landed at Alameda on the afternoon of November 22. I rejoined my family there at the apartment in which they were living and called as many of the wives as I could to tell them of their husbands' arrival on November 25.

The ship's C-1A flew in to Alameda on Sunday, November 24, to bring the arrival planning crew of officers and to pick up the necessary U.S. Customs officers who would return to the ship to clear it and all the crew officially for reentry into the United States. That forethought saved a great deal of time after the ship arrived. More importantly, it saved a lot of anguish as sailors looked at the dock and dependents looked up at the ship, waiting for the laborious customs process to be completed. The customs ritual was necessary because of the length of time that we had been out of the States and because of all the purchases that had been made overseas.

I returned to *Coral Sea* in the C-1A with the customs officers on Sunday, November 24, and reported to the captain concerning the intelligence debrief. He asked me why I had returned and not stayed ashore when I could have been with Mary, and I replied, "I left in *Coral Sea*, and I wanted to return in *Coral Sea*." At that time he produced some captain's eagles and announced that the ship had received a message that I could be promoted. I was to be promoted to captain as of November 1, 1963. That was a big step for me, and I appreciated all that Captain Roemer had done for me to make that cruise memorable. Also, he had been understanding of the many separations Mary and I had endured over the previous four years of sea duty, and I was deeply grateful to him for that and the many opportunities he had provided me to learn ship handling. That afternoon the air group was launched for each squadron's respective airfield. The next morning, Monday, November 25, *Coral Sea* entered San Francisco Bay, to be saluted by lofty water streams from San Francisco's fire and police boats, and tied up at Alameda where crew members were reunited with many happy family members.

Our four children were with us for the 1963 holiday season. Travis was home from MIT, and Candace was home from the University of Minnesota where she was a freshman. My work on board *Coral Sea* was minimal during that period as Commander Tom Mix and I prepared for him to become operations officer. Captain Pierre Charbonnet was ordered to relieve Charles Roemer later in January 1964. Our family enjoyed not only Thanksgiving but also Christmas and the New Year. In early December I flew the ship's C-1A to Washington to learn about the new job and to house hunt for our family.

We packed up our household effects during the first week of January, said good-bye to our many friends, and watched our moving van leave our apartment with our worldly possessions. We had purchased a 1964 Volkswagen Beetle while in Hong Kong for delivery in Baltimore after we arrived on the East Coast. This was to be Mary's car, and she really looked forward to a new one to replace the little black Beetle she had driven for the past nine years. I detached from USS *Coral Sea* on January 6, 1964, as the ship prepared to go to sea for carrier qualifications. We planned to leave the next day to drive to Washington. Things seemed to be in place, and even though the last four years had been tough on the family, we knew we could look forward to a great time in Washington.

14. BLACK SHOES
JANUARY 1964 TO JULY 1965

The Warren Commission reported there was no conspiracy in the assassination of President Kennedy. The United Nations intervened in Cyprus and brought about a cease-fire between warring Greek and Turkish Cypriots. Three North Vietnamese PT boats attacked the U.S. destroyer Maddox *in the Gulf of Tonkin, and the Navy retaliated, after which Congress gave President Johnson the power to use any action necessary to repel armed attack on U.S. forces. Lyndon Johnson was reelected president. Cassius Clay won the heavyweight title from Sonny Liston. The Vietcong attacked a military compound in South Vietnam, and President Johnson ordered air raids on the North and sent more troops to South Vietnam. Martin Luther King led a march from Selma to Montgomery, Alabama, to protest discrimination against blacks, and there were riots for six days in the Watts area of Los Angeles.*

There were 17,125 pilots, 130,742 aviation ratings, and 25 aircraft carriers of all types in the Navy. Patrol seaplanes were phased out in the Atlantic Fleet. A Pacific Fleet task group led by Bon Homme Richard *cruised the Indian Ocean. Chief photographer's mate Clara B. Johnson became the first official female aircrewman, and USS* Franklin *was stricken from the Navy register, the first Essex class ship to be retired. USS* Enterprise, Long Beach, *and* Bainbridge *completed an around-the-world cruise. Some 3,500 Marines were placed ashore at Da Nang and Chu Lai, South Vietnam, and USS* Independence *arrived in the South China Sea while the carriers off Vietnam delivered ordnance faster than it could be supplied.*

Mary, I, and the movers had spent the first week of January 1964 packing up our household effects, and the moving truck left Alameda on January 7. The next morning, as we walked through the house for a last check, the telephone rang with a sound that reverberated throughout the empty apartment. It was Captain Mickey Wiesner, the captain detailer in Washington, and he said, "Don, have you left yet?" We sorted that one out, and then he told me that my orders were being changed as we spoke. I would be taking command of a ship in Concord, California, instead of coming to Washington for duty on the Navy staff. That evening I received telegraphic orders to command USS *Mount Katmai*, a Navy ammunition ship.

The supply officer at NAS Alameda caught our moving truck with the help of the Arizona State Police and returned it to Alameda. We searched rapidly for a house and luckily found a nice one in Alameda. When our confused moving truck driver returned, we moved into our new house and reentered the children in their Alameda schools. With the family back on track, I took stock of what I must do next.

My orders told me to proceed to San Diego, to report to Commander Service Squadron (COMSERVRON) 1 for about nine weeks of instruction and training, and then to take command of *Mount Katmai* when the ship returned from deployment to the western Pacific. I dutifully reported to COMSERVRON 1 in San Diego and entered a new world—the world of the black shoes. At times during the next eighteen months I wondered if I was still in the same Navy.

Unknown to me, a controversy over my orders erupted between my big boss in Honolulu, Rear Admiral William Irwin, the commander of Service Force Pacific Fleet (SERVPAC), and the detailers in the Bureau of Naval Personnel. The current commanding officer of *Mount Katmai* was Captain Jack Grayson, a patrol plane aviator, and Rear Admiral Irwin took strong exception to the bureau ordering another aviator to that ship. The agreed rotation policy for aviators and surface officers was one for one. He felt that two aviators in a row would cause the ship's material condition to slip seriously. More probably, underlying this was a concern over reduced command opportunities for surface and submarine officers. The dialogue between the bureau and SERVPAC transpired without my knowing it, while I blithely continued my training in San Diego. In retrospect the head of steam that was developing was appreciable.

I completed my training (steam engineering school, indoctrination into the navigational rules of the road, and ship-handling school, where probably the most valuable thing I learned was that single-screw ships always back to port, unless you want them to) and returned to Alameda where, according to plan, I reported for further temporary duty on board USS *Mount Vesuvius*, a sister ship of *Mount Katmai*. Captain J. E. (Blackie) Kennedy was commanding officer. Blackie, of course, had previously been staff operations officer for Rear Admiral Dan Smith in *Coral Sea* and was a great friend. He had taken command several months earlier, and we had a good time together as he showed me the ropes.

Up to that time, all Navy ammunition ships had been named after volcanoes, hence *Shasta*, *Baker*, *Vesuvius*, *Katmai*, etc. A lesson in that naming process was not lost on all who served in them. Mount Katmai was a mountain in southwestern Alaska that, on June 6, 1912, erupted for sixty hours, throwing a column of pumice and ash 25 miles high into the stratosphere. Thirty thousand square miles of Alaska and Canada were covered in ash, as deep as 700 feet in some places, and Earth's climate was affected for years. On a smaller and more personal scale, an ammunition ship exploded at Port Chicago in 1944 with such force that it killed 300 people and blew the ship's anchor several miles away onto the side of a mountain.

I rode with Blackie and observed *Mount Vesuvius* work for two weeks, while among other things we traveled the tortuous route to sea: down the Sacramento River, under the Benicia and Carquinez bridges, past Mare Island, down the San Pablo Bay, past Tiburon peninsula and Angel and Alcatraz Islands, and then out under the Golden Gate Bridge. It was more fun watching it than doing it, but I found ship handling easy. I also found that I could get the same rush of adrenaline in ship handling as in flying an airplane. The trick was to think in two, not three, planes. Later I would wish more than once that I could pull back on the stick to miss another ship. The situations between ships just developed much slower and lasted longer. They could be just as excruciating.

After two weeks *Mount Vesuvius* returned to Concord, and I found *Mount Katmai* moored there. The ship looked like the World War II cargo ship that it was. Up close, the normal wear and tear of recent deployment showed. *Mount Katmai* had been built by the North Carolina Shipbuilding Company of Wilmington, North Carolina, in fifty-five days and then delivered to the Navy on February 13, 1945. In 1949 *Mount Katmai* had transited the Panama Canal to the Pacific Fleet where the ship served during and after the Korean War. Two aviators had served as commanding officer before me; the first, Captain Charles Irrabino in 1961, was still remembered for carrying a .45-caliber pistol on his hip. The second was Jack Grayson. Lieutenant Commander R. G. Delozier was executive officer. There were 16 officers and a crew of 195 men. On an aviation scale, the size of the complement was comparable to a carrier squadron.

Captain Jack Grayson had done a great job as commanding officer, and the crew's spirit seemed high. He was most engaging in conversation, and among other things he told me that he had stopped in Pearl Harbor on the way back and had found the air at COMSERVPAC chilly because another aviator would be taking over *Mount Katmai*. He suggested that I fly out there and call on Rear Admiral William Irwin to smooth things over. Jack failed to tell me that Rear Admiral Irwin, a submariner, had earned a nickname: Sweet Old Bill.

One day a week later I flew to Pearl Harbor. The next morning, after getting my bearings, I went to SERVPAC headquarters at about 0830 and presented myself to the chief of staff, Captain Rydeen. We chatted briefly while I waited, and I waited, to call on the admiral. I saw other people entering his office, but my turn never seemed to come. Finally, about noon, his aide very apologetically told me that the admiral had left to play golf. He did not want to see me. This was the first time in my Navy career that my new ultimate commander had refused to see me. With nothing else to do, I flew back to the States, thinking about my upcoming tour of duty. I made up my mind that I would do my best as commanding officer of *Mount Katmai* and stay as far away from Sweet Old Bill as I could. Fortunately, there were several echelons of command between us.

After the change of command ceremony on April 8, I officially entered an entirely different Navy world. We spent the month of April in port, which gave me a chance to learn the ship from stem to stern. *Mount Katmai* had steam, not electric, winches because of the ammunition on board. The steel decks were worn slick, and I wondered why there was no nonskid paint as we had on carriers. I noted a lack of lighting on deck and in the holds and the crew's lack of steel-toed shoes for personal protection. The ship showed little of the technological improvements that had occurred since World War II, and I decided to change that.

An event that occurred in the first week characterized the talent of those who unloaded ammunition and showed the raw concern of those who live in ammunition ships. A civilian worker, unloading some light ammunition from the ship into a railroad car on the pier, pulled the pin on a hand grenade and dropped it to see what would happen. He was smart enough to run from the boxcar, and the reverberation of the exploding hand grenade caused the hearts of every officer and man in *Mount Katmai* to fly into their mouths. At the time, *Mount Katmai* carried about 2,900 tons of high explosive. There was a brief investigation by the weapons station, because the incident occurred on the pier and not in the ship, and the worker was told to find employment someplace else, far away.

On May 6 I made my first sojourn to sea as captain of a ship. I took a harbor pilot for the first part of the trip down the Sacramento River into the San Francisco Bay. After passing Alcatraz, we lay to to let the pilot off. He was slow, and as we waited for him to leave the ship, almost unnoticed the ship's head twisted, and we were set down on the Golden Gate by the fast, ebbing tide. After the few minutes it took him to leave the ship, I looked up in great surprise to see that if I did not do something quickly, we would pass under the Golden Gate Bridge sideways, and a large Japanese merchant freighter was steaming directly at us. My first command to the helmsman of my new ship was "all ahead, full; left full rudder!" *Mount Katmai*, slowly responding, straightened up, and we went to sea in relative safety.

The next day *Coral Sea* came along our port side to receive a token amount of ammunition. My troops showed that they were a little shaky after the April stand-down period but still were good at slinging ammunition across the 80-foot distance between the two ships. We also practiced making UNREP approaches with *Procyon* commanded by Captain Paul Stevens, and the next day we returned to Concord.

In mid-May we went to sea to train in the Southern California operating areas. Some Navy BIS members came on board to evaluate the ship for what should be done during a yard period in the coming winter. I put on a full-court press to have our UNREP capability improved by adding a helicopter deck aft.

My aviation compatriots found *Mount Katmai* at sea in May. Like all service force ships, *Mount Katmai* had large identifying hull numbers painted on the bow. Some of the F-8 pilots from *Kitty Hawk* and *Coral Sea* flying from Miramar saw us at sea and passed the word around the squadrons. Lieutenant Chuck Diamond probably made the first pass. He approached the ship from behind, on the starboard side and low on the water. No one in the ship suspected what was about to happen. As he passed the ship's bridge, he moved the throttle outboard to light the afterburner and pulled up to cross over the ship in a steep left bank. The resounding explosion from lighting the afterburner got everyone's attention. Its effect was similar to stepping on that proverbial anthill. The crew spilled out on the main deck with great alacrity and wildly searching eyes. They had never had an airplane do that to them before. That afternoon I explained the afterburner to them. To put a little levity into it, I said, "If the ship is going to blow up, we will never hear the echo." There was not a lot of laughter. Our attraction for F-8 pilots would continue wherever we went in the Pacific.

For the remainder of May and into June we remained moored in San Diego harbor to put our people into training programs ashore. At the same time I continued to fly with my friends in the fighter and attack communities. Admittedly it was much less flying than I wanted, but at every opportunity I would go to Lemoore to fly the A-4 and to Miramar to fly the F-8D. I had begun to forget until then how much flying meant to me and just how much I missed it. The F-8D was still a Cadillac of an airplane, so much more capable than those we had had just ten years before.

On June 9 we left San Diego and returned to Concord. During that trip I vowed to put down nonskid deck covering for the crew. The swells off the coast of California made many lose their footing on the slick decks, and we had some bad sprains, but no broken bones. There had to be a better way to prevent such potential and needless accidents.

In July we trained and operated with USS *Mount Baker*. Captain Tom Gallagher, an old friend from VX-3 days, was commanding officer, and he and I conspired to experiment with a new luminescent chemical light to see if we could enhance our ability to make night approaches to another ship. The chemical light helped a little, but there had to be a better way. The carrier fleet had given up trying to conduct flight operations in absolute darkness, and I was trying to formulate how to sell the service force on using the red lighting like that which Bob Elder had installed in *Coral Sea* to enhance our abilities to UNREP more safely at night. Hampered by darkness, too many crewmen were being hurt by rolling bombs or were being hit by forklifts while below deck. I discussed how we might do this with my brain trust: executive officer, Dick Delozier; engineering officer, Lieutenant Frank R. Darling; operations officer, Lieutenant Don J. Montgomery; and first lieutenant, Lieutenant Junior Grade Dennis J. Knutson. They were beginning to catch my enthusiasm to upgrade *Mount Katmai*. Each time *Mount Katmai* went to sea, we placed some makeshift red lighting on the king posts, trying to find the best location.

Fog is the predominant weather phenomenon off Northern California, and we had our share of it. I was well versed in ship's radar, so my cross to bear was an antiquated Philco radar repeater that must have been on the bridge of *Mount Katmai* since World War II. It was so old that I thought Thomas Edison might have used it. Although it was cumbersome to use, it was still better than nothing.

Mount Baker and *Mount Katmai* returned to Concord on July 24 with Tom just ahead of me so that, as I came around the bend in the Sacramento River to see the Benicia Bridge, I was just in time to see a train climbing the long approach to the bridge and to watch the bridge as it did not open for Tom's three short whistle blasts. I held my breath as he dropped his anchor for the stern to swing just a few feet away from a collision with the railway bridge and a date with a court-martial. Better he than I, but later we could laugh about it. We both tied up at Concord about the same time.

In August, in company with *Mount Vesuvius*, we were under way for some night UNREPs off the Farallon Islands. Then *Mount Katmai* rendezvoused with *Midway* for a long night-rearming session. Later we moved down the coast toward San Diego to moor there on the evening of August 14. The next day, a Saturday, we began some vital work with the new, first-of-the-class USS *Sacramento*, a combination ammunition ship and oiler.

Lieutenant Junior Grade Henry Kane was my ship's navigator and a golfer of some local repute. We kidded him a lot about his golf, so it was my idea to rig up a golf ball with a screw eye in it to which we attached some fishing line for our first messenger line over to another ship. To the fishing line we tied string, then light line, and gradually worked up to manila line for an UNREP messenger line. For one of our many approaches to *Sacramento*, Henry stood on the number 2 hatch facing aft to address his ball resting on a fiber door mat as I made the approach alongside *Sacramento*. As we drew abreast, First Lieutenant Dennis Knutson sounded the obligatory two blasts on his handheld police whistle and received the necessary one-whistle response from *Sacramento*. Henry then let fly his golf shot with a number 6 iron. The golf ball and line went true, and the crew in Sacramento laughed and began pulling in the line for the UNREP trials. When *Sacramento* tensioned up the three rigs, there was so much power that *Mount Katmai* was pulled into a three- or four-degree starboard list.

We were alongside *Sacramento* day and night for most of three days. For one period we conned for eighteen hours while alongside, and I qualified all my officers of the deck and department heads in their ability to maintain an UNREP station on another ship. After those days alongside, my crew was tired from the continuous work. We went into San Diego for a two-day respite and then went to sea again to provide the same services to a new dry stores class of ship, USS *Mars*. After a three-day replay of what we had done with *Sacramento*, we returned to Concord. Both *Sacramento* and *Mars* sent glowing reports to COMSERVRON 1. Those reports brought accolades for the crew from the commodore in San Diego and from our commodore, Bill Gentry, in Alameda. I never heard from SERVPAC, but I hoped some of this news was filtering up to Sweet Old Bill. *Mount Katmai* was making its reputation.

In the second week of September we were under way to try another new idea. To refuel at sea, ships passed over an eight-inch rubber fuel oil hose with a metal gasket on the end that had ten holes in it. That gasket was mated with a similar heavy gasket on the receiving ship and fastened with ten bolts and nuts to make the firm connection. It was slow and laborious to do or undo the bolts and nuts, but we had always done it that way. My black shoe friends must have observed the aviators' air refueling and noticed the ease with which we hooked up and unhooked. More probably some aviator captain of an oiler had had the idea of applying aviation refueling techniques to ship refueling. At any rate I heard about it from Bill Gentry and volunteered to try it out with *Mount Katmai*. I was given the necessary test female fitting to install on *Mount Katmai* that would fit the male fitting to be sent from the fleet oiler USS *Neches*.

When we met at sea, we passed shot lines across to *Neches*. The *Neches*'s crew sent over the new refueling hose to my one and only refueling station where Frank Darling, as chief engineer, was on deck to make this trial happen. Having never seen air refueling, he was not convinced as to its viability, but he was doing it because I had made such a big thing out of it. The *Neches*'s probe was rammed home into our female receptacle located just below the starboard bridge wing on the main deck, and *Neches* started pumping. Soon a little black oil oozed from the fitting. As Frank leaned over to get a better look at it, the probe suddenly blew out of its lock in the female fitting, and black oil shot all over the main deck and Frank Darling. When *Neches* stopped pumping and the oil was no longer squirting all over our ship, Frank looked up at me, just above him and relatively untouched. He was totally black from head to foot, but I could see pure anger in those white eyes as he stared at me. I had to laugh, which did not help the situation much. But after showering and putting on clean clothes, Frank came up to the bridge, and we both had a good laugh. Today the concept has become standard practice and has proved its worth over tens of thousands of ship refuelings.

On Friday, September 11, we held our *Mount Katmai* family-day cruise, during which we anchored in south San Francisco Bay and early that morning brought out forty-seven guests by ship's boats to go to sea for the day. We exercised the ship at sea, conducted tours throughout the ship, provided lunch on the mess deck, and afterwards returned through the bay and up the Sacramento River to Concord with tired but happy families.

Later in September we went to sea for two weeks for our major First Fleet exercise, during which we provided support for a series of armament and fuel replenishments. As before, Frank Darling reconfigured our temporary red lights on the king posts and winch booms to try to position the red floodlights to provide the best working conditions for the crew. By the time of this exercise we were pretty sure of where we wanted to install our permanent red lights.

On the evening of October 6 *Mount Katmai* left the First Fleet exercise to steam up the California coast to return to Concord. On this return trip I observed an event that showed how far we had not progressed in low visibility navigation. As we approached the San Francisco lightship, we were in heavy fog. Because of that fog I lay to by the lightship to take on a bar pilot. When he appeared out of the gloom, I was studying the old Philco radarscope. On agreement between the two of us, the pilot assumed the conn and said to the lee helm, "All ahead full." I made some inane statement such as "are you sure you want to do that?" He did not look at the radar but began to sound the ship's whistle periodically to position *Mount Katmai* by the sound of the echo of the whistle bouncing back from the cliffs on either side of the Golden Gate. He heard things I did not. Without looking once at the radar the pilot guided *Mount Katmai* through the Golden Gate so smoothly that the first recognizable thing I saw was the south stanchion of the Golden Gate Bridge not 100 feet away as we glided by in the predawn darkness. That was piloting! I took my hat off to the pilot, but I preferred to use radar.

In late October we were under way from Concord for the last time to conduct a graded battle problem before we entered a shipyard for our ship's overhaul. Such exercises were required to ensure that each ship was tactically sound, trained, and ready and were a big part of the ship's yearly grade. We received a good mark for such an old ship, and I felt pleased at the performance of my crew. We returned to Concord to off-load ammunition before going into the shipyard.

During that shipyard time I learned that I had been considered and selected for a major command at a later date. That cleared the decks for me to have command of what I hoped would be an aircraft carrier sometime in the future, and I was appropriately happy. I was told that I probably would be sent to the Naval War College in Newport, Rhode Island, for a year first. Since I was well into my fourth consecutive set of sea duty orders, that sounded pretty good to me. Mary and I could use some time together in a nice environment. With that knowledge I set about with renewed vigor to keep improving *Mount Katmai*. The crew was responding nicely, and we were making good progress.

While *Mount Katmai* was in dry dock, I took the opportunity to inspect the hull, which normally drew 18 feet of water forward and a little more than 24 feet aft. The hull was sandblasted and painted, the lignite-wood shaft water seal and bearing for the single-propeller shaft were replaced, and the screw was renewed and polished. After *Mount Katmai* was refloated, more improvements were made. The communications spaces were expanded, the mess decks and berthing compartments were vastly improved, and repairs were made in the holds and to the platform decks. Permanent and first-of-a-kind (for a service force ship) red lighting was installed to improve our night underway rearming capability, and a new helicopter deck was installed for day vertical rearming by helicopter. That deck was a real coup. I had persuaded the BIS team to go the distance and to allow us to install that new capability. *Mount Katmai* would never have its own helicopter, but we could send and receive ammunition using other ships' helicopters, thus greatly increasing our capability.

During the shipyard period I visited the Coast Guard to propose that they provide vessel separation and guidance by radar for ships in the bay in poor visibility, much like the Navy's GCA for aircraft. I received an incredulous look and a resounding statement of "we can't do that because of maritime law." I informed the port captain that I thought this attitude showed a lack of concern for vessel safety, but I could not interest them in such a service in 1964. Almost twenty years later, as a member of the National Transportation Safety Board, I observed just such a facility on Yerba Buena Island in San Francisco Bay. At least someone saw the light, eventually.

Finally, in February 1965, after what seemed an eternity, the ship started to come alive again. The fires were relit in the number 2 boiler. All topside surfaces were stripped and given a new coat of gray paint. Nonskid paint was put down on the deck walkways and helicopter deck, and all winches were overhauled. The ship looked virtually new. The crew and I felt proud of *Mount Kat-*

mai. After a one-day sea trial we returned to Concord to begin intensive load-ing for our last training period off Southern California during which we would try out our new red lighting and helicopter deck. In that training our red light-ing was a great success and, as *Mount Katmai* was the first service force ship to have it, gave the crew something else to be proud of. We even received high marks on our lighting from the other ships alongside. It was good.

During all this outfitting and training, the crew was changing too. New offi-cers and petty officers arrived, and old ones left. Commanding officers seem at times to be at the mercy of the staff personnel people. I resisted so many con-current changes, but to no avail. Ship's navigator Henry Kane would stay for our trip to the Philippines, but he would detach as soon as we arrived in Subic Bay. The stalwarts, Lieutenants Darling and Montgomery and Lieutenant Ju-nior Grade Knutson, remained to help train a new set of junior officers while we were deployed. We loaded the ship with new ammunition and stores and were ready.

On March 27 *Mount Katmai* returned to Concord to make final preparations for our deployment to the western Pacific. On the day before our departure I noted a large box, whose packing information proclaimed it to be a Navy SPA-4 radar repeater, sitting on the pier, consigned to another ship. I had al-most given up on our Philco radar, but a new one would cost some $40,000, and we needed to spend that kind of money on even more pressing priorities. So, when I happened to see the packing information on the radar repeater in the box, I called Lieutenant Don Montgomery and told him what I had just found. Within minutes of my fortuitous discovery a crew of men had converged on the box and unpacked it, while another crew went to the bridge and disconnected the old Philco. In almost one synchronous motion the bosun at our number 2 starboard winch gently raised the old Philco from the bridge wing, carefully set it in the box on the dock, and swung the brand new radar repeater up onto the bridge. The crate on the dock was quickly put back together and rebanded with steel tape, and the area around it was cleaned up. The whole maneuver was done so quickly and smoothly that no one observing was much the wiser, and no one would be until sometime in the future when the packing crate would re-veal an old radar repeater. Then someone might wonder if they had used the wrong federal stock number when they had ordered that new radar repeater. *Mount Katmai* was now ready to deploy to the western Pacific.

On Monday, April 19, at the turn of the tide, the families present said good-bye, and *Mount Katmai* was under way for Pearl Harbor. The ship shone in the new paint and polished brass, and we were loaded to a draft of 18 feet forward and 24 feet aft. The seven-day transit to Pearl Harbor was foggy until three days out, when the Pacific high took hold to give clear skies and gentle breezes. On the day before we were due to arrive in Pearl Harbor, we spotted a 60-foot sailboat headed west. I altered course a few degrees to starboard to swing by the port side of the sailboat and saw four men in the aft cockpit, each holding a cold beer in his hand, seemingly without a care in the world. They may have staged this for the dry *Mount Katmai*. They said they were out of Los Angeles, and I told them they had 218 miles to go to Honolulu. They thanked us and went back to drinking their beers, and we moved on to arrive in Pearl Harbor on April 26.

While we were en route, Vietnam War activity heightened. Aircraft carriers and other ships were converging on the South China Sea, and flight operations in support of the war were increased. SERVPAC determined that *Mount Katmai* should take as many low-drag bombs from Naval Ammunition Depot Pearl as possible to transport them to Naval Magazine Subic Bay. The difference between low-drag and general-purpose bombs lay in the aerodynamic shape of the low-drag bombs. They were designed to be carried by jet airplanes. The older, fatter general-purpose bombs were still kept in great numbers from the Korean War and used by the propeller-driven A-1s. Captain Rydeen from SERVPAC met *Mount Katmai* and informed me of this need. I told him that we would take as many bombs as we could, and Frank Darling and I sat down to compute the metacentric height and stability of *Mount Katmai* with a load that, to my knowledge, was larger than had ever been carried before.

We loaded day and night to fill our holds, and when those were filled to the overhead of each deck, we started stacking 1,000- and 2,000-pound bombs on the main deck of the ship. The ship began to sit lower and lower in the water, and Frank and I figured and refigured our calculations on the ship's stability. Two typhoons were moving across the western Pacific. The ship could turn turtle and sink in those heavy seas. Finally, we cleaned out the Naval Ammunition Depot of all low-drag bombs. The ship's draft was well over 20 feet forward and 26 feet aft, and the depot workers had to build wooden walkways over the bombs on deck so the crew could get to the anchor windlass and helicopter deck.

I received my orders to the Naval War College by mail while in Pearl Harbor, freeing Mary to arrange the move of our household effects from Alameda to Newport. I was to be relieved in July 1965. We both agreed that it would be best if she were to move early, because the Naval War College would start in August, and if we were late in arriving, there would be no houses left to rent. Through friends Mary rented a house, sight unseen, and planned to move in during May and June.

Mount Katmai departed Pearl Harbor on Friday, April 30, for Subic Bay, some 4,300 nautical miles to the west. Almost immediately, I could tell that the ship was tender sided. *Mount Katmai* rolled slowly and at the maximum amplitude of the roll would hang up before beginning to roll back. The motion was unsettling, but we moved west at 15 knots to cross north of the typhoons.

Although the main deck was filled to the brim with low-drag bombs, we could still use our winches, and the bosuns spent hours and hours training our rearming teams for the work we knew was ahead. I held briefings for the officers so that they would fully understand the importance of our coming mission. The wind was 15 knots from the east. This, coupled with the ship's speed of 15 knots and the tropical sun over the Pacific, made the non-air-conditioned ship hotter and hotter. I noted that the number of bombs on deck sporting chalk messages to whoever might receive them grew daily—an indication of the crew's interest and good morale. As we passed 165° east longitude, we chopped our operational control to the Seventh Fleet, specifically to Commander Service Group (COMSERVGRU) 3, Rear Admiral Williams, who was also CTF 73 and was based on board ship at Subic Bay. I noted the operational message traffic increasing as we drew closer and closer to the South China Sea. Finally, after fifteen days, we entered Subic Bay on Saturday, May 15.

Subic Bay was a little like old home week because Commodore Bill Gentry of COMSERVRON 7 was deployed there, as were Captains Blackie Kennedy in *Mount Vesuvius*, Tom Gallagher in *Mount Baker*, and about ten other contemporary aviators. Captain Pierre Charbonnet came in with *Coral Sea*. Rear Admiral Bush Bringle was the embarked COMCARDIV, and Commander Dickie Wieland was still navigator. Commander Shorty Short was strike warfare officer in *Bon Homme Richard*, Tom Cassidy was aircraft-handling officer, and the list went on and on.

We began unloading all our low-drag bombs as soon as we could get lighters alongside. There was a universal need for the bombs, and I was severely limited in my UNREP capability with so many of them lying on my decks. I have the deepest respect for the Philippine nation and for Filipinos. I have served with many Filipinos and to this day count them among my staunchest friends. However, the Filipino stevedores at Naval Magazine Subic had developed a dangerous disregard for the sensitivity of explosives. I could never attribute their lack of fear to anything other than lack of knowledge. I wondered if anyone had ever explained what could happen if the explosive inside a bomb was cracked. They would drop bombs a foot or two, move them by rolling them over great distances, drag them across metal decks, and push them with forklifts. I am not sure why we all were not killed in one great explosion by their inexpert handling. Consequently, I developed a great concern for and distrust of the abilities of Naval Magazine Subic, which was reinforced with each succeeding visit until I sent a message to CTF 73 about the situation. This also did not sit well with Sweet Old Bill, who somehow received a copy.

We also had trouble getting the needed ammunition barged out to *Mount Katmai* from Naval Magazine Subic, and once the lighters were alongside, the loading was sporadic and uncoordinated. It was a peacetime slow pace in

Subic, while a war was on at sea. The two attitudes were in direct conflict. Finally, I was able to get the Naval Magazine's commanding officer to recognize that I must meet schedules, and on one occasion we loaded bombs for fifty-six hours straight. Unfortunately, there was no rest at sea for my troops, and there certainly was no rest in port. The two attitudes were not going to work, and I sent COMSERVGRU 3 a message with suggestions as to how we might improve the situation.

For the next two months *Mount Katmai* departed Subic Bay five times to proceed to the carrier stations where we would rearm Navy ships operating in the South China Sea, such as *Coral Sea*, *Bon Homme Richard*, *Midway*, and *Oriskany*. We averaged four days in port to replenish our supplies and then ten days at various rearming stations. In between rearming the carriers, *Mount Katmai* would cruise along the Vietnamese coast looking for minesweepers to distribute mail to them and to give them ice cream and looking for destroyers that needed five-inch ammunition to shell Vietcong positions.

The carriers operated at two stations west of the major sea-lane from Singapore, Japan, and China. That sea-lane was like the Los Angeles freeway, and when we were departing from or returning to Subic, it was difficult just getting through all that north-south traffic. But once we were with the carriers, everyone seemed to be going in the same direction—into the wind. Frequently, the carriers conducted launches and recoveries while we were alongside, wind permitting. We had constant bridge-to-bridge communications, and I could keep up with the air war and learn the fates of my aviator friends, such as Commanders Bob Hessom and Jim Stockdale, and others who were shot down. Each day someone else's name was added to the list. We were beginning to lose a lot of pilots.

On May 28 we had a destroyer alongside to give it five-inch ammunition. While we held course at 12 knots and some 50 to 60 feet apart, its little five-piece band began playing "Happy Birthday," and the commanding officer picked up his megaphone and sang the words. Unknown to me, one of my bosun mates had passed over the word that it was my forty-first birthday.

On our second time out we ran low on bombs. We gave *Midway* our last bombs to make the necessary air strikes the very next day. It was that close. Clearly, we were using bombs faster than they could be replenished. All the low-drag bombs that I had brought from Pearl Harbor were loaded in the other ammunition ships as well as *Mount Katmai*. There were no more low-drag bombs. All airplanes were carrying general-purpose bombs, and even they were in short supply. I was reduced to going ashore at Naval Magazine Subic to help identify individual general-purpose bombs that had been missed by the Filipino workers. I found perhaps 150 to 200 general-purpose 500-pound bombs in the tall grass that way. The forward supply was gone, and the war was dependent upon the long supply lines from the United States for any bombs that we might get. I would learn later while at the Naval War College that many senior officers in Washington did not believe that we were out of bombs!

In mid-June my message to COMSERVGRU 3 about the poor conditions for ammunition ships serviced by Naval Magazine Subic elicited a response directly from Rear Admiral Irwin in Hawaii. It came in the form of a message blast. He then directed COMSERVGRU 3 to write me a letter bordering on censure for what he obviously thought was insubordination, or something. Rear Admiral Williams knew of the conditions and seemed to agree with my early assessment. He was caught in the middle, and he dutifully wrote the letter to me, but he made it much softer than I believe Sweet Old Bill had intended. By that time I was fed up with working for black shoes, particularly at the SERVPAC level, but I will give Rear Admiral Irwin some credit. After his blast he sent his chief of staff out to see Naval Magazine Subic and subsequently changed the conditions there. So my message produced two things: the change that I sought and unexpected heat for me. On balance, we made progress.

Destroyers shelling along the Vietnamese coast found that they had defective five-inch ammunition, which could and did explode prematurely in the barrel. The problem was traced to a specific series of five-inch ammunition, and the ammunition ships set about to replace it. The destroyer *Rupertus* was in particular trouble manning the northern search and rescue (SAR) station up in the Gulf of Tonkin, about 35 miles off Hanoi. The commanding officer reported that he could not determine if he had bad ammunition or not. *Mount Katmai* was sent north to help out, and we planned the exchange of ammunition at 0200 so as not to interrupt the destroyer's daily SAR duties. Besides, because *Rupertus* was so close to Hanoi, it was better to do the exchange on a dark night.

We rendezvoused, and *Rupertus* came along the port side of *Mount Katmai*. As we were heavily into exchanging ammunition, both ships detected on radar three fast moving surface targets coming out of Hanoi harbor. They were moving at 45 knots, just like PT boats. Neither *Rupertus*'s commanding officer nor I had seen such a thing before, but something about the three blips did not look right. Each blip did not seem particularly sharp and clear, and I wondered if what we saw might not be several flights of ducks. Both ships set extra lookouts and went to modified general quarters stations, as best as we could while replenishing under way. The radar blips closed to 12,000 yards on our port beam, but we could see nothing. *Rupertus* wanted to break off, but I prevailed on the commanding officer to hang on longer while we sent over more ammunition. If we got into a fight, he needed that ammunition. The three blips moved ahead along our course while we continued to pass ammunition as fast as we could. Finally, the blips cut across our bows about 4,000 yards ahead and then passed down our starboard sides, but try as we might, we could not see anything. Some form of radar ghost images were on both ships' radarscopes. The blips disappeared astern toward Hanoi and did not return. We continued to rearm, determined to sort out just what electronic gimmickry might have caused the phenomenon later. I have often wondered if some of the previous Gulf of Tonkin night incidents that heightened the Vietnam War could have been related to any radar ghosts.

In late June I learned that Captain Jesse Naylor, a submariner, had been named to be my relief as commanding officer, and he would report to the ship near the end of July. We would spend five days together, and then he would relieve me. Then I would fly to San Francisco and on to Boston to meet Mary. Also, I even received a relatively benign and rather formulaic letter from Rear Admiral Irwin noting the end of my command tour in SERVPAC. I could not tell if he was happy or not.

We were occasionally brushed by typhoons. In a storm the relatively shallow South China Sea made underway replenishment very difficult. Handling ammunition seemed particularly hard. Gradually, more and more toes were mashed or broken and fingers smashed by the rolling bombs. Generally, we assigned those who were hurt to jobs in support of those moving the ammunition. The *Mount Katmai* crew began to resemble those principals in paintings of revolutionary war soldiers with bandages and crutches, but the sailors, like their forebearers, worked on. There was no other way to get the job done. The hours were long at sea, and on occasion we would work for thirty-six hours at a stretch. At times like that the men would finish rearming one ship and then fall asleep at their winches or on deck while waiting for the next ship to come along side.

After rearming *Oriskany* on July 8, *Mount Katmai* was sent to Con Son, and I had no idea where it was. That name was not on any chart that I had, so I asked Tom Gallagher in *Mount Baker* where it was. I received some mumbo jumbo back by flashing light message to the effect that I should head southwest and look for some seaplanes, which I did, because we were to rearm *Currituck*, the seaplane tender. Captain Butch O'Neil was commanding officer, and Rear Admiral Dick Fowler was the embarked flag officer as CTF 72 in charge of all patrol seaplanes. Heading toward the coast of Vietnam, I finally asked an ocean mine sweeper (MSO) that we passed, and that ship gave me the name of an island in the bay we were seeking—Poulo Condore. We headed for Poulo Condore, and low and behold, on July 9, we found the *Currituck* at anchor in the lee of the island with a seaplane runway laid out with buoys in the bay. We delivered the jet assisted takeoff (JATO) bottles for the P5M flying boats and then left to meet the carriers.

On July 13, while we were rearming in Subic Bay, Typhoon Freda threatened Luzon. All ships were directed to sortie. Ours was a polyglot group: two tenders, an oiler, *Mount Katmai*, two destroyers, and two amphibious ships. We sortied to the safety of the open sea and enough maneuvering room to avoid typhoon damage. As we formed up to steam together, we seemed to be more of a menace to each other than salvation. I was relieved when Freda changed course and allowed us to return to Subic Bay.

By 2030 on Saturday, July 17, we were loaded at the Naval Magazine and under way for the carriers in the South China Sea. This would be my last at-sea period. Captain Naylor would come on board by helicopter from one of the carriers before we entered port again. *Mount Katmai* had given away more than six million pounds of bombs since we arrived. Our winch operators and the deck teams had become top notch. We were fast, and the carriers liked us to rearm them because it meant less time alongside.

With each ship that came alongside now, I was saying good-bye. A great amount of camaraderie existed between those on the line, who were all working so hard, and I regretted leaving this dedicated team. Captain Jesse Naylor arrived by helicopter from *Coral Sea* on July 27, and we began our process of turning over the ship from one commanding officer to another. I liked Jesse and was pleased that he would take *Mount Katmai*. Since he was a submariner, I thought that maybe he would get along with Sweet Old Bill better than I had, but he told me Sweet Old Bill was known throughout the submarine force in the same way.

Saying good-bye to such a fine crew was difficult because they had been so much a part of my life for the past year, but we forged on toward the inevitable change of command ceremony. On Saturday, July 31, we held the ceremony in *Mount Katmai* at anchor in Subic Bay. *Coral Sea* was in port so Commander Jake Ward, then commanding officer of VF-21, now an F-4 squadron, and a few other aviator friends came over. I left the ship in the gig immediately afterwards to catch a flight from Clark AFB to Travis AFB, California, followed by an American Airlines flight from San Francisco to Boston. I traveled almost halfway around the world to return to Mary and our family in Newport.

Later that summer I heard that the SERVPAC awards for the competitive year July 1964 to July 1965 were announced after I left the ship. *Mount Katmai* had never won the Battle E for efficiency before, but for that year, the year that I was privileged to be commanding officer, the ship outshined all other ammunition ships in the Pacific Fleet and won the Battle E as number 1. Sweet Old Bill and I never talked face to face, and he never wrote me later to say he gave us the E, but I like to think that in that act he ate some humble pie and admitted that aviators can be good as commanding officers of service force ships. Of course, maybe the sun will rise in the west tomorrow, too.

15. *AMERICA* THE BEAUTIFUL
AUGUST 1965 TO AUGUST 1967

The war in Vietnam required increasing commitment on the part of the United States, and racial violence erupted in sixteen U.S. cities. In France Charles de Gaulle was inaugurated for a second term. RCA introduced integrated circuits in its new TVs, and color TV became available and popular. Edward W. Brooke was elected senator from Massachusetts, the first black U.S. senator since the Reconstruction. In a crash off the coast of Spain, a U.S. B-52 bomber was lost along with four unarmed hydrogen bombs. Soviet navy ships deployed to the Mediterranean for the first time in numbers. The Six Day War erupted between Israel and the Arab nations, while the Soviet and U.S. navies maintained watch on each other's ships in the Mediterranean. Israel was victorious in its war.

There were 16,613 pilots, 126,988 aviation ratings, and 26 aircraft carriers of all classes in the U.S. Navy. The secretary of the Navy authorized extra hazardous duty pay for flight deck crewmen. USS Enterprise first deployed to the western Pacific. Fire broke out on the hangar deck of USS Oriskany in the South China Sea with the loss of forty-four officers and men. U.S. involvement in the Vietnam War continued to expand. There was a major fire in USS Forrestal off Vietnam, killing 134 and injuring 62, and USS Currituck, the last seaplane tender, was decommissioned. Aircraft from USS America and Saratoga were launched to support USS Liberty under attack off the Israeli coast.

Flying east from the Philippines on August 1, 1965, I had a few hours to change mental gears from the driving and all-encompassing responsibility of command at sea in a war to a homecoming with my family for a year of far different responsibilities. This would be a year to spend with my family in a new environment with new and old friends. Mary met me in Boston, and we drove south along the coast through those great, dying mill towns of Massachusetts toward Newport, Rhode Island, and a house that I had never seen.

Through good friends and some luck on our part, our home was nice. It was an old three-bedroom, wood-frame house that faced the Atlantic Ocean and had a grand view of Newport's large mansions across the bay. The rolling green grass of the front lawn led to the water. Our two younger boys had already become well ensconced with the locals. Candace decided to leave the University of Minnesota and become a flight attendant and was busy trying to find a position with any major airline. Travis visited with us briefly before returning to MIT in early August. I had purchased an English MGB car through the mail while deployed in the Pacific, and Mary and Travis had collected it in New York before my arrival. We all had a good time unwinding together.

Living in Newport, Rhode Island, can be nice. The small historic seaport was a perfect place to establish the Naval War College. Here, over the years, naval officers have come to study naval strategy and tactics and international politics. Rear Admiral Alfred Thayer Mahan was responsible for the initial esteem in which the Naval War College was held, and the subsequent commandants tried to build on that reputation. Some were more successful than others. Naval officer correspondence courses were administered at the war college, and the naval staff officers and senior naval warfare courses of study were held. It would be safe to say that the senior naval warfare course was a gentleman's course, but still it was intellectually stimulating.

Vice Admiral Charles Melson, formerly commander of the Second Fleet, was commandant of the war college in 1965. The senior course had ninety-one Navy and Marine Corps officers and fifty-six Army, Air Force, Coast Guard, and State Department officers of the rank of commander–lieutenant colonel and above. The purpose was clear to see: to stimulate your thinking and to provide studies, lectures, and projects that would allow you to broaden professionally and intellectually. There were also opportunities to work on advanced degrees. I was able to take evening courses at the University of Rhode Island in Providence toward my long-unfinished baccalaureate degree.

After a week of family fun, I reported for duty on August 8, 1965, and the academic year began the following Monday. I found many old friends and made new ones among Captains Joe Moorer, Jack Godfrey, Mort Cooley, John Ford, Bob Osterholm, Bill Simcox, Bob Bergner, Harry Swinburne, and Bill Wacker; Commanders Fran Babineau, Norm Green, Bob Hanks, Dave Hancock, Charlie Kiser, Len Kojm, Joe Konzen, Bob Roemer, and Garrett White; as well as many others from the Army, State Department, and Air Force. Our schedule was busy but not overly demanding. We aviators flew at NAS Quonset Point in TV-2 airplanes to maintain our flight currency.

Within a week of the course's start, Mary gave the family a great scare. While swimming in front of our house, the boys threw a starfish onto the rocks for Mary to see, and in looking at it, she slipped on the rocks, fell backward, and literally broke her neck. She was put into a body cast in an improper position and sent home. We almost lost her that night when intransigent doctors failed to respond to our calls about her extreme discomfort, and I cut off the cast before getting her to the hospital. In an act of contrition the medics took her into an experimental National Institutes of Health program involving the controversial drug DMSO. Over a period of six months and many, many visits to the hospital, Mary did achieve a truly miraculous healing of her neck.

In September Joe Moorer and I flew a TV-2 to Norfolk and had lunch with his brother, Admiral Tom Moorer, then commander in chief, Atlantic and U.S. Atlantic Fleet, and supreme allied commander Atlantic. Commander Francis Babineau and I also flew together frequently. One night, as Fran and I returned from Jacksonville, we flew over New York City at 32,000 feet but could not even see the lights on that clear moonless night. We marveled at this oddity. After landing at Quonset Point, we learned of the great 1965 power outage along the eastern seaboard. We aviators enjoyed flying and really worked at maintaining our currency. For me it was particularly good after my time spent in *Mount Katmai*.

Also, in September, Vice Admiral Charles Martell, then deputy chief of naval operations (logistics), came to the Naval War College as a guest lecturer. I had difficulty listening to his easy explanation of the logistic support picture for the Seventh Fleet operating off Vietnam and particularly had trouble with his statement that "there was not a shortage of bombs for the fleet." My fellow students egged me to get up and challenge the good admiral, but since the year was to be a great learning experience, I did not. I took his statement to mean that he really was not aware of what was or was not going on in the Seventh Fleet. The lesson for me was that "the further you are from a crisis, the more apt you are to believe the average is an absolute fact." We had a problem in Washington, certainly with respect to logistic support.

Winter came, and Mary's neck healed. We played duplicate bridge one evening each week and partied with our friends on the weekends at the officers club. I attended University of Rhode Island night classes in Providence. Travis graduated from MIT and worked for Bell Laboratories in Buffalo, and Candace began training as a flight attendant for United Airlines. Gradually, our family life returned to normal.

Each student in the war college was required to research and write a paper on a subject he wished to explore intellectually. I chose Secretary of Defense

Robert McNamara's planning, programming, and budgeting system, which was patterned after an economic decision model devised by Professor C. J. Hitch. The secretary's system was creating great consternation in Washington naval circles, and I wanted to learn more, particularly about the decision process.

The topic for my research paper was risky, but I clothed myself in the mantle of academic freedom and took on DOD policy and decision making in the then rapidly growing office of the secretary of defense. As I proceeded further with my research, it became clearer to me that McNamara; Dr. Harold Brown, then director of defense research and engineering; and finally Dr. Alain Enthoven, then an assistant secretary of defense, and other inexperienced hangers-on were taking DOD for a ride. That ride was enjoyed by the Army and Air Force at the Navy's expense. I titled the research paper "The Department of Defense Program Management and Its Effect on the United States Navy."

My subject was a topical one in 1965 because Secretary McNamara had levied on all services a system to provide him autonomous control of the nation's military, while he seemingly disregarded military experience. I came to the conclusion that, even though well intended, the office of the secretary of defense grew unreasonably in size, assumed decision authority previously held by the services, lengthened the acquisition process, made it more complex and costly, and was negatively influencing our country's war-fighting ability—all in the name of improvement! I turned the paper in on March 1, 1966. To my amazement, it was one of several chosen to be presented to the staff and student body.

Subsequently, the *Proceedings* of the U.S. Naval Institute asked to publish my paper, and I politely refused. Taking on the serving secretary of defense and his system was not the credit that I wanted on my career tombstone. I was perfectly willing not to achieve notoriety as the Navy captain who said the "emperor wore no clothes" and have my head lopped off. The Johnson administration had its thumb firmly on every military officer's career, certainly those that chose to challenge it. To my knowledge that research paper still gathers dust in the library stacks at the Naval War College and is much less topical now. But I stand by what I wrote then and perhaps with the wisdom of age now feel I should have allowed the Naval Institute to publish it. Secretary McNamara's and my views differed appreciably.

Concurrently with my finishing the paper in February, Captain Damon W. (Hutch) Cooper, the aviation captain's personnel detailer from the Bureau of Naval Personnel, visited the Naval War College to tell each of us captains what we might expect in the way of orders when we graduated on July 1, 1966. His words were pseudo-official, and we would receive the real orders later. I knew that I had screened for a major command in 1965, before I attended the Naval War College, but I was very junior as a captain and expected that first I would be ordered to Washington as a payback tour for having attended the Naval War College.

Hutch interviewed each of us captains. When my turn came to meet privately with him, he ruffled through some papers as if he were looking for something, then looked me in the eyes, and said, "Don, we are going to give you command of USS *America*. You will take command this summer!" He smiled a sly smile. I could not believe what I had just heard. *America* was the newest, largest, and finest aircraft carrier in the Navy. I would be the first captain in my year group to get a major command and would relieve Captain Lawrence Heyworth to be *America*'s second commanding officer. I had just heard the words that would make any captain envious—I had hit the jackpot! I walked out of the office in a daze, and my compatriots were suitably nice and congratulatory. I floated home on silver clouds to tell Mary, and she seemed as pleased as I.

In the spring Captain Ralph Werner died from cancer. Joe Moorer and I flew to Mayport, Florida, where Ralph previously was homeported as commanding officer of USS *Shangri-La*. Joe and I were two of the pallbearers at the service in the Navy chapel. That day was really sad for both of us. We had lost a friend whom we both admired. Each of us had attended many memorial and funeral services for our friends over the years, but this was my first for someone who had not been killed in an aircraft accident.

Vice Admiral A. S. (Chick) Heyward relieved Vice Admiral Melson as commandant of the Naval War College, and that seemed to resolve a developing problem concerning my orders. The Bureau of Naval Personnel wanted me to attend some schools in April, and Admiral Melson resisted this as interrupting my studies at the Naval War College. Those war college studies were not that demanding, and I think the admiral resisted more on principle. Of course, I feared I would lose the great opportunity of commanding *America*. Admiral Heyward saw the wisdom of not denying me the opportunity and permitted me to spend the last two weeks of April on temporary duty at steam engineering schools in the Norfolk area.

Every ship depends on the plant to provide steam not only for propulsion but also for potable water, heating, cooling, cooking, and the myriad AC/DC voltages for the many systems in a ship to support its war-fighting ability. An aircraft carrier, in its complexity, has requirements for ship's power far in excess of other ships—for steam catapults, for 400-cycle power for a new Terrier surface-to-air missile system, for exotic radars for detection, for aircraft carrier landing-speed control, and on and on. *America* had the more complex 1,200-pound steam pressure system, as opposed to the earlier 600-pound system in *Forrestal* class ships. So I spent those two weeks learning the major strengths and weaknesses of the engineering plant.

After I returned to the Naval War College on April 30, the remainder of the academic year went fast. On graduation day, Wednesday, June 15, 1966, 147 of us gathered in the large naval station theater along with families and friends who had come to see father, son, or husband graduate. Alphabetically, we were called to the stage to receive our diplomas from Admiral Heyward. An unexpected surprise came when seven were named first to graduate with distinction. I was one of those seven and, I must say, very surprised! Admiral Heyward was particularly nice in his handshake and words and seemed to identify with my future career route, which was one that he had taken.

Mary, Charles, and I were down to a family of three, and we immediately drove to Norfolk for me to report to COMNAVAIRLANT for duty on Thursday, June 23. We camped out in temporary lodgings until a small set of quarters on the naval air station became available. Travis happily fell heir to my MGB because I would not be needing it.

The succeeding two weeks of temporary duty passed in a blur of activity as I learned about helicopter ASW in San Diego [*America* would have six SH-3As, the first attack carrier (CVA) to do so], attended school at the Naval Boiler-Turbine Laboratory in Philadelphia, and received indoctrination at the catapult facility at NAS Lakehurst, New Jersey. Those courses were a prelude to my joining *America* in the mid Atlantic as the ship returned to Norfolk from deployment to the Mediterranean. On Friday, July 8, I flew by commercial airliner to Bermuda and there was picked up by *America*'s C-1A to be flown directly on board. After the C-1A landed on *America*, I went to the bridge to pay my respects to Captain Lawrence (Lawry) Heyworth. For the next two days as *America* continued toward Norfolk, I toured the vast ship and met many of the almost 5,000 officers and men. It was much like old home week because I knew many of the officers in the ship and air wing. Captain Lawry Heyworth was most gracious as he explained *America*'s routine, conducted a last underway refueling from an oiler, and provided me briefings on a variety of matters. *America* entered the Chesapeake Bay and then the Hampton Roads where a harbor pilot boarded and with the aid of eight tugs breasted *America* into pier 12 on Sunday, July 10.

The first order of business for all was a joyful homecoming after the six-month cruise. The air wing had flown off on July 9 to its respective home airfields along the eastern seaboard. The second order of business was to get ready and enter the Portsmouth Naval Shipyard for some much-needed repairs and to rectify a few shipbuilder's shortcomings found during the deployment. Lawry and I planned to have our change of command while *America* was in the shipyard. After all ammunition was unloaded over several days at anchor in the Hampton Roads, a harbor pilot guided *America* up the Elizabeth River to the naval shipyard where the yard pilot took the ship across the sill and into dry dock on July 18. *America*'s draft was so great that high tide was needed for the ship to clear the sill and the large reinforced concrete blocks that were set strategically according to ship's plan on the bottom of the dry dock to support the ship.

On Wednesday, July 20, on the hangar deck before the assembled crew, I relieved Captain Heyworth and reported my assumption of command to Rear Admiral J. O. Cobb, commander of Carrier Division 2, while the guest speaker, Vice Admiral C. T. Booth, commander, Naval Air Force Atlantic Fleet, and Vice Admiral K. S. Masterson, commander of the Second Fleet, looked on before *America*'s officers and crew. I had just assumed full responsibility for the largest and newest naval ship in the world and its crew, and I was grateful to Lawry Heyworth for the thoughtful way in which he had helped me to do that.

My priorities in the yard were to get the best and most productive yard period we could while learning all I could about the ship, the officers, and the crew. It is difficult to convey the size of a ship as large and complex as *America*. The flight deck was 4½ acres. The hangar deck was longer than two full-sized football fields. Each of the four aircraft elevators was the size of two suburban home lots. Walking on the floor of the dry dock and looking up at a ship 1,047 feet in overall length with four screws—each 22 feet in diameter, 69,000 pounds, and balanced at the ends of four long shafts—can be mind boggling. *America*'s bulbous underwater bow contained an SQS-23 underwater sonar, the only one installed in a CVA. The displacement was 77,600 tons. The underwater hull was cleaned and painted. Two of the four screws, or wheels, were rotated with those kept in a special *America* pool so they could be examined and refurbished. The wheels of very large ships must be dedicated to the individual ship.

Because the overall number of people in naval aviation was not large, I already knew the naval aviator department heads in *America*. The executive officer, Wiley Scott, and I had been squadron mates in VF-51 in 1949–50 and in sister FJ-3 squadrons at Oceana in 1956–57. Commander Fredrick G. Bouwman, operations officer, was a night-fighter pilot. Commander Hugh B. Baumann, navigator, was ably supported by assistant navigator Lieutenant Commander Roger Box. The air officer was Commander Nicholas A. Castruccio, a flight test pilot at Carrier Suitability. Commander W. W. Ross, a former shipmate of mine in *Coral Sea* and a naval aviator, was weapons officer. Commander C. E. (Ted) Tedholm was engineering officer and the prime mover for our yard period. Commander John J. Gordon, a flight surgeon, was senior medical officer and led the medical team, as well as maintained the eighty-bed complete hospital on board. Commander John W. Beale was the supply officer. Carrier Air Wing 6, commanded by Commander R. E. (Bob) Oechslin, was our assigned air wing and would be shore based until we deployed. Those officers were my brain trust; I relied on them to give us a good yard period and to keep alive the wonderful spirit of *America*.

After what seemed an eternity, the work in dry dock was completed, and on Sunday, August 7, *America* was moved to adjacent piers in the shipyard to complete the work and to undergo our dock trials. Once those were completed and all equipment was found to be working, we moved down the Elizabeth River to anchor in Hampton Roads on August 30. The most impressive sight for me was to see how *America* filled the river and seemed to touch both river-banks as we passed the homes in Norfolk and the grassy shores of the parks in Portsmouth. *America* still smelled new, was easily the most impressive ship in our Navy, and had the name, too.

Going to sea, we completed all trials on September 1. Next would come our refresher training with the fleet training group in Guantánamo, Cuba. But be-fore we moved south, we spent a week at sea off Norfolk providing a deck for carrier qualifications for selected fleet squadrons. That gave us a chance to work out the kinks after two months of flying inactivity.

We loaded a few Air Wing 6 airplanes on board to help us train while at Guantánamo and departed Norfolk on September 20 for the three-day transit to Cuba. Nothing seemed to have changed at the fleet training group since I was last there in *Forrestal* in 1956. We anchored off Fisherman's Point, site of some of naval aviation's earliest flights, and the following Monday, September 26, we started training in earnest. I really felt at home in the captain's chair on the bridge. I had spent most of my adult life in many different aircraft carriers and often could sense developing trouble before it was reported to me. I knew what the operating tempo should be. I had confidence in the crew, and I knew what was going on in the minds of the officers and men as I watched them work.

The flight deck crew in *America* was superb. Whether rigging a barricade, working on the arresting gear engines or steam catapults, or manhandling a simulated deck emergency with an airplane, they were well trained. Because of the noise, wind, and danger on the flight deck, all flight deck crewmen wear colored jerseys that identify their responsibilities. Yellow is a director, blue a plane pusher, brown a squadron plane captain, black and white checkered is a safety checker, and on and on. That color coding makes it easier and much safer to sort out what is going on and who must be responsible. Lieutenant H. L. (Frenchy) Bouchard was flight deck officer. Frenchy had been a flight deck aviation boatswain mate and then a chief petty officer; now, as a commissioned officer and plank owner in *America*, he knew every idiosyncrasy of each piece of equipment relating to the flight deck. He knew every procedure and proba-bly had helped to write most of them. Frenchy was always first to the scene of any flight deck drill that the fleet training group could concoct. Nick Castruccio, his boss, was a good leader and knew when to let Frenchy do his thing and when to step in and help.

Like all other aircraft carriers, *America* had recently acquired helmets with small radios for key flight deck personnel. Because of their large earlike sound suppressor receivers, those helmets were dubbed Mickey Mouse helmets or headsets, and they made a great difference in how the flight deck operated, relieving the need for a large portion of the visual communication while making everything more easily understood. Frenchy used his Mickey Mouse headset to good advantage. It soon became apparent to the fleet training group that Frenchy was the mover and shaker on the flight deck. One day, from my chair on the bridge, I watched a drama unfold below. First, the fleet training group simulated an incoming missile hit on the flight deck. There were simulated deck fires and casualties and simulated aircraft damage. As the flight deck personnel responded, the fleet training group observer wanted to see what the crew could do without the key presence of Frenchy. As I watched, I could see but not hear the observer tell Frenchy he was "dead," whereupon an obvious argument ensued between the dead man and the observer as others responded to the damage and the personnel casualties lay on the flight deck. Finally, the observer forced Frenchy to the deck and a wire basket Stokes litter was dutifully trotted out from the island by two white-jerseyed hospital corpsmen. They put Frenchy in the litter, and as he was carried toward the island, I could see him secretively holding his Mickey Mouse headset microphone close to his mouth while he continued to give direction to his crews. Frenchy was my kind of officer and typified those in *America.*

As planned, Commander Bob Oechslin brought his air wing to *America* for the last part of our shipboard training. It is very important that ship and air wing be one unit and that those in the air wing not feel like guests on board the carrier.

During a high-speed run to determine maximum speed for *America,* I detected a vibration in the island that was foreign. In fact, it became worse and eventually shook the entire island. Later, on October 6, we put divers over the side to look at our screws and found cracks in several blades of two screws. We could continue to operate but would have to replace those two screws before long. We completed our training, and on October 9 the crew manned the rail in dress whites as *America* entered Guantánamo Bay to anchor for the last time. Our gesture was meant to be a morale booster for those at the naval base and was done to show our pride, but it also was done in respect for those at the naval base. The day was warm, clear, and cloudless, and the sight was absolutely impressive. *America*'s spirit was certainly high.

We left the fleet training group and departed Guantánamo on the afternoon of October 10 for the Atlantic Fleet weapons range near Puerto Rico to fire Terrier missiles. After those missile exercises we moved north to Norfolk, flying along the way, and arrived on Tuesday, October 18. Once there, *America* was host to the change of command for the commander of Carrier Division 2; Rear Admiral Harvey Lanham relieved Rear Admiral Joe Cobb.

Earlier during the summer, a budding romance had developed between our daughter and Lieutenant Junior Grade C. C. (Chuck) Parish, an F-4B pilot in VF-102, one of the two F-4B squadrons in the air wing. Candace and Chuck had come to Mary and me just before I left for Guantánamo, saying they wanted to be married. He was a new naval aviator, a graduate of the Naval Academy, and just the kind of fine young man any parent would want a daughter to marry. When I returned from Guantánamo, the wedding was held at the chapel at NAS Norfolk, and Commander Ralph Hopkins, *America*'s senior chaplain, officiated. It was a big event for us and a happy time for all. Candace's bridesmaids were fellow United Airline flight attendants, and I had to laugh at the maneuvering for attention that I observed among Chuck's bachelor squadron mate ushers.

In early November I took *America* up the Elizabeth River one more time to enter dry dock to replace the two faulty ship's wheels. That was accomplished in eight days, and then we went to sea for additional carrier qualification landings for COMNAVAIRLANT and for the initial testing of Bell Laboratories's automatic carrier landing system. That system provided the Navy with hands-off carrier landings, if you had enough guts to trust a black box. We had indeed moved a long way in jet aviation from the first daytime jet landings in 1944 and the first nighttime landings in 1949 to be able to land in zero-zero weather with your hands off the stick. Our oldest son, Travis, then an engineer at Bell Laboratories, came on board to be the resident technical engineer for the automatic carrier landing system, and my new son-in-law, Chuck, was flying F-4Bs from the ship. They took much more of a ribbing because of their relationship than the captain did.

On November 24 the commander of Carrier Division 4, Rear Admiral Dick H. (Tex) Guinn, and his staff embarked. Over the weekend we loaded on board our Air Wing 6 squadrons and departed Norfolk on Monday, November 28, for a major Atlantic Fleet exercise, LANTFLEX 66. A force of some ninety ships was brought together in the Caribbean under the aegis of the commander of the Second Fleet, then Vice Admiral B. A. Clarey. Aside from being a busy time for all, the exercise also brought its challenges. Major fleet exercises can be very complex. The object is to exercise all the ship and aircraft systems, their crews, and decision authorities in as realistic a manner as possible.

Regardless of my friendly dealings with Tex Guinn over the previous years, I found him to be quite intrusive in my ship's business in a micromanagement way. Tex fancied himself to be a good ship handler and maintained tactical command of our task group, TG 20.1, for much of the time. TG 20.1 was composed of *America*, USS *Little Rock*, with the commander of the Second Fleet embarked, and USS *Wainwright*, along with ten destroyers.

December 5, 1966, was a typically ink-black Caribbean night, the kind of night when you could not distinguish sea from sky. Tex Guinn was officer in tactical command, as usual, and intended to maneuver our thirteen-ship TG 20.1 to place it in position to UNREP from TG 23, which consisted of three oilers and two stores ships with six accompanying destroyers. After establishing TG 23 on course and speed for the UNREP, Tex Guinn, as the task group commander, gave signals to maneuver TG 20.1 in close astern of TG 23 where, we understood, he would turn all ships loose to approach preassigned UNREP ships in a predetermined order. Normally, this maneuver works smoothly, and the only ships that have to scramble are the more nimble destroyer screen ships of both task groups.

Tex Guinn was personally maneuvering the combined task groups from his flag bridge in *America*, just below my navigation bridge. For whatever reason, he brought our thirteen-ship task group toward the underway replenishment task group too acutely and with a high rate of closure, and on that black night he somehow lost the visual picture as the two task groups came together. I found *America* approaching the oiler USS *Marias* too fast with steady bearing and decreasing range. In any aviator's or sailor's mind, that means you are going to hit each other if either party does not do something different. In this case the UNREP group was honor bound to maintain course and speed. I estimated *America* would collide with *Marias* in about four minutes unless Tex did that something different, and quickly. I watched with increasing concern as he did nothing. We reached the critical point where soon no matter what I did we would collide with *Marias*. Finally, unable to stand it any longer, I jumped from my chair to the voice communications box in front of me, punched the flag bridge button, and took tactical command of my own ship from the admiral. To some that might seem mutinous, but every commanding officer is responsible for the safety of his ship and crew. He must keep that foremost in his mind, and if his actions later prove to be wrong, he must answer for those actions. That is the price of command responsibility.

We were moving through the inky night and black water at a speed of 25 knots and were about 750 yards from a collision with the port side of *Marias*'s navigation bridge. I came left full rudder, announcing my intentions on the tactical maneuvering frequency so that the other ships and the admiral would know what I intended to do. *America* heeled over to starboard as the bow started coming left. The range was now 200 yards. At this point an unknown destroyer from either TG 20.1 or 23, whose commanding officer was probably as confused as I was, passed between *America* and *Marias* on an opposite course! Our rate of closure was 50 knots, and we missed disaster by about 80 or 90 yards. In fact, we all missed, I am not sure how, and then collected ourselves again to do it right. After that I noticed Tex Guinn did not assume tactical command of the task group nearly as often, and he was a little less intrusive into my business. Perhaps, more importantly, he became more prudent in maneuvering a task group. That was fine with me.

When jets fly from aircraft carriers, sometimes unusual things happen. I thought I had seen about everything until December 7, 1966, when Lieutenant Junior Grade K. W. Leuffen made a normal trap on board. He taxied out of the arresting gear smartly, perhaps too smartly, at the direction of the fly one yellow shirt, and at this critical juncture his wheel brakes failed. Fortunately, no airplanes were parked forward.

Lieutenant Junior Grade Leuffen, in a moment of sheer panic, knew he could not stop and did what he was trained to do. He dropped his tail hook as the signal that he had no brakes, while crewmen responded and ran toward his moving A-4C to grab anything they could to slow down his movement. The airplane continued up the deck between catapults 1 and 2 at seemingly undiminished speed, which I am sure seemed near sonic to Lieutenant Junior Grade Leuffen. One crewman grabbed the right main landing gear, and the wheel rolled over his foot. Another tried to grab the flaps and cut his hands, while two others grabbed the tail hook. The A-4C relentlessly moved on the centerline toward the forward edge of the flight deck, where the nose wheel dropped over and the airplane's two drop tanks stuck in the braided bronze-wire personnel safety nets. The airplane stopped in a fully vertical attitude and hung with its nose pointed straight down at the water 80 feet below. Lieutenant Junior Grade Leuffen was gingerly removed through judicious use of Tilly, the flight deck crash crane, and the A-4C was lifted upright. The brakes were fixed, wing slats were replaced, and the airplane flew again several days later.

After the task group conducted missile shoots for ships and airplanes in the missile firing areas, the fleet exercise began to wind down. LANTFLEX 66 became successful history on December 14, and we returned to Norfolk on December 16 for the holidays. Next on the schedule for *America* was deployment to the Mediterranean.

America, with the commander of Carrier Division 4 and his staff embarked, deployed to the Mediterranean and the U.S. Sixth Fleet on January 10, 1967. The Atlantic transit was uneventful. *America*, *Wainwright*, and *Yarnell* were designated TG 25.3 and moved toward the Mediterranean on a rhumb line course from Norfolk. I insisted that we fly each day to keep Air Wing 6 crew sharp and their spirits high. On January 16 Lieutenant Rufus Freeman of VF-102 collapsed the nose wheel of his F-4B while landing and then boltered to become airborne again. The flight deck crew rigged the 30-foot nylon strap barricade, and Rufus did a masterful job of catching the number 1 wire and putting his airplane safely into the barricade in the mid Atlantic. You cannot throw multimillion dollar airplanes over the side as we had the less expensive variety in World War II, so we kept the airplane on board to be repaired later.

On January 19 two Soviet Bear four-engined turboprop maritime patrol airplanes flew around the northern tip of Norway, through the Iceland-U.K. gap, into the North Atlantic, and down toward the transiting *America*. They were detected hundreds of miles away, intercepted by our own VF-33 and VF-102 F-4Bs, and escorted all the way to *America*, where they turned around, flew by the ship at 1,000 feet, and returned from whence they came. The Soviets did this to demonstrate their own maritime patrol ability and to show presence to counter what they perceived as U.S. dominance over the oceans of the world. The Bear flight was Soviet national showmanship at its best, with the veiled implication that they could launch offensive missiles at *America* if they chose. I am not sure whether or not they realized that they would be shot down long before they could get those missiles off the rails.

We continued across the Atlantic toward Gibraltar and the Mediterranean. I had already noted many differences from the ways of the Pacific Fleet, and even greater differences would appear once we were inside the geographically restricted Mediterranean. One day Tex Guinn said to me, "Don, this is the noisiest ship I have ever been in!" Now, an admiral's comment like that hurts a flag captain, and I watched for what might be bugging him. We were flying every day, so I wondered if that was the reason. One evening, after all was secure, I wandered down onto the then-quiet flight deck. Tex Guinn's in-port cabin was inboard of my cabin and directly under the flight deck, so I walked out over the general area of his cabin, not really knowing what I was looking for. There, painted on the deck in neat precise small white letters, was this sign: "Throw your chocks here."

Aircraft wheel chocks on board ships are made of heavy metal and are expandable to fit any of the different sizes of wheels of the aircraft on board. They are built to last the heavy operating tempo of the flight deck and weigh about 25 pounds each. Some enterprising aviation boatswain mate knew exactly where the admiral's cabin was and had found a way to get his attention. Nick Castruccio carefully painted out the instruction with magical Navy haze gray deck paint, and I never heard the noise complaint from Tex Guinn again.

A number of fine officers were on the Carrier Division 4 staff. Principal among them was Captain Quentin Crommelin, one of five naval officer brothers. He was chief of staff and a true gentleman. I had a great respect for this fine naval aviator and naval officer, and he was a saving grace in dealing with the admiral and some of his staff.

Just before we turned more easterly to pass south of the Iberian Peninsula and through the Straits of Gibraltar, we experienced giant swells from a large North Atlantic storm. Those large swells were of a size and period that started *America* rolling in a dynamic way on our last night in the Atlantic. I was particularly concerned that the rolls were so great that we might drag the tails of a few North American Aviation A-5s parked aft and athwartships with tails over the starboard side. They did not drag, but we must have come close. The admiral called me on the bridge to ask, in his words, "What the hell is going on?" He said I had almost thrown him out of his bed. I gave a brief explanation and thought that the sea can be terribly unforgiving, yet at times subtly rewarding.

We entered the Mediterranean about midnight to make a 25-knot dash for the Bay of Pollensa, Majorca, to rendezvous with USS *Independence* for the turnover of responsibilities. A small Soviet intelligence-gathering trawler, an AGI, made a purposeful fighter-pilot-style high side pass at *America*. That pass presaged six months of deliberate ship-handling incidents concocted by the Soviet navy in an attempt to embarrass *America* while we operated in the Mediterranean. We anchored alongside *Independence* in the Bay of Pollensa early the next morning, Sunday, January 22. Our turnover was fast and businesslike. Rear Admiral V. G. Lambert, commander of Carrier Division 6 and CTF 60 in charge of all carriers in the Mediterranean, formally relinquished his operational responsibilities to Rear Admiral Guinn. Captain John Fox, commanding officer of *Independence*, and I were much less formal, and our turnover was more conversational, along the lines of watch out for this or that. *Independence* left the Bay of Pollensa that afternoon and headed west, and *America*, as a unit of TF 60.1, with CTF 60 embarked, headed east.

Experiences in the Mediterranean—good, bad, nerve racking, exciting, and challenging—would abound. To this Pacific Fleet sailor everything seemed to be bunched up and closer together compared with my previous operating experience. Islands, island nations, and other littoral nations carved up the air and sea space appreciably. Things seemed to happen with more rapidity. Operations as a carrier in the Sixth Fleet were entirely different from the far-ranging operations of the Seventh Fleet in the Pacific. I was careful not to say that too loudly but tried to instill a much more operational air in the ship than the diplomatic air that I sensed was normal. I pressed for as much flying for the air wing and *America* as I could.

Our at-sea periods would range from seven to fourteen or twenty days. Each period was characterized by day and night flight operations in relatively restricted waters with frequent underway replenishments so that all U.S. Navy ships remained independent from any shore support. We mostly conducted national and occasionally NATO operations. Fleet anchorages, near some remote Greek island or in some bay, were used to conserve the ship's fuel. We generally stayed in the central or northwestern portion of the Mediterranean. The northern coast of Africa contained many nations bent on embarrassing U.S. national policy, and we stayed clear, unless we wanted to send a clear diplomatic message, which on occasion we did.

Our in-port periods would be stereotypical as well, usually four to seven days in length. The first day was spent in making calls on U.S. and foreign dignitaries and receiving reciprocal calls on board the ship. Rear Admiral Guinn took the heavy load, and I was appreciative of his doing so because that gave me some breathing room after a stint at sea without much sleep. The first or second evening in port we frequently held an evening show featuring our Marine detachment. The Marine detachment's commanding officer was Captain Lundy Sherretz, who, along with his executive officer, Captain Ken Russom, and some fifty Marines, principally provided special onboard security but also ran the brig, provided the captain's and executive officer's orderlies, and made up the principal armed might of our shore and boarding parties.

For the evening show the forward bay of the hangar deck was emptied and dressed in the fifty state flags of the United States. Commander Wiley Scott made sure it was spotless, probably becoming the bane of the existence of the hangar deck officer, Lieutenant Jim Burns. On the hangar deck the official guests and dignitaries were received and then seated facing outboard before the broad opening on the starboard side for the number 1 elevator. Precisely at sunset the elevator would suddenly and silently descend with twenty Marines in full dress blues holding rifles with polished bayonets at parade rest, their heads bowed. Once descended, they performed a silent drill that was an absolute showstopper against the backdrop of twilight and either harbor lights or open sea, depending how *America* swung to anchor. After the silent drill, Captain Sherretz invited the senior dignitary to inspect the Marines. Once the brief inspection was completed and the senior guest was seated again, the elevator would rise as silently and impressively as it had descended, the carrier division band might give a short concert, and the show would be over. Receptions on board or on shore would follow. In each port the officers and men were visible ambassadors of goodwill. The ship's chaplain organized various civic help programs. A major part of the Sixth Fleet's presence was to assure our allies continually that the United States was there to preserve peace and to support the nations we visited. Port visits were an important part of conveying that message.

From the Bay of Pollensa, we moved east and south of Sicily along the superhighway shipping lanes leading from the Black Sea and the Suez Canal. Those converged near the Malta Channel, which runs between Malta and Sicily, and then flowed toward Gibraltar. On January 31, while we were launching aircraft at night south of Sicily, Lieutenant J. C. Berenti and his radar intercept officer (RIO) from VF-102 were catapulted only to unexpectedly eject from their F-4B just after being launched. Both pilot and RIO floated down out of the darkness in their parachutes and landed in the water along the port side, but their now pilotless F-4B climbed to 3,000 feet and circled the task group. There was some momentary confusion until we determined that we had an F-4B flying around the ship in afterburner without a pilot!

We theorized that Lieutenant Berenti may have overreacted when he became disoriented after the night catapult launch and command ejected both himself and his RIO from a perfectly good airplane. They were rescued quickly, but there was nothing we could do but watch the bright yellow afterburner flames of the pilotless airplane as it eerily flew in circles over the ship. After ten minutes of that random pilotless flight, the airplane flew into the water several miles ahead of *America*, extinguishing the bright afterburner plumes and allowing us all to breathe easier. I had visions of the airplane flying to some nation and crashing or, worse yet, hitting one of the many ships in the Malta Channel.

On February 4 TG 60.1 dispersed to enter various Greek ports for seven-day port visits, our first in the Mediterranean. *America* entered Phaleron Bay of Piraeus near Athens. The visit was a great hit with sailors and Athenians alike and was led off by our evening show on the first night. The king of Greece was a pilot, and through the U.S. ambassador to Greece, Ambassador Talbot, I sent him a personal note to ask if he wished to fly in our C-1A. He declined with thanks. When *America* sortied from Phaleron Bay on February 11, a baby-blue Grumman Gulfstream I made a first-class low pass down the flight deck and pulled up in a sweeping chandelle. That evening I received a message from the U.S. ambassador asking if I had received the king's salute as *America* left Piraeus. I responded affirmatively by message and thought, this was going to be some other kind of cruise!

In the winter of 1967 the Greek and Turkish Cypriots were again headed toward direct confrontation on Cyprus, and *America* was made the secret meeting place for three U.S. ambassadors so that they could plan how to head off open conflict. Ambassador Talbot from Greece slipped on board a U.S. destroyer in Piraeus and was subsequently high lined from the destroyer to *America*. Ambassador Hart from Turkey secretly boarded a C-1A in Ankara to fly to an "unknown" destination, and Ambassador Belcher from Cyprus did the same from Nicosia. They subsequently landed on board *America* and met on February 12 and 13. Tex Guinn, Quentin Crommelin, and I gave them our respective in-port cabins, and they used my vacant in-port cabin lounge for their ultrasecret discussions. I was never privy to those discussions, nor did I ask about them, but I hope they led to the subsequent cease-fire in Cyprus and the lessening of tensions between Greece and Turkey in 1967. All three ambassadors left *America* as they came on February 13 to return unnoticed to their respective posts. Each left glowing praise for the opportunity to be on board and were struck by the might and the importance of a carrier such as *America*. The fact that we were conducting combat training while they met in my cabin was not lost on them.

Our next stop, on February 21, was in Naples, Italy, where we put ashore the damaged F-4B from VF-102 to be repaired at the U.S. naval air station and brought on board senior officers of the Italian navy and the NATO defense college for a one-day demonstration of flight operations. We anchored that evening for our seven-day port visit. Also, in Naples Commander Wiley Scott was relieved by Commander Max Malan as executive officer and returned to the United States. I would miss his affability and friendship. Lieutenant Commander Frenchy Bouchard was relieved by Lieutenant Commander H. N. Osborn, formerly a fighter pilot in VF-114 in Air Group 11. The plank owners were slowly leaving the ship, but strong capable officers were moving in behind them. The spirit of *America* was in tact.

America left Naples on February 28 and operated in the Tyrrhenian Sea before transiting through the Strait of Bonifacio, between Corsica and Sardinia, to move toward Spain. As we were about to enter the strait, I had twenty airplanes airborne flying on normal cyclic operations when suddenly the wind arose to 60 knots just as we were to recover them. That wind was far too high for the safety of those who had to be on deck, and I quickly planned to back down the ship to lessen the wind across the deck while recovering aircraft. I had read of that tactic being used in the 1930s. I stopped all engines and then rang up all astern two-thirds to back down at 12 knots. That maneuver would place the wind at a safer 48 knots across the deck. No sooner had I started backing down but the wind stopped just as suddenly as it had come up. So it was all ahead full to make the recovery in the normal fashion. You have to be adaptive and flexible to operate a moving airfield at sea. The Mediterranean seemed to present more opportunities for challenges such as that than the Pacific.

We moved west and south of France toward Valencia, Spain. Mary and Charles paid their own way to fly to Europe with the intent of following the ship throughout the summer. They arrived in Valencia as *America* entered the port on March 5. Mary had enrolled Charles in the Calvert School of Home Study with the intention of teaching him his seventh grade subjects while they drove in her new Volkswagen from port to port following the ship. She reasoned that there could be no better opportunity for a young boy to learn a great deal, and I had to agree. They planned to live in hotels and tour historic sights, and that worked reasonably well. However, when all was said and done, she felt Charles finished the seventh grade, but she had graduated!

Leaving Valencia, we moved east again through the Malta Channel to visit Taranto, Italy, and then returned to sea for more flight and joint operations before anchoring at Valletta, Malta. In 1967 the British were in the act of pulling out of historic Malta after hundreds of years of influence and rule, and Admiral Sir John Hamilton, the last commander in chief of the Allied Forces Mediterranean, would leave Malta in May for good.

Departing Malta on April 10, *America* operated at sea before anchoring at Aranci Bay in northeastern Sardinia. There, on April 20, Vice Admiral C. T. Booth, commander, Naval Air Force Atlantic Fleet, came on board to award *America* the Atlantic Fleet Battle E for 1966. *America* had outshined all other carriers. In addition, the ship swept the excellence awards for the operations, air, communications, engineering, and weapons departments. Commander F. Z. Ozburn's VF-102 was awarded the E as well for all-weather fighter squadrons. The crews were very proud. Following the one day at anchor in Aranci Bay, *America* and *Saratoga* task groups completed Operation Poopdeck, a nine-day NATO naval exercise in the Ionian Sea. During that exercise several Soviet navy ships, notably turbine-powered guided missile cruisers, became quite aggressive and obstructive. It was clear that the Soviets were bent on creating some form of incident at sea and were pressing their luck. We watched them closely, not trusting their seamanship.

On April 29, once the exercise was completed, Rear Admiral Guinn was relieved at sea by Rear Admiral Lawrence R. Geis as commander of Carrier Division 4. Almost immediately, my life as flag captain became considerably more pleasant. Rear Admiral Geis was a true gentleman and a highly respected officer. Two days later, on May 1, we anchored just outside the Gulf of Taranto, Italy, the site of the Italian navy debacle at the hands of the Royal Navy air arm in 1940. There was not much for sailors to do in Taranto. It was an old navy town. More notably, close by was the boyhood home of Rudolph Valentino. While there, Captain John Ford, commanding officer of the fleet oiler USS *Caloosahatchee*, and I met to reminisce about our long ago tour through North Korea.

In Taranto Commander Bob Oechslin was relieved as commander of Carrier Air Wing 6 by Commander R. C. Boyd. There were also changes of command in the squadrons, with squadron executive officers fleeting up to relieve the commanding officers, who in turn returned to the States. One exception to this was Commander J. E. Kneale of VA-64, who was relieved later in June to become CATCC officer in *America*. The air wing was well seasoned, and it was clear that the operating tempo had sharpened everyone's ability. I had to agree that the system of level readiness in naval aviation, which I had originally doubted, was indeed working. Occasionally, a weak commanding officer or pilot would slip through the system, but the NATOPS and level readiness programs generally seemed alive and well, as viewed from where I sat on the bridge. I tried to communicate with as many of the crew of *America* and Air Wing 6 as possible and would visit ready rooms and walk the flight and hangar decks, mess decks, and engineering spaces after securing from flight quarters. Those visits paid off handsomely in understanding the needs and concerns of all hands.

Completing the next at-sea period, we held a one-day demonstration at sea for the Italian naval academy in Livorno, Italy, on May 15 and then anchored off shore to host local dignitaries that evening. We stayed in Livorno until May 22, allowing the crew to visit Rome, Pisa, Florence, and other areas. As we left Livorno, there was building intelligence that all was not well between Israel and many Arab nations. On May 25 *America* moved from east of Spain again through the Malta Channel to operate south of Crete. There, both carrier task groups of TF 60 were placed on alert and prepared for national tasking for any contingency, although just what it would be we were not sure. Over the next week Egypt moved troops into the Gaza Strip and demanded that the United Nations peacekeeping force there be withdrawn. Israel beefed up its forces, and neighboring Arab countries put their armed forces on alert. Finally, Egypt closed the Gulf of ʿAqaba to Israeli shipping.

America's May port visit to Cannes, France, was canceled as we continued flight operations at sea, while remaining topped off with fuel and stores. On Monday, May 29, the first seven newsmen of what became a contingent of twenty-nine arrived by C-1A. The three major television networks, the wire services, and a number of news publications, such as the *Los Angeles Times*, the *New York Times*, *Newsweek*, *Time*, and others, were represented. Having them on board while we girded the ship and air wing for possible combat, against which side we did not know, was exceedingly difficult for all hands. Because of the sensitive nature of our position and operations, Rear Admiral Geis asked that all stories be cleared before they left the ship. We placed an embargo on individual electronic filing of stories because of the already heavy workload on ship's communicator Lieutenant Commander Don Moxley and his communications crew. In fairness to all concerned, we scheduled a dedicated C-1A each day for the sole convenience of getting the news media stories ashore. Rear Admiral Geis had been chief of information for the CNO and was wise and empathetic to the newsmen's needs. They appreciated this attitude.

The stellar array of media people made the best of the waiting game in *America*. Each evening on the ship's closed TV station, WMAR-TV, Bill Gill of ABC and Bob Goralski of NBC, two well-known news personalities, provided the evening news just as was seen on TV stations at home. Bill and Bob did this gratis, and it was fun for all. They even announced at ringside for a hangar deck boxing smoker that Max Malan organized for all hands. The other reporters wrote many stories datelined *America*, and their work was seen and heard around the world.

Only one incident broke the trust that we placed in those great newsmen.

One newsman of a major New York newspaper tried to bribe a C-1A aircrewman to get his story ashore secretly earlier than the others. I guess he did not count on the veracity of the aircrewman, who promptly reported that he had been offered money to get the story ashore before the normal airplane flew in. I personally favored sending the reporter ashore on the next airplane because he had broken the trust we had placed in him. Rear Admiral Geis, perhaps wisely, opted for a warning instead. I thought back to the trust that Hanson Baldwin of the *New York Times* had garnered and displayed during his long stint leading up to and throughout World War II. He had had great integrity.

The incident notwithstanding, the newsmen had the run of the ship and dutifully recorded every event from flight operations to UNREPs. Associated Press reporter Bob Horton grew tired of the lack of newsworthy happenings as we waited, and he wrote a tongue-in-cheek news story entitled "Closing the Fantail," drawing his title from the intonement of the boatswain mate of the watch on the bridge during flight operations. That story was his way of protesting the dearth of newsworthy items available during the slower buildup phase of the Arab-Israeli War. The uncertainty was just as hard on the reporters as it was on us.

A Soviet guided missile destroyer, DDG-381, joined TG 60.1 and brought a whole new dimension to the cliff-hanging atmosphere at sea in the Mediterranean. In addition to becoming a complete nuisance as the captain tried to embarrass *America* during flight operations and to precipitate an incident, the ship carried new surface-to-surface missiles that were a direct concern to me. Occasionally, at sea, "might makes right." I had the advantage in *America* in that sense, but my ship was far less maneuverable. Rear Admiral Geis directed one of our destroyer screen, a DDG, to take on the role of shouldering the Soviet ship aside when it approached too closely to *America*, and we had some close calls between the Soviet ship and our ships. A year later Captain Ray Lygo RN, then commanding officer of HMS *Ark Royal*, did run down a smaller Soviet ship, damaging but not sinking it. I was told that then the Soviets began to keep their distance.

While *America* was refueling from USS *Truckee* on the morning of June 5, 1967, the word came that the Arabs and Israelis were at war. That afternoon *America* went to general quarters for a drill, but when we secured from that drill, we maintained a higher state of readiness in the ship, which was not made known to our press guests. Events began to move fast on shore and at sea, and I felt we did not have particularly good intelligence on what was transpiring in the land battle. On Wednesday, June 7, USS *Lloyd Thomas* made sonar contact with a submarine—not ours. USS *Sampson*, which was sent to help, also gained and then maintained contact, and our SH-3A ASW helicopters were launched and tracked the contact as well. During that night all units maintained contact on the submarine, and maritime patrol airplanes from the U.S. naval air station at Sigonella, Sicily, also joined the effort and held contact. That probable Soviet submarine under and around the task group further added to the tensions in the Sixth Fleet.

Shortly after 1200 on June 7, Vice Admiral William Martin, commander of the Sixth Fleet, who was embarked in *Little Rock*, warned the Soviet DDG by flashing light message in Russian and English to cease and desist actions inside our task group. Vice Admiral Martin went on in his message to accuse the commanding officer of imperiling his own ship and ours. In essence, the Sixth Fleet was in a combat-at-sea position, not knowing who might be the enemy— the Soviets and their submarine, the Israelis, or the Arabs. Whomever it might be, we would not know who it was until we were attacked first. To say that things were tense would be an understatement.

At about 1400 on June 7, Bob Goralski was visiting on the navigation bridge when CIC called me on the squawk box to say that a U.S. ship, the USS *Liberty*, had been attacked by unknown naval motor torpedo boats and aircraft. Up to that time I had no knowledge of any U.S. ship named *Liberty*, let alone that it was in the Mediterranean. I later learned that our covert intelligence gathering ships were in a different "navy," and subsequently, because of the *Pueblo* and *Liberty* incidents, the Navy would learn not to have two distinct lines of authority and responsibility for signals intelligence operations and line command. Up to that time, each was not aware of what the other was doing. Bob Goralski's eyes became as big as saucers, and I asked him to leave the bridge. At that time *America* was conducting a CTG 60.1–directed no-launch weapons readiness drill, which involved the movement of many different weapons about the flight and hangar decks.

Thus the notification about *Liberty* came at the exact wrong time for *America*, thus adding a certain amount of additional complexity. I found Rear Admiral Geis in his war room and informed him that unless otherwise directed I was stopping the training exercise to strike below those weapons and to arm the air group airplanes with more flexible and appropriate loads of ammunition. He was so busy that he hardly answered me, but his staff agreed. Along the way, Rear Admiral Geis, as CTF 60, directed *America* and *Saratoga* to launch a specific number of airplanes against whoever was attacking *Liberty*. In *America* there ensued about an hour's effort to move some bombs below and bring up others and to launch four A-4Cs fully loaded along with F-4B escorts. That group was judged to be the correct size for a response—not too large and warlike, but still large enough to protect *Liberty*. As our airplanes departed the task group, I heard the flight leader announce on the departure frequency, "We are on the way. Who is the enemy?" Our knowledge was such that no one knew yet who had attacked *Liberty*.

Within minutes the national command authority—President Johnson—was on the radio telephone from the White House direct to Rear Admiral Geis directing that the aircraft be recalled. The president told Rear Admiral Geis that the Israelis had admitted they had mistakenly strafed and torpedoed the ship. The Israelis had said they had believed *Liberty* to be an Arab intelligence ship. That recall of our airplanes presented an additional but far less serious problem. The A-4Cs were armed with Bull Pup air-to-surface missiles with highly volatile hypergolic rocket fuel that could not safely be brought back on board ship. Rather than jettisoning perfectly good and perhaps soon-to-be-needed Bull Pup missiles, the A-4Cs were directed to land at the NATO airfield at Souda Bay, Crete. The airplanes were recovered later; the missiles, much later.

Captain Joe Tully, commanding officer of *Saratoga* in TG 60.2, which was positioned some 100 miles east of us, was able to launch his airplanes before we in *America* could. But the airplanes from both ships were recalled before ever reaching *Liberty*. Vice Admiral Bill Martin issued a public denial to those nations that claimed U.S. Navy airplanes were supporting the Israeli forces. In a way, the Soviet navy ships, through their presence, could confirm that to their own government and as a result may have helped reduce U.S.-Soviet tensions.

During the evening of June 7 *Liberty* was directed by Vice Admiral Martin to steam as best as the ship could north out of reach of any further attack, and he sent USS *Davis* and USS *Massey* to escort the intelligence ship. Commander John Gordon, senior medical officer in *America*, remained on board to prepare our eighty-bed hospital to receive the wounded. Lieutenant Commander Peter A. Flynn, second most senior medical officer in *America* and an accomplished surgeon, and two medical corpsmen were sent in *Davis* to help *Liberty*'s heavily taxed ship's doctor and two corpsmen.

The two destroyers rendezvoused with *Liberty* at 0600 on June 9, transferred the medical personnel, and then assumed the difficult task of following in *Liberty*'s wake to pick up any bodies that floated from the ship and to destroy any highly classified papers that the commanding officer of *Liberty* was concerned might be coming from the underwater holes in the ship's sides. The Soviets were definitely interested.

At 1030 on June 9 two *America* helicopters rendezvoused over *Liberty* and began transferring the more seriously wounded to *America*, where Commander John Gordon and his doctors and corpsmen were well prepared for their arrival. After the helicopters touched down on the flight deck, the patients were carried in Stokes litters directly to nearby bomb elevators already prepared to take them down five decks to the hospital. At 1130 *America* rendezvoused with *Liberty*, and we put our boats in the water to facilitate damage assessment and the transfer of the dead. I took *America* slowly down the port side of *Liberty* from bow to stern and about 200 yards away. Two thousand *America* crewmen lined *America*'s port side flight deck, and there was dead silence as reporters and crew alike visually assessed the major damage that *Liberty* had sustained. As we slowly passed abeam, I called Nick Castruccio, coordinating helicopter traffic in Primary Fly, and said, "Let's give them three cheers!" Nick then led the two thousand officers and sailors on the flight deck in a cheer by using the flight deck speaker system. "Let's hear it for *Liberty*! "Hip, hip," keying them to a thunderous "hooray." Three times that rousing cheer of two thousand voices rose from the flight deck of USS *America* and roared across the 200 yards of water between the two ships, saluting those in *Liberty*. I will never forget that sound. It made the hair stand up on the back of my neck and made me proud to be in the Navy. Thirty-four *Liberty* crew members lost their lives, and seventy-five were wounded, fifteen seriously, when *Liberty* was attacked.

The transfer of the dead and wounded to *America* was completed. Rear Admiral Isaac Campbell Kidd Jr., then assigned in Naples, was appointed by the commander in chief of U.S. Naval Forces Europe to be the investigative officer of the entire incident in accordance with Navy regulations, and he boarded *Liberty* with a small number of officers. On the afternoon of June 9, *Liberty* was under way for Valletta, Malta, with *Davis* and *Massey* continuing their silent and watchful trail astern. The Soviet ships stayed respectfully clear. Valletta was chosen as the port to assess damage and to administer those repairs needed to return to the United States, principally because it was remote and the British still had not left the major shipyard there. On Saturday, June 10, Commander Ralph Hopkins and I officiated at a well-attended memorial service held on the flight deck of *America* for those *Liberty* crewmen who were killed. Also in attendance were forty of their less seriously wounded shipmates.

Over several days C-1A airplanes transferred the wounded to shore airfields where they were later flown to Air Force and Army hospitals in Europe and then returned to the United States. [Subsequently, several authors have written about the attack on *Liberty*. One or two have been highly emotional and have written less than factual books that failed to understand the why or to explore factually the actions of the Sixth Fleet and its aircraft carriers. For those interested in the full story, the most scholarly and factual treatise is the doctoral thesis of Rear Admiral Jay Crystol USNR (ret), currently the chief judge in the federal bankruptcy court in Miami.]

It is amazing how fast a fleet can return to normal operations from a crisis position. We had almost gone to war with the Soviet Union, might have attacked Israel, and had risked war with one or more of the Arab nations. The Mediterranean, locus of conflict for thousands of years, had spawned yet another one. As a result of the Arab-Israeli War, the Suez Canal would remain closed until 1975, and severely bruised international political egos would take a decade to heal to the point of returning to open discourse. On June 19 *Amer-*

ica was headed toward a port visit in İstanbul after thirty days of operations on station south of Crete. Two days earlier I had asked a C-1A pilot to see if Mary was in Athens. I did not know where she might be but surmised that she might have moved closer to the central Mediterranean. In a stroke of pure luck, on the day the pilot flew in, Mary drove up to a hotel in Glyfada, a seacoast suburb of Athens, just as she was paged by the pilot at that hotel. He gave her my message, which simply said, "Go to İstanbul." She, Charles, and Candace—who was following her husband—did just that. They drove through Greece, Yugoslavia, and Turkey and arrived in İstanbul the day that *America* arrived, June 21.

After transiting the Dardanelles and the Sea of Marmara, *America* anchored in the Bosporus at a place that almost seemed to be downtown İstanbul. The Bosporus is the only natural exit or entrance to the Black Sea, and the current from the Black Sea toward the Mediterranean was a respectable and continuous seven knots. I anchored *America* about 100 yards from the European side of the Bosporus and let out 135 fathoms of chain so that the ship rode nicely to the anchor, headed into the current from the Black Sea. *America* returned easily to our port visit routine of a first-evening silent drill and the following social and diplomatic whirl that had accompanied all of our previous port visits.

A number of ship and staff officers and families stayed at the İstanbul Hilton, from which we could see the picturesque minarets of İstanbul's skyline as well as *America* riding well at anchor. With the dress lights, peaked at the top of the mast and strung the 1,000 feet from bow to stern, *America* was the picture of U.S. national power, certainly an impressive peacekeeper.

The cruise was rapidly winding down for me because I would leave *America* before the ship returned to the United States. I received orders to report to Washington, DC, to attend the George Washington University to complete my long-sought baccalaureate degree, before subsequently reporting to the staff of the CNO in the Pentagon. It had been highly unusual for a former aviation cadet with a high school diploma to have commanded our Navy's newest and finest aircraft carrier. I would have to pay my dues if I was to become competitive for flag rank and have a chance to move on in naval aviation. I began to prepare *America* for the change of command, but first came matters of daily operations.

Departing İstanbul was not as simple as arriving. The Bosporus was like a superhighway coming from the Black Sea. So many large Soviet ships were exiting the Black Sea that there was hardly room to fit in between them, let alone turn a 1,000-foot ship around in a space about 2,500 feet wide, before exiting the Dardanelles. On the morning of our departure, I watched the large Soviet ships coming down the Bosporus in an unending stream for thirty minutes and finally felt I had the tempo. I hauled in to short stay on the anchor, which left 25 fathoms of chain out, sounded one long, deep-throated blast on the ship's whistle to indicate the international change-of-status signal, and went all ahead two-thirds on the main engines. We raised the anchor at exactly the appointed time of 0800 on June 26.

My departure plan was to fit *America* in between two 900-foot Soviet ships, both of which looked like they could care less what I did. To compound the challenge of ship handling, there also were 400-foot-long ferries busily moving back and forth at many points between the European and the Asian sides of the Bosporus. To solve that problem, I advised the officer of the deck, Lieutenant Junior Grade Thompson, to advise me only of those ships that were 500 feet long or longer. This time might was going to have to be right. Other ships smaller than 500 feet in length would just have to get out of the way. I propitiously began to spin the ship to head down the Bosporus by using right full rudder, ahead two-thirds on the port engines and back two-thirds on the starboard engines. *America*'s great bow began to move to starboard as I fought to gain a place behind the next Soviet ship and ahead of another. Finally, as *America* was swept down the Bosporus by the current, the ship's head completed its swing round, and I went all ahead two-thirds on all engines to fall in behind the chosen Soviet ships. Those Soviet ships and I adjusted interval, and *America* left İstanbul as we came.

Without the thrill and surprises associated with the exceedingly fast action of the Arab-Israeli War, our operations seemed less challenging. Even the Soviet navy seemed less interested in what we did. We operated in the eastern Mediterranean for five days after passing through the Dardenelles and then anchored off Thessaloníki, Greece, on July 1, 1967. This port was not large enough to support liberty parties from the entire task group, so, by choice, the destroyers opted to visit smaller Greek islands. The new Greek military government went out of its way to convey a strong message of welcome to TG 60.1, and we were appreciative.

On July 7 we sortied from Thessaloníki to regroup with our destroyers and operate in and around Crete for ten days. More and more I was occupied with the thought that my seagoing Navy life was going to end. I knew I would never have command of another aircraft carrier, and my active involvement with flying in the Navy was slipping away. I was forty-three years old, and I would have been happy to start all over again, and even to make the same mistakes I had made before, but that was not to be. So I enjoyed my final days in command of *America*.

The air wing was solicitous and seemed to sense my feelings of impending departure, and I was reminded of an event earlier in the cruise. Lieutenant Commander John R. C. Mitchell loved to boom the ship by flying supersonic directly at the ship and low on the water. He would lay his sonic boom directly on the beam, and the entire ship would reverberate from that high-energy boom. I did not encourage this display, but I did not discourage it either. *America* was designed to take a lot of punishment, and overpressure from a sonic boom could be easily withstood. However, one time John did break the SPS-30 radar dish rotating mechanism. We fixed it, and John was suitably less aggressive after that.

It is important not to kill aggressive initiative in pilots and aircrew. One of the great flexibilities of the Navy's high combat potential is directly related to the fact that a carrier at sea can set its own rules without being bound by the restrictive flying covenants found on land because of cities or other air traffic. Carrier-based naval aviators are lucky to operate so freely at sea, and commanding officers need to honor that freedom carefully.

My relief as commanding officer, Captain F. C. Turner, flew on board by C-1A before we anchored at Valletta, Malta, on Saturday, July 29. I did everything I could to give Fred the best opportunity to see and learn about *America* during my last few days at sea. Now it would be his opportunity to add to the spirit of *America*.

Changes of command are generally sad for those who are leaving and happy for those who are arriving. I kept the tone of my relations with all those on board *America* lighthearted to the last. Rear Admiral Geis was understanding and gave me a lot of latitude. Even so, I noted a somberness in the faces of the officers and crew as the time came for me to leave.

Ambassador Feldman and his family, other notables, and officers from the task group and NATO commands arrived by boat to attend the change of command in the festively bedecked hangar bay 1. Mary and Charles sat in the front row with Candace and Chuck, and the wives who followed the ship were all there. My remarks were very short; I do not believe in long speeches. I admonished the officers and crew to do their best in the future, thanked them for their great service in the past, and read my orders. I saluted Fred Turner, reported to Rear Admiral Geis that I had been relieved, and left the ship as soon as I could. We had a reception at the Valletta Hilton, and Mary, Charles, and I later flew to Rome and eventually returned to the United States, while Candace remained in Europe.

It is fitting to end my story here. In 1967 *America* embodied all that we had learned in carrier aviation over the last twenty-five years. The new equipment in the ship that enabled the near simultaneous launch of four jet airplanes every minute and recovery rate of one airplane every twenty-eight seconds, the vastly increased performance of the airplanes, the improved maintenance and jet-engine buildup shops, the magnificent ready rooms for pilots, the jet fuel now carried, and the new weapons that made carrier-based airplanes so effective and respected by nations throughout the world, and on and on, were magnificent testimony to our progress. Our carrier-based jet airplanes were now flying at twice the speed of sound and carrying four times as much ordnance as the earlier jets.

That progress had not come easily. As I said earlier, the rules and procedures of flying from carriers are written in the blood of the many who have gone before. It is a credit that the Navy learned and did not forget the mistakes and experience of those fine officers and men who made it possible to fly jet airplanes at sea.

America remained a mainstay and symbol for attack aircraft carriers for years, preserving that wonderful spirit, which is truly the reflection of the Navy personnel who manned the ship—captains, officers, and magnificent crews. On July 9, 1996, *America*, in the carrier's thirty-first year, was decommissioned and placed in reserve status. New and mightier nuclear-powered aircraft carriers are taking that ship's place, enabling this nation to help preserve world peace. However, the spirit of *America* now lives on in the hearts and souls of those who served in that great ship.

EPILOGUE

Stories never really end, for tomorrow can modify what we might think today. After leaving *America*, I forged on. In 1967 I attended George Washington University to complete my bachelor's degree and then labored as a captain in the Pentagon. In 1968 both our eldest son, Travis, and our son-in-law, Chuck Parish, were in *America* off Vietnam when Chuck's F-4J was shot down by a Soviet missile and he was listed as missing in action, just days after his own son, Hunter, was born. Candace then fought valiantly in the international arena to support U.S. foreign policy and later found that her husband, indeed, had not survived. Candace later married Lieutenant R. E. Ellis, and today Hunter is a lieutenant and, as I write, an F-18 pilot flying from USS *Carl Vinson* in the Pacific.

In 1969 I was selected for flag rank and ordered to a plans and policy position on the Navy staff and in 1971 escaped Washington to return to sea, where, like Rear Admirals Guinn, Geis, and others before me, I became commander of Carrier Division 4 in the Atlantic Fleet. Subsequently I deployed to the Mediterranean as commander of TF 60 in command of our aircraft carrier task groups. After that we moved to London where I was deputy commander in chief, U.S. Naval Forces Europe. My final tour in the Navy, before I retired in 1978, was as deputy commander in chief, U.S. Atlantic Command and U.S. Atlantic Fleet, where I worked for that respected and delightful officer Admiral Isaac Campbell Kidd Jr.

Retirement has brought a succession of jobs and new learning experiences. I manufactured cabin-class general aviation airplanes for the Piper Aircraft Corporation in Florida and then returned to Washington to help old friend and former chief of the Center for Naval Analysis Erwin Kapos in his war-gaming efforts. In 1982 President Ronald Reagan appointed me to be a member of the National Transportation Safety Board, and then in 1984 he appointed me to be administrator of the FAA, where I was doing what I enjoyed most—improving aviation and, not inconsequentially, flying airplanes in our great national airspace system. I made many new aviation friends.

That period of public service ended in 1987, and I soon received the challenge and opportunity to create a renewed Aircraft Owners and Pilots Association Air Safety Foundation. Working with many of the 600,000 civil pilots on the federal registry and supported by many leaders in general and commercial aviation, we created new practical safety initiatives for all those who fly in the United States. I accepted the Dewitt Ramsey chair for naval aviation history at the Smithsonian Institution's National Air and Space Museum in Washington, D.C., where I wrote this book. In 1996 the secretary of the Smithsonian Institution named me to be the director of the National Air and Space Museum, where today I continue to labor with dedication now to air and space.

I fly my standard class glider, which I keep in Nevada. Mary—my partner of fifty-four years, who declares that she will not carry water for, nor wipe bugs from, any glider—suffers my incurable aviation addiction kindly. We have now lived in one place for seventeen years, which she professes to be far too long. Early every morning, as I enter the National Air and Space Museum's empty and quiet great halls, which will soon be filled with thousands of visitors, I savor the cool air and walk among the many aviation and space exhibits in awe. Many of the airplanes I have flown. I have not traveled in space, yet—other than for those fleeting moments in the Phantom II when I failed to escape the fabled surly bonds of Earth. I can identify with so much of our ninety-four years of powered flight that when I stand silent and alone in those exhibit halls before the awesome presence of aviation history, I hear ghosts. Many, many designers, engineers, pilots, and other dreamers, who preceded me, made possible what I chose to do. All the foregoing is another story.

Knowing the past, today I marvel at what pilots and astronauts will know and do in air and space during the years to come.

GLOSSARY

AA antiaircraft
AAA automatic antiaircraft
ADF automatic direction finding
AEDO aeronautical engineering
    duty officer
AFB air force base
AGI intelligence gathering trawler
AIRLANT Air Force Atlantic Fleet
air ops air operations
AIRPAC Air Force Pacific Fleet
ALPA Air Line Pilots Association
ASW antisubmarine
ATG air task group
BAR Bureau of Aeronautics
    representative
BIS Board of Inspection and
    Survey
BOQ bachelor officers quarters
Btu British thermal unit
CAA Civil Aeronautics Authority
CAB Civil Aeronautics Board
CAG commander of an air group
CAP combat air patrol
CARDIV carrier division

CASU carrier aircraft service unit
CATCC carrier air traffic
    control center
CAW carrier air wing
CFIT controlled flight into terrain
CIC combat information center
CINCNELM Commander in Chief
    Northeastern Atlantic and
    Mediterranean
CINCPAC Commander in Chief
    Pacific
CINCPACFLEET Commander in
    Chief Pacific Fleet
CNO chief of naval operations
CO commanding officer
COMCARDIV Commander
    Carrier Division
COMDESDIV Commander
    Destroyer Division
COMFAIR Commander Fleet Air
COMNAVAIRLANT Commander
    Naval Air Force Atlantic
COMNAVAIRPAC Commander
    Naval Air Force Pacific

COMNAVMARIANAS Commander Naval Forces Marianas

COMOPTEVFOR Commander Operational Test and Evaluation Force

COMSERVGRU Commander Service Group

COMSERVRON Commander Service Squadron

CPT Civilian Pilot Training

CRAG combat readiness air group

CTF commander of a task force

CTG commander of a task group

CVA attack carrier

CVE escort carrier

CVL light carrier built on a cruiser hull

DDG guided missile destroyer

DESDIV destroyer division

DOD Department of Defense

E and E escape and evasion training

ETPS Empire Test Pilots School

FAA Federal Aviation Administration

FAI Federation Aeronautique Internationale

FAWTUPAC Fleet All-Weather Training Unit Pacific

FCLP field carrier landing practice

FQ&P Flying Qualities and Performance Branch

FRP fleet replacement pilots

GCA ground controlled approach

GCI ground controlled intercept

HVAR high-velocity aircraft rocket

IFR instrument flight rules

ILS instrument landing system

IMN indicated Mach number

JATO jet assisted takeoff

kias knots indicated airspeed

LABS loft angle bombing system

LAES Landing Aids Experimental Station

LCM landing craft medium

LSO landing signal officer

LSP launch sequence plan

LTV Ling-TEMCO-Vought

MAC military airlift command

MCAAS Marine Corps auxiliary air station

MSO ocean mine sweeper

NAAS naval auxiliary air station

NAS naval air station

NASA National Air and Space Administration

NATC Naval Air Test Center

NATOPS naval aviation tactical operating procedures

NAVAIRPAC Naval Air Force Pacific

NFO naval flight officer

NPE Navy preliminary evaluation

ORI operational readiness inspection

PAR precision approach radar

PIM a ship's current position and intended movement

PLAT pilot landing aid television

POW prisoner of war

RAAF Royal Australian Air Force

RAE Royal Aircraft Establishment

RAF United Kingdom's Royal Air Force

RAG replacement air group

RESCAP rescue combat air patrol

RIO radar intercept officer, generally an NFO

RN Royal Navy

RNAS Royal Naval Air Station

SAR search and rescue
SBAC Society of British Aircraft Companies
SDO squadron duty officer
SEATO South East Asia Treaty Organization
SERVPAC Service Force Pacific Fleet
SETP Society of Experimental Test Pilots
SpecOps special operations
TACAN tactical air navigation

TEMCO Texas Engineering and Manufacturing Company
TF task force
TG task group
UNREP underway replenishment
VFR visual flight rules
VOR VHF Omni-directional Range
VORTAC combined civil VOR and military TACAN
WEPTRAEX weapons training exercise

INDEX

Moreland, H. H. (Speed), 157
Morgan, Ed, 162–63
Mount Baker, USS, 289, 298
Mount Katmai, USS, 285–99
Mount Vesuvius, USS, 285, 286, 289
Mow, Doug, 248
Moxley, Don, 318
Muckenthaler, C. P. (Charlie), 77, 78, 80, 82, 206
Murphy, D. J. (Spud), 143
Murrill, Robert, 191–92

Naylor, Jesse, 298, 299
Neches, USS, 290–91
New Jersey, USS, 48
Newlin, John, 229
Newman, E. E., 54
Nial, John A. (Jack), 198, 204
Nichols, Bill, 210
Nichols, L. L. (Nick), 63, 68
Niemeyer, Robert D., 38, 56, 61
Nitze, Paul H., 279
Northrop, Jack, 35
Nyhuis, John, 113, 114, 116, 117, 118; disappearance, 118–19, 125–26

O'Connor, Harry, 263
O'Neil, A. C., 210
O'Neil, Butch, 298
O'Neil, Red, 88
O'Neil, Warren, 260, 264
Oechslin, R. E. (Bob), 90, 306, 308, 317
Oldfield, Barney, 114
Olney, A. C., 133, 137
Oriskany, USS, 262, 276, 280, 296, 298; carrier qualification landings, 228, 249; fire, 300; missile shoot, 229, 253
Osborn, H. N., 316
Osterholm, Robert, 248, 249, 252, 260, 301
Ours, S. R., 198
Ozburn, F. Z., 317

P-47 Thunderbolt airplanes, 133, 135
P-80 jet airplanes, 72, 87–89, 91, 102, 116
Parish, C. C. (Chuck), 309, 327
Parish, Hunter, 327
Parker, Robert B., 49, 59
Parks, John, 187, 191
Pawka, Edward J., 88, 103
Peabody, Eddie, 60
Pearce, Jim, 167, 176
Peck, George, 25
Penland, J. R., 27

Perkins, A. N., 72
Perry, Frank C., 62, 107
Peterson, Forrest (Pete), 129, 207–8
Philippine Sea, USS, 11, 118, 122, 127
Pierozzi, Nello, 90
Pirie, Robert B., 214, 218, 245
Pittman, Bill, 137
Plog, Leonard, 92, 113, 131
Pollock, A. D. (Dave), 88, 101, 105, 106, 136; commander of Fighter Squadron 51, 90, 94; death, 93; night jet carrier landings, 103
Princeton, USS, 45, 49, 54, 105
Prothro, Randall, 164

Radford, Arthur, 99
Rahn, Bob, 154
Rahn, Doug, 130
Ramsey, Paul, 78
Randolph, Bev, 202–3
Ranger, USS, 253–54, 264; carrier air traffic control center (CATCC) procedures, 233, 235, 242, 254
Rash, Dick, 237
Rassmusen, Bob, 129
Ratte, Paul, 269
Regan, Louis, 11
Reith, George, 236, 239
Reynolds, R. J. (Dickie), 156
Rich, Dick, 263
Robinson, Jack, 179, 185, 187–88
Roemer, Bob, 301
Roemer, Charles E.: commander of USS *Coral Sea,* 269–76, 282, 283; landing signal officer in USS *Lexington,* 31, 272
Ross, Bill, 199
Ross, W. W., 306
Rostine, Bob, 129
Roth, J. S., 269, 271, 276
Rothrock, George, 248
Rupertus, 297–98
Rushworth, Bob, 207
Russell, Allard (Slim), 197, 245
Russell, Hawley (Monk), 156, 158–59, 161
Russell, T. B., 278
Russom, Ken, 314
Ryan, John, 133

Sable, USS, 30, 31
Sacramento, USS, 289–90
Sahaj, Joe, 132
San Jacinto, USS, 55, 58
Saratoga, USS, 172, 196, 216, 317, 320
Satterfield, Butch, 207, 208